Visions of Hope

VISIONS *of* HOPE

An Anthology of Reflections

Compiled by William Sykes

Published by
The Bible Reading Fellowship
Peter's Way
Sandy Lane West
Oxford OX4 5HG
ISBN 0 7459 2591 X
Albatross Books Pty Ltd
PO Box 320, Sutherland
NSW 2232, Australia
ISBN 0 7324 0753 2

First edition 1993

Acknowledgments

Unless otherwise stated, Scripture is taken from The Revised Standard Version of the Bible, copyright © 1946, 1952, 1971 by the Division of Christian Education of the National Council of the Churches of Christ in the USA.

Every effort has been made to trace and contact copyright owners. If there are any inadvertent omissions in the acknowledgments we apologize to those concerned.

A catalogue record for this book is available from the British Library

Printed and bound in Great Britain
by Biddles Limited, Guildford

Contents

Acknowledgments

We would like to thank all those who have given us permission to reproduce extracts from publications in this book, as indicated in the list below.

Extracts from the Authorized Bible (The King James Bible) the rights in which are vested in the Crown, are reproduced by permission of the Crown's patentee, Cambridge University Press.

Routledge & Kegan Paul: C.G. Jung, *Psychological Reflections*, edited by Jolande Jacobi

Reprint from Albert Schweitzer, *Memoirs of Childhood and Youth*, by permission from the Estate of Albert Schweitzer. Copyright © Rhena Schweitzer Miller.

Faith in the City: The Report of the Archbishop of Canterbury's Commission on Urban Priority Areas (Church House Publishing 1985), © The Central Board of Finance of the Church of England 1985.

Jean Vanier, *Community and Growth*, by permission of Darton, Longman and Todd. In Australia, by permission of St Paul Publications. In US and Canada, by permission of Paulist Press.

The Words of Martin Luther King by permission of Robson Books Ltd.

Mother Teresa, *Jesus, the Word to be Spoken*, compiled by Brother Angelo Devanando, by permission of Collins Fount, and imprint of HarperCollins Publishers Limited.

George Appleton, *Journey for a Soul*, by permission of Collins Fount, and imprint of HarperCollins Publishers Limited.

Dag Hammarskjöld, *Markings*, translated by W.H. Auden and Leif Sjöberg, by permission of Faber and Faber Ltd.

Michael Ramsey, *Through the Year with Michael Ramsey*, edited by Margaret Duggan, by permission of Margaret Duggan.

Michel Quoist, *With Open Heart*, by permission of the publishers, Gill and Macmillan, Dublin.

William Barclay, *Letters to Titus and Timothy*, 1965, and *The Gospel of Matthew*, 1975, by permission of Saint Andrew Press

Michael Hollings and Etta Gullick, *The One Who Listens*, Mayhew-McCrimmon Ltd, 1972, with permission.

SCM Press Ltd for permission to use material from: Olive Wyon, *On the Way*, James F. Childress and John Macquarrie, editors, *A New Dictionary of Christian Ethics*, Gordon S. Wakefield, editor, *A Dictionary of Christian Spirituality*, and Alan Richardson and John Bowden, editors, *A New Dictionary of Christian Theology*

Thomas Merton, *New Seeds of Contemplation* (1962), and *Thoughts in Solitude* (1958), Burns and Oates Ltd, © Copyright by the Abbey of Our Lady of Gethsemani, (1961). With permission of the Merton Legacy Trust.

Preface

A READER'S VIEW

Steve Sheppard practises and teaches law in Mississippi in the United States. He was at University College, Oxford, pursuing his D.Phil from 1989–1992. Last year he wrote a preface for *Visions of Love.* This is what he has now written about *Visions of Hope.*

'Bill Sykes has grappled with our demons—not the hoary Old Testament demons of Hollywood movies, but the mundane, modern demons that stalk the early hours of doubt and fear. This extraordinary book, and its two companion volumes, are a record of his struggles, taken from his remarkable readings across the spectrum of Christian and other writings, from saints and from sinners. Each topic is introduced by our sturdy pilgrim, placing the idea into the world as he experienced it.

'I first met Bill when *Visions of Hope* was still in massive files, heaped behind the couch in his set of rooms in University College. I and my accomplices would meet for an ominously named 'reflection group' weekly during the academic term, and we would haul these tomes out to consider their themes. We were rarely prepared to admit how eagerly we sought these meetings. A bunch of cynical Oxford students are not easily focused on the role of *Anxiety*, or *Courage*, or *Personality*, in their own lives, at least not in front of witnesses. We would much rather sort out the lives of everyone else. Still, someone would volunteer a topic from the index, and we would each nurse cups of Bill's tea while digesting the material from these pages for about twenty-five minutes. With Bill's gentle prodding, the discussion would begin, the student on the hot seat inventing a quick lie to explain why the topic was chosen. The conversations that followed could be predictable, but at times were a furnace of inspiration, driven by these readings and catalyzed by Bill's insightful questions.

When I left Oxford a few years ago, with my doctoral thesis above me in its Damoclean way, I thought I had left reflection groups behind. I was, luckily, wrong, and when *Visions of Love* was published, I found that it re-entered my life like an old friend. I've given copies away as gifts, and I've been amazed by the number of conversations the book later provoked from its recipients. None of them have reacted to it in the same way, but all seem amazed at the thoughts they find in themselves when they put it down. I've lent it to friends in gloom, and I've re-read it myself in dark impatient hours.

Visions of Hope is more than a sequel, it is an extension of *Visions of Love*'s exploration, presenting the artefacts of a once-troubled priest's journey through millennia of thought in search of understanding. Thankfully, he has shared his account of this journey with us.

Steve Sheppard

HOW A SCHOOLMASTER USES AN ANTHOLOGY OF REFLECTIONS

Robert Aldred is a housemaster at St Edward's School, a boys' boarding school in Oxford. A few years ago his wife, Alison, was the nurse at University College, and working closely in that capacity with the chaplain of the college, Bill Sykes. Through that contact Robert discovered Bill Sykes' first anthology, *Visions of Faith* (now out of print) and from the moment he read it he realized what an invaluable resource it was. He has been using it for various groups in the school ever since and I asked him how.

'I use it in just one way,' he told me. 'We have copies of the book for the boys. We had a set of about forty at one stage, but over the years they have diminished. It is a very stimulating book, and sometimes a boy will say "Can I borrow it?" And he will take it away for a while and then bring it back—but not always!

'What I do is to give them just one section of quotations to look at in one period, which usually lasts for forty minutes. They stay in the class room and I ask them just to go through the quotations, to think about them, and to make notes. Then the following week they come back and we discuss them. I use the book two or three times a year, and I try to choose subjects which the boys themselves are interested in pursuing.

'Basically, I use the same method that Bill uses himself, in order to get people to think about whatever subject it is, and to meditate upon it. I actually use the word meditate, and I say to them, "To meditate means to chew it over and to thrash it through: to ask yourself whether you agree with it, and to ask yourself: *What is it actually saying? What does it mean by this phrase, and that phrase?*" I find that it raises the intellectual level of discussion to a much more serious one.

'Quite often a group will tend to treat things at the level where they are, which can be rather shallow. But I have found that this book forces them to go to a level which is more mature and more demanding, and there is a greater level of seriousness in the discussion. This year I have got four groups. Three of them are fine, but one is rather hard work, because of the level of input (or the lack of it) from the various members. There is a group within the group who are somewhat immature, and they tend to be flippant and a bit silly. But using Bill's book has forced them to be more thoughtful.

'It is enormously stimulating, and it provides a broad spectrum of types of writing. To give you an example, I wanted to do something with the sixth form on marriage and sexuality, and when I was looking through those sections I found this marvellous quotation from *The Prophet*, by Kahlil Gibran:

But let there be spaces in your togetherness,
and let the winds of heaven dance between you.

'Brilliant! First of all I found it strange to see that juxtaposed against the Christian view of marriage. But then I thought, "Well, there's nothing much wrong with that!" And it made me realize how good it was to read people who were writing from all backgrounds, and from all walks of life and all the Church traditions. It's an enlarging experience.

'It is interesting how the pupils invariably pick out that passage from *The Prophet.* And when we are looking at the theme of suffering they almost always pick out the passage said to have been written by a young cancer patient (and often known as Footprints):

> One night a man had a dream. He dreamt he was walking along the beach with his Lord. Across the sky flashed scenes from his life. For each scene he noticed two sets of footprints in the sand, one belonging to him, the other to the Lord. When the last scene in his life flashed before him he looked back at the footprints on the sand. He noticed that many times along the path of his life there was only one set of footprints. He also noticed that it happened at the very lowest and saddest times of his life. This really bothered him, and he questioned the Lord about it. 'Lord, you said that, once I decided to follow you, you would walk with me all the way. But I've noticed that during the most difficult times in my life there is only one set of footprints. I don't understand why, in times when I needed you most, you would leave me.' The Lord replied, 'My precious child, I love you and would never leave you during your trials and sufferings; when you see only one set of footprints, it was then that I carried you.'

The Reverend Shelagh Brown
Bible Reading Fellowship

The story behind Visions of Hope

HOW IT CAME INTO BEING AND HOW TO USE IT

A priest who lost his faith

What happens when a priest thinks he has lost his faith? I was thirty years old and, faced with this situation, saw three options: leave the Church; stay put in the Church and go through the motions; or stand my ground and fight. I had one thing on my side in making the choice—fresh memories from being a Gurkha officer. I had to fight.

Where he started the fight to find it

I started anew in the book of Genesis. In the story of the creation of man God is depicted as fashioning and shaping man in his own image. He breathed into man and man became a living being. I was fascinated by this simple story. I took it to mean that God breathed something of his own nature into man, giving a divine potential for life.

Then I turned to the Gospels and found 'something of God in man' worked out in the man—Jesus Christ. He found the Father in the depths of himself. He tried to explain this to the disciples: 'Do you not believe that I am in the Father and the Father in me?... the Father who dwells in me does his works' (John 14:10). As I struggled with what these words meant, I began to understand Jesus as the image of the invisible God.

Starting to see the way of hope

This understanding brought me a new insight. Jesus discovered not only the presence of 'the Father' in himself, but also discovered that this presence is love, not just an abstraction, but for people individually: 'As the Father loved me, so have I loved you; abide in my love' (John 15:9). This is the basis for the two great commandments: 'You shall love the Lord your God with all your heart... and you shall love your neighbour as yourself' (Matthew 22:37–39). He made this simpler: 'A new commandment I give to you, that you love one another; even as I have loved you' (John 13:34). Living in love, he lived in hope, and hope prevailed to the end of his life, to his death on the cross: 'Father, into thy hands I commit my spirit!' The vision of hope was beginning to take shape.

I went back to the Epistles. Paul discovered that what Christ had experienced in his life, we can all experience in some measure. Some time after his conversion on the Damascus road, Paul wrote: 'It is no longer I who live, but Christ who lives in me...' (Galatians 2:20). 'In him the whole fullness of deity dwells bodily, and you have come to fullness of life in him' (Colossians 2:9–10). I knew this meant much to me, that the whole power of the Trinity could be found in each of us as well as such attributes as life, light, truth, joy, love—and hope. I found to my delight that Paul had discovered this hope and expressed it concisely in his Epistle to the Romans: 'Through him we have obtained access to this grace in which we stand, and we rejoice in our hope of sharing the glory of God... and hope does not disappoint us, because God's love has been poured into our hearts through the Holy Spirit which has been given to us' (Romans 5:2, 5). Later in the same letter this hope comes out even more clearly: 'May the God of hope fill you with all joy and peace in believing, so that by the power of the Holy Spirit you may abound in hope' (Romans 15:13). It was neatly summed up: 'Christ in you, the hope of glory' (Colossians 1:27). But I still felt that I was missing some part of his vision for me.

Dust and divinity

Then something in Genesis clicked into place: *that which was fashioned and shaped in the image and likeness of God was taken from the dust of the earth.* I saw then that in addition to being born with a 'divine' potential, we are still earthy and creaturely. This was no news to me, but now I saw that if either side was repressed or allowed too much sway the consequences would be negative and destructive.

But how could I make such a balance? I went back again to the Gospels. What do we find in the life of Christ? An integration of the divine and the earthy, the godly and the creaturely—'very God and very Man'—a perfect combination of the divine and the human. I now began to understand why he was called 'the second Adam'. By his life, death, and resurrection he had pioneered a way of integrating both sides of his nature, and so became the prototype of a new humanity. The vision of hope underlying this anthology finally made sense.

In many people over many years

Granted this vision of hope, I thought I might find evidence of it in the experience of men and women in the last two thousand years. I started searching for signs of this vision in the thoughts and words of others. First I sought it in the recorded experience of saints and theologians. Secondly from poets, novelists, playwrights, musicians and artists. Thirdly, of philosophers, scientists, statesmen, historians, politicians, economists and psychologists.

The material found has been set out in seventy-five topics. These contain many aspects of hope, and their opposites—with some related topics.

How to grow in this vision

The aim of the anthology is to provide a means to grow in this vision of hope. This is done primarily through the practice of reflection. Hence the subtitle, *An Anthology of Reflections.*

The *Concise Oxford Dictionary* defines 'reflection' as to 'go back in thought, meditate, or consult with oneself, remind oneself, or consider'. Reflection indicates a way of thinking with the mind, the imagination, intuition and feelings. It includes 'lateral thinking' and 'vertical thinking'—thinking which takes into account the spiritual dimension. A good description comes from the Collect for the Second Sunday in Advent (a prayer for the study of the Scriptures) '... Grant that we may in such wise hear them, read, mark, learn and inwardly digest them.' Reflection can have a devotional aspect, and merge into meditation and contemplation. I hope *Visions of Hope* can be used in many ways—as a book to dip into from time to time—as a bedside book—as a guide in time of need—as an aid in keeping a journal—as a personal book of devotion.

How to run a reflection group

As chaplain and fellow of an Oxford college, I have used the material for 'reflection groups'. These have been very popular, and in term-time at least thirty groups of up to five students meet each week.

I have been asked to describe in detail how these groups function. We meet for an hour a week at a mutually convenient time. We begin with a cup of tea, coffee or hot chocolate and briefly catch up on news. A list of topics is circulated and after two or three minutes a topic is chosen by consensus. Each topic consists of an introduction and some twenty quotations, two from the Old Testament, two from the New Testament, and the remaining sixteen from a wide variety of sources. Each person in the group is then given a copy of this material and the reflection group gets under way.

We then have about half an hour of silence. We look through the quotations thinking them through, and working out what they mean to us individually. Some of our participants are not used to being quiet and find silence difficult at first, so I make available a clipboard, pen and paper. We have found that writing down thoughts and insights has eased this period of silence and been a useful way of developing ideas.

As convenor of the group, I use this half-hour period to go through the quotations in the same way as the others, but in addition to formulate some questions. These can be useful for stimulating discussion in the second half of the reflection group.

At the half-way stage, I ask if everyone has completed the material. I then ask, 'Was there any particular reason for choosing this topic?' Someone usually comes forward with a reason. My next question is: 'Did you find anything helpful?' The person who has chosen the topic responds, and then the other members of the group join in. Having reflected on the same material, conversation comes fairly easily. As convenor, my role is mainly to listen and make sure everyone has an opportunity to contribute. Sometimes the questions formulated by me earlier are a help; often they are not needed. The group ends promptly on the hour. (Time is precious in an eight-week term.)

How a reflection group begins

I usually start a new group with one person. Before long he or she usually suggests a person to join. Sometimes the addition is actually uninterested in religion but a good thinker. Sometimes it is someone committed to a particular creed, often not that of the first in the group. The two of them then invite a third member and so on. So the groups are based on trust and friendship, not orthodoxy. In the groups we have Roman Catholics, Methodists, members of the Church of England, the United Reformed Church, and the Christian Union, and the occasional Jew, Hindu, Muslim, Buddhist, atheist and agnostic.

Sometimes a group doesn't grow. Some people are shy, and are not ready for the group experience. Others want to go forward slowly. A few need individual attention. Some function quite happily in twos and threes. I reckon four or five is the best working number. Trust can still be maintained, and everyone can fully participate. Above this number, communication tends to break down.

I see *Visions of Hope* as a skeleton (or framework) of hope—and I leave it to the individual to put upon it (to clothe it with) his or her own flesh and blood.

Bill Sykes

ACCEPTANCE

Acceptance—favourable reception, approval, belief

At the age of ten I had a firm conviction that there was one job I would never do—that of being a priest.

In my teens, in the midst of a very active life, I became aware of a growing faith. This led to a commitment in my early twenties and a conviction that from now on, whatever happened, I was going to lead a Christian life. What particularly stimulated me was a quiet but encouraging awareness of the Holy Spirit.

At that time I was wrestling with the problem of what to do in life. Being a solicitor in the family firm had already been considered and rejected. I was keen to work overseas and wondered about applying to Shell, but my heart was not in oil so that was that. Whilst pondering over other possibilities I was suddenly challenged with the thought that if my Christian faith was so important to me, perhaps instead of just living it I ought to be actively engaged in spreading it?

A chord had been struck. There followed a great deal of kicking and struggling. Could I possibly work for such an archaic institution? Much to my surprise, in the space of a few days, my former firm conviction was overthrown and a state of acceptance reached. I was to be a priest after all. Over the years I have become aware of another area of acceptance which is something of a paradox. It involves at one level accepting the worst that life can throw at you, and at another level, facing disaster in the most creative way possible. Another facet of acceptance is being accepted by God and by other people. The passages which follow deal with both these aspects of acceptance, and so provide us with grounds for hope.

The beloved of the Lord, he dwells in safety by him; he encompasses him all the day long, and makes his dwelling between his shoulders.

Deuteronomy 33:12

Naked I came from my mother's womb, and naked shall I return; the Lord gave, and the Lord has taken away; blessed be the name of the Lord.

Job 1:21

Keep your life free from love of money, and be content with what you have; for he has said, 'I will never fail you nor forsake you.' Hence we can confidently say, 'The Lord is my helper, I will not be afraid; what can man do to me?'

Hebrews 13:5–6

Therefore put away all filthiness and rank growth of wickedness and receive with meekness the implanted word, which is able to save your souls.

James 1:21

It is so, it cannot be otherwise.

Anon.

What will be, will be.

Anon.

We must accept finite disappointment, but we must never lose infinite hope.

Martin Luther King, *The Words of Martin Luther King*, selected by Coretta Scott King, William Collins Sons & Co., 1986, page 25

The will of God... cannot be simply that we accept the situations of life but must be rather that we go through them and emerge from them.

John S. Dunne, *The Reasons of the Heart*, SCM Press, 1978, page 26

You often try to run away from your life, but you're wasting your time.

If you sincerely believe that your life is worthwhile and necessary, then you will have accepted it.

Michel Quoist, *With Open Heart*, translated by Colette Copeland, Gill and Macmillan, 1983, page 183

The self-accepting person has a realistic appraisal of his resources combined with appreciation of his own worth; assurance about standards and convictions of his own without being a slave to the opinions of others; and realistic assessment of limitations without irrational self-reproach.

Arthur T. Jersild, *The Psychology of Adolescence*, The Macmillan Company, 1963, page 34

One could say that the courage to be is the courage to accept oneself as accepted in spite of being unacceptable. One does not need to remind the theologians of the fact that this is the genuine meaning of the Paulinian-Lutheran doctrine of 'justification by faith.'

Paul Tillich, *The Courage to Be*, Nisbet & Co., 1952, page 156

As I see it, to live a day at a time means to accept the happiness which each day brings without spoiling it by deploring that I may not be able to enjoy the pleasures which I supposed the years had in store for me. It means to do that bit of my task which is within my power today without worrying about whether I shall be able to finish it, and leaving it in God's hands to make what use of it He can. It means bearing the day's suffering, if suffering there is to be, in the strength that the day brings, without wondering how I shall endure the more severe trials that may come, but believing that 'as thy days, so shall thy strength be'.

Leslie J. Tizard, *Facing Life and Death*, George Allen and Unwin, 1959, page 162

Out of evil, much good has come to me. By keeping quiet, repressing nothing, remaining attentive, and by accepting reality—taking things as they are, and not as I wanted them to be—by doing all this, unusual knowledge has come to me, and unusual powers as well, such as I could never have imagined before. I always thought that when we accepted things they overpowered us in some way or other. This turns out not to be true at all, and it is only by accepting them that one can assume an attitude toward them. So now I intend to play the game of life, being receptive to whatever comes to me, good and bad, sun and shadow that are forever alternating, and, in this way, also accepting my own nature with its positive and negative sides.

Thus everything becomes more alive to me. What a fool I was! How I tried to force everything to go according to the way I thought it ought to!

Richard Wilhelm & C.G. Jung, extract from a former patient, in *The Secret of the Golden Flower*, Routledge & Kegan Paul, 1972, page 126

There is more to be said for the Stoic 'resignation', which takes refuge in a grim refusal to lower one's head under the 'bludgeonings of chance', when the attitude is genuine, and not—as I suspect is more often the case—the mere self-conscious theatrical 'pose'. But I think we all know of a better way, which is followed in practice by thousands of humble souls under burdens more grievous than those which send the sentimentalists of literature to whining or cursing, according to temperament, and the literary Stoics to admiration of their own fortitude. It is possible to do better than to abstain from complaints or to cultivate pride; it is possible, and we all know of cases in which it is finely done, to make acceptance of the worst fortune has to bestow a means to the development of a sweetness, patience, and serene joyousness which are to be learned nowhere but in the school of sharp suffering... But this attitude is possible only on one condition: the affliction must be regarded as 'God's messenger'.

A.E. Taylor, *The Faith of a Moralist*, Macmillan and Co., 1930, volume I, page 153

Sometimes... a wave of light breaks into our darkness, and it is as though a voice were saying: 'You are accepted. *You are accepted*, accepted by that which is greater than you, and the name of which we do not know. Do not ask for the name now; perhaps you will find it later. Do not try to do anything now; perhaps later you will do much. Do not seek for anything; do not perform anything; do not intend anything. *Simply accept the fact that you are accepted!*' If that happens to us, we experience grace. After such an experience we may not be better than before, and we may not believe more than before. But everything is transformed. In that moment, grace conquers sin, and reconciliation bridges the gulf of estrangement. And nothing is demanded of this experience, no religious or moral or intellectual presupposition, nothing but *acceptance*.

Paul Tillich, *The Shaking of the Foundations*, SCM Press, 1949, page 162

And who will venture to say that the highest insight of the spirit is even half as constant as the highest action of the mind? Ask the saintliest men and women of this world, whether their holy watch was continuous, and their faith and love as reliable as their thought; and they will tell you how long, even when they went up to be with the Saviour on the mount, have been the slumbers of unconsciousness, compared with the priceless instants when they were awake and beheld his glory. In every earnest life, there are weary flats to tread, with the heavens out of sight,—no sun, no moon,—and not a tint of light upon the path below; when the only guidance is the faith of brighter hours, and the secret Hand we are too numb and dark to feel. But to the meek and faithful it is not always so. Now and then, something touches the dull dream of sense and custom, and the desolation vanishes away: the spirit leaves its witness with us: the divine realities come up from the past and straightway enter the present: the ear into which we poured our prayer is not deaf; the infinite eye to which we turned is not blind, but looks in with answering mercy on us. The mystery of life and the grievousness of death are gone: we know now the little from the great, the transient from the eternal: we can possess our souls in patience; and neither the waving palms and scattered flowers of triumph can elate us, nor the weight of any cross appear too hard to bear. Tell me not that these undulations of the soul are the mere instability of enthusiasm and infirmity. Are they not found characteristically in the greatest and deepest men,—Augustine, Tauler, Luther? Nay did not the Son of God himself, the very type of our humanity, experience them more than all?

Did he not quit the daily path, now for a Transfiguration, and now for a Gethsemene? did not his voice burst into the exclamation, 'I beheld Satan as lightning fall from heaven,' yet also confess, 'Now is my soul troubled'? and had he not his hours on the mountain all night? and what, think you, passed beneath those stars? Ah no! those intermittent movements are the sign of divine gifts, not of human weakness. God has so arranged the chronometry of our spirits that there shall be thousands of silent moments between the striking hours.

James Martineau, ***Hours of Thought on Sacred Things,*** **Longmans, Green, Reader and Dyer, 1880, volume I, page 10**

One of the deepest needs of the human heart is the need to be appreciated. Every human being wants to be valued... Every human being craves to be accepted, accepted for what he is... When I am not accepted, then something in me is broken... Acceptance means that the people with whom I live give me a feeling of self-respect, a feeling that I am worthwhile. They are happy that I am who I am. Acceptance means that I am welcome to be myself. Acceptance means that though there is need for growth, I am not forced. I do not have to be the person I am not! Neither am I locked in, by my past or present. Rather I am given room to unfold, to outgrow the mistakes of the past. In a way we can say that acceptance is an unveiling. Every one of us is born with many potentialities. But unless they are drawn out by the warm touch of another's acceptance, they will remain dormant. Acceptance liberates everything that is in me. Only when I am loved in that deep sense of complete acceptance can I become myself. The love, the acceptance of other persons, makes me the unique person that I am meant to be. When a person is appreciated for what he *does,* he is not unique; someone else can do the same work perhaps better than the other. But when a person is loved for what he *is,* then he becomes a unique and irreplaceable personality. So indeed, I need that acceptance in order to be myself. When I am not accepted, I am a nobody. I cannot come to fulfillment. An accepted person is a happy person because he is opened up, because he can grow.

To accept a person does not mean that I deny his defects, that I gloss over them or try to explain them away. Neither does acceptance mean to say that everything the person does is beautiful and fine. Just the opposite is true. When I deny the defects of the person, then I certainly do not accept him. I have not touched the depth of that person. Only when I accept a person can I truly face his defects...

I am accepted by God as I am—*as I am,* and not as I should be... He loves me with my ideals and disappointments, my sacrifices and my joys, my successes and my failures. God is himself the deepest Ground of my being. It is one thing to know I am accepted and quite another thing to realize it. It is not enough to have but just once touched the love of God. There is more required to build one's life on God's love. It takes a long time to believe that I am accepted by God as I am.

Peter G. van Breemen, S.J., ***As Bread That Is Broken,*** **Dimension Books, Inc., 1978, page 9**

ACTION

Action—process of acting, exertion, of energy or influence, as men of action, thing done, act

In 1969 I was appointed chaplain to University College, London, by the then Bishop of London—Robert Stopford. This was a college of 6,000 students, with an academic and administrative staff of approximately 2,000. I was greatly privileged to have a monk as a part-time assistant—Fr Simon Holden, of the Community of the Resurrection, Mirfield. We immediately struck up a rapport and over the years established a good working relationship.

Up to the point of meeting Simon I had been very active in my work, but not really effective. In him I soon became aware of a more passive approach to ministry. He was a man of deep insight and understanding. At university he had read English, and was currently involved in a research project concerned with the psychology of C.G. Jung. He was a good listener, and a man of great wisdom and discernment. As a monk his life was rooted in prayer and devotion. No wonder people with problems sought him out far and wide. I certainly learnt more from him than from anyone else, and greatly missed him when he returned to Mirfield five years later.

I still continued to meet students in an active way, playing in the college hockey and cricket teams, but inwardly a significant corner had been turned—the beginning of reflection and a blending of the passive and active. The future pattern of ministry began to emerge with an emphasis on individual and group work leading on to the development of the reflection groups.

Arise and be doing! The Lord be with you!

1 Chronicles 22:16

... but the people who know their God shall stand firm and take action.

Daniel 11:32

And let us not grow weary in well-doing, for in due season we shall reap, if we do not lose heart.

Galatians 6:9

You see that a man is justified by works and not by faith alone.

James 2:24

Pray, with *humility*; and do, with *diligence*.

Benjamin Whichcote, *Moral and Religious Aphorisms*, century x, number 912, Elkin Mathews & Marrot, 1930

There is nothing like active work for relieving and steadying the mind.

A.C. Benson, *Extracts from the Letters of Dr. A.C. Benson to M.E.A.*, Jarrold Publishing, 1927, page 6

No man can read the Gospels without being impressed with the immense activity of Christ.

Henry Ward Beecher, *Proverbs from Plymouth Pulpit*, Charles Burnet & Co., 1887, page 151

We cannot sit down and be devotional, while acquiescing in conditions which make it impossible for other souls even to obey the moral law.

Evelyn Underhill, in John Stobbart, editor, *The Wisdom of Evelyn Underhill*, A.R. Mowbray & Co., 1951, page 27

What frightens me most is the glorification of activity, especially when it happens in the Church. How can anything grow in us without passivity, the long, dull wait for birth?

Monica Furlong, *Travelling In*, Hodder and Stoughton, 1971, page 59

He who is morally active does not exert himself in vain, for much more of the seed falls on fertile ground than the Gospel all too modestly estimates in the parable of the sower.

Johann Wolfgang von Goethe, *Wisdom and Experience*, selected by Ludwig Curtius, translated and edited by Hermann J. Weigand, Routledge & Kegan Paul, 1949, page 210

I therefore go and join head, heart, and hand,
Active and firm, to fight the bloodless fight
Of Science, Freedom, and the Truth in Christ.

Samuel Taylor Coleridge, 'Reflections on Having left a place of Retirement', in Ernest Hartley Coleridge, editor, *The Complete Poetical Works of Samuel Taylor Coleridge*, Oxford at the Clarendon Press, 1975, volume I, page 100

Before giving the floor to 'thinkers' at meetings, let's give it to the 'doers'.
Yes... but the problem is they're not present—they're out working.

Michel Quoist, *With Open Heart*, translated by Colette Copeland, Gill and Macmillan, 1983, page 99

The means that heaven yields must be embraced
And not neglected. Else if heaven would
And we will not. Heavens offer, we refuse
The proffered means of succour and redress.

William Shakespeare, *Richard II*, III. ii. 29

All passion becomes strength when it has an outlet from the narrow limits of our personal lot in the labour of our right arm, the cunning of our right hand, or the still, creative activity of our thought.

George Eliot, *Adam Bede*, Virtue & Co., 1908, volume I, page 318

In Church and State alike one sees the results of action severed from its roots of passivity, the quiet brooding joy and agony which is anaesthetised by busyness... The real leaders in the coming years will be... those who know that the road to action lies through holiness and wholeness.

Monica Furlong, *Travelling In*, Hodder and Stoughton, 1971, page 37

The pressure of business is very good for the soul. After it has discharged its task the soul moves with greater ease and enjoys life. There is nothing more wretched than well-being without work. This is enough to make the finest of nature's gifts turn sour.

Johann Wolfgang von Goethe, *Wisdom and Experience*, selected by Ludwig Curtius, translated and edited by Hermann J. Weigand, Routledge & Kegan Paul, 1949, page 212

To save the mind from preying inwardly upon itself, it must be encouraged to some outward pursuit. There is no other way to elude apathy, or escape discontent; none other to guard the temper from that quarrel with itself, which ultimately ends in quarrelling with all mankind.

Fanny Burney, *Camilla*, edited by Edward A. Bloom and Lillian D. Bloom, Oxford University Press, 1983, page 41

No one need search for a programme of action or a crusade. The world and suffering humanity create the agenda for those who have eyes for human misery, ears for the stories of oppression and degradation and hearts to respond to the distress of our human family.

Basil Hume, OSB., *To Be a Pilgrim*, St Paul Publications, 1984, page 157

... Solitude has but few sacrifices to make, and may be innocent, but can hardly be greatly virtuous like Abraham, like Job, like the Roman Regulus or the apostle Paul. Great actions, from their nature, are not done in the closet; they are performed in the face of the sun, and on behalf of the world.

Ralph Waldo Emerson, *Journals*, Constable & Co., 1909, volume I, page 118

These two lives, action and contemplation, instead of excluding each other, call for each other's help, implement and complete each other. Action, to be productive, has need of contemplation. The latter, when it gets to a certain degree of intensity, diffuses some of its excess on the first. By contemplation the soul draws directly from the heart of God the graces which the active life must distribute.

Mother Teresa, *Jesus, the Word to be Spoken*, compiled by Brother Angelo Devananda, William Collins Sons & Co., 1990, page 8

Action and contemplation now grow together into one life and one unity. They become two aspects of the same thing. Action is charity looking outward to other men, and contemplation is charity drawn inward to its own divine source. Action is the stream, and contemplation is the spring. The spring remains more important than the stream, for the only thing that really matters is for love to spring up inexhaustibly from the infinite abyss of Christ and of God.

Thomas Merton, *No Man is an Island*, Burns & Oates, 1974, page 61

Let us make life one poem—not of dreams or sentiments—but of actions, not done Byronically as proofs of genius, but for our own self-education, alone, in secret, awaiting the crisis which shall call us forth to the battle to do just what other people do, only, perhaps, by an utterly different self-education. That is the life of great spirits, after, perhaps, many many years of seclusion, of select training in the lower paths of God's vineyard, till their hearts have settled into a still, deep, yet swift current, and those who have been faithful over a few things are made rulers over many things.

Charles Kingsley, *Daily Thoughts*, Macmillan and Co., 1884, page 215

Here we have no abiding-place—and I feel it more as I grow older and the days for service and for doing and for making often seem so few ahead and so few behind too. It is amazing and most puzzling when one tries to think what is the object of our short life on earth—a mere visit—and how desperately this must represent our effect on the little part of the world with which we come into contact. I get such a feeling of the absolute necessity to be at something always, and at every hour, day and night, before the end may come or I have done a decent portion of what I was expected to do; each minute is of value, though we so often waste hours and hours, not because we want rest, not because as sometimes it is a duty, but out of sheer want of application.

Edward Wilson, in George Seaver, *Edward Wilson of the Antarctic*, John Murray, 1935, page 169

When we have said all that we can, the secret mysteries of a new nature and divine life can never be sufficiently expressed; language and words cannot reach them; nor can they be truly understood, but by those souls that are inkindled within, and awakened into the sense and relish of spiritual things: *there is a spirit in man*, and *the inspiration of the Almighty giveth this understanding*. The power and life of religion may be better expressed in actions than in words, because actions are more lively things and do better represent the inward principle whence they proceed; and therefore we may take the best measure of those gracious endowments, from the department of those in whom they reside, especially as they are perfectly exemplified in the holy life of our blessed Saviour, a main part of whose business in this world was to teach by his practice what he did require of others, and to make his own conversation an exact resemblance of those unparalleled rules which he prescribed; so that if ever true goodness was visible to mortal eyes, it was then when his presence did beautify and illustrate this lower world.

Henry Scougal, ***The Life of God in the Soul of Man*****, C.J.G. & F. Rivington, 1829, page 16**

The appearances of doing good are often profoundly deceptive. Souls are saved by the holy, not by the busy. 'Action must never be allowed to be an obstacle to our union with God, but must serve rather to bind us more closely and lovingly to Him.' For 'just as there are certain humours which, when they are too abundant, cause the death of the body, so in the religious life, when action predominates to excess and is not tempered by prayer and meditation, it infallibly stifles the spirit.' Hence the fruitlessness of so many lives, seemingly so meritorious, so brilliant and so productive. Without the selfless inwardness which is the condition of inspiration, talent is fruitless, zeal and hard work produce nothing of spiritual value. 'A man of prayer can do more in a single year than another can accomplish in a whole lifetime.'

Exclusively outward work may be effective in changing outward circumstances; but the worker who wishes to change men's reactions to circumstances—and one can react destructively and suicidally to even the best environment—must begin by purifying his own soul and making it capable of inspiration. A merely outward man may work like a Trojan and talk like Demosthenes; but 'an inward man will make more impression of hearts and minds by a single word animated by the spirit of God' than the other can do by all his efforts, all his cleverness and learning.

Aldous Huxley, ***The Devils of Loudun*****, Penguin Books, 1973, page 91**

ADVERSITY

Adversity—condition of adverse fortune, misfortune

At University College, London, as chaplain to the college, I used to meet students following up my own interests. This seemed to me the most natural way of approach. Being musical I used to sing in the college choir.

After the first week or so, I met a member of the choir in the lunch queue in the lower refectory. He was a fresher, and terribly lonely and depressed. His home was in Suffolk. It was his first time away from home, and the transition from village life to the heart of London was just too much for him. He had no friends. He was feeling utterly miserable. He was reading law and felt he had made a mistake in his choice of subject. In short he was right up against adversity. I saw him a number of times over the next week or so. He eventually requested to leave college, take a year out, and hoped to try again next year. His plans were to work in a Rudolf Steiner School for handicapped young people in Switzerland, and try to work through his depression.

The following February there was a knock on my door, and there he was. Relaxing over a cup of coffee he explained he had suddenly realized in Switzerland that the subject he really wanted to read was history, not law, and wondered if I could do anything to effect the transition. As it happened one of the history lecturers had been a contemporary at Balliol College. I rang him, arranged a meeting, and he was accepted there and then for the following year. On his return to UCL, he never looked back and even went on to become a history teacher.

Sooner or later, we all come up against adversity in some shape or form. If faced with courage and determination, it can be put to good use and in turn be a great source of hope.

Even though I walk through the valley of the shadow of death, I will fear no evil; for thou art with me; thy rod and thy staff, they comfort me.

Psalm 23:4

God is our refuge and strength, a very present help in trouble.

Psalm 46:1

Blessed be the God and Father of our Lord Jesus Christ, the Father of mercies and God of all comfort, who comforts us in all our affliction, so that we may be able to comfort those who are in any affliction, with the comfort with which we ourselves are comforted by God.

2 Corinthians 1:3–4

Count it all joy, my brethren, when you meet various trials, for you know that the testing of your faith produces steadfastness. And let steadfastness have its full effect, that you may be perfect and complete, lacking in nothing.

James 1:2–4

. . . Turning past evils to advantages.

William Shakespeare, *II King Henry IV*, IV. iv. 78

He knows himself, and all that's in him, who knows adversity.

Herman Melville, *Mardi*, The New American Library of World Literature, 1964, page 491

. . .those
That would make good of bad and friends of foes.

William Shakespeare, *Macbeth*, II. iv. 40

God makes the life fertile by disappointment, as He makes its ground fertile by frost.

Henry Ward Beecher, *Proverbs from Plymouth Pulpit*, Charles Burnet & Co., 1887, page 209

Adversity's sweet milk, philosophy,
To comfort thee.

William Shakespeare, *Romeo and Juliet*, III. iii, 55

Henceforth I'll bear
Affliction till it do cry out itself
'Enough, enough,' and die.

William Shakespeare, *King Lear*, IV. vi. 74

All torment, trouble, wonder, and amazement,
Inhabits here. Some heavenly power guide us
Out of this fearful country!

William Shakespeare, *The Tempest*, V. i. 103

Affliction is the good man's shining scene!
Prosperity conceals his brightest ray;
As Night to stars, Woe lustre gives to man.

Edward Young, 'Night Thoughts', Night ix, in *The Complete Works of Edward Young*, William Tegg and Co., 1854, page 195

He went like one that hath been stunned,
And is of sense forlorn:
A sadder and a wiser man
He rose the morrow morn.

Samuel Taylor Coleridge, 'The Rime of the Ancient Mariner', Part 11, in Ernest Hartley Coleridge, editor, *The Complete Poetical Works of Samuel Taylor Coleridge*, Oxford at the Clarendon Press, 1975, volume I, page 209

Adversity is like the period of the former and of the latter rain cold, comfortless, unfriendly to man and to animal; yet from that season have their birth the flower and the fruit, the date, the rose, and the pomegranate.

Sir Walter Scott, *The Talisman*, Oxford University Press, 1912, page 168

. . . yet famine,
Ere clean it o'erthrow nature, makes it valiant.
Plenty, and peace, breeds cowards; hardness ever
Of hardiness is mother.

William Shakespeare, *Cymbeline*, III. vi. 19

Thus sometimes hath the brightest day a cloud,
And after summer evermore succeeds
Barren winter, with his wrathful nipping cold;
So cares and joys abound, as seasons fleet.

William Shakespeare, *II King Henry VI*, II. iv. 1

He that has never known adversity is but half acquainted with others, or with himself. Constant success shows us but one side of the world. For, as it surrounds us with friends, who will tell us only our merits, so it silences those enemies from whom alone we can learn our defects.

Charles Caleb Colton, *Lacon*, William Tegg, 1866, page 5

I have touched the highest point of all my greatness,
And from that full meridian of my glory
I haste now to my setting. I shall fall
Like a bright exhalation in the evening,
And no man see me more.

William Shakespeare, *Henry VIII*, III. ii. 223

The Gods, in bounty, work up storms about us,
That give mankind occasion to exert
Their hidden strength, and throw out into practice

Virtues, which shun the day, and lie conceal'd
In the smooth seasons and the calms of life.

Joseph Addison, *Cato*, II. iv. 54, in A.C. Guthkelch, editor, *The Miscellaneous Works of Joseph Addison*, G. Bell and Sons, Volume 1, 'Poems and Plays', page 379

... who never heard the voice of reproof, or felt the keen blast of the wintry wind, is usually a slave to himself, and a tyrant to his vassals; while, on the contrary, he that, by adversity, has been taught that he is no more than his fellows, treats his dependents with gentleness, and becomes a blessing to all.

Elizabeth Helme, *St. Margaret's Cove: or, The Nun's Story*, printed for Earle and Hement, 1801, page 122

... as the icy fang
And churlish chiding of the winter's wind,
Which, when it bites and blows upon my body
Even till I shrink with cold, I smile, and say...
These are counsellors...
And this our life...
Finds tongues in trees, books in the running brooks,
Sermons in stones, and good in every thing.

William Shakespeare, *As You Like It*, II. i. 5

Farewell, a long farewell to all my greatness!
This is the state of man; today he puts forth
The tender leaves of hope, tomorrow blossoms,
And bears his blushing honours thick upon him:
The third day comes a frost, a killing frost,
And when he thinks, good easy man, full surely
His greatness is a-ripening, nips his root,
And then he falls as I do.

William Shakespeare, *Henry VIII*, III. ii. 351

I saw him beat the surges under him,
And ride upon their backs; he trod the water,
Whose enmity he flung aside, and breasted
The surge most swoln that met him; his bold head
'Bove the contentious waves he kept, and oared
Himself with his good arms in lusty stroke
To th'shore, that o'er his wave-worn basis bowed...
He came alive to land.

William Shakespeare, *The Tempest*, II. i. 109

The virtue of prosperity, is temperance; the virtue of adversity, is fortitude: which in morals is the more heroical virtue. Prosperity is the blessing of the Old Testament; adversity is the blessing of the New; which carrieth the greater Benediction, and the clearer revelation of God's favour... and the pencil of the holy ghost, hath laboured more, in describing the afflictions of Job than the felicities of Solomon. Prosperity is not without many fears and distastes; and adversity is not without comforts and hopes.

Francis Bacon, *The Essays or Counsels, Civil and Moral*, Clarendon Press, 1985, page 18

I am sick—if I should die what would become of me? We forget ourselves and our destinies in health, and the chief use of temporary sickness is to remind us of these concerns. I must improve my time better. I must prepare myself for the great profession I have purposed to undertake. I am to give my soul to God and withdraw from sin and the world the idle or vicious time and thoughts I have sacrificed to them; and let me consider this as a resolution by which I pledge myself to act in all variety of circumstances, and to which I must recur often in times of carelessness and temptation, to measure my conduct by the rule of conscience.

Ralph Waldo Emerson, *Journals*, Constable & Co., 1909, volume I, page 78

Why then, you princes,
Do you with cheeks abash'd behold our works
And call them shames, which are, indeed, naught else
But the protractive trials of great Jove
To find persistive constancy in men;
The fineness of which metal is not found
In fortune's love? For then the bold and coward,
The wise and fool, the artist and unread,
The hard and soft, seem all affin'd and kin.
But in the wind and tempest of her frown,
Distinction, with a broad and powerful fan,
Puffing at all, winnows the light away;
And what hath mass or matter, by itself
Lies rich in virtue and unmingled.

William Shakespeare, *Troilus and Cressida*, I. iii. 17

AGE

Age—length of time or of existence, duration of life required for a purpose, latter part of life

One of our dons recently took early retirement. In some ways he has led a conventional life. Having completed his degree and doctorate he got married and he and his wife produced three children. In his working life he continued his research and was a tutor in college for the best part of thirty years. He then had a serious illness which required major surgery, and following this decided to take early retirement. His wife in her professional life worked for several years as a college secretary.

By this time the children had grown up and left home. They no longer needed to be supported. The first major step was to acquire a property in a remote part of Scotland which required considerable renovation. All kinds of skills were required to make a successful transformation. They both found this creative and rejuvenating.

Now that they had another base, the question arose as to what to do next? It was at this point that they took up hobbies, the husband began to paint and the wife worked full-time with silver and jewelry. Both have recently taken part in an art exhibition, and have begun to market their creations. An exciting new life has evolved for this couple. This section is largely concerned with the latter part of life. Nowadays enormous emphasis is put on the importance of youth and the active life, but the latter part of life is equally important and a valuable source of hope.

So teach us to number our days that we may get a heart of wisdom.

Psalm 90:12

He will not much remember the days of his life because God keeps him occupied with joy in his heart.

Ecclesiastes 5:20

Stay with us, for it is toward evening and the day is now far spent.

Luke 24:29

But as for you, teach what benefits sound doctrine. Bid the older men be temperate, serious, sensible, sound in faith, in love, and in steadfastness. Bid the older women likewise to be reverent in behaviour, not to be slanderers or slaves to drink; they are to teach what is good.

Titus 2:1–3

The weakness of age... is the penalty paid by the folly of youth.

Anthony Trollope, *He Knew He Was Right*, Oxford University Press, 1948, page 436

The best part of the art of living is to know how to grow old gracefully.

Eric Hoffer, *The Passionate State of Mind*, Secker & Warburg, 1956, page 108

Thirty-nine. It is a good age. One begins to appreciate things at their true value.

Norman Douglas, *An Almanac*, Chatto & Windus in association with Martin Secker & Warburg, 1945, page 66

Many a mourner over a wasted life may yet be shown that he was fruitful of good when he knew it not.

Henry Ward Beecher, *Proverbs from Plymouth Pulpit*, Charles Burnet & Co., 1887, page 43

My day is done, and I am like a boat drawn on the beach, listening to the dance-music of the tide in the evening.

Rabindranath Tagore, 'Stray Birds', LV, in *Collected Poems & Plays of Rabindranath Tagore*, Macmillan & Co., 1936, page 294

I like your account of his tranquillity in declining years. That is, or should be, the normal and happy outcome of a useful life.

A.C. Benson, *Extracts from the Letters of Dr. A.C. Benson to M.E.A.*, Jarrold Publishing, 1927, page 35

Things look dim to old folks: they'd need have some young eyes about 'em, to let 'em know the world's the same as it used to be.

George Eliot, *Silas Marner*, Virtue & Co., 1912, page 271

It ought to be lovely to be old
to be full of the peace that comes of experience
and wrinkled ripe fulfilment.

D.H. Lawrence, 'Beautiful Old Age', in Vivian de Sola Pinto and Warren Roberts, editors, *The Complete Poems of D.H. Lawrence*, William Heinemann, 1967, volume I, page 503

It is a criminal blunder of our maturer years that we so tamely, and without frantic and habitual struggles to retain it, allow *The ecstasy of the unbounded* to slip away out of our lives.

John Cowper Powys, *Autobiography*, Macdonald and Co. (Publishers), 1967, page 2

To love playthings well as a child, to lead an adventurous and honourable youth, and to settle when the time arrives, into a green and smiling age, is to be a good artist in life and deserve well of yourself and your neighbour.

Robert Louis Stevenson, *Virginibus Puerisque*, Chatto & Windus, 1906, page 64

Yet Time, who changes all, had altered him
His soul and aspect as in age: years steal
Fire from the mind as vigour from the limb;
And Life's enchanted cup but sparkles near the brim.

Lord Byron, 'Childe Harold', Canto III, viii, in Ernest Hartley Coleridge, editor, *The Poetical Works of Lord Byron*, John Murray, 1905, page 186

I have scaled the peak and found no shelter in fame's bleak and barren height. Lead me, my Guide, before the light fades, into the valley of quiet where life's harvest mellows into golden wisdom.

Rabindranath Tagore, 'Stray Birds', CCCXX, in *Collected Poems & Plays of Rabindranath Tagore*, Macmillan & Co., 1936, page 328

Tho' old, he still retain'd
His manly sense, and energy of mind.
Virtuous and wise he was, but not severe;
He still remember'd that he once was young.

John Armstrong, *The Art of Preserving Health*, printed for T. Cadell, Jun. and W. Davies, 1795, book IV, page 135

All the world's a stage,
And all the men and women merely players.
They have their exits and their entrances,
And one man in his time plays many parts,
His acts being seven ages.

William Shakespeare, *As You Like It*, II. vii. 139

Our religions were always 'schools for forty-year-olds' in the past, but how many people regard them as such today? How many of us older persons have really been brought up in such a school and prepared for the second half of life, for old age, death, and eternity?

C.G. Jung, *Psychological Reflections*, selected and edited by Jolande Jacobi, Routledge & Kegan Paul, 1953, page 124

A venerable aspect!
Age sits with decent grace upon his visage,
And worthily become his silver locks;
He wears the marks of many years well spent,
Of virtue, truth well try'd, and wise experience.

Nicholas Rowe, *Dolby's British Theatre*, T. Dolby, Britannia Press, *Jane Shore*, page 10

Learn to live well, or fairly make your Will;
You've play'd, and lov'd, and eat, and drank your fill:
Walk sober off, before a sprightlier Age,
Comes titt'ring on, and shoves you from the stage:
Leave such to trifle with more grace and ease,
Whom Folly pleases, and whose Follies please.

Alexander Pope, 'Imitations of Horace', epistle II. ii. 322, in *The Poems of Alexander Pope*, Methuen & Co., 1969, volume IV, page 187

Of no distemper, of no blast he dy'd,
But fell like Autumn-Fruit that mellow'd long:
Even wonder'd at, because he dropt no sooner.
Fate seem'd to wind him up for fourscore years;
Yet freshly ran he on ten Winters more:
Till, like a Clock worn out with eating time,
The Wheels of weary life at last stood still.

John Dryden, *Oedipus*, IV. i. 228, in *The Works of John Dryden*, University of California Press, 1984, volume XIII, page 184

In the second half of life there is a natural movement of the imagination towards being rather than doing, away from prestige-motivated acquisition and accomplishment, and tentatively towards life's meaning, whether or not conscious religion has been important in the preceding years. There is usually a growth of concern about what things need more tenderness than they are getting, how much one's marriage needs re-shaping, how you are to bear the world's beauty when you have reached that point in the journey when you have a strong suspicion that the end of your life is following you.

J. Neville Ward, *Friday Afternoon*, Epworth Press, 1982, page 117

Let us have done with vain regrets and longings for the days that never will be ours again. Our work lies in front, not behind us; again 'Forward!' is our motto. Let us not sit with folded hands, gazing upon the past as if it were the building: it is but the foundation. Let us not waste heart and life, thinking of what might have been, and forgetting the maybe that lies before us. Opportunities flit by while we sit regretting the chances we have lost, and the happiness that comes to us we heed not, because of the happiness that is gone.

Jerome K. Jerome, *Idle Thoughts of an Idle Fellow*, J.M. Dent & Sons, 1983, page 163

Whom the gods love, die young.
How the gods must hate most of the old, old men today,
the rancid old men that don't die
because the gods don't want them
won't have them
leave them to stale on earth.

Old people fixed in a rancid resistence
to life, fixed to the letter of the law.

The gods, who are life, and the fluidity of living change
leave the old ones fixed to their ugly, cogged self-will
which turns on and on, the same, and is hell on earth.

D.H. Lawrence, 'Old Men', in Vivian de Sola Pinto and Warren Roberts, editors, *The Complete Poems of D.H. Lawrence*, William Heinemann, 1967, volume II, page 662

To grow old is more difficult than to die, because to renounce a good once and for all, costs less than to renew the sacrifice day by day and in detail. To bear with one's own decay, to accept one's own lessening capacity, is a harder and rarer virtue than to face death. There is a halo round tragic and premature death; there is but a long sadness in declining strength. But look closer; so studied, a resigned and religious old age will often move us more than the heroic ardour of young years. The maturity of the soul is worth more than the first brilliance of its faculties, or the plenitude of its strength, and the eternal in us can but profit from all the ravages made by time. There is comfort in this thought.

Henri Frédéric Amiel, *Amiel's Journal*, translated by Mrs Humphry Ward, Macmillan & Co., 1918, page 77

Christianity alone deprives old age of its bitterness, making it the gate of heaven. Our bodies will fade and grow weak and shapeless, just when we shall not want them, being ready and in close expectation of that resurrection of the flesh which is the great promise of Christianity (no miserable fancies about 'pure souls' escaped from matter, but)—of bodies, *our* bodies, beloved, beautiful, ministers to us in all our joys, sufferers with us in all our sorrows—yea, our own selves raised up again to live and love in a manner inconceivable from its perfection.

. . . No! I can wait:
Another body!—Ah, new limbs are ready,
Free, pure, instinct with soul through every nerve,
Kept for us in the treasuries of God!

Charles Kingsley, *Daily Thoughts*, Macmillan and Co., 1884, page 63

Old age is the most precious time of life, the one nearest eternity. There are two ways of growing old. There are old people who are anxious and bitter, living in the past and illusion, who criticise everything that goes on around them. Young people are repulsed by them; they are shut away in their sadness and loneliness, shrivelled up in themselves. But there are also old people with a child's heart, who have used their freedom from function and responsibility to find a new youth. They have the wonder of a child, but the wisdom of maturity as well. They have integrated their years of activity and so can live without being attached to power. Their freedom of heart and their acceptance of their limitations and weakness makes them people whose radiance illuminates the whole community. They are gentle and merciful, symbols of compassion and forgiveness. They become a community's hidden treasures, sources of unity and life. They are true contemplatives at the heart of community.

Jean Vanier, *Community and Growth*, Darton, Longman and Todd, 1991, page 140

AMBITION

Ambition—ardent desire for distinction; aspiration (to be, to do); object of such desire

A new academic year began at University College, London. I went out to our sports ground at Shenley for our first hockey match of the season. The omens were encouraging. Our First XI were usually pretty good, but the Second XI tended to be mediocre. This year we were pleasantly surprised when our Second XI chalked up a 14–0 victory, and apparently eleven of these goals had been scored by one person. He was immediately promoted to the First XI, where he proved to be a great success. He was particularly good at scoring goals. He used to aim at the top corner of the net, and could do this effortlessly by perfect timing. Gradually we learnt that hockey was not his main sport. He was reputed to be a promising cricketer and there were whispers he might be playing for Leicestershire in the summer, and perhaps one day for England. You might already have guessed who this was—David Gower. He went on to captain England and score more runs in test cricket than any other Englishman. At our time of knowing him none of us classified him as an overtly ambitious person. He was pleasant and unassuming, merely someone needing an outlet for his considerable talents.

Looking through the material of this section there seem to be two main views on ambition—one in which there is an ardent desire for distinction (and possibly the presence of selfishness)—and the other, which is merely the outworking of particular gifts and talents, exercised for the common good, and as such, sources of hope.

A man's mind plans his way,
but the Lord directs his steps.

Proverbs 16:9

A faithful man will abound with blessings, but he who hastens to be rich will not go unpunished.

Proverbs 28:20

For what does it profit a man, to gain the whole world and forfeit his life?

Mark 8:36

For where jealousy and selfish ambition exist, there will be disorder and every vile practice.

James 3:16

Ambition makes people diligent.

Proverb

Few things are impossible to diligence and skill.

Samuel Johnson, *The History of Rasselas*, Oxford University Press, 1971, page 37

... God's gifts put man's best dreams to shame.

Elizabeth Barrett Browning, 'Sonnets from the Portuguese', xxvi. 14, *The Poetical Works of Elizabeth Barrett Browning*, Henry Froude, 1904, page 323

A man without ambition is worse than dough that has no yeast in it to raise it.

Henry Ward Beecher, *Proverbs from Plymouth Pulpit*, Charles Burnet & Co., 1887, page 8

Ambition is the spur that makes man struggle with destiny. It is heaven's own incentive to make purpose great and achievement greater.

Anon.

The world owes all its onward impulses to men ill at ease. The happy man inevitably confines himself within ancient limits.

Nathaniel Hawthorne, *House of the Seven Gables*, Harper & Row, Publishers, 1965, page 206

If men could regard the events of their own lives with more open minds they would frequently discover that they did not really desire the things they failed to obtain.

André Maurois, *The Art of Living*, The English Universities Press, 1940, page 206

I charge thee, fling away ambition;
By that sin fell the angels. How can man then,
The image of his Maker, hope to win by it?

William Shakespeare, *Henry VIII*, III. ii. 440

He that seeketh to be eminent amongst able men, hath a great task; but that is ever good for the public. But he that plots, to be the only figure among ciphers, is the decay of an whole age.

Francis Bacon, 'Of Ambition', in *The Essays or Counsels, Civil and Moral*, Clarendon Press, 1985, page 116

I have no spur
To prick the sides of my intent, but only
Vaulting ambition, which o'er-leaps itself,
And falls on th'other.

William Shakespeare, *Macbeth*, I. vii. 25

Oh sons of earth! attempt ye still to rise,
By mountains pil'd on mountains, to the skies?
Heav'n still with laughter the vain toil surveys,
And buries madmen in the heaps they raise.

Alexander Pope, 'An Essay on Man', iv. 73, in *The Poems of Alexander Pope*, Methuen & Co., volume III–I, page 135

It is not at all necessary to be great, so long as we are in harmony with the order of the universe. Moral ambition has no pride; it only desires to fill its place, and make its note duly heard in the universal concert of the God of love.

Henri Frédéric Amiel, *Amiel's Journal*, translated by Mrs Humphry Ward, Macmillan & Co., 1918, page 165

Unnumber'd suppliants crowd Preferment's gate,
Athirst for wealth, and burning to be great;
Delusive Fortune hears th'incessant call.
They mount, they shine, evaporate and fall.

Samuel Johnson, 'The Vanity of Human Wishes', in *The Yale Edition of the Works of Samuel Johnson*, Yale University Press, 1964, volume VI, 'Poems', page 95

The grand secret of enjoying yourself with a free heart is to get rid of ambition, rid of even the most trifling competitions with other poor devils. But we must have our pride; and we must have a very deep pride. We must have a pride in simply being ourselves and beyond any conceivable competition.

John Cowper Powys, *Autobiography*, Macdonald & Co. (Publishers), 1967, page 622

Ambition makes the same mistake concerning power, that avarice makes concerning wealth; she begins by accumulating power as a means to happiness, and she finishes by continuing to accumulate it as an end. Ambition is, in fact, the avarice of power, and happiness herself is soon sacrificed to that very lust of dominion which was first encouraged only as the best mode of attaining it.

Charles Caleb Colton, *Lacon*, William Tegg, 1866, page 7

... what is called ambition had no room or time to sprout. Ambitious people are forced—as one learns from reading their lives—to cut down rigidly upon their contemplative tendencies, to harden themselves *against* their momentary sensations. I *lived* for sensations; and have always, in my deepest heart regarded such a life as the only adequate return we can make to Nature for giving us birth!

John Cowper Powys, *Autobiography*, Macdonald & Co. (Publishers), 1967, page 237

The true Ambition there alone resides,
Where Justice vindicates, and Wisdom guides;
Where inward dignity joins outward state;
Our purpose good, as our achievement great;
Where public blessings public praise attend;
Where glory is our motive, not our end.
Wouldst thou be famed? have those high acts in view
Brave men would act, though scandal should ensue.

Edward Young, 'Love of Fame, the Universal Passion', vii. 175, in *The Complete Works of Edward Young*, William Tegg and Co., 1854, volume I, page 408

... Ambition is a good thing, but I think that one may take it as one's aim only in things which one has set one's-self to achieve, has made the reason for one's existence. In anything else it's nonsense. The only essential is to live with ease; and moreover one must sympathize with one's fellow-creatures, and strive to win their sympathy in return. And if, indeed, one had no other determined aim, this would by itself more than suffice.

Fyodor Dostoyevsky, *Letters of Fyodor Michailovitch Dostoyevsky to his Family and Friends*, translated by Ethel Colburn Mayne, Peter Owen, 1962, page 104

He who ascends to mountain tops, shall find
The loftiest peaks most wrapt in clouds and snow;
He who surpassed or subdues mankind,
Must look down on the hate of those below.
Though high *above* the Sun of Glory glow,
And far *beneath* the Earth and Ocean spread,
Round him are icy rocks, and loudly blow
Contending tempests on his naked head,
And thus reward the toils which to those summits led.

Lord Byron, 'Childe Harold', canto III. xlv, in Ernest Hartley Coleridge, editor, *The Poetical Works of Lord Byron*, John Murray, 1905, page 191

Ambition is to the mind what the cap is to the falcon; it *blinds* us first, and then compels us to tower by reason of our blindness. But, alas! when we are at the summit of a vain ambition, we are also at the *depth* of real misery. We are placed where time cannot improve, but must impair us; where chance and change cannot befriend, but may betray us. In short, by attaining all we wish, and gaining all we want, we have only reached a pinnacle where we have nothing to hope, but everything to fear.

Charles Caleb Colton, *Lacon*, William Tegg, 1866, page 8

They that soar too high, often fall hard; which makes a low and level dwelling preferable. The tallest trees are most in the power of the winds; and ambitious men, of the blast of fortune. They are most seen and observed, and most envied; least quiet, but most talked of, and not often to their advantage. Those builders had need of a good foundation, that lie so much exposed to weather. Good works are a rock that will support their credit; but ill ones, a sandy foundation, that yields to calamities. And truly they ought to expect no pity in their fall, who, when in power, had no bowels for the unhappy.

The worst of distempers; always craving and thirsty, restless and hated: a perfect delirium in the mind, unsufferable in success, and in disappointment most revengeful.

William Penn, *Fruits of Solitude*, A.W. Bennett, 1863, page 77

ANXIETY

Anxiety—uneasiness, concern; solicitous desire (for a thing, to do)

Towards the end of my two-year period of National Service, the Battalion was sent off to patrol a jungle area for a month. We were required to do this mostly on foot, but commandeered some power boats for river surveillance and communication. I spent the first part of this manoeuvre with my platoon in the jungle and for the second part stayed close to the CO. With the rivers in flood and small patrols scattered over a vast area, it became important to remain in touch by radio. My task was to keep him briefed so that he could transmit fresh orders for the following day.

It was early evening. Progress reports were coming in. One patrol had a major problem. They were required to reach a village the next day to collect a boat. The area through which they had to go was flooded. During that day they had already covered jungle with water up to their chests. (Gurkhas are notoriously bad swimmers). What should they do? I discussed it briefly with the patrol commander. This was difficult because of radio interference—always an occupational hazard with evening atmospherics in that part of the world. My last words before we lost complete contact were—they must go ahead as planned.

An acute state of anxiety then set in. Had I in fact committed these men to their doom? A sleepless night ensued. In the early hours I could envisage the words of a court of enquiry—a dishonourable discharge seemed inevitable. There was nothing I could do to change the situation. It was out of my control.

The following evening the report came in. They had collected the boat—but the water had been at chin-level for some of them.

Anxiety hits us all from time to time. The quotations have been selected to help us face anxiety in a constructive and hopeful way.

Cast your burden on the Lord, and he will sustain you.

Psalm 55:22

Anxiety in a man's heart weighs him down, but a good word makes him glad.

Proverbs 12:25

Do not be anxious about your life, what you shall eat or what you shall drink, nor about your body, what you shall put on. Is not life more than food, and the body more than clothing? Look at the birds of the air: they neither sow nor reap nor gather into barns, and yet your heavenly Father feeds them. Are you not of more value than they? And which of you by being anxious can add one cubit to his span of life? And why are you anxious about clothing? Consider the lilies of the field, how they grow; they neither toil nor spin; yet I tell you, even Solomon in all his glory was not arrayed like one of these. But if God so clothes the grass of the field, which today is alive and tomorrow is thrown into the oven, will he not much more clothe you, O men of little faith? Therefore do not be anxious, saying, 'What shall we eat?' or 'What shall we drink?' or 'What shall we wear?' For the Gentiles seek all these things; and your heavenly Father knows that you need them all. But seek first his kingdom and his righteousness, and all these things shall be yours as well. Therefore do not be anxious about tomorrow, for tomorrow will be anxious for itself. Let the day's own trouble be sufficient for the day.

Matthew 6:25–34

Have no anxiety about anything, but in everything by prayer and supplication with thanksgiving let your requests be made known to God.

Philippians 4:6

People often do the idlest acts of their lifetimes in their heaviest and most anxious moments.

Nathaniel Hawthorne, *The Marble Faun*, The Bobbs-Merrill Company, 1971, page 197

In the depth of the anxiety of having to die is the anxiety of being eternally forgotten.

Paul Tillich, *The Eternal Now*, SCM Press, 1963, page 24

It is a help to have something to do, and not to creep about in a dim fatiguing dream of anxiety.

A.C. Benson, *Extracts from the Letters of Dr. A.C. Benson to M.E.A.*, Jarrold Publishing, 1927, page 69

Anxiety, fear, ill-fated desire are signatures on the human face. Suffering and anxious care are written there.

Henry Ward Beecher, *Proverbs from Plymouth Pulpit*, Charles Burnet & Co., 1887, page 18

Anxiety usually comes from strain, and strain is caused by too complete a dependence on ourselves, on our own devices, our own plans, our own idea of what we are able to do.

Thomas Merton, *No Man Is an Island*, Burns & Oates, 1974, page 197

If what we have we receive as a gift, and if what we have is to be cared for by God, and if what we have is available to others, then we will possess freedom from anxiety.

Richard Foster, *The Celebration of Discipline*, Hodder and Stoughton, 1982, page 77

In our age everything has to be a 'problem.' Ours is a time of anxiety because we have willed it to be so. Our anxiety is not imposed on us by force from outside. We impose it on our world and upon one another from within ourselves.

Thomas Merton, *Thoughts in Solitude*, Burns & Oates, 1958, page 71

It is probably good for most people to have an occasional shock of fright with reference to their shortcomings; but there is no doubt that to live under the constant pressure of fear—in the sense of anxiety concerning one's self—is deeply demoralising.

William Temple, *Nature, Man and God*, Macmillan & Co., 1934, page 460

The release of anxiety is to turn cares into prayers. If we feel anxious about somebody, ill or in danger or need, that anxiety does no good to us or to them. But if that anxiety is turned into a prayer, it widens and enriches our spiritual life, it turns a thought which is depressing into a thought which is uplifting, and it helps the person we are praying for.

Geoffrey Harding, in George Appleton, *Journey for a Soul*, William Collins Sons & Co., 1976, page 114

... if God has you, then He has your yesterdays and your tomorrows. He has your yesterdays and forgives all that has been amiss in them; He has your tomorrows and will provide grace and power to meet them. But only as they come. He will not provide for what is not yet here. His grace is like manna—when kept over for the next day, it spoiled. It had to be eaten day by day.

E. Stanley Jones, *Growing Spiritually*, Hodder and Stoughton, 1954, page 45

In my own life, anxiety, trouble, and sorrow have been allotted to me at times in such abundant measure that had my nerves not been so strong, I must have broken down under the weight. Heavy is the burden of fatigue and responsibility which has lain upon me without a break for years. I have not much of my life for myself, not even the hours I should like to devote to my wife and child.

Albert Schweitzer, *My Life and Thought*, translated by C.T. Campion, Allen & Unwin, 1924, page 281

God is a Being, joyful, satisfied, and blessed. Let your spirit therefore be glad and satisfied. Avoid all anxious cares, all taking of offence, all murmuring and gloominess, which cloud the heart, and make it unfit for intercourse with God. Turn gently away when you perceive any of these things likely to beset you. Let the world and passing things be strange and foreign to your heart; but let it be at home with God, in the intimacy of love. Be as strict as you will with yourself, and your evil passions and self-love and self-will; but with God be free as a loving child with a Father, confiding restfully in Him, seeing in Him the Friend of your innermost heart, and imagining in Him nothing but perfect love.

Gerhard Tersteegen, in Frances Bevan, *Sketches of the Quiet in the Land*, John F. Shaw and Co., 1891, page 401

To live thus, to cram today with eternity and not with the next day, the Christian has learnt and continues to learn (for the Christian is always learning) from the Pattern. How did He manage to live without anxiety for the next day—He who from the first instant of His public life when He stepped forward as a teacher knew how His life would end, that the next day was His crucifixion, knew this while the people exultantly hailed Him as King (ah, bitter knowledge to have at precisely that moment!), knew when they were crying, 'Hosanna!', at His entry into Jerusalem that they would cry, 'Crucify Him!', and that it was to this end He made His entry; He who bore every day the prodigious weight of this superhuman knowledge—how did He manage to live without anxiety for the next day?

Søren Kierkegaard, *Christian Discourses*, translated by Walter Lowrie, Princeton University Press, 1974, page 78

The secret of happiness lies in the avoidance of Angst (anxiety, spleen, noia, guilt, fear, remorse...). It is a mistake to consider happiness as a positive state. By removing Angst, the condition of all unhappiness, we are then prepared to receive any blessings to which we are entitled. We know very little about Angst, which may even proceed from the birth trauma, or be a primitive version of the sense of original sin, but we can try to find out what makes it worse. Angst may take the form of remorse about the past, guilt about the present, anxiety about the future. Often it is due to our acceptance of conventional habits of living, through an imperfect knowledge of ourselves...

Fatigue is a cause of Angst, which often disappears if the tired person is able to lie down; bad air is another... a frequent cause of Angst is an awareness of the waste of our time and ability.

Cyril Connolly, *The Unquiet Grave*, Hamish Hamilton, 1945, page 22

The problem of anxiety has become a major problem of our time. How many forms of anxiety there are! There is anxiety about the delicately poised balance within the marriage situation. How many marriages are near to breaking-point, with few outside the family circle aware of the tragedy that threatens! There is anxiety about success. Ambition can be a disease. There is anxiety about our health. The duodenal ulcer has been described in America as the 'wound-stripe of our civilization' since it seems to be caused, partly at least, by the pace and problems of to-day. There is the anxiety which parents find it so easy to justify, anxiety about the children—their health, their future, their schooling, their happiness, their success. This very anxiety prevents parents from being the kind of companions to their children they want to be, and subtly, communicates itself to the children. That will-o'-the-wisp we call security is breeding edginess that makes security worthless when it is found. And underground all the time, burrowing at the roots of life, is the great nameless anxiety about the possibility of an atomic war that would wreck our civilization.

Charles S. Duthie, *God in His World*, Independent Press, 1955, page 15

The anxiety of meaninglessness is anxiety about the loss of an ultimate concern, of a meaning which gives meaning to all meanings. This anxiety is aroused by the loss of a spiritual centre, of an answer, however symbolic and indirect, to the question of the meaning of existence.

The anxiety of emptiness is aroused by the threat of non-being to the special contents of the spiritual life. A belief breaks down through external events or inner processes: one is cut off from creative participation in a sphere of culture, one feels frustrated about something which one had passionately affirmed, one is driven from devotion to one object of devotion to another and again on to another, because the meaning of each of them vanishes and the creative eros is transformed into indifference or aversion. Everything is tried and nothing satisfied. The contents of the tradition, however excellent, however praised, however loved once, lose their power to give content *to-day*. And present culture is even less able to provide the content. Anxiously one turns away from all concrete contents and looks for an ultimate meaning, only to discover that it was precisely the loss of a spiritual centre which took away the meaning from the special contents of the spiritual life. But a spiritual centre cannot be produced intentionally, and the attempt to produce it only produces deeper anxiety. The anxiety of emptiness drives us to the abyss of meaninglessness.

Paul Tillich, *The Courage To Be*, Nisbet & Co., 1952, page 44

ART

Art—skill applied to imitation and design, as in painting, etc., of artistic design, etc., thing in which skill may be exercised

At theological college, we were each assigned a pastoral task to give us some experience of the 'real world' before ordination. I was a member of a small team which went to an experimental boarding school for boys with problems. We used to go there twice a week—once on a Wednesday evening to get to know the boys, and then on a Sunday morning to take a service.

The school had a mid-term break. There was one boy who had no home to go to, and was stuck at school for the brief holiday. We invited him to come and stay with us at college for a couple of days. As you can imagine, it was not long before he was bored stiff. One of our team knew he had an artistic streak so bought him brushes and paints, and offered him a wall of his room, for a mural.

This fourteen-year-old boy got down to work. He became thoroughly engrossed in the assignment. He spent all day painting, refused all meals, and forbade all entry into the room by curious onlookers. He laboured on throughout the night, and at nine o'clock the following morning, we were invited in for a showing. We were spell-bound and completely taken aback by what we saw. What he had produced was a magnificent picture of the nativity. It was the work of a genius. He claimed he had no prior knowledge of ever having seen a picture of the nativity.

Where had this artistic 'gift' and inspiration come from? I wonder if this is yet another consequence of 'the divine inbreathing' of the Genesis story of the creation of man. This is what many of the quotations are suggesting. Many of us may have latent artistic gifts in the depths of our being, of which we may not yet be aware.

I have filled him with the Spirit of God, with ability and intelligence, with knowledge and all craftsmanship, to devise artistic designs, to work in gold, silver, and bronze, in cutting stones for setting, and in carving wood, for work in every craft.

Exodus 31:3–5

He has filled them with ability to do every sort of work done by a craftsman or by a designer or by an embroiderer in blue and purple and scarlet stuff and fine twined linen, or by a weaver—by any sort of workman or skilled designer.

Exodus 35:35

... and there are varieties of working, but it is the same God who inspires them all in every one.

1 Corinthians 12:6

For we are his workmanship, created in Christ Jesus for good works, which God prepared beforehand, that we should walk in them.

Ephesians 2:10

The artist must possess the courageous soul that dares and defies.

Kate Chopin, *The Awakening and Other Stories*, edited with an Introduction by Lewis Leary, Holt, Rinehart and Winston, 1970, page 340

Every artist dips his brush in his own soul, and paints his own nature into his pictures.

Henry Ward Beecher, *Proverbs from Plymouth Pulpit*, Charles Burnet & Co., 1887, page 223

The artist, of whatever kind, is a man so much aware of the beauty of the universe that he must impart the same beauty to whatever he makes.

A. Clutton Brock, *The Ultimate Belief*, Constable and Company, 1916, page 101

All true Art is the expression of the soul. The outward forms have value only in so far as they are the expression of the inner spirit of man.

Mohandas K. Gandhi, in C.F. Andrews, *Mahatma Gandhi's Ideas*, George Allen & Unwin, 1929, page 332

Art is the true and happy science of the soul,
exploring nature for spiritual influences,
as doth physical science for comforting powers,
advancing so to a sure knowledge with life progress.

Robert Bridges, *The Testament of Beauty*, iii. 1058, Oxford at the Clarendon Press, page 126

A picture, however admirable the painter's art, and wonderful his power, requires of the spectator a surrender of himself, in due proportion with the miracle which has been wrought. Let the canvas glow as it may, you must love with the eye of faith, or its highest excellence escapes you.

Nathaniel Hawthorne, *The Marble Faun*, The Bobbs-Merrill Company, 1971, page 324

Not everything has a name. Some things lead us into a realm beyond words. Art thaws even the frozen, darkened soul, opening it to lofty spiritual experience. Through Art we are sometimes sent—indistinctly, briefly—revelations not to be achieved by rational thought.

Alexander Solzhenitsyn, *One Word of Truth, The Nobel Speech on Literature*, The Bodley Head, 1970, page 5

... our human speech is naught
Our human testimony false, our fame
And human estimation words and wind.
Why take the artistic way to prove so much?
Because, it is the glory and good of Art,
That Art remains the one way possible
Of speaking truth, to mouths like mine at least.

Robert Browning, 'The Ring and the Book', xii. 838, from *The Poetical Works of Robert Browning*, Smith, Elder & Co., 1897, volume I

It is important... that great art teaches us how real things can be looked at and loved without being seized and used, without being appropriated into the greedy organism of the self. This exercise of *detachment* is difficult and valuable whether the thing contemplated is a human being or the root of a tree or the vibration of a colour or a sound. Unsentimental contemplation of nature exhibits the same quality of detachment: selfish concerns vanish, nothing exists except the things which are seen.

Iris Murdoch, *The Sovereignty of Good*, Routledge & Kegan Paul, 1970, page 65

In every human being there is the artist, and whatever his activity, he has an equal chance with any to express the result of his growth and his contact with life. I don't believe any real artist cares whether what he does is 'art' or not. Who, after all, knows what is art?...

I think the real artists are too busy with just being and growing and acting (on canvas or however) like themselves to worry about the end. This end is what it will be. The object is intense living, fufillment, the greatest happiness in creation.

Robert Henri, *The Art Spirit*, compiled by Margery A. Ryerson, J.P. Lippencott Company, 1960, page 226

... the value of art is not merely the value of works of art. It is the value of the aesthetic activity of the spirit, and we must all value that before we can value works of art rightly; and ultimately we must value this glory of the universe, to which we give the name of beauty when we apprehend it. For it is, ultimately, a glory of what is outside us and not merely of our own mental processes...

All the richness and health of our lives depend upon this discovery, this recognition. We live in our relation to the universe, and not merely in our effort to go on living. All this relation of ours is threefold (intellectual, moral and aesthetic) and must be threefold if it is to be right and sane.

A. Clutton Brock, *The Ultimate Belief*, Constable and Company, 1916, page 76

... the highest beauty of form must be taken from Nature; but it is an art of long deduction and great experience, to know how to find it. We must not content ourselves with merely admiring and relishing; we must enter into the principles on which the work is wrought: these do not swim on the superficies, and consequently are not open to superficial observers.

Art in its perfection is not ostentatious; it lies hid, and works its effect, itself unseen. It is the proper study and labour of an artist to uncover and find out the latent cause of conspicuous beauties, and from thence form principles for his own conduct: such an examination is a continual exertion of the mind; as great, perhaps, as that of the artist whose works he is thus studying.

Sir Joshua Reynolds, 'Sixth Discourse', in *Discourses*, Seeley & Co., 1905, page 152

Upon the whole it seems to me, that the object and intention of all the Arts is to supply the natural imperfection of things, and often to gratify the mind by realising and embodying what never existed but in the imagination.

It is allowed on all hands, that facts, and events, however they may bind the historian, have no dominion over the poet or the painter. With us, history is made to bend and conform to this great idea of art. And why? Because these arts, in their highest province, are not addressed to the gross senses; but to the desires of the mind, to that spark of divinity which we have within, impatient of being circumscribed and pent up by the world which is about us.

Just so much as our art has of this, just so much of dignity, I had almost said of divinity, it exhibits; and those of our artists who possessed this mark of distinction in the highest degree, acquired from thence the glorious appellation of Divine.

Sir Joshua Reynolds, *Sir Joshua Reynolds' Discourses*, Kegan Paul, Trench & Co., 1883, page 247

Art is the remembrance of the universal presence of God. Art is Beauty expressed in ways that can be grasped by the senses. It is the form assumed by the Ideal under the laws of the natural world...

Every artist—every artist worthy of the name—helps the human soul to breathe. Art, to a certain extent and at any given moment, is a force which blows the roof off the cave where we crouch imprisoned. What mighty levers does it employ? What massive weights have been placed at its service? Language! Music! A mere breath from human lips!

Poor fugitive notes, poor syllables caught away by the breeze! How invisible your majesty! How weak you seem! Yet you have power to shake the earth to its foundations, and Heaven itself stoops to listen to you. In the solemn moments when we yield ourselves to your sway, our soul breathes a purer air; she breathes, and she is conscious of herself. She says: 'Yes, my God, I am great, and I had forgotten it.'

Ernest Hello, *Life, Science, and Art*, R. & T. Washbourne, 1913, page 124

There are moments in which it is suddenly brought home to me why creative artists take to drink, become dissipated, lose their way, etc. The artist really needs a very strong character if he is not to go to pieces morally, not to lose his bearings. I don't quite know how to put it properly, but I feel it very strongly in myself at certain moments. All my tenderness, all my emotions, this whole swirling soul-lake, soul-sea, soul-ocean, or whatever you want to call it, wants to pour out then, to be allowed to flow forth into just one short poem, but I also feel, if only I could, like flinging myself headlong into an abyss, losing myself in drink. After each creative act one has to be sustained by one's strength of character, by a moral sense, by I don't know what, lest one tumble, God knows how far. And pushed by what dark impulse? I sense it inside me; even in my most fruitful and most creative inner moments, there are raging demons and self-destructive forces. Still, I feel that I am learning to control myself, even in those moments. That is when I suddenly have the urge to kneel down in some quiet corner, to rein myself in and to make sure that my energies are not wildly dissipated.

Etty Hillesum, *A Diary, 1941–43*, translated by Arnold J. Pomerans, Jonathan Cape, 1983, page 76

ASPIRATION

Aspiration—draw of breath; desire earnestly—for or after

I wonder where aspiration comes from? This question came to me whilst observing someone I came across. By profession he is a neuro-physiologist. At school, he was a promising sportsman and specialized as a gymnast. He has excelled in rowing and rugby, and can still play squash in respectable company. He can converse on almost any topic, and does so regularly with one of our elderly retired professors. He is a talented flamenco guitarist, and has recently written a biography of an artist—unusual for a scientist. His latest interest began with parachute jumping but quickly moved on to sky-diving. He is skilful with his hands and re-wired his house whilst installing a central heating system. He is a brilliant cook and goes in for original recipes. He also has a friendly and engaging personality, rounded off with a pleasant sense of humour. Where does it all come from?

An insight occurred to me when we went skiing one Easter vacation in Switzerland. He gazed, almost with an eye of envy, at the effortless movements of a ski instructor. The spirit of aspiration was stirring deeply inside him. 'I'd give anything to ski like that,' he muttered. A close friend quickly retorted, 'Yes, and I bet he wishes he could be a brilliant neuro-physiologist too.' The point was taken—but his aspiration to be a brilliant skier also took off as well. What a valuable source of hope aspiration can be for us.

But earnestly desire the higher gifts.

1 Corinthians 12:31

I press on toward the goal for the prize of the upward call of God in Christ Jesus.

Philippians 3:14

To aspire to live quietly, to mind your own affairs, and to work with your hands, as we charged you; so that you may command the respect of outsiders, and be dependent on nobody.

1 Thessalonians 4:11–12

Thou, who canst *think* as well as *feel*.
Mount from the earth. Aspire! Aspire!

William Wordsworth, *Devotional Incitements*, 25

It's not a matter of chasing sensations, but welcoming those which come to us legitimately, and directing them towards the goals we aspire to.

Michel Quoist, *With Open Heart*, translated by Colette Copeland, Gill and Macmillan, 1983, page 66

'Tis he, I ken the manner of his gait:
He rises on the toe; that spirit of his
In aspiration lifts him from the earth.

William Shakespeare, *Troilus and Cressida*, IV. v. 14

By the word soul, or psyche, I mean that inner consciousness which aspires. By prayer I do not mean a request for anything preferred to a deity; I mean soul-emotion, intense aspiration.

Richard Jefferies, *The Story of My Heart*, Macmillan & Co., 1968, page 142

But I do hold to a something more, far higher than the actual human, something to which it is human to aspire and to seek to translate into life individual and communal; this something translates itself to me best as the Holy Spirit.

Stephen MacKenna, *Journal and Letters*, Constable and Company, 1936, page 276

It is true, no doubt... that many persons 'go through life' without being consciously aware of their high endowment, they accumulate 'things', live in their outside world, 'make good'... but... the *push for the beyond* is always there in us...

Rufus Jones, in H. Loukes, *The Quaker Contribution*, SCM Press, 1965, page 91

The Divine Being brings comfort and consolation to men. He is a God for men that are weak, and want to be strong; for men that are impure, and want to be pure; for men that are unjust, and want to be just; for men that are unloving, and want to be loving; for men that aspire to all the greatness and glory of which the soul is capable.

Henry Ward Beecher, *Proverbs from Plymouth Pulpit*, Charles Burnet & Co., 1887, page 136

From such an encounter with God, what emerges? That we are indeed made in His image, and, though fallen creatures and inheritors of Adam's curse, we may aspire to participate in His purposes. What those purposes are we cannot know, what they portend we cannot imagine. Nevertheless, knowing God brings with it the requisite faith to surrender wholly to His purposes. Then at last we can pray, really meaning it, fully accepting its implications, that line in the Lord's Prayer—*Thy will be done*—which is all there is to say to God, then or at any time.

Malcolm Muggeridge, *A Twentieth Century Testimony*, William Collins Sons & Co., 1979, page 55

A root set in the finest soil, in the best climate, and blessed with all that sun, and air, and rain can do for it, is not in so sure a way of its growth to perfection as every man may be whose spirit aspires after all that which God is ready and infinitely desirous to give him. For the sun meets not the springing bud that stretches towards him with half that certainty as God, the source of all good, communicates Himself to the soul that longs to partake of Him.

William Law, in Stephen Hobhouse, editor, *Selected Mystical Writings of William Law*, Rockliff, 1948, page 68

In thoughts like these true Wisdom may discern
Longings sublime, and aspirations high,
Which some are born with, but the most part learn
To plague themselves withal, they know not why:

'Twas strange that one so young should thus concern
His brain about the action of the sky;
If *you* think't was Philosophy that this did,
I can't help thinking puberty assisted.

Lord Byron, 'Don Juan', canto I. xciii, in Ernest Hartley Coleridge, editor, *The Poetical Works of Lord Byron*, John Murray, 1905, page 790

All religions, arts and sciences are branches of the same tree. All these aspirations are directed toward ennobling man's life, lifting it from the sphere of mere physical existence and leading the individual toward freedom. It is no mere chance that our older universities have developed from clerical schools. Both churches and universities—insofar as they live up to their true function—serve the ennoblement of the individual. They seek to fulfill this great task by spreading moral and cultural understanding, renouncing the use of brute force.

Albert Einstein, *Out of my Later Years*, Thames and Hudson, 1950, page 9

Each sphere of being tends towards a higher sphere, and has already revelations and presentiments of it. The ideal under all its forms is the anticipation and the prophetic vision of that existence, higher than his own, toward which every being perpetually aspires. And this higher and more dignified existence is more inward in character—that is to say, more spiritual. Just as volcanoes reveal to us the secrets of the interior of the globe, so enthusiasm and ecstasy are the passing explosions of this inner world of the soul; and human life is but the preparation and the means of approach to this spiritual life.

Henri Frédéric Amiel, *Amiel's Journal*, translated by Mrs Humphry Ward, Macmillan & Co., 1918, page 27

I stood at first where all aspire at last
To stand: the secret of the world was mine.
I knew, I felt, (perception unexpressed,
Uncomprehended by our narrow thought,
But somehow felt and known in every shift
And change in the spirit,—nay, in every pore
Of the body, even,)—what God is, what we are,
What life is—how God tastes an infinite joy
In infinite ways—one everlasting bliss,
From whom all being emanates, all power
Proceeds; in whom is life for evermore,
Yet whom existence in its lowest form
Includes; where dwells enjoyment there is he.

Robert Browning, 'Paracelsus', V, in *The Poetical Works of Robert Browning*, Oxford University Press, 1947, page 60

To every man and woman the inevitable choice comes. Indeed, it is coming constantly. 'Which is first in my life—the spiritual or the material?' We know that within ourselves there are two warring elements. There are the highest aspirations of our soul, and the lower, coarser tendencies of our nature. We are constantly legislating between the two. Our best self points out the hard and costly way; our lower self derides it and urges us to 'play for safety'. Our best self challenges us to be the highest we have power to be; our lower self tells us that we must always take care of 'number one'. So the struggle goes on. So our essential character is shaped. The light of eternity will reveal what we have become.

W.E. Sangster, *They Met at Calvary*, The Epworth Press, 1956, page 54

'Whosoever exalteth himself shall be abased, and he that humbleth himself shall be exalted.'

Do we desire glory?—let us seek it in its true place; let us seek that which will endure for ever. Oh noble ambition, to dwell eternally with the Son of God! But how weak, how childish, this eager desire for distinction in the world; for a name, a reputation, more evanescent than the vapour that is the sport of the winds! Is a vain show worth so much pains? Let us aspire after true greatness, that is only found in humility. God rebukes the proud even in this world, and in the world to come they are abased; but the humble, even in this life, shall receive the respect that they have not sought for, and eternal glory shall be the recompense of their contempt of false and perishing honours.

François de la M. Fénelon, *Selections from the Writings of Fénelon*, 'Mrs Follen', Edward T. Whitfield, 1850, page 255

AUTHORITY

Authority—power, right, to enforce obedience, person having authority; personal influence, especially over opinion, weight of testimony; person whose opinion is accepted

I was recently invited to join the crew of a yacht that was taking part in a race in the Solent starting off from Cowes. The yacht itself was impressive—fifty-seven feet long, built in 1903, restored to prime condition, and manned on this occasion by a crew of ten.

Little did I realize at the time, but in retrospect the captain of our boat epitomized 'authority'. I suppose he was helped by the fact that he was the owner, though this was not immediately apparent. His authority lay far more in his thorough knowledge of the boat, and how to make her speed through the water. To this knowledge of the boat was added his thorough knowledge of people. For instance, he handed over the helm to the most experienced 'sailor' on board, so that he was free during the race to work out the most effective tactics bearing in mind changing weather conditions. He was skilful in interpreting tide patterns, and 'reading' clouds and sea to verify future directions of the wind. He had a good pair of hands, and was immediately available whenever there was a practical problem to be solved. He had an intimate knowledge of the area, the flow of currents and depth of the water, and well versed in the terms and conditions of the race. He was the only person on board who was master of all aspects of sailing and who spoke with authority.

Such was the authority of this particular captain, confirmed when we were the first boat to cross the finishing line. But what about 'authority' in the deeper aspects of life? Is this where the words, life and person of Jesus Christ speak with authority?

The Lord our God we will serve, and his voice we will obey.

Joshua 24:24

Where there is no prophecy the people cast off restraint.

Proverbs 29:18

And call no man your father on earth, for you have one Father, who is in heaven. Neither be called masters, for you have one master, the Christ. He who is greatest among you shall be your servant; whoever exalts himself will be humbled, and whoever humbles himself will be exalted.

Matthew 23:9–12

And they were astonished at his teaching, for he taught them as one who had authority, and not as the scribes.

Mark 1:22

The New Testament is certainly not a blue-print for twentieth-century Christian behaviour.

F.R. Barry, *Christian Ethics and Secular Society*, Hodder and Stoughton, 1966, page 77

And certain it is, that nothing destroyeth Authority so much, as the unequal and untimely interchange of power pressed too far, and relaxed too much.

Francis Bacon, 'Of Empire', in *The Essays or Counsels, Civil and Moral*, Clarendon Press, 1985, page 59

The Gospel stories are not to be treated as something sacred, as a final authority, but as the means whereby we can come in touch with the living Christ who is the same yesterday, today, and for ever.

William Temple, *Basic Convictions*, Hamish Hamilton, 1937, page 46

Authority is not the static manifestation of power at one particular point in time giving unquestionable directions to all generations. Authority is the name for an element in a living relationship and consequently eludes exact definition.

R.E.C. Browne, *The Ministry of the Word*, SCM Press, 1958, page 28

The authority of the Bible reposes in the fact that, in statements some right and some wrong, and in practical application some of which is disputable and some even more dubious, a unified witness is borne to Him who is at the centre of the Gospel.

J.K.S. Reid, *The Authority of Scripture*, Methuen & Co., 1962, page 267

Nothing that somebody else says is true will be of use to any of us in an hour of trial. Nothing will hold us as an anchor in a stormy sea save that little bit of the truth of God which we have made our very own. The very Greek word for 'authority' is 'exousia' namely 'out of that which is one's very own'. But what we have made our own will hold us. Nothing can ever destroy truth.

Leslie D. Weatherhead, *The Christian Agnostic*, Hodder and Stoughton, 1965, page 34

To exercise authority is to feel truly responsible for others and their growth, knowing too that the 'others' are not their property, are not objects but people with hearts in whom resides the light of God, and who are called to grow to the freedom of truth and love. The greatest danger for someone in authority is to manipulate people and to control them for his or her own goals and need for power.

Jean Vanier, *Community and Growth*, Darton, Longman and Todd, 1991, page 207

One of the most important things for people in authority is to be clear about their priorities. If they lose themselves in a thousand details, they are in danger of losing the vision. They have to keep their eyes fixed firmly on essentials. The best authority is the one which does very little itself but reminds others of these essentials in their activities and their life, calls them to assume responsibilities, supports them, confirms them, and directs them.

Jean Vanier, *Community and Growth*, Darton, Longman and Todd, 1991, page 220

'All authority has been given unto me in heaven and on earth,' the Lord is recorded to have said; 'go ye, *therefore*, and preach the Gospel to all nations.' 'Therefore,' because the authority is His; because the only right and wise way for men to order life is under His authority; if they order it otherwise, they are ordering it foolishly and wrong. That is why He will say of those who hear His words and live by them that they are building upon the rock, the rock of truth and reality.

William Temple, *Basic Convictions*, Hamish Hamilton, 1937, page 78

A general during the war was sitting in a first-class carriage which was quite full, save for one seat. His moustaches could be heard faintly bristling behind a *Daily Telegraph*.

Enter a Leading Aircraftsman, uncommissioned, but dead tired. He swung his webbing on the rack and slumped into the vacant seat. Enter from the corridor a young and whippersnapper Captain.

'Give me that seat, young man,' he said to the aircraftsman. 'It's an order.'

The order was obeyed: the aircraftsman withdrew into the corridor.

Then, from behind the *Daily Telegraph* the steady bristling of the moustache assumed almost the crackle of a forest fire.

'Give that man back his seat,' he said with immense authority. The whipper-snapper demurred. 'It's an order,' roared the General. The order was obeyed. The whippersnapper withdrew into the corridor. And out into the corridor came the General.

'Now,' he said to the whippersnapper, 'you take my seat and I'll stand out here.'

The crestfallen Captain demurred.

'It's an order,' said the General, and stood outside the rest of the journey.

That is what is meant by spiritual authority.

George Macleod, in Ronald Ferguson, editor, *Daily Readings with George Macleod*, HarperCollins, 1991, page 99

Many people seem to have a strange concept of authority. They are afraid of it and of taking it on. To them authority seems to lack tenderness and relationship. They see it only as bad and bullying. Perhaps they had an authoritarian father who was neither tender nor trusting. Perhaps too, this is one of the ills of our times; the tendency everywhere seems to be to separate authority from love and to make it legalistic.

True authority is exercised in the context of justice for all, with special attention to the weakest people, who cannot defend themselves and are part of the oppressed minority. This is an authority ready to give its life, which does not accept any compromise with evil, deceit, and the forces of oppression. A family or community authority, as well as having this sense of justice and truth, needs personal relationships, sensitivity in its action and the ability to listen, trust, and forgive. None of this, of course, excludes moments of firmness.

At the same time, and perhaps for the same reasons, many people confuse authority and the power of efficiency, as if the first role of people with responsibility is to take decisions, command effectively and so exercise power. But their role is first of all to be a person to whom others can turn to for help and advice, to provide security, to affirm, to support, to encourage and to guide.

In biblical language authority is a *rock*; it is solid and gives support. It is a *source of water*, giving life, cleansing, forgiving, nourishing. It is the *shepherd* leading the flock to green pastures. It is a *gardener* watering seeds so that they may bear fruit.

Jean Vanier, *Community and Growth*, Darton, Longman and Todd, 1991, page 207

The problem of the future is really, 'What are men going to obey?' In the medieval world the authority of king and Pope was absolute, but that world has passed away, and we do not believe that any one would honestly wish it back again. What then is the ultimate authority, to which we can trust as a sure guide, leading us more and more into all truth? For each soul this must be the ultimate authority of his own spiritual experience.

The Church's treasure is the spiritual experience of her saints, and it is to this really that the Church points as her claim to hold the truth that is the solution of the world's needs. The plenary inspiration of the Bible, the scientific interpretation of life, individual declarations of doctrine from the greatest theologians, all these would not help unless they tallied with the fundamental experience of the human soul. Christ Himself is the interpreter of experience, and experience finds its interpretation in Christ. As the Church seeks, interprets, and nourishes spiritual experience, so she leads her children to the ultimate union for which we pray.

S. Paul spoke of his own individual life as God's revelation of His Son in him. 'When it was the good pleasure of God to reveal His Son in me,' he writes, 'immediately I conferred not with flesh and blood... I went to Arabia' (Gal.1). Out of his spiritual experience came his submission to the Catholic Church. A sane submission to the Church is just the attitude of humility in the presence of great spiritual experience, and the glad contribution of one's own to the welcoming experience of the rest.

Father Andrew, SDC, *Meditations for Every Day*, A.R. Mowbray & Co., 1941, page 189

The impression of 'authority,' and of an authority of an altogether unique kind, produced by His earlier ministry is deepened as His teaching becomes fuller and more explicit. There is a new accent in all His words, even in the simplest of them; and there are passages in His discourses in which He assumes prerogatives and powers such as no prophet had ever claimed before. He forgives the sins of men. He calls to Himself all that labour and are heavy-laden, and promises that He will give them rest. He declares that where two or three are gathered together in His name, He is in the midst of them; reminding us of the great Jewish saying, which was perhaps already current in our Lord's time, that where two of the devout sons of Abraham are studying the Divine law together, *there* is the Shechinah, the glory which is an assurance of the presence of the God of Israel. He is the Shepherd of the flock of God, whether they are in the Jewish fold, or scattered over the great waste and wilderness of heathenism; He has come to lay down His life for the sheep, and they are to become one flock under one Shepherd.

To all that listen to His voice and follow Him He gives eternal life; and He says that they shall 'never perish, and no one shall snatch them out of My hands.' The life which He gives is not given once for all; those who receive it are continuously dependent upon Him; 'apart' from Him they wither and die, like the branches apart from the vine. He Himself is 'the Way, the Truth, and the Life'; 'no one cometh to the Father' but by Him. He is in the Father, and the Father is in Him. To have seen Him is to have seen the Father. He will pray the Father, and the Father will send His disciples another Comforter—a Divine Person—to teach, strengthen, and defend them. He Himself will send the Comforter, and the Comforter will glorify Him. He associates Himself with the Eternal: 'He that loveth Me shall be loved of My Father; and I will love him, and will manifest Myself unto him... My Father will love him, and We will come to him, and make Our abode with him.'

R.W. Dale, *The Living Christ and the Four Gospels*, Hodder and Stoughton, 1890, page 59

BEAUTY

Beauty—combination of qualities, as shape, proportion, colour, in human face or form, or in other objects, that delight the sight; combined qualities, delighting the other senses, the moral sense, or the intellect

I wonder if 'beauty' is yet another consequence of the divine inbreathing in the Genesis story of the creation of man. The psalmist in the verse below suggests that the nature and essence of God is beauty. Out of the divine bounty we all have a spark or seed of this beauty 'breathed' into us. If we want to see this fully worked out in a life we go to the Gospels. There we discern a person of great moral, spiritual and intellectual beauty. Jesus worked out in his own experience of life what it meant to be made in the image and likeness of God. As such he became a pioneer, a prototype, an incarnation of beauty.

This spark or seed of beauty in us needs to be catalyzed or triggered off in such a way that 'beauty' comes alive for us and transforms us. Traditionally this happens in our baptism and confirmation. This sacrament is concerned primarily with spiritual rebirth. Nurtured by communion and prayer it should lead to a regular experience of beauty, felt primarily as the divine within us, a great opening of the eyes to the beauty around us, and leading to ourselves becoming incarnations of beauty.

For many people today, beauty is seen as something outside us, in nature, in such things as music, poetry and art, and in the beauty of another person. As such it can greatly enrich our lives. However, we seem to have lost the awareness that the essence of beauty lies in the depths of our being, and rarely do we become the beauty we observe and long for. Of all the quotations in this section the last one by C.S. Lewis comes closest to expressing this hope. Reflecting on beauty can give direct access to this beauty residing within us and enables us to become the beauty we observe.

One thing have I asked of the Lord, that will I seek after; that I may dwell in the house of the Lord all the days of my life, to behold the beauty of the Lord, and to inquire in his temple.

Psalm 27:4

He has made everything beautiful in its time.

Ecclesiastes 3:11

Woe to you, scribes and Pharisees, hypocrites! for you are like whitewashed tombs, which outwardly appear beautiful, but within they are full of dead men's bones and all uncleanness.

Matthew 23:27

Finally, brethren, whatever is true, whatever is honorable, whatever is just, whatever is pure, whatever is lovely, whatever is gracious, if there is any excellence, if there is anything worthy of praise, think about these things.

Philippians 4:8

Beauty may be said to be God's trade mark in creation.

Henry Ward Beecher, *Proverbs from Plymouth Pulpit*, Charles Burnet & Co., 1887, page 101

Beauty is one of the few things which don't shake one's faith in God.

Jean Anouilh, *Becket*, translated by Lucienne Hill, Methuen & Co., 1963, page 29

This world is the world of wild storm kept tame with the music of beauty.

Rabindranath Tagore, 'Stray Birds', CXCV, in *Collected Poems & Plays of Rabindranath Tagore*, Macmillan & Co., 1936, page 312

When you reach the heart of life you shall find beauty in all things, even in the eyes that are blind to beauty.

Kahlil Gibran, *Sand and Foam*, William Heinemann, 1927, page 23

It is part and parcel of every man's life to develop beauty in himself. All perfect things have in them an element of beauty.

Henry Ward Beecher, *Proverbs from Plymouth Pulpit*, Charles Burnet & Co., 1887, page 187

Ultimately we long to love the beauty of the world in the form of a living, responding being; and this is essentially the longing for the Incarnation.

J. Neville Ward, *The Use of Praying*, Epworth Press, 1967, page 33

Flowers, shade, a fine view, a sunset sky, joy, grace, feeling, abundance, and serenity, tenderness, and song,—here you have the element of beauty.

Henri Frédéric Amiel, *Amiel's Journal*, translated by Mrs Humphry Ward, Macmillan & Co., 1918, page 68

Spirit of BEAUTY, that dost consecrate
With thine own hues all thou dost shine upon
Of human thought or form—where art thou gone?

Percy Bysshe Shelley, 'Hymn to Intellectual Beauty', verse 11, in *The Complete Poems of Percy Bysshe Shelley*, Oxford University Press, 1935, page 526

I feel more and more that the instinct for beauty (spiritual and moral as well as natural) is the most trustworthy of all instincts, and the surest sign of the nearness of God.

A.C. Benson, *Extracts from the Letters of Dr. A.C. Benson to M.E.A.*, Jarrold Publishing, 1927, page 77

I see and find beauty through Truth. All Truths, not merely true ideas, but truthful faces, truthful pictures, truthful songs, are highly beautiful. Whenever men begin to see Beauty in Truth, then Art will arise.

Mohandas K. Gandhi, in C.F. Andrews, *Mahatma Gandhi's Ideas*, George Allen & Unwin, 1927, page 333

Man comes into life to seek and find his sufficient beauty, to serve it, to win and increase it, to fight for it, to face anything and dare anything for it, counting death as nothing so long as the dying eyes still turn to it.

H.G. Wells, *The History of Mr Polly*, Thomas Nelson and Sons, 1910, page 321

O how much more doth beauty beauteous seem,
By that sweet ornament which truth doth give!
The rose looks fair, but fairer we it deem
For that sweet odour, which doth in it live.

William Shakespeare, Sonnet 54

The first Puritans had a forbidding sort of holiness, and some of them had a great regard for truth, but what about beauty? The empty niches, the ancient glass and beautiful buildings that they destroyed, all cry out against them.

Father Andrew, SDC., *Meditations for Every Day*, A.R. Mowbray & Co., 1941, page 193

In Lourdes, I realized for the first time something that would be confirmed to me in my teens and later as an adult in Africa. Mankind at its most desperate is often at its best. When the physical is reduced to an ugly irrelevance the possibilities of blinding human beauty emerge.

Bob Geldof, *Is That It?*, Penguin Books, 1986, page 20

There comes a moment in life... when moral beauty seems more urgent, more penetrating, than intellectual beauty; when all that the mind has treasured must be bathed in the greatness of soul, lest it perish in the sandy, desert, forlorn as the river that seeks in vain for the sea.

Maurice Maeterlinck, *Wisdom and Destiny*, translated by A. Sutro, George Allen, 1898, page xiii

The aesthetic sense is very close to the religious: beauty has a great educative power. When it takes the form of sacrifice, heroism and holiness it irresistibly attracts men towards the heights. It is this beauty which gives life its meaning, nobility and joy. We must show every child that any existence, however humble and painful it may be, becomes radiant when it is illuminated by an ideal of beauty and love.

Alexis Carrel, *Reflections on Life*, Hamish Hamilton, 1952, page 176

Heroism, ecstacy, prayer, love, enthusiasm, weave a halo round the brow, for they are a setting free of the soul, which through them gains force to make its envelope transparent and shine through upon all around it. Beauty is, then, a phenomenon belonging to the spiritualisation of matter. It is a momentary transfiguration of the privileged object or being—a token fallen from heaven to earth in order to remind us of the ideal world.

Henri Frédéric Amiel, *Amiel's Journal*, translated by Mrs Humphry Ward, Macmillan & Co., 1918, page 105

I believe that there is nothing lovelier, deeper, more sympathetic, more rational, more manly, and more perfect than the Saviour; I say to myself with jealous love that not only is there no one else like Him, but that there could be no one. I would say even more: If anyone could prove to me that Christ is outside the truth, and if the truth really did exclude Christ, I should prefer to stay with Christ and not with truth... There is in the world only one figure of absolute beauty: Christ. That infinitely lovely figure, is as a matter of course, an infinite marvel.

Fyodor Dostoyevsky, *Letters of Fyodor Michailovitch Dostoyevsky to his Family and Friends*, translated by Ethel Colburn Mayne, Peter Owen, 1962, pages 71 and 142

It is a righteous instinct which bids us welcome and honour beauty, whether in man or woman, as something of real worth—divine, heavenly, ay, though we know not how, in a most deep sense Eternal; which makes our reason give the lie to all merely logical and sentimental maunderings of moralists about 'the fleeting hues of this our painted clay;' and tell men, as the old Hebrew Scriptures told them, that physical beauty is the deepest of all spiritual symbols; and that though beauty without discretion be the jewel of gold in the swine's snout, yet the jewel of gold it is still, the sacrament of an inward beauty, which ought to be, perhaps hereafter may be, fulfilled in spirit and in truth.

Charles Kingsley, *Daily Thoughts*, Macmillan & Co., 1884, page 213

We do not want merely to see beauty, though, God knows, even that is bounty enough. We want something else which can hardly be put into words—to be united with the beauty we see, to pass into it, to receive it into ourselves, to bathe in it, to become part of it. That is why we have peopled air and earth and water with gods and goddesses and nymphs and elves—that, though we cannot, yet these projections can enjoy in themselves that beauty, grace, and power of which Nature is the image... For if we take the imagery of Scripture seriously, if we believe that God will one day *give* us the Morning Star and cause us to *put on* the splendour of the sun, then we may surmise that both the ancient myths and the modern poetry, so false as history, may be very near the truth as prophecy. At present we are on the outside of the world, the wrong side of the door. We discern the freshness and purity of morning, but they do not make us fresh and pure. We cannot mingle with the splendours we see. But all the leaves of the New Testament are rustling with the rumour that it will not always be so. Someday, God willing, we shall get *in*. When human souls have become as perfect in voluntary obedience as the inanimate creation is in its lifeless obedience, they will put on its glory, or rather that greater glory of which Nature is only the first sketch. We are summoned to pass in through Nature, beyond her, into that splendour which she fitfully reflects.

C.S. Lewis, *The Weight of Glory*, Macmillan Publishing Co., 1980, page 16

CHARACTER

Character—moral strength, back-bone; reputation, good reputation; description of person's qualities

I have always been influenced by people of character. When I first went away to school, I was assigned a 'guardian'—a slightly older boy, who was to keep an eye on me and help me settle down. We became firm friends. Years later he became captain of school, played rugby for English Schoolboys, and has recently been made a bishop. He's always been to me a person of quality and character.

Two biographies, both by George Seaver, have been about men of character, and have influenced me a great deal. The first was *Edward Wilson of the Antarctic*—the life story of the doctor, zoologist and artist, on Scott's expedition to the Antarctic. Although Scott was the official leader, the qualities of Edward Wilson's character exercised a quiet but decisive influence on the members of the expedition. The second was *Albert Schweitzer: The Man and His Mind.* Here was portrayed the character of a man with four doctorates, in philosophy, theology, music and medicine, who went on to found and run a mission hospital in a remote part of equatorial West Africa. He was described as a man of moral strength, with impressive qualities.

Recently I've been moved by the writings of Mother Teresa of Calcutta, and several years ago, was privileged to attend a meeting at which she was present. One glance showed me she was a woman of quality and character. A few months ago Jean Vanier and Sheila Cassidy ran a university mission in Oxford. Both spend their lives working for people in need—the physically and mentally handicapped, and the terminally ill. What came over in both of them, was character.

Character has been a source of hope from time immemorial—the character of God, the greatest of all.

As he thinketh in his heart, so is he.

Proverbs 23:7 (AV)

And I heard the voice of the Lord saying, 'Whom shall I send, and who will go for us? Then I said, 'Here am I! Send me.'

Isaiah 6:8

And the Word became flesh and dwelt among us, full of grace and truth.

John 1:14

Do you not know that you are God's temple and that God's Spirit dwells in you?

1 Corinthians 3:16

To shame the guise o' th' world, I will begin
The fashion—less without and more within.

William Shakespeare, *Cymbeline*, V. i. 32

Religion is only another word for character, and it is developed in man. Religious education is a growth, and requires time.

Henry Ward Beecher, *Proverbs from Plymouth Pulpit*, Charles Burnet & Co., 1887, page 122

Character—in things great and small—is indicated when a man pursues with sustained follow-through what he feels himself capable of doing.

Johann Wolfgang von Goethe, *Wisdom and Experience*, selected by Ludwig Curtius, translated and edited by Hermann J. Weigand, Routledge & Kegan Paul, 1949, page 217

A truer, nobler, trustier heart,
More loving, or more loyal, never beat
Within a human breast.

Lord Byron, 'The Two Foscari', II. i. 154, in Ernest Hartley Coleridge, editor, *The Poetical Works of Lord Byron*, John Murray, 1905, page 603

In Christ was comprehended the fullest conception of greatness and nobleness of character. Every idea of true manhood is in Him.

Henry Ward Beecher, *Proverbs from Plymouth Pulpit*, Charles Burnet & Co., 1887, page 150

It is held
That valour is the chiefest virtue and
Most dignifies the haver.

William Shakespeare, *Coriolanus*, II. ii. 81

There is no sight more beautiful than a character which has been steadfastly growing in every direction, and has come to old age rich and ripe.

Henry Ward Beecher, *Proverbs from Plymouth Pulpit*, Charles Burnet & Co., 1887, page 43

There is no point so critical of Christian character as the power to maintain love toward all men—not a love of personal attraction, but a love of benevolence, that begets a willingness to bear with them and work for them.

Henry Ward Beecher, *Proverbs from Plymouth Pulpit*, Charles Burnet & Co., 1887, page 164

Supreme and tremendous energy and positiveness enter into the spiritual delineation of Christian character. Intense virtues and self-denials, bearing yokes, bearing the cross, sacrificing, crucifying, are enjoined.

Henry Ward Beecher, *Proverbs from Plymouth Pulpit*, Charles Burnet & Co., 1887, page 166

Quality and power of emotion are the noblest elements of character; and reason and knowledge and experience work to and for that which is the essential being—namely, emotion, out of which comes disposition.

Henry Ward Beecher, *Proverbs from Plymouth Pulpit*, Charles Burnet & Co., 1887, page 45

The character I admire is a character that is a rod of iron to itself and a well-spring of tenderness and pity for others; a character that forces itself to be happy in itself, blames no one but itself, and compels itself to clear away obstacles from the path to happiness for every organism it encounters.

John Cowper Powys, *Autobiography*, Macdonald & Co. (Publishers), 1967, page 376

People's characters are tested in three ways: by the circumstances in which they live, by the people whom they meet, and by the experience of their own failures. Their characters are tested by the degree in which these things draw forth from them love and not bitterness, a humble penitence and dependence upon God and not despair.

Father Andrew, SDC., *A Gift of Light*, selected and edited by Harry C. Griffith, A.R. Mowbray & Co., 1968, page 84

I do not think that there can be any life quite so demonstrative of character as that which we had on these expeditions (to the Antarctic). One sees a remarkable reassortment of values. Under ordinary conditions it is so easy to carry a point with a little bounce; self-assertion is a mask which covers many a weakness. As a rule we have neither the time nor the desire to look beneath it, and so it is that commonly we accept people on their own valuation. Here the outward show is nothing, it is the inward purpose that counts. So the 'Gods' dwindle and the humble supplant them. Pretence is useless.

Edward Wilson, in George Seaver, *Edward Wilson of the Antarctic*, John Murray, 1935, page 232

[The Beatitudes] give the picture of the Christian character in its wonderful attractiveness—that detachment, that readiness to enter into the heritage of human pain, that self-suppressing meekness and humility towards our fellow-men, that strong passion for righteousness, that effective compassion, that singleness of heart, that striving for peace. Yet, where it is not welcomed, it stings by its very beauty, it hardens by its very holiness. Thus there came about the strange result, that when that character was set in its perfection before men's eyes in the person of our Lord, they would not have it. They set upon Him and slew Him. It is in full view of this consequence of being righteous that our Lord speaks this last beatitude, and He gives it pointed and particular application to His disciples.

'Blessed are ye when men shall reproach you, and persecute you, and say all manner of evil against you falsely, for my sake. Rejoice, and be exceeding glad: for great is your reward in heaven: for so persecuted they the prophets which were before you.'

Charles Gore, *The Sermon on the Mount*, John Murray, 1897, page 43

As soon as ever a man sets himself seriously to aim at this Christian character, the devil at once puts this thought into his mind—Am I not aiming at what is too high to be practicable? Am I not aiming too high to do any good? If I am to help men, surely I must be like them? I must not be so unworldly, if I am to help men in this sort of world. Now our Lord at once anticipates this kind of argument. He says at once, as it were, No, you are to help men by being unlike them. You are to help men, not by offering them a character which they feel to be a little more respectable than their own, but by offering them a character filled with the love of God. They may mock it for a while; but in the 'day of visitation,' in the day when trouble comes, in the day when they are thrown back on what lies behind respectability, in the day when first principles emerge, they will glorify God for the example you have given them. They will turn to you then, because they will feel that you have something to show them that will really hold water, something that is really and eternally worth having.

Thus our Lord at once proceeds to answer the question, How is a character such as the beatitudes describe, planted in a world such as this, to effect good? It is to purify by its own distinctive savour, it is to be conspicuous by its own splendid truth to its ideal, it is to arrest attention by its powerful contrast to the world about it. This is the meaning of the metaphors which follow the beatitudes...

'Ye are the salt of the earth.' Salt is that which keeps things pure by its emphatic antagonistic savour. 'Ye are the light of the world.' Light is that which burns distinctively in the darkness. 'A city that is set on a hill' is a marked object, arresting attention over a whole country-side.

Charles Gore, *The Sermon on the Mount*, John Murray, 1897, page 44

The springs of human character lie beyond the reach of outward observation. External action is but an inadequate and often deceptive measure of inward spiritual capacity. What a man does or has done, or within the limits of our brief and bounded life can ever accomplish, is but an imperfect and often blurred and confused expression of the hidden potentialities of the spirit. Of that which constitutes the essence and reality of a human soul an outward observer may easily form a mistaken, can only form a partial and inadequate estimate. Only to an eye which penetrates to the root of character, which can embrace in its judgment the unrealized and boundless possibilities of the future as well as truly interpret the meaning of the past, only to an eye which measures life, not by action merely, but by the principles from which action springs and the inexhaustible productive force that is in them—only to such an eye does the true complexion and character of a human soul lie open. It is perhaps on this principle, translating the technical language of theology into our ordinary forms of expression, that we may represent to ourselves what is meant by being justified not by works but by faith. Stated generally the principle is this, that the true criterion of a human spirit is not outward performances but the ideal to which it is devoted; and, in its application to religion, it is the principle that the divine measure of a Christian life is not outward works or doings but devotion to Christ as its ideal... What we are in God's sight... is determined not by what we do or have done but by the presence in the soul of that inward spirit, principle, characteristic motive and aim—in one word, by that self-surrender, that identification with a divine ideal, which constitutes the Christian faith. Poor, imperfect, fluctuating, inadequate may be our attempts to realize that ideal in action, the very best which the best of men do can be only a gradual approximation to it; but all they fain would be, all the splendour of the spirit's future career is already and virtually contained in it. In the soul in which that divine principle dwells, in the soul in which devotion to Christ has become the one supreme, all-dominating motive and aim, it is *that*, and not the dim imperfect life, the blurred, confused medium through which it struggles into expression—it is *that* which determines God's judgment of us, makes us what in his sight we are. Underneath the poverty and meanness of the present life, its manifold imperfections and shortcomings, its feeble virtues, its often abortive aspirations and ever imperfect attainments,—all that is but as the beggar's raiment disguising an inward nobility,—underneath all that, what the omniscient eye beholds is the radiant image of a son of God, the hidden splendour of a Christlike purity, the transfigured glory of a soul that has already washed its robes and made them white in the blood of the Lamb.

John Caird, *University Sermons*, James MacLehose and Sons, 1898, volume I, page 116

CHRISTIANITY

Christianity—the Christian faith, doctrines of Christ and his apostles; a Christian religious system; being a Christian, Christian quality of character

There was a tentative knock on my door at University College, Oxford. The door opened and one of our undergraduates entered the room. I was shocked by his appearance. His face was ashen white. Clearly something was seriously wrong. I invited him to sit down and made him a cup of tea.

He was someone I hardly knew. He was in his second year and I had only just arrived. I was aware that he was a gifted flautist and the recent winner of a much coveted university English essay prize. He could hardly speak to start off with. 'You are the chaplain aren't you,' he stammered out, 'and you are here to help?' 'Yes,' I said quietly, 'what seems to be the problem?'

He had been through a very bad patch—four days of utter darkness and terror. I listened carefully to his account, and suggested he see the college doctor. It looked to me as though he was anaemic and had been through some kind of a breakdown. He was in need of professional medical help. This meeting was the start of a valuable friendship. It took him some time to recover but over the next few months we became firm friends. He had a very dry sense of humour and a marvellous way of expressing himself, often reducing me to helpless laughter. Eventually he took a step of faith and shared with me a valuable insight he had discovered in this awful experience. 'Bill,' he said, 'Christianity is not the easy way out, it's the difficult way in.'

The quotes in this section have been selected with this in mind. They are true to the cross and the crown of Christianity.

Afterward he appeared to the eleven themselves as they sat at table; and he upbraided them for their unbelief and hardness of heart, because they had not believed those who saw him after he had risen. And he said to them, 'Go into all the world and preach the gospel to the whole creation.'

Mark 16:14–15

For I am not ashamed of the gospel: it is the power of God for salvation to every one who has faith, to the Jew first and also to the Greek.

Romans 1:16

For if I preach the gospel, that gives me no ground for boasting. For necessity is laid upon me. Woe to me, if I do not preach the gospel!

1 Corinthians 9:16

Beloved, being very eager to write to you of our common salvation, I found it necessary to write appealing to you to contend for the faith which was once for all delivered to the saints.

Jude 3

Love is the hardest lesson in Christianity; but for that reason, it should be most our care to learn it.

William Penn, *Fruits of Solitude*, A.W. Bennett, 1863, page 65

Christianity... had come into the world with a double purpose, to offer men the vision of God, and to call them to the pursuit of that vision.

Kenneth E. Kirk, *The Vision of God*, Longmans, Green and Co., 1932, page 1

Unless Christianity be viewed and felt in a high and comprehensive way, how large a portion of our intellectual and moral nature does it leave without object and action!

Samuel Taylor Coleridge, *The Table Talk and Omniana of Samuel Taylor Coleridge*, Oxford University Press, 1917, page 284

Christianity, as I see it, is first and foremost the response to Christ's invitation to live in the Kingdom; from within that Kingdom there can be no moral answers, only imaginative and loving living.

W.B.J. Martin, *Five Minutes to Twelve*, William Collins Sons & Co., 1957, page 121

Again there are signs that organised Christianity is unaware, or perhaps afraid of, the treasure that lies at its heart, and it might be that others may find it and live in the light of it before the guardians of the treasure see what it is they guard. Maybe this is the way the harlots go first into the kingdom of God.

Monica Furlong, *The End of our Exploring*, Hodder and Stoughton, 1973, page 21

One of the distinctive marks of Christianity at its best is that it teaches men to hold a very lofty opinion of themselves. They are children of God, made in his image, destined for his character. Not an outward temple, but an inward shrine of man's personality with all its possibilities and powers is seen to be infinitely sacred.

Harry Emerson Fosdick, *Twelve Tests of Character*, Hodder and Stoughton, 1923, page 47

... Christianity is the most encouraging, the most joyous, the least repressive and the least forbidding of all the religions of mankind. There is no religion which throws off the burden of life so completely, which escapes so swiftly from sad moods, which gives so large a scope for the high spirits of the soul, and welcomes to its bosom with so warm an embrace those things of beauty which are joys for ever... Christianity does not brood upon the sorrows of mankind. It is always music that you hear, and sometimes dancing as well.

L.P. Jacks, *The Lost Radiance of the Christian Religion*, The Lindsay Press, 1921, pages 5 and 15

At a time when a great part of mankind is beginning to lay aside Christianity, it is worth while to realize clearly why it was ever actually accepted. It was accepted in order to escape at last from the brutality of antiquity. If we put Christianity aside, then that wantonness appears again of which life in our great modern cities gives us an impressive foretaste. This step is not progress but regression. It is like the case of an individual who lays aside some form of transference and has no new form; he will unfailingly regress to the old path of transference, to his own great detriment, for the surrounding world will have changed considerably in the meantime.

C.G. Jung, *Psychological Reflections*, selected and edited by Jolande Jacobi, Routledge & Kegan Paul, 1953, page 306

Christianity: by that I understand a distinctive belief and way of life connected with the Bible, the belief that there is one God, supreme and righteous, who created the world, and therein the human race, which is distinct from the Creator in its utter creaturely dependence upon him, yet akin to him as made 'in his own image' for fellowship with him; that mankind has wilfully deviated from the divine will and brought catastrophe upon itself; that Jesus Christ came as the perfect revelation of God and as—by his death and resurrection and the gift of the Spirit—the restorer of mankind; that Jesus Christ is the living, contemporary Lord, through whom we have eternal life here already and beyond the grave.

Michael Ramsey, in Margaret Duggan, editor, *Through the Year With Michael Ramsey*, Hodder and Stoughton, 1975, page 215

We too often forget that Christian faith is a principle of questioning and struggle before it becomes a principle of certitude and of peace. One has to doubt and reject everything else in order to believe firmly in Christ, and after one has begun to believe, one's faith itself must be tested and purified. Christianity is not merely a set of foregone conclusions. The Christian mind is a mind that risks intolerable purifications, and sometimes, indeed very often, the risk turns out to be too great to be tolerated. Faith tends to be defeated by the burning presence of God in mystery, and seeks refuge from him, flying to comfortable social forms and safe conventions in which purification is no longer an inner battle but a matter of outward gesture.

Thomas Merton, ***Conjectures of a Guilty Bystander*****, Burns & Oates, 1968, page 58**

My contention is that besides the combative Catholic and Protestant elements in the Churches, there has always been a third element, with very honourable traditions, which came to life again at the Renaissance, but really reaches back to the Greek Fathers, to St. Paul and St. John, and further back still. The characteristics of this type of Christianity are—a spiritual religion, based on a firm belief in absolute and eternal values as the most real things in the universe—a confidence that these values are knowable by man—a belief that they can nevertheless be known only by whole-hearted consecration of the intellect, will, and affections to the great quest—an entirely open mind towards the discoveries of science—a reverent and receptive attitude to the beauty, sublimity, and wisdom of the creation, as a revelation of the mind and character of the Creator—a complete indifference to the current valuations of the worldling.

W.R. Inge, ***The Platonic Tradition in English Religious Thought*****, Longmans, Green and Co., 1926, page 33**

The essential element in Christianity as it was preached by Jesus and as it is comprehended in thought, is this, that it is only through love that we can attain to communion with God. All living knowledge of God rests upon this foundation: that we experience Him in our lives as Will-to-Love.

Anyone who has recognized that the idea of Love is the spiritual beam of light which reaches us from the Infinite, ceases to demand from religion that it shall offer him complete knowledge of the supra-sensible. He ponders, indeed, on the great questions: what the meaning is of evil in the world; how in God, the great First Cause, the will-to-create and the will-to-love are one; in what relation the spiritual and the material life stand to one another, and in what way our existence is transitory and yet eternal. But he is able to leave these questions on one side, however painful it may be to give up all hope of answers to them. In the knowledge of spiritual existence in God through love he possesses the one thing needful.—

'Love never faileth: but . . . whether there be knowledge it shall be done away,' says S. Paul.

The deeper piety is, the humbler are its claims with regard to knowledge of the supra-sensible.

Albert Schweitzer, ***My Life and Thought*****, translated by C.T. Campion, George Allen & Unwin, 1933, page 277**

As I understand it, Christianity is above all religions, and religion is not a method, it is a life, a higher and supernatural life, mystical in its root and practical in its fruits, a communion with God, a calm and deep enthusiasm, a love which radiates, a force which acts, a happiness which overflows. Religion, in short, is a state of the soul. These quarrels as to method have their value, but it is a secondary value; they will never console a heart or edify a conscience. This is why I feel so little interest in these ecclesiastical struggles. Whether the one party or the other gain the majority and the victory, what is essential is in no way profited, for dogma, criticism, the Church, are not religion; and it is religion, the sense of a divine life, which matters. 'Seek ye first the kingdom of God and his righteousness, and all these things shall be added unto you.' The most holy is the most Christian; this will always be the criterion which is least deceptive. 'By this ye shall know my disciples, if they have love one to another.'

As is the worth of the individual, so is the worth of his religion. Popular instinct and philosophic reason are at one on this point. Be good and pious, patient and heroic, faithful and devoted, humble and charitable; the catechism which has taught you these things is beyond the reach of blame. By religion we live in God; but all these quarrels lead to nothing but life with men or with cassocks. There is therefore no equivalence between the two points of view. Perfection as an end,—a noble example for sustenance on the way,—the divine proved by its own excellence,—is not this the whole of Christianity? God manifest in all men, is not this its true goal and consummation?

Henri Frédéric Amiel, *Amiel's Journal*, translated by Mrs Humphry Ward, Macmillan & Co., 1918, page 121

... to come to the plain words of Jesus of Nazareth, Christianity is a simple thing, very simple. It is absolute, pure morality; absolute, pure religion; the love of man; the love of God acting without let or hindrance. The only creed it lays down is the great truth which springs up spontaneous in the holy heart—there is a God. Its watchword is, Be perfect as your Father in heaven. The only form it demands is a divine life; doing the best thing in the best way, from the highest motives; perfect obedience to the great law of God. Its sanction is the voice of God in your heart; the perpetual presence of him who made us and the stars over our head; Christ and the Father abiding within us. All this is very simple—a little child can understand it; very beautiful—the loftiest mind can find nothing so lovely. Try it by reason, conscience, and faith—things highest in man's nature—we see no redundance, we feel no deficiency. Examine the particular duties it enjoins; humility, reverence, sobriety, gentleness, charity, forgiveness, fortitude, resignation, faith, and active love; try the whole extent of Christianity, so well summed up in the command, 'Thou shalt love the Lord thy God with all thy heart and with all thy soul, and with all thy mind—thou shalt love thy neighbour as thyself'; and is there anything therein that can perish? No, the very opponents of Christianity have rarely found fault with the teachings of Jesus. The end of Christianity seems to be to make all men one with God as Christ was one with him; to bring them to such a state of obedience and goodness, that we shall think divine thoughts and feel divine sentiments, and so keep the law of God by living a life of truth and love. Its means are purity and prayer; getting strength from God, and using it for our fellow-men as well as ourselves. It allows perfect freedom. It does not demand all men to *think* alike, but to think uprightly, and get as near as possible at truth; not all men to *live* alike, but to live holy, to a life perfectly divine.

Theodore Parker, *The Transient and Permanent in Christianity*, British and Foreign Unitarian Association, 1908, page 32

COURAGE

Courage—bravery, boldness, nerve oneself to a venture

In my teenage years I read a book by Paul Brickhill entitled *Reach for the Sky*. It is a book about courage and is the life story of Douglas Bader, a fighter pilot of the Second World War. A lively character, he was involved in a serious flying accident in the 1930s. Both legs were amputated, and his short flying career was over. He struggled against the odds. Over a period of months he managed to walk again with the help of artificial limbs. In the desperate times of the Battle of Britain, he managed to persuade the RAF to let him fly again. As is well known he went on to become an ace fighter pilot, with many enemy aircraft to his credit. He was eventually shot down, taken prison, escaped, recaptured, transferred to Colditz, and the only way he could be contained was by the removal of his artificial limbs. All this to me epitomized courage. This was reinforced by my time in the Gurkhas. Again in the last war, there was a Gurkha deemed not to be pulling his weight. He was hauled up before his Company Commander and told to pull his finger out. Next day he won the Victoria Cross in an extraordinary display of courage.

Later, whilst serving as a curate in Bradford I came across a different form of courage. As a part-time chaplain to the Bradford Royal Infirmary, visiting about a hundred patients a week, I found many instances of quiet courage and fortitude, and this was repeated in numerous visits to high-rise flats and back-to-back houses in the parish. It was a part of everyday life and very common, and as such a great resource of hope.

Be strong and of good courage; be not frightened, neither be dismayed; for the Lord your God is with you wherever you go.

Joshua 1:9

His heart was courageous in the ways of the Lord.

2 Chronicles 17:6

Be watchful, stand firm in your faith, be courageous, be strong. Let all that you do be done in love.

1 Corinthians 16:13–14

He who has prepared us for this very thing is God, who has given us the Spirit as a guarantee. So we are always of good courage.

2 Corinthians 5:5–6

... but there is a higher sort of bravery, the bravery of self-control.

Thomas Bailey Aldrich, *The Stillwater Tragedy*, David Douglas, 1886, volume I, page 172

How few there are who have courage enough to own their Faults, or resolution enough to mend them.

Benjamin Franklin, *Poor Richard's Almanack*, Taurus Press, 1962, page 6

The most precious thing about Jesus is the fact that he is not the great discourager, but the great encourager.

William Barclay, *The Gospel of Matthew*, The Saint Andrew Press, 1975, volume II, page 37

One has to be courageous not to let oneself be carried along by the world's march; one needs faith and will-power to go cross-current.

Carlo Carretto, *Letters from the Desert*, translated by Rose Mary Hancock, Darton, Longman and Todd, 1972, page 130

People talk about the courage of condemned men walking to the place of execution: sometimes it needs as much courage to walk with any kind of bearing towards another person's habitual misery.

Graham Greene, *The Heart of the Matter*, William Heinemann, 1959, page 61

…be like our Saviour, unwearied: who when He was abused and had often been evil-intreated among men, proceeded courageously through all treacheries and deceits to die for them.

Thomas Traherne, *Centuries*, The Faith Press, 1969, page 43

One who never turned his back but marched breast forward,
Never doubted clouds would break,
Never dreamed, though right were worsted, wrong would triumph,
Held we fall to rise, are baffled to fight better,
Sleep to wake.

Robert Browning, 'Epilogue', in *The Poetical Works of Robert Browning*, Oxford University Press, 1949, page 688

God is no refuge for the coward, cringing soul. He is the goal and the sustainer of those who dare. 'Whosoever doth not bear his cross and come after Me cannot be My disciple.' Come then, let us get our backs beneath it—whatever it is. Our God demands courage! May he observe that courage in us all!

W.E. Sangster, *Why Jesus Never Wrote a Book*, The Epworth Press, 1932, page 112

The world seems somehow so made as to suit best the adventurous and courageous, the men who, like Nelson, wear all their stars, like Napoleon's marshals their most splendid uniforms, not that they may be less but more conspicuous and incur greater dangers than their fellows.

W. Macneile Dixon, *The Human Situation*, Edward Arnold & Co., 1937, page 89

Life, willing to surpass itself, is the good life, and the good life is courageous life. It is the life of the 'powerful soul' and the 'triumphant body' whose self-enjoyment is virtue. Such a soul banishes everything cowardly; it says: 'bad—that is cowardly.'

Paul Tillich, *The Courage to Be*, Nisbet & Co., 1952, page 28

The affirmation of one's essential being in spite of desires and anxieties creates joy… it is the happiness of a soul which is 'lifted above every circumstance'. Joy accompanies the self-affirmation of our essential being in spite of the inhibitions coming from the accidental elements in us. Joy is the emotional expression of the courageous Yes to one's own being.

Paul Tillich, *The Courage to Be*, Nisbet & Co., 1952, page 14

Courage is far more common than is commonly supposed, and it belongs as much, and more, to the ordinary events of life than to the spectacular. Every man who lives in intimate contact with other people, especially the unprivileged people, is amazed at the quiet bravery of obscure folk. To those who have eyes to see, there is evidence of courage on every hand.

W.E. Sangster, *These Things Abide*, Hodder and Stoughton, 1939, page 157

I know a man who had to encounter three successive trials of all the courage and inventive faculty in him. If he had failed in one he would have been ruined. The odds were desperate against him in each, and against ultimate victory were overwhelming. Nevertheless he made the attempt and was triumphant almost by a miracle in each struggle. How often calculation is folly and cowardice!

Mark Rutherford, *More Pages From a Journal*, Oxford University Press, 1910, page 222

O! what a thing it is, in a time of danger, and in the presence of death, the shining of a face upon a face! I have heard it broached that orders should be given in great new ships by electric telegraph. I admire machinery as much as any man, and am as thankful to it as any man can be for what it does for us. But it will never be a substitute for the face of a man, with his soul in it, encouraging another man to be brave and true.

Charles Dickens and Wilkie Collins, *The Wreck of the Golden Mary*, Arthur Barker, 1955, page 53

The Italians call it *Coraggio*, or greatness of heart; the Spaniards, *Corage*; the French, *Courage*, from whom we have borrowed it. And we understand it to mean manliness, bravery, boldness, fearlessness, springing not from a sense of physical power, or from insensibility to danger or pain, but from the moral habit of self-command, with deliberation, fully weighing present dangers, and clearly foreseeing future consequences, and yet in the path of duty advancing unmoved to its execution.

Cardinal Manning, *Pastime Papers*, Burns & Oates, 1892, page 79

The one word 'courage' must cover such a great range of situations and responses—running all the way from coping to daring, resignation to resistance—that, like the character trait it represents, the word must have both flexible and firm possibilities of meaning. Perhaps therefore the best definition of courage would be one couched in the language of explicit metaphor and parable, evoking what it describes, but always in terms of that resilient steadfastness out of which human courage is made.

Roger Hazelton, in James F. Childress and John Macquarrie, editors, *A New Dictionary of Christian Ethics*, SCM Press, 1986, page 135

Strange is the vigour of a brave man's soul. The strength of his spirit and his irresistible power, the greatness of his heart and the height of his condition, his mighty confidence and contempt of danger, his true security and repose in himself, his liberty to dare and do what he pleaseth, his alacrity in the midst of fears, his invincible temper, are advantages which make him master of fortune. His courage fits him for all attempts, renders him serviceable to God and man, and makes him the bulwark and defence of his king and country.

Thomas Traherne, *The Way to Blessedness*, the spelling and punctuation by Margaret Bottrall, The Faith Press, 1962, page 178

Without courage we can never attain to true simplicity. Cowardice keeps us 'double-minded'—hesitating between the world and God. In this hesitation, there is no true faith—faith remains an opinion. We are never certain, because we never quite give in to the authority of an invisible God. This hesitation is the death of hope. We never let go of those visible supports which, we well know, must one day surely fail us. And this hesitation makes true prayer impossible—it never quite dares to ask for anything, or if it asks, it is so uncertain of being heard that in the very act of asking it surreptitiously seeks by human prudence to construct a makeshift answer.

Thomas Merton, *Thoughts in Solitude*, Burns & Oates, 1958, page 31

In the modern period the face of the world has changed profoundly, and it is hard for it to keep its balance between the attractions and the perils of a constant and almost exclusive pursuit of material goods, and in the midst of a total neglect or watering down of the supernatural, spiritual principles that characterized the implanting and spread of Christian civilization throughout the centuries. In this modern period, the question is not so much one of some particular point or other of doctrine or of discipline that has to be brought back to the pure fonts of revelation and tradition, as it is of restoring the substance of humane and Christian thinking and living (for which the Church has served as custodian and teacher through the centuries) to full force and to its proper splendour.

On the other hand, it is certainly important and even obligatory for us to deplore the errors and faults of a human spirit that is being tempted and pushed in the direction of concentrating completely on enjoyment of the earthly goods that modern scientific research now puts within the easy grasp of the man of our age. But may God keep us from exaggerating the extent of this to the point of making ourselves believe that God's heavens have now closed over our heads once and for all, that, as a matter of fact, 'darkness has covered the whole earth' and that there is nothing left for us to do but shed tears as we plod along our difficult path.

Instead, we must take courage.

No, Christ, the Son of God and our saviour, has not departed from the world that he redeemed; and the Church that he founded, one, holy, catholic, and apostolic, remains forever *his mystical body*, with him as its head, and each of us who believe is closely related to it, each of us belongs to it. This is the important point that every baptized person must keep in mind: belonging to the Church of Christ is not just something of an individual nature for each person but it has an eminently social nature for everybody. This is the meaning of saying, in effect, that in Christ Jesus, in the Church of Jesus, each and every one of us really belongs to the same family, we are all sons and brothers, 'whom [the Father] has destined from the first to be moulded into the image of his son, who is thus to become the eldest born among many brethren.'

Pope John XXIII, in Vincent A. Yzermans, editor, *Readings from Pope John*, A.R. Mowbray & Co., 1968, page 17

DARKNESS

Darkness—with no or relatively little light, unilluminated, gloomy, sombre; evil, atrocious, cheerless side to things; sad, sullen

A lady in her mid-fifties came to see me. She was going through a time of darkness in her life, and asked me if there was anything I could do to help her.

I put her on to an anthology appropriately entitled *From Darkness to Light* by the publisher, Victor Gollancz. Apparently he had gone through a very dark period in his life in which he had lost all hope. Somehow he had managed to come through, and compiled this anthology to help fellow-sufferers. She cautiously accepted the book and went away to look through it in her own time.

She returned several weeks later, and was a little better. She had found the first part of the book on 'darkness' particularly helpful and hadn't realized how many people suffered from this condition. People's recorded experiences of despair, depression, desolation and darkness fell in very much with what she was feeling. That in itself had been a great help. She wasn't the only person in the world to have gone through these awful feelings. Perhaps she was fairly normal after all?

There was now a little movement stirring in the depths below, a movement away from gloominess and sadness. She felt she was beginning to move away from darkness to light, but complained that progress was very slow. I reminded her of some words of a spiritual director—'you can't hurry the dawn'—and encouraged her to go forward slowly. It took her several months to work through the darkness, but eventually she succeeded, and regained her composed demeanour.

Visions of Hope has its 'dark' side, but the main emphasis of the book points in the direction of light.

Yea, thou dost light my lamp; the Lord my God lightens my darkness.

Psalm 18:28

The people who walked in darkness have seen a great light; those who dwelt in a land of deep darkness, on them has light shined.

Isaiah 9:2

In him was life, and the life was the light of men. The light shines in the darkness, and the darkness has not overcome it.

John 1:4–5

...who has called you out of darkness into his marvellous light.

1 Peter 2:9

Darkness travels toward light, but blindness towards death.

Rabindranath Tagore, 'Stray Birds', CLXXVIII, in *Collected Poems & Plays of Rabindranath Tagore*, Macmillan & Co., 1936, page 311

I believe there is a way out of dark experiences though one cannot see it, and that all the suffering does not come in vain.

A.C. Benson, ***Extracts from the Letters of Dr. A.C. Benson to M.E.A.,*** **Jarrold Publishing, 1927, page 14**

The Powers of Darkness are the Workings of Nature or Self: for Nature, Darkness, and Self, are but three different Expressions for one and the same Thing.

William Law, in Sidney Spencer, editor, ***The Spirit of Prayer and the Spirit of Love,*** **James Clarke & Co., 1969, page 275**

If I enter the darkness of my own heart... I am entering the region of my being where I am ordinarily inaccessible to human beings; I am entering where God enters. I am using the sense of being accessible to God to become accessible to myself and to others.

John S. Dunne, ***The Reasons of the Heart,*** **SCM Press, 1978, page 57**

The idea sometimes heard today that darkness can be avoided and we should find God only in joy and celebration, in peace and comfort, is a grave delusion that perhaps reveals our present lack of experience. We are apt either to begin this way in some darkness and depression or else caught up by it somewhere along the way. Celebration is fine and comes after deliverance. Beforehand, celebration is often hollow and false and naïve.

Morton T. Kelsey, ***The Other Side of Silence,*** **SPCK, 1977, page 47**

Mingle with a crowd, especially a town crowd; look into those harassed, agitated, sickly faces; recall your own life and those of whom you have known intimately; remember the violent deaths, the cases of suicide of which you have heard,—and then ask yourself the cause of all those miseries, and of that despair which ends in self-murder. You will see, terrible as it seems, that nine-tenths of human sufferings spring from the teaching of the world; that all these sufferings are really needless, and yet unavoidable, and that the majority of men are martyrs to the teaching of the world.

Leo Tolstoy, ***What I Believe ('My Religion'),*** **C.W. Daniel, 1922, page 160**

Thus with the Year
Seasons return, but not to me returns
Day, or the sweet approach of Ev'n or Morn,
Or sight of vernal bloom, or Summer's Rose,
Or flocks, or herds, or human face divine;
But cloud in stead, and ever-during dark
Surrounds me, from the cheerful ways of men
Cut off, and, for the Book of knowledge fair,
Presented with a Universal blank
Of Nature's works to me expung'd and rais'd,
And wisdom at one entrance quite shut out.
So much the rather thou, Celestial light
Shine inward, and the mind through all her powers
Irradiate, there plant eyes, all mist from thence
Purge and disperse, that I may see and tell
Of things invisible to mortal sight.

John Milton, ***Paradise Lost,*** **iii. 40, in** ***The Poetical Works of John Milton,*** **Oxford at the Clarendon Press, 1900, page 228**

What of the Darkness? Is it very fair?
Are there great calms, and find ye silence there?
Like soft-shut lilies all your faces glow
With some strange peace our faces never know,
With some great faith our faces never dare:
Dwells it in Darkness? Do ye find it there?

Is it a Bosom where tired heads may lie?
Is it a Mouth to kiss our weeping dry?
Is it a Hand to still the pulse's leap?
Is it a Voice that holds the runes of sleep?
Day shows us not such comfort anywhere:
Dwells it in Darkness? Do ye find it there?

Out of the Day's deceiving light we call,
Day, that shows man so great and God so small,
That hides the stars and magnifies the grass,
O is the Darkness too a lying glass,
Or, undistracted, do ye find truth there?
What of the Darkness? Is it very fair?

R. Le Gallienne, in J.T. Hackett, *My Commonplace Book*, Macmillan and Co., 1923, page 57

'Darkness' in the spiritual life may be due to several causes. It may be 'psycho-physical'—that is, the result of illness or overstrain. Here common sense, rest and refreshment, coupled with quiet confidence in God, is the only line to take. It may be due to sin: to self-will or to lack of love or truth. This cause can soon be discovered by one who is sensitive to the voice of the Spirit; the only way back is through repentance, followed by the humble effort to wait for God, to follow at His pace, and not to try to force ours. But the 'darkness' of which writers like St John of the Cross speak with such authority is a normal experience, and must be patiently endured. For, just as we cannot look directly at God, who is Light; the glare would be too much for us; we must direct our gaze to Him indirectly. The whole principle of the spiritual life is this: 'that progress will be measured by what is felt to be defeat... that the blind who walk in the darkness of prayer are those who are really seeing most... that light doesn't make things clearer but less clear... that knowledge is perfected in ignorance.' In the words of St John of the Cross: 'The soul makes greatest progress when it travels in the dark, not knowing the way. The truth is that the nearer the soul comes to Him it perceives that the darkness is deeper and greater because of its own weakness... So the further a penitent advances, the further from himself he must go—walking by faith and not seeing.'

In such darkness there is nothing to fear. The trial is severe, it is true, and there is no getting away from the fact that the darkness is real, and the way seems hard. Often we feel as though we were travelling in the wrong direction; but by faith we know that we are not alone; that God is with us, leading and sustaining us all the time. Gradually, as we learn to adjust ourselves to this new way of living, we begin to understand why God must work in us in this secret way: He has to do so, because if we could see what He was doing we might become far too much interested in the process, and then we would spoil His work by looking at ourselves instead of at Him. All we are asked to do is to keep moving: 'Some run swiftly; some walk; some creep painfully; but everyone who keeps on will reach the goal'.

Olive Wyon, *On the Way*, SCM Press, 1958, page 63

The term 'darkness' is one which comes at different stages and has different meanings. It is, however, very much a part of growth in prayer, and needs to be looked at, if not fully understood. Why? Because if you are going to go on, you will need to go through it, and let it go through you.

In the beginning, there may be the darkness which is really blankness—unbelief. The soul can be shattered from God's light, not knowing how to begin to pray, not even wanting to, or thinking it possible. Faced with this impossibility, the impossible is demanded; you must 'Begin, all the same'... somehow, anyhow, however falteringly, however little.

When a person has set off in rather a different mood—filled with joy and eagerness, the honeymoon period which seems so full of light and promise gives way in most cases to loss of light, greyness and aridity. It is not quite dark, but it is like those days when a blight comes over the weather and nothing is quite so good or so worth while. The difficulty at that point is to avoid going back or trying to do so, starting all over again, trying to recapture the first taste of God which was so good. But this is the one thing you must not do, for it is necessary to go on through it—not back. Later there may be a deeper darkness as you move into the unknown—a loss of images, an intensification of aridity.

Again this, though difficult and even painful and tasteless, like eating sawdust while you pray, must be gone through. It is right, however wrong it feels; so keep on. You may be partly experiencing that God is immense—that is, too big for your mind to grasp or focus upon, and therefore everything blurs, becomes indistinct. Perhaps, too, in the greater penetration of God's light into the soul there must ensue darkness, as happens with the naked eye moving from darkness to sudden sunshine.

There is another darkness (or is it part of the same? Who knows!). This is desolation. It can be a sense of the loss of God or of sin separating you from God; when it is really bad, it can seem that God is abandoning you. In some cases the intensity grows to the point where the horror and blackness of it stems from the idea that God hates you and appears to will your destruction. When God is lost, then faith is deeply tested. It is not at all unusual—in fact it is to be expected—that you seem no longer able to believe that God exists.

Needless to say, much of this is very painful and almost puts the soul into a panic. There is genuine need for a guide at these times—even if only to give support and encouragement to go on. It can appear to be a real agony. Only God fully knows the purpose of it. But the soul, which is humble enough to endure in faith, later glimpses what it is all about—but only later.

The message at these points is to live through, groan, let yourself be broken open or be ignored by God. Above all, trust.

Michael Hollings and Etta Gullick, *The One Who Listens*, Mayhew-McCrimmon, 1972, page 144

EDUCATION

Education—bringing up (young persons); giving intellectual and moral training; development of character or mental powers

A quotation about higher education (which I've been unable to track down) suggests we are in danger of producing intellectual giants who remain spiritual and emotional pygmies.

Over the years I have been impressed with the intellectual qualities of our fellows, post-graduates and undergraduates. University College is one of the top academic Oxford colleges, usually performing well in the Norrington table, until it was abolished recently. However I sometimes wonder if we are too one-sided in our system of education. The emphasis tends to be on developing critical and analytical skills, and the powers of reason and the intellect. In formal education, the spiritual dimension barely gets a mention, and we even seem to have abandoned responsibility for moral training and development of character. As a chaplain, most of the problems that come before me are emotional in essence, and as an academic institution we do very little in the realm of educating feelings. It is largely left to the individual. Our main task is training the mind in one particular academic discipline.

Reflection groups are an attempt to educate the 'whole' person. They are based on the original meaning of the Latin word *educere*—to draw out, lead out—and concentrate on developing latent gifts and talents. A typical reflection group meets for an hour a week, chooses a topic, mulls over the contents in silence and then talks it through. Much is learned from the other members of the group. The intellectual content is still present, but the spiritual and moral contents are also there, and development of character takes place unconsciously. The reflection group thus makes its contribution in the academic institution which aims to educate the whole person, body, mind and spirit.

I will instruct you and teach you the way you should go; I will counsel you with my eye upon you.

Psalm 32:8

The wise man also may hear and increase in learning, and the man of understanding acquire skill.

Proverbs 1:5

About the middle of the feast Jesus went up into the temple and taught. The Jews marvelled at it, saying, 'How is it that this man has learning, when he has never studied?'

John 7:14–15

To them God chose to make known how great among the Gentiles are the riches of the glory of this mystery, which is Christ in you, the hope of glory. Him we proclaim, warning every man and teaching every man in all wisdom, that we may present every man mature in Christ. For this I toil, striving with all the energy which he mightily inspires within me.

Colossians 1:27–29

Learning is its own exceeding great reward.

William Hazlitt, 'The Plain Speaker', in *The Collected Works of William Hazlitt*, J.M. Dent & Co., 1903, volume VII, page 320

Unemployment has dealt us a stunning and crushing blow... there is little motivation... truancy is high.

Headmaster of a Midlands Comprehensive, in *Faith in the City*, Church House Publishing, 1985, page 293

... he is perfectly educated who is taught all the will of God concerning him, and enabled, through life, to execute it.

Thomas Arnold, *Sermons*, Longmans, Green, and Co., volume III, xvi, page 131

The highest education is that which teaches us to guide ourselves by motives which are intangible, remote, incapable of direct and material appreciation.

Mark Rutherford, *More Pages From a Journal*, Oxford University Press, 1910, page 220

A child is not educated who has not physical education, social education, intellectual education, industrial education, professional education, spiritual education.

Henry Ward Beecher, *Proverbs from Plymouth Pulpit*, Charles Burnet & Co., 1887, page 76

The task of religious education is to fashion a religious life-style, and to nurture in people that creative spirit of love that will help them to grow up and live wisely without a rule-book.

Roy Stevens, *On Education and the Death of Love*, Epworth Press, 1978, page 136

... if but the teacher be himself
virtuous or musical—an exemplar as such,
he will be keenly follow'd, and often in his love
that his pupil surpass him is his best reward.

Robert Bridges, *The Testament of Beauty*, iv. 685, Oxford at the Clarendon Press, 1930, page 160

A man is a great bundle of tools. He is born into this life without the knowledge of how to use them. Education is the process of learning their use, and dangers and troubles are God's whetstones with which to keep them sharp.

Henry Ward Beecher, *Proverbs from Plymouth Pulpit*, Charles Burnet & Co., 1887, page 9

Education: by that I understand not merely the imparting of knowledge, but the drawing out of the powers of the mind, spirit, and body; the evoking of a reverence for the truth, and the use of the imagination in its pursuit.

Michael Ramsey, in Margaret Duggan, editor, *Through the Year with Michael Ramsey*, Hodder and Stoughton, 1975, page 215

Education ought to teach how to be in love always and what to be in love with. The great things of history have been done by the great lovers, by the saints and men of science and artists; and the problem of civilisation is to give every man a chance of being a saint, a man of science, or an artist.

A. Clutton Brock, *The Ultimate Belief*, Constable and Company, 1916, page 99

... the modern educationalist is forever pointing out that *educere* means to lead forth, or to draw out, a student's potentiality, as opposed to the old-style education that was content to stuff a head full of presumed facts. If there is any analogy with spiritual direction, then it is very up-to-date indeed, for this has always been its aim; to develop innate gifts and graces.

Martin Thornton, *Spiritual Direction*, SPCK, 1984, page 11

The primary object of all religious education today, as of Bible reading, is to open the door into this Bible experience of God, so that its wealth of religious experience, the achievements of its creative personalities, and its enduring religious insight may become available to living people today; and so that the spiritual power of the same living God may be released into the modern world.

J.N. Schofield, *Introducing Old Testament Theology*, SCM Press, 1966, page 11

Ordinary, secular education, as it deals only with the comprehensible, puts the pupil in a wrong position. He has to do with nothing which may not be mastered, and becomes insensible to that which is beyond. Worse—he is affected only by reasons which appeal to his understanding, by what is immediate, and his conduct is not governed, as it so often should be, by that which is intangible, shadowy, and remote.

Mark Rutherford, *Last Pages From a Journal*, Oxford University Press, 1915, page 279

The development of general ability for independent thinking and judgment should always be placed foremost, not the acquisition of special knowledge. If a person masters the fundamentals of his subject and has learnt to think and work independently, he will surely find his way and besides will be better able to adapt himself to progress and changes than the person whose training principally consists in the acquiring of detailed knowledge.

Albert Einstein, *Out of My Later Years*, Thames and Hudson, 1950, page 36

The purpose of education is not simply the transmission of information but the bringing into being of persons of responsibility and integrity who, in a world of persons and things, can be instruments of a love which, in the words of Paul Tillich, 'moves everything toward everything else that is.' The educator's responsibility is to recognize that each single unique person is the bearer of a special task of being which can be fulfilled through him and him alone.

Reuel L. Howe, *The Miracle of Dialogue*, The Saint Andrew Press, 1969, page 77

The word 'relaxation' is vital. Somehow we must help students to relax, to get away from the worry, to get off the excess alcohol and the cigarettes, and rest creatively so that they can work better. Relaxation, deep meditation, physical movement as therapy: things like these can lead us, for part of our education time, away from the over-stressed intellect towards wholeness of mind and body and a sense of the body's grandeur. Keats spoke of 'diligent indolence'. It is a largely unrecognized educational virtue.

Roy Stevens, *Education and the Death of Love*, Epworth Press, 1978, page 103

This silence without which no enduring progress can be built must enter into all education that is worthy of the name: it is the reason why climbing or walking or sailing should come, if possible, into the life of every child:

'The thought of death sits easy on the man
Who has been born and dies among the mountains.'

Some people, out of strength or weakness, come to love such solitude as the breath of life. Many, strangers to their own souls, shun it with fear. But the well-strung creature, finds in it a tonic, a pause from which he comes refreshed. With the mountain air still in his eyes and feet, he is happy to return from the wilderness and to find himself again among the paths and dwellings and habits, the rites and symbols which in their long trail of history have made him what he is.

Freya Stark, *Perseus in the Wind*, John Murray, 1948, page 7

... A Church which seeks to take seriously its mission to the nation's young people will wish to uphold a system of schooling in which young people are helped to realise their human potential implanted by God, attain maturity and be prepared for life in the wider community.

Education has a part to play in making human self-centredness less disastrous. The capacity to grasp and experience the redemptive work of Christ is fundamental to the task of the Church. Although the maintained sector of education cannot be in the business of evangelising in the full sense, the Church... in partnership, must have commitment to a school system which allows the fullest possible individual development. It must seek to exercise its influence in upholding within the system an organisation, ethos and learning environment which reflects the reality of the presence of the living God in all. The Church must also speak out when it believes that what it holds to be precious is under threat.

Faith in the City, Church House Publishing, 1985, page 293

I often wonder whether or not education is fulfilling its purpose. A great majority of the so-called education people do not think logically and scientifically. Even the press, the classroom, the platform, and the pulpit in many instances do not give us objective and unbiased truths. To save man from the morass of propaganda, in my opinion, is one of the chief aims of education. Education must enable one to sift and weigh evidence, to discern the true from the false, the real from the unreal, and the facts from fiction.

The function of education, therefore, is to teach one to think intensively and to think critically. But education which stops with efficiency may prove the greatest menace to society. The most dangerous criminal may be the man gifted with reason but with no morals.

We must remember that intelligence is not enough. Intelligence plus character—that is the goal of true education. The complete education gives one not only power of concentration but worthy objectives upon which to concentrate. The broad education will, therefore, transmit to one not only the accumulated knowledge of the race but also the accumulated experience of social living.

Martin Luther King, *The Words of Martin Luther King*, selected by Coretta Scott King, William Collins Sons & Co., 1986, page 41

How far is this or that kind of education giving a chance for the appreciation of religion—the attitude of religion—to form itself and grow in a child's mind? It is not simply a question of whether this or that is being taught; it is a question of what modes of thought, what processes of knowing and appreciation are being elicited, and what ideas about life and its purpose are being stimulated.

There is the tragic fact that a good deal of education gives little or no place to the processes of thought, knowledge, and imagination whereby religion can be appreciated. The mind is stuffed with facts, but the use of the imagination in wonder and in the sense of mystery is not evoked.

The mind is trained to approach knowledge exclusively along one or two tracks, the tracks of science or technology: and to a mind so trained the language of religion is a foreign language conveying little or nothing.

We must face the fact that there are thousands of young people so educated that our problem is not just that they don't know the Christian faith, but that their minds are so formed that it is the hardest thing for the Christian faith to be intelligible to them.

The attitude of religion is in large part the sense of wonder: wonder at man, wonder at the marvel of his capacities and his frailties; wonder at man as he learns about the universe around him, and uses and misuses his knowledge. Hence we pass from wonder about man to wonder about the world with its astonishing range of content from atom to saint, and then to wonder about the Maker, both of man and of the world.

Michael Ramsey, in Margaret Duggan, editor, *Through the Year with Michael Ramsey*, Hodder and Stoughton, 1975, page 127

ENDURANCE

Endurance—power of enduring, undergoing pain etc.; bearing up

Shortly after arriving in London to work as chaplain to University College, I met a man, roughly my age, asking for help. I listened to him carefully. His parents had split up several years ago. He had been thrown out of St Andrew's University for drunken violent behaviour. This was followed by a breakdown and a period in mental hospital where he was diagnosed as schizophrenic. At the time he was on medication and living in a hostel. He had no money and was terribly hungry, and his clothes were in tatters. I gave him something to eat and fixed him up with some clothes, and that started an acquaintanceship which was to last for more than twenty years.

From then onwards he saw me regularly. The only job he could hold down was washing up, and this only for a short time before his health broke down again. He was seeing a doctor on a regular basis and taking all sorts of drugs—tranquillizers, anti-depressants and sleeping tablets.

Things did not improve for him. He appeared on one occasion with an impressive black eye. He had been involved in a fight and beaten up. He went through a long phase in which he suffered from paranoia in which he feared the Russians were after him. He unfortunately phoned the police with a bomb hoax, and didn't get away quickly enough. They caught him as he was leaving the phone-box. He experienced life in prison for a time. And so it went on. When I left London he managed to track me down in Oxford, and he continued to see me as before. By now he was having heart trouble, and the onset of Parkinson's disease. How he managed to endure those twenty years, I shall never know. Life for him was a living hell. Last year his step-mother died, and he went back to live in the country and to settle down on the family farm. Certainly for me he personifies endurance, and I've only given a brief summary of what he went through.

The Lord is a stronghold to him whose way is upright.

Proverbs 10:29

Set thy heart aright, and constantly endure, and make not haste in time of trouble.

Ecclesiasticus 2:2 (AV)

By your endurance you will gain your lives.

Luke 21:19

Love bears all things, believes all things, hopes all things, endures all things.

1 Corinthians 13:7

Some strains are bearable and even bracing, but others are deadly.

A.C. Benson, *Extracts from the Letters of Dr. A.C. Benson to M.E.A.*, Jarrold Publishing, 1927, page 41

Life should be a voluntary overcoming of difficulties, those met with and those voluntarily created, otherwise it is just a dice-game.

A.R. Orage, *On Love*, The Janus Press, 1957, page 61

I often wish there were some index or inward monitor showing me when I had not reached the limit of my power of resistance and endurance in trouble. Sometimes, I dare say, I fancy I can hold out no longer when, in reality, I am nowhere near falling.

Mark Rutherford, *Last Pages From a Journal*, Oxford University Press, 1915, page 316

To endure is greater than to dare; to tire out hostile fortune; to be daunted by no difficulty; to keep heart when all have lost it; to go through intrigue spotless; to forego even ambition when the end is gained—who can say this is not greatness?

William Makepeace Thackeray, *The Virginians*, Smith, Elder, & Co., 1894, page 761

There remain times when one can only endure. One lives on, one doesn't die, and the only thing that one can do, is to fill one's mind and time as far as possible with the concerns of other people. It doesn't bring immediate peace, but it brings the dawn nearer.

A.C. Benson, *Extracts from the Letters of Dr. A.C. Benson to M.E.A.*, Jarrold Publishing, 1927, page 14

The years should temper a man like steel, so that he can bear more and more and emerge more and more the conqueror over life. In the nature of things we must grow weaker in body, but in the divine nature of things we must grow ever stronger in the faith which can endure the slings and arrows of life, and not fail.

William Barclay, *The Letters to Timothy and Titus*, The Saint Andrew Press, 1965, page 283

He's truly valiant that can wisely suffer
The worst that man can breathe, and make his wrongs his outsides;
To wear them like his raiment carelessly,
And ne'er prefer his injuries to his heart
To bring it into danger.

William Shakespeare, *Timon of Athens*, III. v. 31

The value of such moral teaching lies in a man learning what others have experienced and what he too may expect of life. Whatever happens to him, he will realize that he is meeting the common lot of mankind and not a peculiar fate, fortunate or unfortunate. Even if this knowledge does not help us to escape sorrows, it shows us how to endure them and, perhaps, how to conquer them.

Johann Wolfgang von Goethe, *The Practical Wisdom of Goethe*, chosen by Emil Ludwig, George Allen & Unwin, 1933, page 159

Why should I murmur at my lot forlorn?
The self-same Fate that doom'd me to be poor
Endues me with a spirit to endure
All, and much more, than is or has been borne
By better men, of want, or worldly scorn.
My soul has faith.

Hartley Coleridge, 'Sonnet XIV' in *New Poems*, Oxford University Press, 1942, page 11

Life makes many an attempt to take away our faith. Things happen to us and to others which baffle our understanding; life has its problems to which there seems no solution and its questions to which there seems no answer; life has its dark places where there seems to be nothing to do but hold on. Faith is always a *victory*, the victory of the soul which tenaciously maintains its clutch on God.

William Barclay, *The Letters to the Corinthians*, The Saint Andrew Press, 1988, page 143

Provided we attain at last to the truly heroic and divine life, which is the life of virtue, it will matter little to us by what wild and weary ways, or through what painful and humiliating processes, we have arrived thither. If God has loved us, if God will receive us, then let us submit loyally and humbly to His law—'whom the Lord loveth He chasteneth, and scourgeth every son whom he receiveth.'

Charles Kingsley, *Daily Thoughts*, Macmillan & Co., 1884, page 41

The answer to this suffering lies in endurance. The Greek word for this endurance is *hupomone*. The keynote of *hupomone* is not grim, bleak acceptance of trouble but triumph. It describes the spirit which can not only accept suffering but triumph over it. Someone once said to a sufferer, 'Suffering colours life, doesn't it?' The sufferer replied, 'Yes, but I propose to choose the colour.' As the silver comes purer from the fire, so the Christian can emerge finer and stronger from hard days. The Christian is the athlete of God whose spiritual muscles become stronger from the discipline of difficulties.

William Barclay, *The Letters to the Corinthians*, The Saint Andrew Press, 1988, page 170

He [Paul] begins with one triumphant word of the Christian life—*endurance (hupomone)*. It is untranslatable. It does not describe the frame of mind which can sit down with folded hands and bowed head and let a torrent of troubles sweep over it in passive resignation. It describes the ability to bear things in such a triumphant way that it transfigures them... It is the courageous and triumphant ability to pass the breaking-point and not to break and always to greet the unseen with a cheer. It is the alchemy which transmutes tribulation into strength and glory.

William Barclay, *The Letters to the Corinthians*, The Saint Andrew Press, 1988, page 212

How do the saints endure? By what divine strategy do they maintain their faith?

They believe that God is in their suffering all the time! They do not see events as happening apart from God, nor put an undue stress on the difference between what God does and what God permits. They find God even in what He *allows*. Because the Universe is God's at the last, they see Him as taking ultimate responsibility for *whatever* happens. If it were possible to conceive of anything utterly sterile of good, God, they believe, would not permit it. Anything that happens, rightly met with God, is fecund of good. Therefore, they find God even in suffering; even in suffering prolonged, undeserved and bitter.

W.E. Sangster, *The Pure in Heart*, The Epworth Press, 1954, page 150

There is a spirit, which I feel, that delights to do no evil nor to revenge any wrong, but delights to endure all things, in hope to enjoy its own in the end. Its hope is to outlive all wrath and contention, and to weary out all exaltation and cruelty, or whatever is of a nature contrary to itself. It sees to the end of all temptations: As it bears no evil in itself, so it conceives none in thoughts to any other: If it be betrayed, it bears it; for its ground and spring is the mercies and forgiveness of God. Its crown is meekness, its life is everlasting love unfeigned, and it takes its kingdom with entreaty and not with contention, and keeps it by lowliness of mind. In God alone it can rejoice, though none else regard it or can own its life. It is conceived in sorrow and brought forth without any to pity it; nor doth it murmur at grief and oppression. It never rejoiceth but through sufferings; for with the world's joy it is murdered. I found it alone, being forsaken: I have fellowship therein with them who lived in dens and desolate places in the earth; who through death obtained their resurrection and eternal holy life.

James Naylor, A Quaker Saint. This is 'His last testimony, said to be delivered by him about two hours before his Departure'. From 'A Collection of Sundry Books, Epistles and Papers', &c., London, 1715. It seems to rely on oral tradition. I have followed the text in the Book, except that that has *and takes its kingdom*, and *obtained this resurrection.*

Robert Bridges, in *Spirit of Man*, Longman, Green & Co., 1973, number 372

They came as for a blessing, and they found a work. They are soldiers in Christ's army; they fight against 'things that are seen,' and they have 'all these things against them.' To their surprise, as time goes on, they find that their lot is changed. They find that in one shape or other adversity happens to them. If they refuse to afflict themselves, God afflicts them. One blow falls, they are startled; it passes over, it is well; they expect nothing more. Another comes; they wonder; 'why is this?' they ask; they think that the first should be their security against the second; they bear it however; and it passes too. Then a third comes; they almost murmur; they have not yet mastered the great doctrine that endurance is their portion. O simple soul, is it not the law of thy being to endure since thou camest to Christ? Why camest thou but to endure? Why didst thou taste His heavenly feast, but that it might work in thee? Why didst thou kneel beneath His hand, but that He might leave on thee the print of His wounds? Why wonder then that one sorrow does not buy off the next? Does one drop of rain absorb the second?

Does the storm cease because it has begun? Understand thy place in God's kingdom, and rejoice, not complain, that in thy day thou hast thy lot with Prophets and Apostles.

John Henry Newman, *Plain and Parochial Sermons*, J.G.F. & J. Rivington, 1840, volume 5, page 335

If you can keep your head when all about you
Are losing theirs and blaming it on you,
If you can trust yourself when all men doubt you,
But make allowance for their doubting too;
If you can wait and not be tired of waiting,

Or being lied about, don't deal in lies,
Or being hated, don't give way to hating,
And yet don't look too good, nor talk too wise:

If you can dream—and not make dreams your master;
If you can think—and not make thoughts your aim;

If you can meet with Triumph and Disaster
And treat those two impostors just the same.
If you can make one heap of all your winnings
And risk it on one turn of pitch-and-toss,
And lose, and start again at your beginnings
And never breathe a word about your loss.

If you can talk with crowds and keep your virtue,
Or walk with Kings—nor lose the common touch,
If neither foes nor loving friends can hurt you,
If all men count with you, but none too much;
If you can fill the unforgiving minute
With sixty seconds' worth of distance run,
Yours is the Earth and everything that's in it,
And—which is more—you'll be a Man, my son!

Rudyard Kipling, 'If'

FAILURE

Failure—non-occurrence, non-performance; running short, breaking down; ill success; unsuccessful person, thing, or attempt

I was walking with two of our undergraduates on a chalet reading/walking party in the French Alps, and asked them if they had any ideas of new topics for this anthology. One of their suggestions was 'failure'. I was quite surprised but they were both equally emphatic. They assured me that the fear of failure was quite common amongst undergraduates.

They reminded me of a remarkably successful organist and choirmaster at Bradford Cathedral. I once asked him what motivated him. 'It's the fear of failure,' he replied, 'it's getting up in front of a congregation, and the choir breaking down in the middle of an anthem, or of me making a complete mess of an organ voluntary.' I appreciated what he was saying. It shed light on my experience of sermon preparation. It also made me look back over my life and realize the fear of failure had been a main source of motivation as regards exam preparation—not exactly healthy.

How then can we best cope with failure when it happens? We shall probably have to make changes. Some of the world's greatest pioneers were failures in their early years—Florence Nightingale, for instance. I know of at least three undergraduates sent down for failing exams, who went on to get firsts in other universities. Perseverance is important. I came across a brief summary of the life of Abraham Lincoln. It's a long depressing list of failures, and then it ends up on a note of success—President of the United States of America.

The quotations which follow are designed to enable us to make a creative use of our failures.

The Lord upholds all who are falling, and raises up all who are bowed down.

Psalm 145:14

For a righteous man falls seven times, and rises again; but the wicked are overthrown by calamity.

Proverbs 24:16

And then many will fall away, and betray one another, and hate one another... But he who endures to the end will be saved.

Matthew 24:10, 13

Beware lest you be carried away with the error of lawless men and lose your own stability.

2 Peter 3:17

A minute's success pays for the failure of years.

Robert Browning, 'Apollo and the Fates', in *The Poetical Works of Robert Browning*, Smith, Elder & Co., 1897, volume II, page 689

They fail, and they alone, who have not striven.

Thomas Bailey Aldrich, 'Enamored Architect of Airy Rhyme', in *The Poems of Thomas Bailey Aldrich*, Houghton Mifflin and Company, 1882, page 240

In the world who does not know how to swim, goes to the bottom.

George Herbert, 'Outlandish Proverbs', number 285, in F.E. Hutchinson, editor, *The Works of George Herbert*, Oxford at the Clarendon Press, 1945, page 330

Do not be one of those who, rather than risk failure, never attempt anything.

Thomas Merton, *New Seeds of Contemplation*, Burns & Oates, 1962, page 80

It is often the failure who is a pioneer in new lands, new undertakings and new forms of expression.

Eric Hoffer, *The Passionate State of Mind*, Secker & Warburg, 1956, page 87

There is no loneliness greater than the loneliness of a failure. The failure is a stranger in his own house.

Eric Hoffer, *The Passionate State of Mind*, Secker & Warburg, 1956, page 104

We learn wisdom from failure much more than from success. We often discover what *will* do, by finding out what will not do.

Samuel Smiles, *Self Help*, S.W. Partridge & Co., 1912, page 251

Failure after long perseverance is much grander than never to have a striving good enough to be called a failure.

George Eliot, *Middlemarch*, edited by W.J. Harvey, Penguin Books, 1985, book II, page 254

Have you heard that it was good to gain the day?
I also say it is good to fall, battles are lost in the same spirit in which they are won.

Walt Whitman, 'Song of Myself', section 18, in Francis Murphy, editor, *The Complete Poems*, Penguin Books, 1982, page 80

But I'm proof against that word failure. I've seen behind it. The only failure a man ought to fear is failure in cleaving to the purpose he sees to be best.

George Eliot, *Felix Holt*, J.M. Dent & Co., 1909, page 404

Failure is as much part of life as success is and by no means something in front of which one sits down and howls as though it is a scandal and a shame.

J. Neville Ward, *Five for Sorrow, Ten for Joy*, Epworth Press, 1971, page 74

... I know that all this failure is somehow in the ultimate purpose of God, and He will use it for His own ultimate glory and for the ultimate good of men.

William Barclay, *The Gospel of Matthew*, The Saint Andrew Press, 1975, volume II, page 79

We are undefeated as long as we keep on trying, as long as we have some source of movement within ourselves and are not just moved by outside forces, as long as we retain the freedom of right decision and action, whatever the circumstances.

George Appleton, *Journey for a Soul*, William Collins Sons & Co., 1976, page 46

You're discouraged because somewhere in your life, or in the life of others, love has failed. If you want to recover, you must try offering a loving gesture. It will put you back on the road to hope, and life. For a failed love is death, and love itself is life.

Michel Quoist, *With Open Heart*, translated by Colette Copeland, Gill and Macmillan, 1983, page 182

If a man has a talent and cannot use it, he has failed. If he has a talent and uses only half of it, he has partly failed. If he has a talent and learns somehow to use the whole of it, he has gloriously succeeded, and won a satisfaction and a triumph few men ever know.

Thomas Wolfe, *The Web and the Rock*, William Heinemann, 1947, page 431

They never fail who die
In a great cause: the block may soak their gore;
Their heads may sodden in the sun; their limbs
Be strung in city gates and castle walls—
But still their spirit walks abroad.

Lord Byron, *Marino Faliero*, II. ii. 93, in Jerome J. McGann, editor, *The Complete Poetical Works*, Clarendon Press, Oxford, 1986, volume IV, page 356

It is good for a man to be brought once, at least, in his life, face to face with *fact*, ultimate fact, however horrible it may be, and to have to confess to himself shuddering, what things are possible on God's earth, when man has forgotten that his only welfare is living after the likeness of God.

Charles Kingsley, *Daily Thoughts*, Macmillan & Co., 1884, page 207

So I am content to have failed. I have learned in the experiment priceless truths concerning myself, my fellow-men, and the city of God, which is eternal in the heavens, for ever coming down among men, and actualising itself more and more in every succeeding age. I only know that I know nothing, but with a hope that Christ, who is the Son of Man, will tell me piecemeal, if I be patient and watchful, what I am and what man is.

Charles Kingsley, *Daily Thoughts*, Macmillan & Co., 1884, page 143

Why not give Christianity a trial? The question seems a hopeless one after 2,000 years of resolute adherence to the old cry of 'Not this man, but Barabbas.' Yet it is beginning to look as if Barabbas was a failure, in spite of his strong right hand, his victories, his empires, his millions of money, and his moralities and churches and political constitutions. 'This man' has not been a failure yet; for nobody has ever been sane enough to try his way.

George Bernard Shaw, Preface to *Androcles and the Lion*, The Bodley Head, 1972, page 458

At any point in his life a man may write under his own life story so far the words 'To be continued'. The final chapter always remains to be written, and it can be written in co-authorship with God, if the man so wills. In the same way God will write the final chapter in human history. A man's character determines and is determined by his response to external circumstances over which he has no control. Similarly the character of a nation and the rise and fall of a civilization.

George Appleton, *Journey for a Soul*, William Collins Sons & Co., 1976, page 45

The great temptation is to use our many obvious failures and disappointments in our lives to convince ourselves that we are really not worth being loved. Because what do we have to show for ourselves?

But for a person of faith the opposite is true. The many failures may open that place in us where we have nothing to brag about but everything to be loved for. It is becoming a child again, a child who is loved simply for being, simply for smiling, simply for reaching out.

This is the way to spiritual maturity: to receive love as a pure, free gift.

Henri J.M. Nouwen, *Seeds of Hope*, edited by Robert Durback, Darton, Longman and Todd, 1989, page 26

At times in the past, religious men have felt that if they are faithful to God, he must grant them success, guaranteeing them against defeat, suffering, failure. Men in misfortune sometimes ask, 'What have I done that God should do this to me?' The answer is probably 'nothing', with the denial that God is responsible at all for the unfortunate happening, though there is still the mystery of his providence and the interlocking of cause and effect in the human scene. God promises that his grace shall be more than sufficient for every happening and that he will always be at work to bring a greater blessing than if the unfortunate thing had never happened.

George Appleton, *Journey for a Soul*, William Collins Sons & Co., 1976, page 44

I feel like writing you a rather bracing, disagreeable, east-windy sort of letter. When I read yours my first impulse was to send you a line begging you only to *let yourself alone*. Don't keep on pulling yourself to pieces: and please burn that dreadful book with the list of your past sins! If the past really oppresses you, you had far better go to confession, and finish that chapter once and for all! It is emphatically your business now to look forwards and not backwards: and also to look forwards in an eager and optimistic spirit. Any other course is mere ingratitude, you know. There is a dispirited tone about your letter as if you were taking your own variations of mood and inevitable failures far too seriously—feeling your pulse too much. You say reading the *Modern Mystic* 'increased your responsibility more than you can bear.' This also is morbid (I am really horribly rude this evening!). Your responsibility ends when you have made sure that you are honest in will and intention, and are doing your best. There are no unbearable responsibilities in this world but those of our own seeking. Once life is realized as a succession of acts of loving service, undertaken in a spirit of joy, all that moonshine vanishes. I nearly quoted a text at you: but instead of that, here is a 'bit' which contains much food for profitable meditation I think. I wonder if you know it already?

'There was a saint who said, "I must rejoice without ceasing, although the world shudder at my joy." *He did not think he could save his soul without it.*'

People seem often to forget that Hope is a cardinal virtue necessary to salvation like Faith and Love: an active principle which ought to dominate life. I do think it would be so much better if you would go on quite simply and *trustfully* for a bit. After all, we value far more in our human relationships the sort of love that gives itself joyously and eagerly without introspection than the sort which is perpetually occupied with its own unworthiness or shortcomings. I wonder whether you are living too lonely a life for your temperament. You sound a bit like it.

Of course you are *quite* right when you say that feeling must precede doing: but unless it finally results in doing, it is mere emotional satisfaction, of no value. The direction and constancy of the *will* is what really matters, and intellect and feeling are only important in so far as they contribute to that. Don't be bullied by Tyrrell: he is often splendid, and also often quite wrong, being cursed with a cleverness that runs away with him.

Evelyn Underhill, 'Letter to M.R.', in *The Letters of Evelyn Underhill*, Longmans, Green & Co., 1907, page 66

FREEDOM

Freedom—personal liberty, non-slavery; independence; liberty of action, right to do; power of self-determination, independence of fate or necessity, freedom of speech and religion, from fear and want

It was two o'clock on a Monday afternoon. I began my weekly visiting on the wards of Bradford Royal Infirmary.

The man in the first bed was rather anxious about a pending operation. We chatted briefly about his condition, the doctors and nurses on the ward, and the likely outcome of the operation. I tried to give him some reassurance and moved on to the next patient. Here was a man of a very different disposition—blunt and direct—a typical Yorkshireman. 'They're not very intelligent in here, padre,' he started off apologetically, 'take yond, for instance, the man you've just been talking to. He came in yesterday, and tried to make conversation with me. "I've worked for thirty-five years for such-and-such a firm," he said. "Really," I replied, "you might just as well have been a cabbage." He hasn't spoken to me since. He was proud of the fact that he'd worked so long for one firm. I don't think of it that way at all. With those sort of people there's no get-up-and-go, no initiative, no intelligence, and certainly no freedom. He might just as well have been a cabbage.'

Well, he certainly gave me something to think about, especially as I've been ordained for twenty-seven years. I wonder if most of us settle down too quickly—in our work, in getting married, and in having families—at the cost of our freedom.

I'm thankful for being single, and being able to enjoy flexibility and freedom in work and in leisure. At the cost of an occasional bout of loneliness, I reckon it is worth it.

Out of my distress I called on the Lord; the Lord answered me and set me free.

Psalm 118:5

The Lord has anointed me... to proclaim liberty to the captives, and the opening of the prison to those who are bound.

Isaiah 61:1

So if the Son makes you free, you will be free indeed.

John 8:36

I want you to be free from anxieties.

1 Corinthians 7:32

Christianity promises to make men free; it never promises to make them independent.

W.R. Inge, *The Philosophy of Plotinus*, Longmans, Green and Co., 1948, volume II, page 192

The hope of the world is still in dedicated minorities. The trailblazers in human, academic, scientific, and religious freedom have always been in the minority.

Martin Luther King, *The Words of Martin Luther King*, selected by Coretta Scott King, William Collins Sons & Co., 1986, page 58

Freedom has always been an expensive thing. History is fit testimony to the fact that freedom is rarely gained without sacrifice and self-denial.

Martin Luther King, *The Words of Martin Luther King*, selected by Coretta Scott King, William Collins Sons & Co., 1986, page 51

You shall be free indeed when your days are not without a care and your nights without a want and a grief,
But rather when these things girdle your life and yet you rise above them named and unbound.

Kahlil Gibran, *The Prophet*, Sheldon Press, 1970, page 56

Men were invited to hear; but none was compelled to listen or to respond. For that is the law of the New Birth. Initiation is free from constraint, because freedom is of the essence of the Spirit-begotten life and the faith which accompanies it.

L.S. Thornton, C.R., *The Common Life in the Body of Christ*, Dacre Press: A. & C. Black, 1950, page 242

The price of freedom for all musicians, both composers and interpreters, is tremendous control, discipline and patience; but perhaps not only for musicians. Do we not all find freedom to improvise, in all art, in all life, along the guiding lines of discipline?

Yehudi Menuhin, *Theme and Variations*, William Heinemann, 1972, page 46

Be sure that if you offer your freedom to God—whether it is a question of time or affection or place or anything else—He will take it, He will take it, and you will no longer be free *in the same way*. But He will give you a far greater liberty instead. You will be free with the liberty of the children of God.

Hubert van Zeller, *Praying While You Work*, Burns, Oates and Washbourne, 1951, page 48

... when we decide to make a move that will liberate us from our enslavement: we must be aware that we shall be attacked by violence, by beguilement, by the inner enemies that are our old habits, our old craving for security, and that nothing is promised us, except the desert beyond. Beyond that is the promised land, but far beyond, and we must accept the risks of the journey.

Anthony Bloom, *The Essence of Prayer*, Darton, Longman and Todd, 1989, page 28

I was free. I belonged to God, not to myself: and to belong to Him is to be free. What was the difference between one place and another, one habit and another, if your life belonged to God, and if you placed yourself completely in His hands? The only thing that mattered was the fact of the sacrifice, the essential dedication of one's will. The rest was only accidental.

Thomas Merton, *Elected Silence*, Hollis and Carter, 1949, page 322

We who lived in concentration camps can remember the men who walked through the huts comforting others, giving away their last piece of bread. They may have been few in number, but they offer sufficient proof that everything can be taken from a man but one thing: the last of the human freedoms—to choose one's attitude in any given set of circumstances, to choose one's own way.

Viktor E. Frankl, *Man's Search for Meaning*, translated by Ilse Lasch, Hodder and Stoughton, 1959, page 65

The human will is free, ultimately, to choose one of two things:
either to stay connected with the tree of life, and submit the human will to the flush

of the vaster impulsion of the tree;
or else to sever the connection, to become self-centred, self-willed, self-motivated—and subject, really, to the draught of every motor-car or the kicking tread of every passer-by.

D.H. Lawrence, 'Free Will', in Vivian de Sola Pinto and Warren Roberts, editors, *The Complete Poems of D.H. Lawrence*, William Heinemann, 1967, volume II, page 617

True freedom doesn't mean being able to do anything you please with your body, heart and soul, when and where you wish, with no restraints or taboos. This sort of freedom only betrays an absence of freedom. It's a form of total alienation; man giving in, on his knees, to all his compulsions. It's going backwards, reverting to his animal condition. An animal lives by its instincts, programmed to fulfil its needs and its growth. But man must master his life and gradually learn how to direct it.

Michel Quoist, *With Open Heart*, translated by Colette Copeland, Gill and Macmillan, 1983, page 128

The disciplined life that is the only effective way to durable freedom involves *firstly* the inner way to a knowledge of God from Whom all freedom comes. Then comes the *second* part that concerns the individual life of mind and body. All is consummated in the *third* part which concentrates its work in relationships with other people. Thus the life of spiritual discipline consists of contemplation, ascetic living and purity of relationships. First comes the love of God, then the loving discipline of oneself, and finally service to our neighbours, who, as Jesus reminds us in the Parable of the Good Samaritan, include everyone in immediate relationship with us.

Martin Israel, *The Spirit of Counsel*, Hodder and Stoughton, 1983, page 111

This is man's great and inalienable freedom—perhaps the only freedom he has—the freedom of his spirit to accept and be at one with life, or to revolt and be in separation. It is a fateful freedom, a tragic freedom if you will, but it is what gives dignity and purpose to the life of man. It is the power to co-operate with God in the work of creation and redemption—which cannot indeed be completed without man's co-operation. Our task is to live fully and wisely 'now,' within the limits of our circumstances and of those relationships which are at once our joy and our sorrow, our opportunity and our restriction.

E. Grahaw Howe and L. Le Mesurier, *The Open Way*, Methuen & Co., 1939, page 173

My freedom does not mean my ability to do what I like as and when I like: it means my ability to choose some goal or end, and to unify all my powers in the consistent pursuit of that goal or end.

That is a freedom for the whole person, a freedom which involves an ideal *for* which one is free; a freedom which involves restraints which a person makes for himself, but which the community can also help him make in a common pursuit of freedom. It is, above all, not only a freedom *from* this and that and the other, but a freedom *for* something greater than oneself. And in so far as it is a freedom *from*, it is freedom from oneself, from the arbitrary tyranny which the self can impose upon itself.

Michael Ramsey, in Margaret Duggan, editor, *Through the Year with Michael Ramsey*, Hodder and Stoughton, 1975, page 212

Some have called me the philosopher of freedom, and a reactionary Russian bishop once said of me that I was 'the captive of freedom'. I do indeed love freedom above all else. Man came forth out of freedom and issues into freedom. Freedom is a primordial source and condition of existence, and, characteristically, I have put Freedom, rather than Being, at the basis of my philosophy. I do not think any other philosopher has done this in such a radical and thorough-going way. The mystery of the world abides in freedom: God desired freedom and freedom gave rise to tragedy in the world. Freedom is at the beginning and at the end. I might say that all my life I was engaged in hammering out a philosophy of freedom. I was moved by the basic conviction that God is truly present and operative only in freedom.

Freedom alone should be recognized as possessing a sacred quality, whilst all the other things to which a sacred character has been assigned by men since history began ought to be made null and void.

I found strength to renounce many things in life, but I have never renounced anything in the name of duty or out of obedience to precepts and prohibitions: I renounced for the sake of freedom, and, maybe, also out of compassion. Nothing could ever tie me down, and this, no doubt, has to some extent weakened my efficiency and diminished my possibilities of self-realization. I always knew, however, that freedom gives birth to suffering, while the refusal to be free diminishes suffering. Freedom is not easy, as its enemies and slanderers allege: freedom is hard; it is a heavy burden. Men... often renounce freedom to ease their lot...

All things in human life should be born of freedom and pass through freedom and be rejected whenever they betray freedom. The true meaning and origin of the fallen condition of man is to be seen in the primordial rejection of freedom.

Nicolas Berdyaev, *Dream and Reality*, translated by Katharine Lampert, Geoffrey Bles, 1950, page 46

GOODNESS

Goodness—virtue; positive or comparative excellence; benevolence, kindness, generosity; what is good in a thing, its essence or strength

Recently I had the privilege of meeting Jean Vanier at a university mission in Oxford. Before that I had heard a lot about him through friends and acquaintances and had read some of his books. From these sources I gleaned he was the son of a Governor-General of Canada, and for a career, had become an officer in the Royal Navy. In later life he left the navy to study for a doctorate in philosophy at the *Institut Catholique* in Paris, and then lectured in a Canadian university. A significant change followed. He bought a dilapidated house in a village outside Paris and invited three handicapped men to come and live with him. This was the start of L'Arche—a community of handicapped and able-bodied people—which came into being in 1964. Since then L'Arche communities have proliferated. Nearly a hundred such communities have sprung up in different parts of the world, all started off by this one man.

One of our former members of Univ. (University College, Oxford) worked in a L'Arche community for six months, as a preparation for the ordained ministry. He popped in to see me on his return to England. Living in such a community had not been easy, but he had learnt such a lot in the short space of time. When I asked him how he had managed to cope he looked at me quizzically, raised an eyebrow, and gave an answer in two words: 'Prayer, Bill.'

With this background I was curious to meet Jean Vanier. I was not disappointed. He has all the qualities, mentioned in the definition of 'goodness' at the start of this paragraph. He comes over as a man of great compassion and understanding, mingled with kindness and sympathy. His form of 'goodness' is extremely attractive—quietly charismatic.

And God saw everything that he had made, and behold, it was very good.
Genesis 1:31

Depart from evil, and do good; seek peace, and pursue it.
Psalm 34:14

I am the good shepherd. The good shepherd lays down his life for the sheep.
John 10:11

He was a good man, full of the Holy Spirit and of faith.
Acts 11:24

Nature meant me to be, on the whole, a good man.
Charlotte Brontë, *Jane Eyre*, Oxford at the Clarendon Press, 1969, page 166

To be good is to be in harmony with one's self.

Oscar Wilde, *The Picture of Dorian Gray*, Chivers Press, 1979, page 128

Good nature is one of the richest fruits of Christianity.

Henry Ward Beecher, *Proverbs from Plymouth Pulpit*, Charles Burnet & Co., 1887, page 107

Goodness is something so simple: always to live for others, never to seek one's own advantage.

Dag Hammarskjöld, *Markings*, translated by W.H. Auden & Leif Sjoberg, foreword by W.H. Auden, Faber and Faber, 1964, page 87

Good in a strong many-compounded nature is of slower growth than any other mortal thing, and must not be forced.

George Meredith, *The Ordeal of Richard Feverel*, The Times Book Club, 1912, page 210

Good is no good, but if it be spend:
God giveth good for none other end.

Edmund Spenser, 'The Shepherd's Calender: May', in J.C. Smith & E. de Selincourt, editors, *Spenser Poetical Works*, Oxford University Press, page 436

Where a man chooses comfort as his 'good' he is in fact choosing to remain at the animal level when he has capacity for more.

William Temple, *Nature, Man and God*, Macmillan & Co., 1934, page 517

Nothing I can do, even if I do my best, can be good. As Jesus said, 'We are unprofitable servants, we have done our duty'. Therefore I shall strive to do my best.

A.R. Orage, *On Love*, The Janus Press, 1957, page 61

Trusting in your goodness and great mercy, Lord, I come—sick I come to my Saviour, hungry and thirsty to the well of life, needy to the King of Heaven.

Thomas à Kempis, *The Imitation of Christ*, translated by Betty I. Knott, William Collins Sons & Co., 1979, page 218

The inclination to goodness is imprinted deeply in the nature of man, insomuch that if it issue not towards men, it will take unto other living creatures.

Francis Bacon, *The Essays*, edited by John Pitcher, Penguin Books, 1985, page 96

In his love he clothes us, enfolds and embraces us; that tender love completely surrounds us, never to leave us. As I saw it he is everything that is good.

Julian of Norwich, *Revelations of Divine Love*, Penguin Books, 1976, page 67

How God is a true, simple, perfect Good, and how He is a Light and a Reason and all virtues, and how what is highest and best, that is, God, ought to be most loved by us.

Theologia Germanica, translated by Susanna Winkworth, Stuart & Watkins, 1966, page 84

Goodness as a fruit of the Divine Spirit is raining satisfaction and happiness upon all around us, not studying our own welfare; a fountain out of which all the time flow streams of delight for others.

Henry Ward Beecher, *Proverbs from Plymouth Pulpit*, Charles Burnet & Co., 1887, page 154

Good men are not those who now and then do a good act, but men who join one good act to another. It is men, the whole tendency of whose lives is the production of good things, kind things, right things.

Henry Ward Beecher, *Proverbs from Plymouth Pulpit*, Charles Burnet & Co., 1887, page 96

By desiring what is perfectly good, even when we don't quite know what it is and cannot do what we would, we are part of the divine power against evil—widening the skirts of light and making the struggle with darkness narrower.

George Eliot, *Middlemarch*, edited by W.J. Harvey, Penguin Books, 1985, page 427

But my life now, my whole life, independently of anything that can happen to me, every minute of it is no longer meaningless as it was before, but has a positive meaning of goodness with which I have the power to invest it.

Leo Tolstoy, *Anna Karenin*, translated by Rosemary Edmonds, Penguin Books, 1983, page 853

It should be a part of our private ritual to devote a quarter of an hour every day to the concentration of the good qualities of our friends. When we are not *active*, we fall back idly upon defects, even of those whom we most love.

Mark Rutherford, *Last Pages From a Journal*, Oxford University Press, 1915, page 319

Dive through the stormy surface of the flood
To the great current flowing underneath;
Explore the countless springs of silent good;
So shall the truth be better understood,
And thy grieved Spirit brighten strong in faith.

William Wordsworth, 'Men of the Western World! in Fate's dark book', in *The Poems*, Penguin Books, 1977, volume II, page 822

Once we enter again into contact with our own deepest self, with an ordinate self-love that is inseparable from the love of God and of His truth, we discover that all good develops from within us, growing up from the hidden depths of our being according to the concrete and existential norms laid down by the Spirit Who is given us from God. This mystical spontaneity (which begins with the free option of faith and grows with our growth in charity) sets the tone for our whole moral life. It is the inward promulgation of God's new law of charity in our hearts.

Thomas Merton, *The New Man*, Burns & Oates, 1962, page 166

You ask, 'What is the Good?' I suppose God Himself is the Good; and it is this, in addition to a thousand things, which makes me feel the absolute certainty of a resurrection, and a hope that this, our present life, instead of being an ultimate one, which is to decide our fate for ever, in which man's faculties are so narrow and cramped, his chances (I speak of the millions, not of units) of knowing the Good so few, that he may have chances hereafter, perhaps continually fresh ones, to all eternity.

Charles Kingsley, *Daily Thoughts*, Macmillan & Co., 1884, page 171

Always say to yourself this one thing, 'Good I will become, whatever it cost me; and in God's goodness I trust to make me good, for I am sure He wishes to see me good more than I do myself.' And you will find that, because you have confessed in that best and most honest of ways that God is good, and have so given Him real glory, and real honour, and real praise, He will save you from the sins which torment you, and you shall never come, either in this world or the world to come, to that worst misery, the being ashamed of yourself.

Charles Kingsley, *Daily Thoughts*, Macmillan & Co., 1884, page 207

The goodness of the saint is a peculiar goodness. It flames with the numinous. It is a goodness which unconsciously proclaims itself. One feels it as an aura around its possessor. It is incandescent. It is *essential* goodness: goodness 'in the inward parts'; it is white with a whiteness 'no fuller on earth can whiten'.

If a man came near to this goodness in a saint and did not feel it, there is nothing one could do about it. It is spiritually discerned. Yet its radiations are so powerful that it may be doubted whether anyone could be near it and quite unaware of it.

W.E. Sangster, *The Pure in Heart*, The Epworth Press, 1954, page 140

God's purpose is like a stream of goodness flowing out into the world and all its needs. But it is our privilege as God's children to help this stream of goodness to reach other people, becoming ourselves like channels. Our good actions can be channels of God's goodness, and so too can our prayers.

We do not bombard God with our desires; no, we bring our desires into tune with his, so that he, waiting upon our co-operation, and using the channel of our prayers, brings the stream of his good purpose into the parched deserts of human need.

Michael Ramsey, in Margaret Duggan, editor, *Through the Year with Michael Ramsey*, Hodder and Stoughton, 1975, page 26

What, then, is the service rendered to the world by Christianity? The proclamation of 'good news.' And what is this 'good news'? The pardon of sin. The God of holiness loving the world and reconciling it to Himself by Jesus, in order to establish the kingdom of God, the city of souls, the life of heaven upon earth,—here you have the whole of it; but in this is a revolution. 'Love one another, as I have loved you;' 'Be ye one with me, as I am one with the Father;' for this is life eternal, here is perfection, salvation, joy. Faith in the fatherly love of God, who punishes and pardons for our good, and who desires not the death of the sinner, but his conversion and his life,—here is the motive power of the redeemed.

Henri Frédéric Amiel, *Amiel's Journal*, translated by Mrs Humphry Ward, Macmillan & Co., 1918, page 147

If we are to say there is only one good, the most promising candidate seems to me to be harmony. When we are in harmony on the feeling side with ourselves and our environment we have happiness; when we are in harmony on the intellectual side with reality, we have truth and wisdom; when in harmony with other men, social virtue and love; when in harmony with God, religious peace. And aesthetic experience is very commonly also regarded as the enjoyment of a kind of harmony. But the claims of harmony to be the sole good are hard to reconcile with the fact that one of the things we must account as most eminently good is a heroic struggle against difficulties and with the fact that a worse man is often more in harmony with himself and with society than a better. All this suggests that it is at least doubtful whether we can produce any tidy list of things good-in-themselves. Even if the different goods belong to the same genus, they are different species and have to be considered separately.

A.C. Ewing, *Ethics*, The English Universities Press, 1975, page 73

GREATNESS

Greatness—of remarkable ability, genius, intellectual or practical qualities, loftiness or integrity of character

I wonder if Albert Schweitzer will be acknowledged as the greatest person of the twentieth century. A man of remarkable academic ability, he had four doctorates—in philosophy, in theology, in music, and in medicine—and three of these were completed in his twenties. On this alone he must be regarded as a person of great intellectual ability. Linked with this, which is rare, were equally important practical skills. He was a surgeon, a self-taught architect and builder, an agriculturalist, a famous organist and a consultant in organ-craft. Later he became a mission doctor in order to devote himself wholeheartedly to philanthropic work. In this he became a skilled administrator in founding, organizing, and maintaining a hospital at Lambarene in the Gabon Province of French Equatorial Africa. He was the recipient of the 1952 Nobel Peace Prize for his efforts on behalf of 'The Brotherhood of Nations'.

What I particularly like about him was his personal philosophy of 'reverence for life'. He saw this as the key ethical principle, linking philosophy and religion, involving all living things. This not only included people—irrespective of race, caste, colour and religion—but was extended to all living things, to the whole of creation. In living out 'reverence for life' to the full, emerged a wholehearted personality with integrity of character. Anyone who wants to do a study of greatness must read *Albert Schweitzer: the Man and His Mind* by George Seaver.

Thine, O Lord, is the greatness, and the power, and the glory, and the victory, and the majesty; for all that is in the heavens and in the earth is thine; thine is the kingdom, O Lord, and thou art exalted as head above all.

1 Chronicles 29:11

Let them know how much better the Lord of them is: for the first author of beauty hath created them... For by the greatness and beauty of the creatures proportionably the maker of them is seen.

Wisdom of Solomon 13:3, 5 (AV)

Whoever would be great among you must be your servant, and whoever would be first among you must be your slave; even as the Son of man came not to be served but to serve, and to give his life as a ransom for many.

Matthew 20:26–28

... and what is the immeasurable greatness of his power in us who believe, according to the working of his great might.

Ephesians 1:19

There is never any easy way to greatness; greatness is always the product of toil.

William Barclay, *The Gospel of Matthew*, The Saint Andrew Press, 1987, volume I, page 278

Some are born great, some achieve greatness,
And some have greatness thrust upon 'em.

William Shakespeare, *Twelfth Night*, II. v. 148

[Jesus] was clear that He had come 'not to make life easy, but to make men great.'

William Barclay, *The Gospel of Matthew*, The Saint Andrew Press, 1987, volume I, page 111

There is a great man who makes every man feel small. But the real great man is the man who makes every man feel great.

G.K. Chesterton, *Charles Dickens*, Methuen & Co., 1906, page 8

Very rarely something may emerge complete and perfect in a flash, but far oftener greatness is the result of long labour and constant attention to detail.

William Barclay, *The Gospel of Matthew*, The Saint Andrew Press, 1987, volume I, page 279

If a man is great in the spiritual elements, he is great everywhere else; but if he is small there, he is small everywhere else. Not animalhood, but manhood, must be measured.

Henry Ward Beecher, *Proverbs from Plymouth Pulpit*, Charles Burnet & Co., 1887, page 16

'Tis meet
The great should have the fame of happiness,
The consolation of a little envy.
'Tis all their pay for those superior cares,
Those pangs of heart, their vassals ne'er can feel.

Edward Young, *The Brothers*, I. i, in *The Complete Works of Edward Young*, William Tegg and Co., 1854, volume II, page 255

Men of genius, in addition to their powers of observation and comprehension, possess other qualities, such as intuition and creative imagination. *Through intuition they learn about other things ignored by other men*, they perceive relations between seemingly isolated phenomena, they unconsciously feel the presence of the unknown treasure. All great men are endowed with intuition. *They know without analysis, without reasoning*, what is important for them to know.

Alexis Carrel, in F.C. Happold, *Religious Faith and Twentieth Century Man*, Darton, Longman and Todd, 1980, page 41

He alone deserves the appellation of great, who either achieves great things himself, or teaches how they may be achieved; or who describes with suitable dignity the great achievements of others. But those things are only great, which either make this life of ours happy, or at least comfortable and agreeable as far as is consistent with honesty, or which lead to another and a happier life.

John Milton, 'Second Defence of the People of England', in *The Works of John Milton*, Columbia University Press, 1933, volume VIII, page 95

I wish I could make you see that you must decide what you will be and do. It does not matter what you choose—be a farmer, business-man, artist, what you will—but know your aim and live for that one thing. We have only one life. The secret of success is concentration; wherever there has been a great life, or a great work, that has gone before. Taste everything a little, look at everything a little; but live for one thing. Anything is possible to a man who knows his end and moves straight for it, and for it alone.

Olive Schreiner, *The Story of an African Farm*, Ernest Benn, 1951, page 202

Wisdom and Spirit of the universe!
Thou Soul that art the eternity of thought,
That givest to forms and images a breath

And everlasting motion, not in vain
By day or star-light thus from my first dawn
Of childhood, didst thou intertwine for me
The passions that build up our human soul;
Not with the mean and vulgar works of man,
But with high objects, with enduring things—
With life and Nature purifying thus
The elements of feeling and of thought,
And sanctifying, by such discipline,
Both pain and fear, until we recognise
A grandeur in the beatings of the heart.

William Wordsworth, *The Prelude*, i. 401, Macmillan and Co., 1932, page 11

I may not count over all the links in the chain which led Isabel to think of Madame Merle's situation as aristocratic—a view of it never expressed in any reference made to it by that lady herself. She had known great things and great people, but she had never played a great part. She was one of the small ones of the earth; she had not been born to honours; she knew the world too well to nourish fatuous illusions on the article of her own place in it. She had encountered many of the fortunate few and was perfectly aware of those points at which their fortune differed from hers. But if by her informed measure she was no figure for a high scene, she had yet to Isabel's imagination a sort of greatness. To be so cultivated and civilized, so wise and so easy, and still make so light of it—that was really to be a great lady, especially when one so carried and presented one's self.

Henry James, *The Portrait of a Lady*, Penguin Books, 1986, page 242

'Ye shall leave Me alone.' Alone then the Son of man was content to be. He threw Himself on His own solitary thought: did not go down to meet the world; but waited, though it might be for ages, till the world should come round to Him. He appealed to the Future—did not aim at seeming consistent: left His contradictions unexplained:—'I came from the Father—I leave the world, and go to the Father.' 'Now,' said they, 'Thou speakest no proverb:' that is, enigma. But many a hard and enigmatical saying before He had spoken, and He left them all. A thread runs through all true acts, stringing them together into one harmonious chain: but it is not for the Son of God to be anxious to prove the consistency with each other.

This is self-reliance—to repose calmly on the thought which is deepest in our bosoms, and be unmoved if the world will not accept it yet. To live on your own convictions against the world, is to overcome the world—to believe that what is truest in you is true for all: to abide by that, and not be over-anxious to be heard or understood, or sympathized with, certain that at last all must acknowledge the same, and that while you stand firm, the world will come round to you: that is independence. It is not difficult to get away into retirement, and there live upon your own convictions: nor is it difficult to mix with men, and follow their convictions: but to enter into the world, and there live out firmly and fearlessly according to your own conscience, that is Christian greatness.

F.W. Robertson, *Sermons on Biblical Subjects*, J.M. Dent & Co., 1906, volume III, page 198

It was a strange, almost a unique, thing to be the idol of a nation and to remain uncorrupted, to be oneself the guardian of the people's rights sometimes against the emotional impulse of the people themselves... There lies his greatest claim to recognition: he sought not to impose his own will on the embryo nation, but to let the nation create and form itself. He belonged in spirit to an earlier, a more generous and more cultured age than this of narrowness and authority, and thin, sectarian hatred. But he belonged also to a later age; his deep and genuine interest in the people he ruled, his faith in their development, his toleration, his convinced belief in government by consent—all these reach out from the medieval world towards a wider time. Few statesmen in any period, none in his own, cared so deeply for the ordinary comfort and the trivial happiness of the thousands of individuals who are 'the people'. He neither idealized nor overestimated them and he knew that they were often wrong, for what political education had they yet had? But he believed in them, not merely as a theoretical concept, but as individuals, as men. Therein lay the secret of the profound and enduring love between him and them. Wise, wary, slow to judge and slow to act, patient, stubborn and undiscouraged, no other man could have sustained so difficult a cause for so long, could have opposed, with so little sacrifice of public right, the concentrated power of a government which disregarded it. He respected in all men what he wished to have respected in himself, the right to an opinion.

There have been politicians more successful, or more subtle; there have been none more tenacious or more tolerant. 'The wisest, gentlest and bravest man who ever led a nation', he is one of that small band of statesmen whose service to humanity is greater than their service to their time or their people. In spite of the differences of speech or political theory, the conventions and complexities which make one age incomprehensible to another, some men have a quality of greatness which gives their lives universal significance. Such men, in whatever walk of life, in whatever chapter of fame, mystic or saint, scientist or doctor, poet or philosopher, and even—but how rarely—soldier or statesmen, exist to shame the cynic, and to renew the faith of humanity in itself.

Of this number was William of Nassau, Prince of Orange, called the Silent.

C.V. Wedgwood, *William the Silent*, Jonathan Cape, 1944, page 252

GROWING

Growth—increasing in size, height, quality, degree, power etc., advancing to maturity, reaching full size

When I was being prepared for confirmation at the age of sixteen, the school chaplain told us our main aim in life was 'to glorify God and enjoy him for ever'. This didn't mean much to me at the time. God was somehow put over as being 'out there' miles away beyond the clouds. 'Glorifying God' suggested an attitude of worship, with hands upraised towards the heavens. I was somehow meant to enjoy this for ever, but I was unable to enjoy it at all.

Years later I was trying to work out what our main aim in life is, in a practical and realistic way. I remember looking at a flower, observing it carefully, and suddenly realizing that if it unfolded, flourished and died, nobody would be particularly upset because it had achieved in what it set out to do. It had actually succeeded in growing to its highest level of development and expression. I wondered if there was a lesson here for human life. Could it be that our main aim in life is to grow a soul (character or personality) which is us at our highest level of development and expression—so that we become most truly and fully ourselves?

I went on to work out how best this could be done. Again the Genesis story of the creation of man became relevant. The divine inbreathing meant we already had an enormous potential of life in the depths of our being. The practice of reflection provided a means of growing. The words of the definition above could then become a reality for us—'increasing in size, height, quantity, degree, power etc., advancing to maturity, reaching full size'. What an exciting prospect, but do not most of us get stunted in our growing and never reach wholeness and maturity?

Blessed are the men whose strength is in thee... They go from strength to strength.

Psalm 84:5, 7

But the path of the righteous is like the light of dawn, which shines brighter and brighter until the full day.

Proverbs 4:18

The kingdom of heaven is like a grain of mustard seed which a man took and sowed in his field; it is the smallest of all seeds, but when it has grown it is the greatest of shrubs and becomes a tree.

Matthew 13:31–32

We are to grow up in every way into him who is the head, into Christ, from whom the whole body, joined and knit together by every joint with which it is supplied, when each part is working properly, makes bodily growth and upbuilds itself in love.

Ephesians 4:15–16

If only I may grow: firmer, simpler—quieter, warmer.

Dag Hammarskjöld, *Markings*, translated by W.H. Auden & Leif Sjoberg, with a foreword by W.H. Auden, Faber and Faber, 1964, page 89

No life is spoiled but one whose growth is arrested.

Oscar Wilde, *The Picture of Dorian Gray*, Chivers Press, 1979, page 122

Only love enables humanity to grow, because love engenders life and it is the only form of energy that lasts forever.

Michel Quoist, *With Open Heart*, translated by Colette Copeland, Gill and Macmillan, 1983, page 202

Men never grow up into manhood as an acorn grows into an oak-tree. Men come to it by re-birth in every faculty, again, and again, and again.

Henry Ward Beecher, *Proverbs from Plymouth Pulpit*, Charles Burnet & Co., 1887, page 8

There is in the universe a provision by which men are helped by the Divine Spirit. God inspires us to the Christian life, and helps to the development of its graces.

Henry Ward Beecher, *Proverbs from Plymouth Pulpit*, Charles Burnet & Co., 1887, page 180

There is little hope for us until we become tough-minded enough to break loose from the shackles of prejudice, half-truths, and downright ignorance.

Martin Luther King, *The Words of Martin Luther King*, selected by Coretta Scott King, William Collins Sons & Co., 1986, page 30

Some individuals need stability in order to grow, and sometimes they simply need the confidence to stay put when change does not mean growth.

Morton T. Kelsey, *The Other Side of Silence*, SPCK, 1977, page 67

I never allow principles to carry me far enough. I do not think that in this I am peculiar. I notice that in the gardens of most men are nothing but arrested buds. How rare it is to see the fully developed flower!

Mark Rutherford, *Last Pages From a Journal*, Oxford University Press, 1915, page 280

If your roots are firmly planted, be sure you know what you're doing before pulling them up and moving on. A plant always suffers when transplanted; it needs time to grow more roots and time to develop before it can bear any fruit.

Michel Quoist, *With Open Heart*, translated by Colette Copeland, Gill and Macmillan, 1983, page 133

Omnipotence as a divine attribute comes to meaning in organic growth. The tree does not develop first at this point and then at the other. *All over* it proceeds to perfection. So should the growth of character be, and so it is when it is divinely prompted.

Mark Rutherford, *Last Pages From a Journal*, Oxford University Press, 1915, page 256

... we need some means by which in time the Eternal grows real, the invisible shines through the seen, God becomes a speaking Presence, conscience is quickened, resources are deepened and hope is renewed, until one hears the trumpets of the soul again and is adequate for life!

Harry Emerson Fosdick, *Successful Christian Living*, SCM Press, 1938, page 16

To grow is to emerge gradually from a land where our vision is limited, where we are seeking and governed by egotistical pleasure, by our sympathies and antipathies, to a land of unlimited horizons and universal love, where we will be open to every person and desire their happiness.

Jean Vanier, *Community and Growth*, Darton, Longman and Todd, 1991, page 105

Only a little seed is needed, a tiny seed: drop it in the soul of a peasant and it will not die. It will live in his soul all his life. It will be hidden inside him amidst the darkness... as a bright spot, as a great reminder. And it is not necessary, it is not necessary to teach and expound a lot. He will understand it all simply.

Fyodor Dostoyevsky, *The Brothers Karamazov*, translated by David Magarshack, Penguin Books, 1963, volume I, page 345

But I had to do it, to live with myself, to be myself, and to continue growing, where others had stopped. I would not be a crippled tree... Indeed it is suffering, to go on growing, to hold to what is, to try to understand, to knock down one's preconceptions. To find one's memories ravaged by time and revolution, one's intimate illusions ripped up, laughter for one's own private desolation the only answer; to realize how difficult, agonizing, is the process of understanding, and how long it takes.

Han Suyin, *The Crippled Tree*, Mayflower Books, 1968, page 18

Prayer... is fellowship with God. *It is being with Him.* He made us for friendship, and His fatherly heart is always seeking for our close companionship.

The sublime fruit of this friendship for men and women is that they grow like Him. All people grow to some extent like those they love, admire, and live with, and one of the most wonderful things about human beings is that they can grow like God.

W.E. Sangster, *Give God a Chance*, Epworth Press, 1968, page 67

I thought that my voyage had come to its end at the last limit of my power,—that the path before me was closed, that provisions were exhausted and the time come to take shelter in a silent obscurity.

But I find that thy will knows no end in me. And when old words die out on the tongue, new melodies break forth from the heart; and where the old tracks are lost, new country is revealed with its wonders.

Rabindranath Tagore, *Gitanjali*, Macmillan & Co., 1971, page 29

The hope is not in our own efforts to love. It is not in psychoanalysis which tries to throw light on the knots and blocks of our life, nor in a more equitable reorganisation of the political and economic structures which have their effects on our personal lives. All this is perhaps necessary. But true growth comes from God, when we cry to him from the depths of the abyss to let his Spirit penetrate us. Growth in love is a growth in the Spirit. The stages through which we must pass in order to grow in love are the stages through which we must pass to become more totally united to God.

Jean Vanier, *Community and Growth*, Darton, Longman and Todd, 1991, page 133

... little is made of the quiet but crucial dimension of growth and sanctification. The impression often given is that once you have made the difficult decision of faith and become a member of the Body of Christ, nothing important remains to be done except perhaps to keep faithfully where you are, and above all, not to 'be missing'. The traditional notion that you are *going* somewhere, on a journey of growth and exploration, seems to have been lost. Paul knew that in spite of being converted and justified, something else remained: 'Forgetting what is behind me, and reaching out for that which lies ahead, I press towards the goal to win the prize which is God's call to the life above, in Christ Jesus' (Philippians 3.13).

Frank Wright, *The Pastoral Nature of the Ministry*, SCM Press, 1980, page 24

The spiritual life means growth. We are called to grow 'unto the measure of the stature of the fulness of Christ'. The end of growth is perfection: this means both purity of heart and maturity of character. Just as the hyacinth in its pure beauty develops from a dark and uninteresting bulb, through all the stages of growth, into a perfect bloom, so this purity or perfection means reaching the end for which we have been made. Thus the mature Christian is not a blameless, insipid kind of person, out of touch with real life, but rather a wise, all-round, 'grown-up' kind of person; one who is always moving on, and finding more in life and in people and in God, to the very end. In other words, 'growth is a continual process of integration; on every level of human life, physical, mental and spiritual'. The Christian ideal, however, is not that of a number of 'integrated' individuals, concerned about their own spiritual progress, but of growth into Christ, as members of the Body of Christ, in which we all live by the same Life, which flows through the Body, and animates us all.

Olive Wyon, *On the Way*, SCM Press, 1958, page 33

Have we not all come across people, grown men and women, who remain on the fringe of life and seem quite content to stay there? They are familiar with the ways of the world, well informed, cultured, authorities perhaps on this and that, yet their lives seem never properly to have set. They are not conscious of lacking anything. On the contrary they often appear to be all too satisfied with what they have found. But what have they found? They have not found either man's true place in the scheme of creation nor, more immediately, their own. They can jog along with their amusements, can meet their troubles more or less philosophically, can manage to get by without going deeply into ends and origins. Passing satisfactions compensate for passing disappointments. But is it good enough? Surely the first lesson of the growing mind is that there must be more in life than would appear on the surface, and that if persons are to be complete beings they must discover what it is. Otherwise they are like children who skim through the book, looking only at the pictures lest they come upon long words which they will not understand. A grown-up person ought to understand, ought to know what he is supposed to be developing into and why. His life should have shape, direction, and destination. Even at this present-day stage in the evolution of the human intelligence there are many who, believing that man is in fact developing, are not at all clear as to the rationale of this development or the goal aimed at.

Hubert van Zeller, *Leave Your Life Alone*, Sheed and Ward, 1973, page 95

HAPPINESS

Happiness—(of person or circumstance) lucky, fortunate, contented with one's lot

When I was young, and looking forward to the future, the one thing I wanted out of life was happiness. At school, happiness came by way of achievement, getting through exams, involvement in sport, and friendships. In National Service, happiness came through a sense of adventure, an involvement with the Gurkhas, and travel. There was the long sea voyage in the troopship the *Empire Fowey* via Gibraltar, the Suez Canal, Aden (now South Yemen), Ceylon (Sri Lanka), and finally Singapore. This led to new experiences in Malaya (Malayasia), Hong Kong and Sarawak. At university, happiness came primarily through being in Oxford. At Balliol College there was greater freedom than at school and in the army, and greater opportunities for learning, sport and friendships. I got a great deal of enjoyment out of listening to music. Happiness peaked on the expedition to the Himalayas. I began to realize how lucky and fortunate I had been throughout the early part of my life.

Whilst at university I did a lot of thinking about what I was going to do in the future. A commitment had been made and a change of priorities had taken place over a period of time. I was not going to pursue happiness as an end in itself, but rather fulfilment. Work as a priest, with its involvement with people, was likely to be costly, but I was guided by the principle that you only get out of life what you are prepared to put into it. Well, I'm still working on it. There have been many ups and downs but from time to time precious moments of contentment and happiness.

Blessed is every one who fears the Lord, who walks in his ways! You shall eat the fruit of the labour of your hands; you shall be happy, and it shall be well with you.

Psalm 128:1–2

I know that there is nothing better for them than to be happy and enjoy themselves as long as they live; also that it is God's gift to man that every one should eat and drink and take pleasure in all his toil.

Ecclesiastes 3:12–13

Happiness lies more in giving than in receiving.

Acts 20:35 (NEB)

... we call those happy who were steadfast.

James 5:11

The happy person is he who is striving to actualize his potentialities.

A.R. Orage, *On Love*, The Janus Press, 1957, page 61

To rush the world over seeking for happiness is a fool's work.

Olive Schreiner, *Undine*, Ernest Benn, 1929, page 191

There is no duty we so much underrate as the duty of being happy.

Robert Louis Stevenson, *Virginibus Puerisque*, Chatto & Windus, 1906, page 80

Happiness... must be something solid and permanent, without fear and without uncertainty.

Samuel Johnson, *The History of Rasselas*, Oxford University Press, 1971, page 48

... to be without some of the things you want is an indispensable part of happiness.

Bertrand Russell, *The Conquest of Happiness*, Unwin Paperbacks, 1984, page 23

We are to give our heart to God that he may make it happy, with a happiness which stretches its capacity to the full.

Gordon S. Wakefield, in *A Dictionary of Christian Spirituality*, SCM Press, 1986, page 68

The largest proportion of the happiness experienced among men on earth has been derived from social relationships.

Henry Ward Beecher, *Proverbs from Plymouth Pulpit*, Charles Burnet & Co., 1887, page 186

... there is a secret belief amongst some men that God is displeased with man's happiness; and in consequence they slink about creation, ashamed and afraid to enjoy themselves.

Arthur Helps, *Companions of my Solitude*, George Routledge & Sons, 1907, page 20

If you will be true to the best of yourself, fearing and desiring nothing, but living up to your nature, standing boldly by the truth of your word, and satisfied therewith, then you will be a happy man.

Marcus Aurelius, *The Meditations of Marcus Aurelius*, translated by Jeremy Collier, Walter Scott, page 42

A loving heart, a genuine sympathy, a pure, unadulterated taste, a life that is not scorched by dissipation or wasted by untimely hours, a good, sound body and a clear conscience, ought to make any man happy.

Henry Ward Beecher, *Proverbs from Plymouth Pulpit*, Charles Burnet & Co., 1887, page 22

The monastery is a school—a school in which we learn from God how to be happy. Our happiness consists in sharing the happiness of God, the perfection of His unlimited freedom, the perfection of His love.

Thomas Merton, *Elected Silence*, Hollis and Carter, 1949, page 332

It is not our level of prosperity that makes for happiness but the kinship of heart to heart and the way we look at the world. Both attitudes lie within our power, so that a man is happy so long as he chooses to be happy and no one can stop him.

Alexander Solzhenitsyn, *Cancer Ward*, translated by Nicholas Bethell and David Burg, Penguin Books, 1972, page 290

There is certainly no greater happiness, than to be able to look back on a life usefully and virtuously employed, to trace our own progress in existence, by such tokens as excite neither shame nor sorrow.

Samuel Johnson, 'The Rambler', number 41, in *The Yale Edition of the Works of Samuel Johnson*, edited by W.J. Bate and Albrecht B. Strauss, Yale University Press, 1969, volume III, page 225

And happiness... what is it? I say it is neither virtue nor pleasure nor this thing nor that, but simply *growth*. We are happy when we are growing. It is this primal law of all nature and the universe, and literature and art are the cosmic movements in the conscious mind.

J.B. Yeats, *Letters to his son, W.B. Yeats and others*, Faber and Faber, 1944, page 121

The way to be happy is to love according to nature, in obedience to that universal and unalterable law with which every heart is originally impressed; which is not written on it by precept, but engraven by destiny, not instilled by education, but infused at our nativity. He that lives according to nature will suffer nothing from the delusions of hope, or importunities of desire: he will receive and reject with equability of temper; or act or suffer as the reason of things shall alternately prescribe.

Samuel Johnson, *The History of Rasselas*, Oxford University Press, 1971, page 59

Happiness cannot be attained directly nor is it what we usually imagine it to be. The only happiness man can attain is that which results from the perfect functioning of body and soul and from the accomplishment of the destiny which the order of things assigns to him.

The only means, therefore, of attaining happiness is to aim at the widest possible fulfilment of life. It is useless to pursue happiness as an end in itself; when life succeeds as a whole, happiness appears as a by-product.

Alexis Carrel, *Reflections on Life*, translated by Antonia White, Hamish Hamilton, 1952, page 183

I do not flatter myself that I hold any very important place in the world's economy. But I believe that I have humbly contributed somewhat to the happiness of others, and I find that the reward of thwarted, wasted ambitions has come in the shape of a daily increasing joy in quiet things and tender simplicities... yet I have proved by experiment that a life beset by many disadvantages, and deprived of most of the stimulus that to some would seem essential, need not drift into being discontented or evil or cold or hard.

A.C. Benson, *The House of Quiet*, John Murray, 1910, page 210

When I looked outside right into the depth of nature and God, then I was happy, really happy... so long as I have that happiness here, the joy in nature, health and a lot more besides, all the while one has that, one can always recapture happiness.

Riches can all be lost, but that happiness in your own heart can only be veiled, and it will still bring you happiness again, as long as you live. As long as you can look fearlessly up into the heavens, as long as you know that you are pure within and that you will still find happiness.

Anne Frank, *The Diary of Anne Frank*, Pan Books, 1954, page 137

The world is best enjoyed and most immediately while we converse blessedly and wisely with men. I am sure it were desirable that they could give and receive infinite treasures: and perhaps they can. For whomsoever I love as myself, to him I give myself, and all my happiness, which I think is infinite: and I receive him and all his happiness. Yea, in him I receive God, for God delighteth me for being His blessedness: so that a man obligeth me infinitely that maketh himself happy; and by making himself happy, giveth me himself and all his happiness.

Thomas Traherne, *Centuries*, The Faith Press, 1969, page 176

This afternoon I walked over to Lanhill.

As I came down from the hill into the valley across the golden meadows and along the flower-scented hedges a great wave of emotion and happiness stirred and rose up within me. I know not why I was so happy, nor what I was expecting, but I was in a delirium of joy, it was one of the supreme moments of existence, a deep delicious draught from the strong sweet cup of life. It came unsought, unbidden, at the meadow stile, it was one of the flowers of happiness scattered for us and found unexpectedly by the wayside of life. It came silently, suddenly, and it went as it came, but it left a long lingering glow and glory behind as it faded slowly like a gorgeous sunset, and I shall ever remember the place and the time in which such great happiness fell upon me.

The Revd Francis Kilvert, entry for 24 May 1875 in *Kilvert's Diary*, chosen, edited and introduced by William Plomer, Jonathan Cape, 1977, volume III, page 190

It is only a poor sort of happiness that could ever come by caring very much about our own narrow pleasures. We can only have the highest happiness, such as goes along with being a great man, by having wide thoughts, and much feeling for the rest of the world, as well as ourselves; and this sort of happiness often brings so much pain with it, that we can only tell it from pain by its being what we would choose before everything else, because our souls see it is good. There are so many things wrong and difficult in the world, that no man can be great—he can hardly keep himself from wickedness—unless he gives up thinking much about pleasures or rewards, and gets strength to endure what is hard and painful. My father had the greatness that belongs to integrity; he chose poverty and obscurity rather than falsehood... And so, if you mean to act nobly and seek to know the best things God has put within reach of men, you must learn to fix your mind on that end, and not on what will happen to you because of it. And remember, if you were to choose something lower, and make it the rule of your life to seek your own pleasure and escape from what is disagreeable, calamity might come just the same; and it would be calamity falling on a base mind, which is the one form of sorrow that has no balm in it, and that may well make a man say,—'It would have been better for me if I had never been born.'

George Eliot, epilogue to *Romola*, Oxford University Press, 1965, page 598

The door [to happiness] is opened by beauty or pain, delight or sorrow, into a universe whose processes are not complete—a divine workshop where one can live in the active partnership of God.

Creativeness, too, we share with the divine in our degree: and because of this partnership which exists only in loving or creating, I believe that these two energies alone can give us happiness.

The power to create does not appear to have grown like love, slowly out of the building of earth; it is our Promethean gift. The delight of it is felt in its simple stages, by the child with his toy boat on the stream, by the mechanic over his screw, or the painter at his easel...

But while there is pleasure in looking back over accomplishment, the word *happiness* must surely be reserved for that which actually allows us to share in the transformation. No mere knowledge, not even the acquisition of new knowledge, can give this firm delight. In it the amateur is joyful, the craftsman content, and the artist free of the weight of age. It is the secret of the pleasure women sometimes find in embroidery and men in gardens.

Something is made, some combination of thoughts, materials, colours, which was not there before: imperfect as love, it shares with love the only divinity we have; it is our partnership in Creation.

Freya Stark, *Perseus in the Wind*, John Murray, 1948, page 24

HEALING

Healing—restoring (person, wound), to health, cure (person of disease); (of wound) become sound or whole; health-giving; conducive to moral or spiritual welfare

An experience of 'healing' affected me greatly. It occurred in the Duke of York's Home in Bradford whilst visiting there as a part-time hospital chaplain. I knocked on a door of a single room and got a rather feeble 'come in.' I found Douglas in an extremely weak condition. He had just undergone major surgery, in which his bowels had been removed, and a catheter fitted. He was in pain and weary, and just wanted to die. He greeted me with the words: 'Do you believe in faith healing?' I told him I did when I felt the circumstances were right. 'Could you please give me the laying on of hands.' I did so, and then took my leave as he was in such a weak condition.

The next day he seemed a little stronger. We had a five-minute conversation in which he told me his life story. He had qualified as a solicitor, but never practised. He realized his heart was not in the law and so became a photographer instead. His aim in life from then onwards was to pursue 'beauty' particularly in nature. He had specialized in the Yorkshire Dales and showed me a book he had written and illustrated—*Yorkshire Revealed*. But he moved on quickly. 'I still don't think I've found the "beauty" I've been looking for. I think its essence is spiritual. Could you please give me the laying on of hands again. I really think it did me some good yesterday.'

I saw him regularly during the next few weeks, and he made a remarkable recovery. On my last visit he said: 'Do you realize you've got the gift of healing in your hands? Whenever you lay hands on my head and pray it is as if an electric shock goes right through my body. I'm convinced it has played a major part in healing me.'

From time to time we need to be reminded that Jesus 'healed' people, and still does so, through others gifted in this way.

I am the Lord, your healer.

Exodus 15:26

Bless the Lord, O my soul, and forget not all his benefits, who forgives all your iniquity, who heals all your diseases.

Psalm 103:2–3

And he went about all Galilee, teaching in the synagogues and preaching the gospel of the kingdom and healing every disease and every infirmity among the people.

Matthew 5:23

Is any among you sick? Let him call for the elders of the church, and let them pray over him, anointing him with oil in the name of the Lord; and the prayer of faith will save the sick man, and the Lord will raise him up; and if he has committed sins, he will be forgiven. Therefore confess your sins to one another, and pray for one another, that you may be healed. The prayer of a righteous man has great power in its effects.

James 5:14–16

Stress has replaced disease as the problem of the day.

GP in Birmingham, in *Faith in the City*, Church House Publishing, 1985, page 265

The crickets sing, and man's o'er-labour'd sense
Repairs itself by rest.

William Shakespeare, *Cymbeline*, II. ii. 11

God is Himself a vast medicine for man. It is the heart of God that carries restoration, inspiration, aspiration, and final victory.

Henry Ward Beecher, *Proverbs from Plymouth Pulpit*, Charles Burnet & Co., 1887, page 137

There is a healing curative nature forever outworking from the Divine Mind upon ours, although we may not co-operate voluntarily upon His will.

Henry Ward Beecher, *Proverbs from Plymouth Pulpit*, Charles Burnet & Co., 1887, page 153

A bodily disease, which we look upon as whole and entire within itself, may, after all, be but a symptom of some ailment in the spiritual part.

Nathaniel Hawthorne, *The Scarlet Letter*, The Gresham Publishing Co., 1900, page 90

... it remains eternally true that we can never be right physically until we are right spiritually, that health in body and peace with God go hand in hand.

William Barclay, *The Gospel of Matthew*, The Saint Andrew Press, 1987, volume I, page 328

Psychosomatic illnesses are illnesses of the soul transmitted to the body; a sick spirit and a healthy body inevitably come into conflict and finally break down.

Michel Quoist, *With Open Heart*, translated by Colette Copeland, Gill and Macmillan, 1983, page 66

It is the infinite, overflowing, swelling impulse of the Divine nature to cure souls of their diseases; to augment that which is good in them; to develop them; to equip them; to perfect them.

Henry Ward Beecher, *Proverbs from Plymouth Pulpit*, Charles Burnet & Co., 1887, page 138

Look to your health: and if you have it, praise God, and value it next to a good conscience; for health is the second blessing that we mortals are capable of; a blessing that money cannot buy; and therefore value it, and be thankful for it.

Izaak Walton, *The Compleat Angler*, The Nonesuch Press, 1929, page 193

The basic idea of inner healing is simply this: that Jesus, who is the same yesterday, today, and forever, can take the memories of our past and
1) *Heal* them from the wounds that still remain and affect our present lives; and
2) Fill with his love all these places in us that have been empty for so long, once they have been healed and drained of the poison of past hurts and resentment.

Francis MacNutt, *Healing*, Ave Maria Press, 1977, page 164

I find great occasion for alarm in very much of that modern practice of psychotherapy from which no doubt we are also going to gain great benefits. But in some of this practice there is a strong suggestion that all we have to do is somehow to become at peace with ourselves, to restore an internal harmony, to become, as they like to say, fully integrated. And I want to ask, about what centre?—with what manner of self is my whole being to be harmonized?

William Temple, *The Preacher's Theme To-day*, SPCK, 1936, page 53

I am not a mechanism, an assembly of various sections.
And it is not because the mechanism is working wrongly, that I am ill.
I am ill because of wounds to the soul, to the deeper emotional self
and the wounds to the soul take a long, long time, only time can help
and patience, and a certain difficult repentance
long, difficult repentance, realisation of life's mistake, and freeing oneself
from the endless repetition of the mistake
which mankind at large has chosen to sanctify.

D.H. Lawrence, in Vivian de Sola Pinto and Warren Roberts, editors, *The Complete Poems of D.H. Lawrence*, William Heinemann, 1967, page 620

The paralysed man (Mark 2:1–12) could not get free from a feeling of guilt and was healed by the word of forgiveness. The paralysed man at the Sheep Gate (John 5:2–9) was asked 'Do you want to be healed? inferring that he preferred to escape from the responsibilities of daily life. The man who called himself Legion (Mark 5:1–20) had his many divisions unified in the acceptance of Christ's authority and encouragement. Many of our troubles are spiritual and will not be healed by treating the physical symptoms but only by tackling the spiritual causes—fear of failure, fear of ridicule, anxiety, frustrated irritation, escapism, inner division, feelings of guilt for which we are not humble enough or wise enough to accept God's forgiveness.

George Appleton, *Journey for a Soul*, William Collins Sons & Co., 1976, page 185

Any community of Christians, will have a concern for all its members. When any member is ill, the others will rally round in sympathy and helpfulness. There will be believing and persistent prayer, calling God's love to the aid of those in trouble, so much greater and more effective than our own. The Church will also be engaged in preventative health, teaching people how to live a disciplined life avoiding over-eating, over-drinking, over-working, a trusting life avoiding anxiety, impatience, frustration, a psychologically healthy life so that they never come to a stage where psychiatric treatment or a period in a mental hospital is needed. Living in Christ's way will enable us to share in Christ's health, and make available to us the abundant life of spirit, mind and body which is God's will for all.

George Appleton, *Journey for a Soul*, William Collins Sons & Co., 1976, page 185

Let us open ourselves to the healing, forgiving Spirit of Jesus. Let us open up all the pains of the past, the wounds that came from the moment of our conception—wanted or unwanted—and from the months we were carried in our mother's womb; the wounds from our early childhood when we felt rejected or stifled, unloved in our being and unrecognized in our gifts; the wounds coming from all the failures of the past; our incapacity to love and give life, the people we have hurt because of our sinfulness, pride or fears, and the barriers we have built around our vulnerability.

Let us allow the healing, forgiving Spirit of Jesus to penetrate our whole being, and lead us to wholeness. Then will rise from that very darkness a new understanding of others.

Jean Vanier, *The Broken Body*, Darton, Longman and Todd, 1988, page 135

What has to be healed in us is our true nature, made in the likeness of God. What we have to learn is love. The healing and the learning are the same thing, for at the very core of our essence we are constituted in God's likeness by our freedom, and the exercise of that freedom is nothing else but the exercise of disinterested love—the love of God for His own sake, because He is God.

The beginning of love is truth, and before He will give us His love, God must cleanse our souls of the lies that are in them. And the most effective way of detaching us from ourselves is to make us detest ourselves as we have made ourselves by sin, in order that we may love Him reflected in our souls as He has re-made them by His love.

That is the meaning of the contemplative life, and the sense of all the apparently meaningless little rules and observances and fasts and obediences and penances and humiliations and labours that go to make up the routine of existence in a contemplative monastery: they all serve to remind us of what we are and who God is—that we may get sick of the sight of ourselves and turn to Him: and in the end, we will find Him in ourselves, in our own purified natures which have become the mirror of His tremendous goodness and of His endless love...

Thomas Merton, *Elected Silence*, Hollis and Carter, 1949, page 325

Dr. Racanelli, of Florence, who has a gift of healing, and who practises the laying on of hands in all kinds of nervous afflictions, has said that he has a very strong sensation of this force working in him and passing out through his hands. Whereas his patients are left with a sense of well-being and calm, he himself experiences such fatigue that he is compelled to a strict austerity of life when he is practising this type of treatment, so as not to become exhausted.

When we discussed this subject, another doctor from Florence told us that he had also practised this kind of healing with success; but, he said, he had had to give it up because he was himself too sensitive to it, 'Thus,' he told us, 'for example, my patient, suffering from angina, would find that his angina had suddenly gone; but I myself at once suffered a similar attack.' When I told my wife about this, we were reminded of a fact we had frequently observed: that we regularly had a quarrel ourselves during the evening of a day in which we had been able to help in the reconciliation of another married couple. One is reminded of the passage in the Gospel recalled by Carl Jung after the collapse of the Nazi regime: that when a devil is cast out he goes somewhere else (Matthew 8:28–34).

Paul Tournier, *A Doctor's Casebook in the Light of the Bible*, SCM Press, 1954, page 152

The idea behind inner healing is simply that we can ask Jesus Christ to walk back to the time we were hurt and to free us from the effects of that wound in the present. This involves two things then:

1) *Bringing to light* the things that have hurt us. Usually this is best done with another person; even the talking out of the problem is in itself a healing process.

2) *Praying* the Lord to heal the binding effects of the hurtful incidents of the past...

Jesus, as Lord of time, is able to do what we cannot: he can heal those wounds of the past that still cause us suffering. The most I was ever able to do as a counsellor was to help the person bring to the foreground of consciousness the things that were buried in the past, so that he could consciously cope with them in the present. Now I am discovering that the Lord can heal these wounds—sometimes immediately—and can bring the counselling process to its completion in a deep healing.

At times, these hurts may seem slight to an adult mind, but we must be sensitive to see things as a child would. I remember once praying for a woman whose complaint was that her inner life was always bleak and boring, even though her professional life was in itself full and exciting. When we finally found what had caused her to shut off the flow of life it was an incident that happened when she was ten years old.

Francis MacNutt, *Healing*, Ave Maria Press, 1977, page 165

HOLINESS

Holiness—consecrated, sacred; belonging to, commissioned by, devoted to, God; of high moral excellence

One of my earliest childhood memories was being taken to a church by my godmother. It must have been just before Christmas, for we went off to see the baby Jesus in the manger. I remember it was dark inside the church and she hushed me to be quiet. In a spirit of awe and reverence we peeped into the manger. A light shone on the baby Jesus. There was a quiet atmosphere of holiness about the whole scene. It made a deep impression on me.

Years later I remember the same feeling of holiness listening to a sermon, preached by a bishop. I can't remember a word he said now, but I can remember his face. It was radiant and energetic. There was something sacred permeating his being, or so it seemed. I again became aware of a spirit of awe and reverence. It was deeply moving and inspiring, and evoked a response. I was never argued into accepting the Christian faith but I was won over by the sight of holiness.

In London, I met Anthony Bloom, or Metropolitan Anthony of Sourozh. He came to take a 'quiet day' for chaplains working in London University. He spoke quietly and deeply. He had a pair of bright shining eyes and a radiant disposition. He had about him an air of awe and reverence—an aura of holiness. What he said was also deeply impressive.

In this section, and in *Visions of Hope* as a whole, I have tried to bring together some of the insights of holiness. The practice of reflection is a way of growing in holiness.

Who is like thee, majestic in holiness, terrible in glorious deeds, doing wonders?

Exodus 15:11

For I am the Lord your God; consecrate yourselves therefore, and be holy, for I am holy.

Leviticus 11:44

... that we, being delivered from the hand of our enemies, might serve him without fear, in holiness and righteousness before him all the days of our life.

Luke 1:74–75

... he disciplines us for our good, that we may share his holiness.

Hebrews 12:10

Real holiness has a fragrance about it which is its own advertisement.

Father Andrew SDC, *The Way of Victory*, A.R. Mowbray & Co., 1938, page 12

Let the remembrance of all the glory wherein I was created make me more serious and humble, more deep and penitent, more pure and holy before Thee.

Thomas Traherne, *Centuries*, The Faith Press, 1969, page 39

We cannot reach our Saviour's puritie,
Yet are we bid, *Be holy e'en as He.*
In both let's do our best.

George Herbert, 'Lent', in F.E. Hutchinson, editor, *The Works of George Herbert*, Oxford at the Clarendon Press, 1953, page 87

Holiness means living within the divine perspective. It comes from attention to God—on your knees in prayer; and it comes from obedience to God—on your feet in action.

Hugh Montefiore, *Sermons from Great St Mary's*, William Collins Sons & Co., 1968, page 16

Jesus wants us to be holy as his Father is. We can become very great saints if we only want to. Holiness is not the luxury of the few, but a simple duty for you and for me.

Mother Teresa, *Jesus, the Word to be Spoken*, compiled by Brother Angelo Devananda, William Collins Sons & Co., 1990, page 49

Holiness... in men, is their dei-formity; likeness to God in goodness, righteousness, and truth. Such real holiness sanctifies the subject by its presence: and where that is, the person is made pure, good, righteous.

Benjamin Whichcote, *Moral and Religious Aphorisms*, century iii, number 262, Elkin Mathews & Marrot, 1930, page 32

The way of holiness was by the gift of the Holy Spirit, and the common use of the word 'saint' waited on the outpouring of the Spirit. The outpouring of the Spirit was the Birthday of the Christian Church.

W.E. Sangster, *The Pure in Heart*, The Epworth Press, 1954, page 28

No one can resist the argument of holiness, brought in a personified form before him, in its gentleness, in its sweetness, in its aspiration, in its love, in all its blossoms and fruits of peace and joy.

Henry Ward Beecher, *Proverbs from Plymouth Pulpit*, Charles Burnet & Co., 1887, page 171

Holiness is the goal of every true Christian. 'Holy' means 'set apart for God'. A holy person is not gloomy and unnatural, but 'whole' and therefore happy. That is why holiness, whenever we see it in others, is always attractive.

Hugh Montefiore, *Confirmation Notebook*, Fifth Edition, SPCK, 1985, page 39

If we earnestly desire holiness, self-denial must enter our lives fully after prayer. The easiest form of self-denial is control over our bodily senses. We must practice interior mortification and bodily penances also. How generous are we with God in our mortifications?

Mother Teresa, *Jesus, the Word to be Spoken*, compiled by Brother Angelo Devananda, William Collins Sons & Co., 1990, page 35

It doesn't matter, he is holy, his heart contains the secret of a renewal for all, the power which will finally establish truth on earth, and all will be holy, and will love each other, and there will be no more rich nor poor, exalted nor humbled, but all men will be as the children of God and the real kingdom of Christ will come.

Fyodor Dostoyevsky, *The Brothers Karamazov*, translated by David Magarshack, Penguin Books, 1962, volume 1, page 32

Let us really take the trouble to learn the lesson of holiness from Jesus, whose heart was meek and humble. The first lesson from this heart is our examination of conscience, and the rest—love and service—follow at once. Examination is not our work alone, but a partnership between us and Jesus. We should not waste our time in useless looks at our own miseries, but should lift our hearts to God and let his light enlighten us and make him to have his way with us.

Mother Teresa, *Jesus, the Word to be Spoken*, compiled by Brother Angelo Devananda, William Collins Sons & Co., 1990, page 122

It is not to the clever folk, nor even to the scientific folk, that the empire over souls belongs, but to those who impress us as having conquered nature by grace, as having passed through the burning bush, and as speaking, not the language of human wisdom, but that of the divine will. In religious matters it is holiness which gives authority; it is love, or the power of devotion and sacrifice, which goes to the heart, which moves and persuades.

Henri Frédéric Amiel, *Amiel's Journal*, translated by Mrs Humphry Ward, Macmillan & Co., 1918, page 155

Christian holiness, whether for the Church or for the individual, can never be a static thing, something gained once for all. It has to be maintained amid conflicts and perils that are renewed day by day. It is a moving thing; it can only exist as a function of pilgrimage. But movement is not haphazard and without direction. The pillar of fire and the pillar of cloud are given. The Spirit has been sent to abide with the Church for ever; but the Church and its members can profit by that divine gift only in so far as they have grasped the significance of the divine 'today'.

Stephen Neill, *Christian Holiness*, Lutterworth Press, 1960, page 112

... all holiness is to consist in this: to receive Divine life from Christ and by Christ, Who possesses its fulness and Who has been constituted the One Mediator; to keep this Divine life and increase it unceasingly by an ever more perfect adhesion, an ever closer union with Him Who is its source.

Holiness then, is a *mystery of Divine life communicated and received*: communicated in God, from the Father to the Son ... communicated by the Son to humanity, which He personally united to Himself in the Incarnation; then restored to souls by this humanity ... so that Christ is truly the life of the soul because He is the source and giver of life.

D. Columba Marmion, *Christ the Life of the Soul*, Sands & Company, 1922, page 7

All holiness is God's holiness in us: it is a holiness that is participation and, in a certain way, more than participation, because as we participate in what we can receive from God, we become a revelation of that which transcends us. Being a limited light, we reveal the Light. But we should also remember that in this life in which we are striving towards holiness, our spirituality should be defined in very objective and precise terms. When we read books on spirituality or engage in studying the subject, we see that spirituality, explicitly or implicitly, is repeatedly defined as an attitude, a state of soul, an inner condition, a type of interiority, and so on. In reality, if you look for the ultimate definition and try to discover the inner core of spirituality, you find that spirituality does not consist of the states of soul that are familiar to us, but that it is the presence and action of the holy spirit in us, by us and through us in the world.

Anthony Bloom, *The Essence of Prayer*, Darton, Longman and Todd, 1989, page 295

What are the marks of holiness of life? First and foremost—and all the time—love. Love is the force which unites and holds together all those qualities and graces which combine to form completeness or maturity in a human life... Another essential sign of holiness is dependence upon God.

Holiness is not the search for an individual perfection, nor for the production of a 'beautiful character' (which—we hope—people will admire). If the pursuit of holiness is begun with any thought of this kind, from the outset it is doomed to fail. For it shows that we are full of spiritual pride, and where this is so the way to true holiness is blocked by our self-importance. Real spiritual life is very personal, it is true, but it is not individualistic or self-regarding. It is a life lived in close touch with other people—in the Church and outside it—but, at the same time, a life that is secretly lived in absolute dependence on God, for everything , at every moment...

Another mark of holiness is creativeness. Those who live in dependence upon God, who is both Love and Life, are themselves filled with vitality. Almost without being aware of it this 'life' pulses through them and overflows into all sorts of channels. It is received and continually renewed in the exercise of prayer and worship; it is poured out in loving service of all kinds, in apostolic work, indeed, in every sphere of human life, whether one is 'gifted' or not. Such people have the power to deal with difficult people and difficult situations. They are people who bring order out of disorder, peace out of strife, beauty out of ugliness. Such 'creativeness' is a positive, healing force springing from the hidden working of the Spirit of God. An essential quality of holiness is that of courage, courage of a special kind, which gives a profound meaning to life and to every human experience...

Although these exalted ideals are perfectly valid and relevant, it is important to remind ourselves that a healthy 'sanctity' is completely normal. The genuine 'saint' is the normal person at the height of his development. We, who lag behind, and suffer from 'arrested development', are the 'abnormal' people. Outwardly a 'saintly' man or woman seems very much like everyone else and very natural, but he or she is always a person who uses all his or her God-given faculties to the utmost limit.

Olive Wyon, *On the Way*, SCM Press, 1958, page 24

HOPE

Hope—expectation and desire combined (of thing, of doing, that); feeling of trust

I remember a programme on TV. A young woman, whose baby son had disappeared a year ago whilst they were on holiday on a Greek island, was being interviewed. She still hoped he would be found and that they would be reunited. There was something inside her which gave her hope, though she didn't know what it was.

An important verse of Scripture is: 'May the God of hope fill you with all joy and peace in believing, so that by the power of the Holy Spirit you may abound in hope.' One of God's attributes is 'hope'. As a consequence of the divine inbreathing a seed or a spark of this 'God of hope' resides in the depths of our being. I wonder if this is meant to be catalyzed or brought to life in baptism and confirmation when we specifically receive the Holy Spirit by the laying on of hands. When we receive bread and wine (the body and blood of Christ) in a Communion service, I wonder if we receive an increase in this 'God of hope'. When we reflect and contemplate on the contents of this topic, or indeed on most topics in *Visions of Hope*, I wonder if the source of all hope already in us comes alive so that 'by the power of the Holy Spirit we may abound in hope'.

The odds were stacked against Jesus, but he was rooted and grounded in hope, and went out to transform the world. His work still goes on, and we are invited to play our part—in hope.

Let thy steadfast love, O Lord, be upon us, even as we hope in thee.

Psalm 33:22

Happy is he . . . whose hope is in the Lord his God.

Psalm 146:5

May the God of hope fill you with all joy and peace in believing, so that by the power of the Holy Spirit you may abound in hope.

Romans 15:13

Blessed be the God and Father of our Lord Jesus Christ! By his great mercy we have been born anew to a living hope through the resurrection of Jesus Christ from the dead, and to an inheritance which is imperishable, undefiled, and unfading, kept in heaven for you.

1 Peter 1:3–4

. . . entertain him with hope . . .

William Shakespeare, *The Merry Wives of Windsor*, II. i. 58

It is perhaps true that the hopeful cannot be tragic figures.

Eric Hoffer, *The Passionate State of Mind*, Secker & Warburg, 1956, page 112

Optimism means faith in men, in the human potentiality; hope means faith in God in His omnipotence.

Carlo Carretto, *The Desert in the City*, translated by Barbara Wall, William Collins Sons & Co., 1983, page 90

Ah! if man would but see that hope is from within and not from without—that he himself must work out his own salvation.

H. Rider Haggard, *She*, William Collins Sons & Co., 1957, page 199

Hope is the best possession. None are completely wretched but those who are without hope; and few are reduced so low as that.

William Hazlitt, 'Characteristics', XXXIV, in *The Collected Works of William Hazlitt*, J.M. Dent & Co., 1902, volume II, page 359

Hope is lived, and it comes alive, when we go outside of ourselves and, in joy and pain take part in the lives of others. It becomes concrete in open community with others.

Jürgen Moltmann, *The Open Church*, SCM Press, 1978, page 35

'Hope,' says St Thomas Aquinas, 'is a divinely infused quality of the soul, whereby with certain trust we expect those good things of the life eternal which are to be attained by the grace of God.'

St Thomas Aquinas, in W.R. Inge, *Personal Religion and the Life of Devotion*, Longmans, Green and Co., 1924, page 54

He is a God who does not make empty promises for the hereafter nor trivialize the present darkness, futility and meaninglessness, but who himself in the midst of darkness, futility and meaninglessness invites us to the venture of hope.

Hans Küng, *On Being a Christian*, translated by Edward Quinn, William Collins Sons & Co., 1977, page 311

Oh, how good a thing it is that the great God who has placed us in this world—where amid so much that is beautiful, there still exists vast bestowal among men of grief, disappointment, and agony—has planted in our bosoms the great sheet-anchor, Hope.

Walt Whitman, from 'The Early Poems and the Fiction', in Thomas L. Brasher, editor, *The Collected Writings of Walt Whitman*, New York University Press, Franklin Evans, 1963, volume VI, page 148

Hope is a completely confident expectation; that sureness and certitude with which the awakened soul aims at God and rests in God. It is the source of that living peace, that zest and alertness, that power of carrying on, which gives its special colour to the genuine Christian life.

Evelyn Underhill, in John Stobbart, editor, *The Wisdom of Evelyn Underhill*, A.R. Mowbray & Co., 1951, page 21

The Christian hope is the hope which has seen everything and endured everything, and still has not despaired, because it believes in God. The Christian hope is not hope in the human spirit, in human goodness, in human endurance, in human achievement; the Christian hope is hope in the power of God.

William Barclay, *The Letter to the Romans*, The Saint Andrew Press, 1969, page 215

Hope, of all passions, most befriends here;
Passions of prouder name befriend us less.
Joy has her tears; and Transport has her death:
Hope, like a cordial, innocent, though strong,
Man's heart at once inspirits and serenes;
Nor makes him pay his wisdom for his joys.

Edward Young, 'Night Thoughts', vii. 1461, in *The Complete Works of Edward Young*, William Tegg and Co., 1854, volume I, page 151

At bottom, everything depends upon the presence or absence of one single element in the soul—hope. All the activity of man, all his efforts and all his enterprises, presuppose a hope in him of attaining an end. Once kill this hope and his movements become senseless, spasmodic, and convulsive, like those of some one falling from a height.

Henri Frédéric Amiel, *Amiel's Journal*, translated by Mrs Humphry Ward, Macmillan & Co., 1918, page 171

The true basis of the soul's hope of God is God's hope for the soul. His confident intention precedes and inspires ours, and gives all its significance to our life. God's hope for souls often seems to us to be thwarted; but it begins again in its power and freshness with every baby born into the world. Each represents a hope of God: a possibility of holiness, a fullness of life.

Evelyn Underhill, in John Stobbart, editor, *The Wisdom of Evelyn Underhill*, A.R. Mowbray & Co., 1951, page 21

... Christian hope can only be so much beating of the air unless we are sustained by some vision which can set alight our minds, excite our imagination and nerve our faith. This is the Church for which I often weep and at which I sometimes rage and am often tempted to quit. But it is still the guardian of a Gospel without which Mankind will be robbed of hope.

Colin Morris, *The Hammer of the Lord*, Epworth Press, 1973, page 58

The Christian hope is that God's way is the best way, that the only happiness, the only peace, the only joy, the only true and lasting reward are to be found in the way of God. Loyalty to Christ may bring trouble here—but that is not the last word. The world may laugh contemptuously at the folly of the way of love—but the foolishness of God is wiser than the wisdom of man. The Christian hope is the certainty that it is better to stake one's life on God than to believe the world.

William Barclay, *The Letter to the Philippians, Colossians and Thessalonians,* The Saint Andrew Press, 1971, page 127

Jesus Christ is final because he is in the way to his final victory. He is God's guarantee and down-payment, and therefore our great sign of hope. Christians do not differ from others as if they had reached the goal. Together with all men we remain on the journey, in via. But we know that there is a goal and a way. Though we cannot offer final solutions for the endless problems of our unredeemed world, nevertheless in the resurrection of Jesus we have discovered the direction for an unceasing struggle for renewal. That is more modest than what we have often pretended to possess, but it is real and sufficient.

Hendrikus Berkhof, in David L. Edwards, *The Last Things Now,* SCM Press, 1969, page 115

Every blade of grass, each leaf, each separate floret and petal, is an inscription of hope. Consider the grasses and the oaks, the swallows, the sweet blue butterfly—they are one and all a sign and token showing before our eyes earth made into life ... my hope becomes as broad as the horizon afar, reiterated by every leaf, sung on every bough, reflected in the gleam of every flower. There is so much for us yet to come, as much to be gathered, and enjoyed. Not for you or me, now, but for our race, who will ultimately use this magical secret for their happiness. Earth holds secrets enough to give them the life of the fabled Immortals. My heart is fixed firm and stable in the belief that ultimately the sunshine and the summer, the flowers and the azure sky, shall become, as it were, interwoven into man's existence. He shall take from all their beauty and enjoy their glory.

Richard Jefferies, *The Pageant of Summer,* Chatto & Windus, 1911, page 10

What is our hope concerning this world in which we are now living? Certainly Christ encourages us to have hope concerning it. We are to pray, 'Thy kingdom come on earth', and so to hope that God's rule may become apparent in the world everywhere.

Thus wc hopc to see races free from injustice to one another, for racial strife is a denial of the divine image in man. We hope to see nations so using the earth's resources and economic structures that all may have enough to eat, instead of some being affluent while others starve. We hope to see war, and the possibility of war, banished. We hope to see family life everywhere secure and stable, happy and unselfish, with sex fulfilling its true use in lifelong marriage. We hope to see chastity, honesty, and compassion prevail. We hope to see these things happen as part of a deep reconciliation between man and God through Jesus Christ. We hope to see people brought everywhere into fellowship with God through him.

In all this we hold in one our hope about earth and our hope about heaven. A Christian can scarcely separate these hopes, as Jesus is the Lord of both earth and heaven.

Michael Ramsey, in Margaret Duggan, editor, *Through the Year with Michael Ramsey,* Hodder and Stoughton, 1975, page 205

We must not disguise from ourselves that God's dealings with this world are still a very difficult problem ... There is a great deal of shallow optimism which 'heals too lightly' the wounds which experience inflicts upon Faith and Hope. It is useless to say, 'God's in His Heaven; All's right with the world,' when many things are obviously all wrong in the world... Eminent literary men in the last century were too secure and comfortable to see what a rough place the world is for the majority of those who live in it. It was only after long travail of soul that the Jews learned their lesson; we shall not learn ours by turning epigrams. Remember that complacent optimism, as well as pessimism, is treason against Hope. The world, as it is, is not good enough to be true. We ought not to be satisfied with it. 'God has prepared some better thing'... This world exists for the realisation in time of God's eternal purposes. Some of these are bound up with individual lives, for God intended each one of us to do and to be something; others have a far wider scope, and require far more time for their fulfilment. The manifold evils in the world are allowed to exist because only through them can the greater good be brought into activity. This greater good is not any external achievement, but the love and heroism and self-sacrifice which the great conflict calls into play. We must try to return to the dauntless spirit of the early Christians.

W.R. Inge, *Personal Religion and the Life of Devotion*, Longmans, Green and Co., 1924, page 60

For when hope does awaken, an entire life awakens along with it. One comes fully to life. It begins to seem indeed that one has never lived before. One awakens to a life that is eternal in prospect, a life that opens up before one all the way to death and beyond, a life that seems able to endure death and survive it. Wherever hope rises, life rises. When one first enters upon the spiritual adventure, hope rises where there was no hope before, where there was a life of 'quiet desperation,' and life rises too, the life of the spiritual adventure, the sense of being on a journey in time. There is *something to live for* where before there was nothing. Yet it proves not to be enough. One's heart is kindled, and yet there is a residue of darkness in it that remains unkindled. That dark residue is touched only when one discovers a new and unknown life in another person. Where one finds the other, a new hope rises and one seems now to have *someone to live for*, but that hope is disappointed. The dark residue in one's heart has been heated but not to the kindling point, the 'fire point' after which it will burn by itself. It reaches the kindling point only 'when we dead awaken,' when one discovers a life that is able to live through death and loss. When the hope of living through death arises, then a life arises within one that appears to be the very life one is hoping for, the life that is spoken of in the words of promise 'and whoever lives and believes in me shall never die.'

John S. Dunne, *The Reasons of the Heart*, SCM Press, 1978, page 120

I

IDEALS

Ideals—answering to one's highest conception; embodying an idea; existing only in idea; visionary, relating to, consisting of, ideas; perfect type; actual thing as standard for imitation

It was the start of a new academic year at University College, London. I went out to our sports ground at Shenley, near St Albans, to watch the rugby trials. A talented centre stood out from the others. He was extremely quick and nimble, and stormed through a gap before the opposition knew what was happening. He scored a try. Play re-started. The ball came out to him again. He tried to make another break, but this time the opposition was ready for him. He was at the receiving end of a crunching crash-tackle. It was some time before he moved from the ground. He was winded and gasping for breath. He tried to stand up but something was wrong with his knee. He was helped off the field, limping badly, and never seen at Shenley again.

Some people are rather like this with ideals. They grow up at home and live a rather sheltered life. They go to school and manage to be successful in their studies and extra-curricular activities. They are motivated by ideals and have a somewhat limited knowledge of the ways of the world. They go out to work or on to university and are shattered by something awful happening to them. Their ideals disappear like the dew on a summer morning and they sometimes become bitter and resentful. The purpose of this section is to enable people to grow into their ideals, and by far the most important contribution is that of Albert Schweitzer in the last quotation. Ideals lived out throughout the duration of a life are a potent source of hope.

When Abram was ninety-nine years old the Lord appeared to Abram, and said to him, 'I am God Almighty; walk before me, and be blameless. And I will make my covenant between me and you, and will multiply you exceedingly.'

Genesis 17:1–2

Mark the blameless man, and behold the upright, for there is posterity for the man of peace.

Psalm 37:37

The kingdom of heaven is like treasure hidden in a field, which a man found and covered up; then in his joy he goes and sells all that he has and buys that field. Again, the kingdom of heaven is like a merchant in search of fine pearls, who, on finding one pearl of great value, went and sold all that he had and bought it.

Matthew 13:44–46

I was not disobedient to the heavenly vision.

Acts 26:19

An ideal is often but a flaming vision of reality.

Joseph Conrad, *Chance*, J.M. Dent and Sons, 1949, page 262

To be happy one must have an ideal and strive to live up to it.

George Moore, *Evelyn Innes*, Bernhard Tauchnitz, 1898, volume II, page 103

The Christian ideal has not been tried and found wanting. It has been found difficult; and left untried.

G.K. Chesterton, *What's Wrong with the World*, Bernhard Tauchnitz, 1910, page 43

Even a rich man is sad if he has no ideals. He may try to hide his sadness from himself and from others, but his efforts only make him sadder still.

Yevgeny Yevtushenko, *A Precocious Autobiography*, translated by Andrew R. MacAndrew, Collins and Harvill Press, 1963, page 39

It is the very ideal of true manhood not to be suppressed. A man should lay it down in his mind, when he begins life, 'I am, and I will be, superior to my circumstances.'

Henry Ward Beecher, *Proverbs from Plymouth Pulpit*, Charles Burnet & Co., 1887, page 22

It is hard for a man to take the ideals of honour, and truth, and rectitude, and plough through life with them. It breeds conflicts with himself and with all others.

Henry Ward Beecher, *Proverbs from Plymouth Pulpit*, Charles Burnet & Co., 1887, page 54

The most consummate ideal that men have ever known, or felt, or thought, is the ideal of one who is supreme and sovereign, guiding nature and in it Providence.

Henry Ward Beecher, *Proverbs from Plymouth Pulpit*, Charles Burnet & Co., 1887, page 127

Christ's ideal of manhood is power in the head, and power in the heart, and art in the hand, with the humiliation of love, and carried down to the lowest and meanest, if thereby they may be helped.

Henry Ward Beecher, *Proverbs from Plymouth Pulpit*, Charles Burnet & Co., 1887, page 23

Every ideal affirms that, in some sense, our supernatural environment is more truly active than the world of our apprehension, and is always offering itself as a world to be possessed and not to be created.

John Oman, *The Natural & the Supernatural*, Cambridge at the University Press, 1931, page 329

The ideal, after all, is truer than the real: for the ideal is the eternal element in perishable things: it is their type, their sum, their *raison d'être*, their formula in the book of the Creator, and therefore at once the most exact and the most condensed expression of them.

Henri Frédéric Amiel, *Amiel's Journal*, translated by Mrs Humphry Ward, Macmillan & Co., 1918, page 105

'The kingdom of heaven is like a merchant seeking precious pearls.' Yes, we have promised great things but greater things are promised us. Be faithful to Christ and pray for perseverance. Remember to say to yourself, 'I have been created for greater things.' Never stoop lower than the ideal. Let nothing satisfy you but God.

Mother Teresa, *Jesus, the Word to be Spoken*, compiled by Brother Angelo Devananda, William Collins Sons & Co., 1990, page 42

Religion cannot remain on the level of ideas alone. Religion must be an expression. It must be an incarnation in the real world of an ideal that is of supreme import to the individual of belief. Religion not only has to be worth living for, it has to be worth living. Faith on a theoretical level is a fossilized faith if it only remains on that level.

Harry James Cargas, *Encountering Myself*, SPCK, 1978, page 54

Our ideal is no one but Jesus. We must think as he thinks, love as he loves, wish as he wishes; we must permit him to use us to the full. It is beautiful to see the humility of Christ—'Who being in the form of God did not think it robbery to be equal with God, but emptied himself, taking the form of a servant, being made in the likeness of men and in habit found as man.'

Mother Teresa, *Jesus, the Word to be Spoken*, compiled by Brother Angelo Devananda, William Collins Sons & Co., 1990, page 41

A high ideal may be presented to a man and he considers whether or not he shall accept it for the guidance of his life. His answer must depend on his character. He may give the truest and wisest answer of which he is then capable; but if he has allowed himself to settle down to a selfish outlook or to materialist standards, this will affect his judgement. He will reject the ideal in perfect sincerity; but that sincerity is not so much a justification of his conduct as a measure of his sin.

William Temple, *Readings in St. John's Gospel* (First and Second Series), Macmillan & Co., 1947, page 284

The astonishing thing about the human being is not so much his intellect and bodily structure, profoundly mysterious as they are. The astonishing and least comprehensible thing about him is his range of vision; his gaze into the infinite distance; his lonely passion for ideas and ideals, far removed from his material surroundings and animal activities, and in no way suggested by them, yet for which, such is his affection, he is willing to endure toils and privations, to sacrifice pleasures, to disdain griefs and frustrations, for which, rating them in value above his own life, he will stand till he dies, the profound conviction he entertains that if nothing be worth dying for nothing is worth living for. The inner truth is that every man is himself a creator, by birth and nature, an artist, an architect and fashioner of worlds.

W. Macneile Dixon, *The Human Situation*, Edward Arnold & Co., 1937, page 190

Grown-up people reconcile themselves too willingly to a supposed duty of preparing young ones for the time when they will regard as illusion what now is an inspiration to heart and mind. Deeper experience of life, however, advises their inexperience differently. It exhorts them to hold fast, their whole life through, to the thoughts which inspire them. It is through the idealism of youth that man catches sight of truth, and in that idealism he possesses a wealth which he must never exchange for anything else. We must all be prepared to find that life tries to take from us our belief in the good and the true, and our enthusiasm for them, but we need not surrender them. That ideals, when they are brought into contact with reality, are usually crushed by facts does not mean that they are bound from the very beginning to capitulate to the facts, but merely that our ideals are not strong enough; and they are not strong enough because they are not pure and strong and stable enough in ourselves.

The power of ideals is incalculable. We see no power in a drop of water. But let it get into a crack in the rock and be turned to ice, and it splits the rocks; turned into steam, it drives the pistons of the most powerful engines. Something has happened to it that makes active and effective the power that is latent in it.

So it is with ideals. Ideals are thoughts. So long as they exist merely as thoughts, the power latent in them remains ineffective, however great the enthusiasm, and however strong the conviction with which the thought is held. Their power only becomes effective when they are taken up into some refined human personality.

The ripeness, then, that our development must aim at is one which makes us simpler, more truthful, purer, more peace-loving, meeker, kinder, more sympathetic. That is the only way in which we are to sober down with age. That is the process in which the soft iron of youthful idealism hardens into the steel of a full-grown idealism which can never be lost.

The most valuable knowledge we can have is how to deal with disappointments. All acts and facts are a product of spiritual power, the successful ones of power which is strong enough; the unsuccessful ones of power which is too weak. Does my behaviour in respect of love effect nothing? That is because there is not enough love in me. Am I powerless against the untruthfulness and the lies which have their being all around me? The reason is that I myself am not truthful enough. Have I to watch dislike and illwill carrying on this sad game? That means that I myself have not yet completely laid aside small-mindedness and envy. Is my love of peace misunderstood and scorned? That means I am not yet sufficiently peace-loving.

The great secret of success is to go through life as a man who never gets used up. That is possible for him who never argues and strives with men and facts, but in all experiences retires upon himself, and looks for the ultimate cause of things in himself.

No one who is always striving to refine his character can ever be robbed of his idealism, for he experiences in himself the power of the ideas of the good and the true. When he sees far too little of the external results at which he is aiming, he knows nevertheless that he is producing as much as his character allows; it is only that success has not yet begun, or that it is as yet hidden from him. Where there is power, there some result or other is produced. No ray of sunlight is ever lost, but the green which it wakes into existence needs time to sprout, and it is not always granted to the sower to live to see the harvest. All work that is worth anything is done in faith.

The knowledge of life, therefore, which we grown-ups have to pass on to the younger generations will not be expressed thus: 'Reality will soon give way before your ideals,' but 'Grow into your ideals, so that life can never rob you of them.' If all of us could become what we were at fourteen, what a different place the world would be!

Albert Schweitzer, *Memoirs of Childhood and Youth*, George Allen & Unwin, 1924, page 99

IMAGINATION

Imagination—imagining, mental faculty forming images of external objects not present to the senses; creative faculty of the mind

A reflection group was under way. There were three of us in this particular group, two undergraduates and me. As usual they had each been given a cup of coffee and a list of topics. After two or three minutes they chose Imagination. We reflected silently on the material for about half an hour. I then asked them if they had got through the material and were they now ready for discussion? They nodded affirmatively. My first question was the usual one. 'Was there any particular reason for choosing Imagination?' 'Yes,' they said. 'In reading law we are encouraged not to use our imagination. We have to stick to the facts and use our powers of critical analysis and reason. It is such an exacting discipline we are beginning to feel more dead than alive, and that is why we chose *imagination.*' 'I see, and did you find anything helpful in this section?' 'Yes, it's very revealing. It seems as though the great people of the past were those with vivid imaginations—the great scientists, philosophers, artists, musicians, writers, poets, playwrights—even lawyers. Most of these quotes stress the importance of the imagination and suggest that it is one of our most valuable faculties. Maybe that has pinpointed our problem of the moment. Instead of dampening down our imaginations in the study of law, we ought to be developing them in other areas of university life.'

They brightened up as they considered the implications of all this. It seemed as though they were beginning to come alive before my eyes. So much of modern education concentrates on the primacy of the intellect that we miss out on the imagination—much to our cost.

... out of my understanding a spirit answers me. Do you not know this from of old, since man was placed upon earth?

Job 20:3–4

For God speaks in one way, and in two, though man does not perceive it. In a dream, in a vision of the night, when deep sleep falls upon men, while they slumber on their beds, then he opens the ears of men.

Job 33:14–16

Do not be conformed to this world but be transformed by the renewal of your mind, that you may prove what is the will of God, what is good and acceptable and perfect.

Romans 12:2

Faith means a sanctified imagination, or the imagination applied to spiritual things.

Henry Ward Beecher, *Proverbs from Plymouth Pulpit*, Charles Burnet & Co., 1887, page 183

There is no power on earth like imagination, and the worst, most obstinate grievances are imagined ones.

Laurens van der Post, *Venture to the Interior*, Penguin Books, 1968, page 26

For God hath made you able to create worlds in your own mind which are more precious unto Him than those which He created.

Thomas Traherne, *Centuries*, The Faith Press Ltd, 1969, page 90

Learn to foster an ardent imagination; so shall you descry beauty which others pass unheeded.

Norman Douglas, *An Almanac*, Chatto & Windus in association with Secker & Warburg, 1945, page 43

Meditation, experience of life, hope, charity, and all the emotions—out of these the imaginative reason speaks.

J.B. Yeats, *Letters to his son, W.B. Yeats and others*, Faber and Faber, 1944, page 87

The imagination is the secret and marrow of civilisation. It is the very eye of faith. The soul without imagination is what an observatory would be without a telescope.

Henry Ward Beecher, *Proverbs from Plymouth Pulpit*, Charles Burnet & Co., 1887, page 25

The proper use of the imagination is not to conjure up false things and foolishly believe them to be true, but to take true things and make them vivid in the life of to-day.

W.E. Sangster, *The Secret of Radiant Life*, Hodder and Stoughton, 1957, page 210

'What is imagination?' asks Rider Haggard in the midst of his narratives. And he answers: 'Perhaps it is a shadow of the intangible truth, perhaps it is the soul's thought!'

Henry Miller, *The Books in My Life*, Village Press, 1974, page 84

When the pioneer in science sends forth the groping fingers of his thoughts, he must have a vivid intuitive imagination, for new ideas are not generated by deduction, but by an artistically creative imagination.

Max Planck, in F.C. Happold, *Religious Faith and Twentieth Century Man*, Darton, Longman and Todd, 1980, page 41

... I cannot tell you how strongly I feel that the kind of imagination which the gods have given me is more than imagination! In fact almost all the power we call 'imagination' may come from an actual tapping of some great reservoir of planetary, if not cosmic, experience.

John Cowper Powys, *Autobiography*, Macdonald & Co. (Publishers), 1967, page 436

Imagination is distinct from the mere dry faculty of reasoning. Imagination is creative—it is an immediate intuition; not a logical analysis—we call it popularly a kind of inspiration. Now imagination is a power of the heart:—Great thoughts originate from a large heart:—a man must have a heart, or he never could create.

F.W. Robertson, *Sermons*, Kegan Paul, Trench, Trubner & Co., 1907, First Series, page 8

I have always believed that the imagination and the will have a creative power. What a person wills and what a person imagines become a mysterious part of what is. It is madness to spend your days trying to eliminate what your own will and spirit and imagination are perpetually adding to the mystery of life.

John Cowper Powys, *Autobiography*, Macdonald & Co. (Publishers), 1967, page 360

... Without imagination—and of the kind that creates—there is no love, whether it be love of a girl or love of a country or love of one's friend or even of children, and of our wives. Lawyers, mathematicians and practical people, that is the minor sort, have logic and can destroy—and the energy of destruction brings with it its own emotion, which is hatred.

J.B. Yeats, *Letters to his son, W.B. Yeats and others*, Faber and Faber, 1944, page 276

If I were asked what has been the most powerful force in the making of history, you would probably adjudge of unbalanced mind were I to answer, as I should have to answer, metaphor figurative expression. It is by imagination that men have lived; imagination rules all our lives. The human mind is not, as philosophers would have you think, a debating hall, but a picture gallery. Around it hang our similes, our concepts.

W. Macneile Dixon, *The Human Situation*, Edward Arnold & Co., 1937, page 65

By imagination I intend the capacity in man to grasp with the whole of his being, by rapport between him and what he is confronting, that which is not himself; I mean his ability to experience at levels deeper than mere sense-perception and deeper than rational awareness; I mean his empathetic identification with some 'other' which comes alive to him and with which he finds himself strangely 'at one'. Call it intuition, if you will, call it sensitive apprehension—whatever it may be called, there is in man an imaginative quality which enables him to see, to hear, to feel, what is not immediately and obviously present on the surface of things.

Norman Pittenger, *The Christian Situation Today*, Epworth Press, 1919, page 85

I do not think we can put the true scientist on the left and the true poet on the right and think of them as in different categories. They are in the same category: they are both artists. In both the main faculty is imagination. Imagination is the power to see what is there... Imagination sees what is there with full concentration in combination with the faculty of love—indeed imagination has also been defined as 'Intellectual Love' and as 'Reason in her most exalted mood.' This is man's highest faculty, the power to see, to be a seer, to fasten upon the total significance of phenomena—and even to image further. It was by his 'wonderful imagination', we are told, that Newton was constantly discerning new tracks and new processes in the region of the unknown. This imaging into the centre of reality seems to belong to the great scientists as much as the great poets. There is nothing to choose here in force of imaginative power between a Rutherford who can penetrate into the very heart of matter and a Tolstoy who can penetrate into the very heart of man.

John Stewart Collis, *The Vision of Glory*, Charles Knight & Co., 1972, page 61

The all-important fact is that imagination is not only superior to the intellect, but *is a different, independent faculty.* It is the source of originality and invention, the framer of hypotheses and cause of discoveries in science and philosophy, and the inspiration of art and poetry. It is the 'divine afflatus' of the ancients, without which, as Cicero said, no man could be truly great. (William Blake thought it the essential attribute of God.) It is clearly differentiated from intellect, since it acts *independently of the conscious mind and will.* An artist will *consciously* plan out his work, but, as it proceeds, he finds his scheme so altered (and improved) that he is startled at the ultimate result....

The difference between intellect and imagination is that between *reason* and *insight.* In the state of knowledge of Newton's time no amount of conscious intellectual work would have given him the idea that the universe was balanced by gravitation. When Shelley wrote those marvellous lines in 'Adonais,'

Life, like a dome of many-coloured glass,
Stains the white radiance of Eternity,

he rose as high as the stars above mere intellect, and gave us a sublime truth whose meaning it would take volumes to adequately express.

J.T. Hackett, *My Commonplace Book*, Macmillan and Co., 1923, page 175

Men are ruled by imagination: imagination makes them into men, capable of madness and of immense labours. We work dreaming. Consider what dreams must have dominated the builders of the Pyramids—dreams geometrical, dreams funereal, dreams of resurrection, dreams of outdoing the pyramid of some other Pharaoh! What dreams occupy that fat man in the street, toddling by under his shabby hat and bedraggled rain-coat? Perhaps he is in love; perhaps he is a Catholic, and imagines that early this morning he has partaken of the body and blood of Christ; perhaps he is a revolutionist, with the millennium in his heart and a bomb in his pocket. The spirit bloweth where it listeth; the wind of inspiration carries our dreams before it and constantly refashions them like clouds. Nothing could be madder, more irresponsible, more dangerous than this guidance of men by dreams. What saves us is the fact that our imaginations, groundless and chimerical as they may seem, are secretly suggested and controlled by shrewd old instincts of our animal nature, and by continual contact with things. The shock of sense, breaking in upon us with a fresh irresistible image, checks wayward imagination and sends it rebounding in a new direction, perhaps more relevant to what is happening in the world outside.

When I speak of being governed by imagination, of course I am indulging in a figure of speech, in an ellipsis; in reality we are governed by that perpetual latent process within us by which imagination itself is created. Actual imaginings—the cloud-like thoughts drifting by—are not masters over themselves nor over anything else. They are like the sound of chimes in the night; they know nothing of whence they came, how they will fall out, or how long they will ring. There is a mechanism in the church tower; there was a theme in the composer's head; there is a beadle who has been winding the thing up. The sound wafted to us, muffled by distance and a thousand obstacles, is but the last lost emanation of this magical bell-ringing. Yet in our dream it is all in all; it is what first entertains and absorbs the mind. Imagination, when it chimes within us, apparently of itself, is no less elaborately grounded; it is a last symptom, a rolling echo, by which we detect and name the obscure operation that occasions it; and not this echo, in its aesthetic impotence, but the whole operation whose last witness it is, receives in science the name of imagination, and may be truly said to rule the human world...

Whilst dreams entertain us, the balance of our character is shifting beneath: we are growing while we sleep. The young think in one way, the drunken in another, and the dead not at all; and I imagine—for I have imagination myself—that they do not die because they stop thinking, but they stop thinking because they die. How much veering and luffing before they make that port! The brain of man, William James used to say, has a hair-trigger organization. His life is terribly experimental. He is perilously dependent on the oscillations of a living needle, imagination, that never points to the true north...

Imagination changes the scale of everything, and makes a thousand patterns of the woof of nature, without disturbing a single thread. Or rather—since it is nature itself that imagines—it turns to music what was only strain; as if the universal vibration, suddenly ashamed of having been so long silent and useless, had burst into tears and laughter at its own folly, and in so doing had become wise.

George Santayana, *Soliloquies in England*, Constable and Company, 1922, page 122

IMMORTALITY

Immortality—undying; divine; unfading, incorruptible; constant, long-lasting

In my last year at school, I managed to come across a book by Ralph Waldo Trine, called *In Tune with the Infinite*. It belonged to my father and I found it hidden away in the cupboard of a display cabinet at home. One of the effects of reading this book was to trigger off a belief in immortality—a belief which has never left me. I find it very difficult to put this belief into words. I can only give an outline of what I felt at the time—a deep sense of peace and joy—a feeling of complete and utter harmony in myself and in the universe at large. A feeling as though everything had suddenly fitted into place in an ultimate unity. I experienced a deep sense of beauty and ecstasy. For a short time I felt something of the delights of heaven—an awareness of immense resources of energy and power and of infinite life. These feelings stayed with me for several weeks and then gradually faded away, though they still continue to exert an influence on me. Perhaps they were a preparation, enabling me to understand something of the mystery of the resurrection which was to hit me with such force later on. I still maintain that a belief in immortality is a great source of hope for us and can effect the quality of our lives here and now.

Depart from evil, and do good; so shall you abide for ever.

Psalm 37:27

God created man to be immortal, and made him to be an image of his own eternity.

Wisdom of Solomon 2:23 (AV)

For this perishable nature must put on the imperishable, and this mortal nature must put on immortality. When the perishable puts on the imperishable, and the mortal puts on immortality, then shall come to pass the saying that is written: 'Death is swallowed up in victory.'

1 Corinthians 15:53–54

... and now has manifested through the appearing of our Saviour Christ Jesus, who abolished death and brought life and immortality to light through the gospel.

2 Timothy 1:10

My comfort is that heaven will take our souls.

William Shakespeare, *King Richard II*, III. i. 33

We were not made to rest in this world. It is not our true native land.

Father Andrew SDC, *In the Silence*, A.R. Mowbray & Co., 1947, page 126

Dust as we are, the immortal spirit grows
Like harmony in music.

William Wordsworth, *The Prelude*, i. 340, Macmillan and Co., 1932, page 9

To believe in immortality is one thing, but it is first needful to believe in life.

Robert Louis Stevenson, *Memories and Portraits*, Chatto & Windus, 1917, page 26

Let the dead have the immortality of fame, but the living the immortality of love.

Rabindranath Tagore, 'Stray Birds', CCLXXIX, in *Collected Poems & Plays of Rabindranath Tagore*, Macmillan & Co., 1936, page 323

Death, with the might of his sunbeam,
Touches the flesh and the soul awakes.

Robert Browning, 'The Flight of the Duchess', in *The Poetical Works of Robert Browning*, Oxford University Press, 1949, page 347

Man is the only animal that contemplates death, and also the only animal that shows any sign of doubt of its finality.

William Ernest Hocking, *The Meaning of Immortality in Human Experience*, Greenwood Press, Publishers, 1975, page 5

. . . all that lives must die,
Passing through nature to eternity.

William Shakespeare, *Hamlet*, I. ii. 72

Death be not proud, though some have called thee
Mighty and dreadfull, for, thou art not soe,
For, those, whom thou think'st, thou dost overthrow,
Die not, poore death, nor yet canst thou kill mee.

John Donne, 'Holy Sonnets', VI, in Sir Herbert Grierson, editor, *Poetical Works*, Oxford University Press, 1977, page 297

Ah Christ, that it were possible
For one short hour to see
The souls we loved, that they might tell us
What and where they be.

Alfred, Lord Tennyson, 'Maud', IV, in *The Works of Alfred Lord Tennyson*, Macmillan and Co. Ltd., 1898, page 303

I feel my immortality o'ersweep
All pains, all tears, all fears, and peal
Like the eternal thunders of the deep,
Into my ears this truth—'Thou liv'st for ever!'

Lord Byron, 'Heaven and Earth', I. ii. 111, in Ernest Hartley Coleridge, editor, *The Poetical Works of Lord Byron*, John Murray, 1905, page 653

If you were to destroy the belief in immortality in mankind, not only love but every living force on which the continuation of all life in the world depended, would dry up at once. Moreover, there would be nothing immoral then, everything would be permitted.

Fyodor Dostoyevsky, *The Brothers Karamazov*, translated by David Magarshack, Penguin Books, 1958, volume I, page 77

Hence in a season of calm weather
Though inland far we be,
Our Souls have sight of that immortal sea
Which brought us hither,
Can in a moment travel thither.

William Wordsworth, 'Ode. Intimations of Immortality', ix. 165, in Thomas Hutchinson, editor, *The Poetical Works of William Wordsworth*, 1904, page 590

On another occasion I was led in imagination down on to the sea-bed, and there I saw green hills and valleys looking as though they were moss-covered with seaweed and sand. This I understood to mean that if a man or woman were under-sea and saw God ever present with him (as indeed God is) he would be safe in body and soul, and take no hurt. Moreover he would know comfort and consolation beyond all power to tell.

Julian of Norwich, *Revelations of Divine Love*, Penguin Books, 1976, page 77

The soul, secured in her existence, smiles
At the drawn dagger, and defies its point.
The stars shall fade away, the sun himself
Grow dim with age, and nature sink in years,
But thou shalt flourish in immortal youth,

Unhurt amidst the war of elements,
The wreck of matter, and the crush of worlds.

Joseph Addison, *Cato*, V. i. 25, in A.C. Guthkelch, editor, *The Miscellaneous Works of Joseph Addison*, G. Bell and Sons, volume I, 'Poems and Plays', page 411

Although man has been developed from a lower to a higher form, yet he has been immortal from the beginning. He did not, however, enjoy his higher capacities until he became conscious of the soul within him. It is also asserted that he has fallen from a childlike simplicity and innocence, while he has made tremendous material progress, and is returning by long, steep ways to the heights where is God, 'the meeting place of all souls.'

Helen Keller, *My Religion*, Hodder and Stoughton, 1927, page 102

Disinclined though many people are to admit it, there is a sense of unease and dissatisfaction in the heart of any man or woman until they are at ease with God. Right at the core of our being there is a hunger for something hard to define, and almost embarrassing to confess, but which still remains when this world has given us its finest things and every tangible fear has been driven away. Some people say that it is the longing in us for the eternal—a kind of homesickness of the soul.

William Watson knew it. He said:

'In this house with starry dome
Shall I never feel at home?'

Never! The fact must be faced that, though man seems to belong to the earth, there is a hunger in him which earth cannot satisfy. It seems to satisfy the birds and the beasts. They eat their fill and are content. But man does not live by bread alone. He has immortal longings in him.

W.E. Sangster, *The Secret of Radiant Life*, Hodder and Stoughton, 1957, page 85

The great aim of all true religion is to transfer the centre of interest and concern from self to God. Until the doctrine of God in its main elements is really established, it would be definitely dangerous to reach a developed doctrine of immortality. Even when the doctrine of God is established in its Christian form, the doctrine of immortality can still, as experience abundantly shows, perpetuate self-centredness in the spiritual life. If my main concern in relation to things eternal is to be with the question of what is going to become of *me*, it might be better that I should have no hope of immortality at all, so that at least as I look forward into the vista of the ages my Self should not be a possible object of primary interest.

For as in order of historical development, so also in order of spiritual value, the hope of immortality is strictly dependent on and subordinate to faith in God. If God is righteous—still more, if God is Love—immortality follows as a consequence. He made me; He loves me; He will not let me perish, so long as there is in me anything that He can love. And that is a wholesome reflection for me if, but only if, the result is that I give greater glory to God in the first place,—and—take comfort to myself only, if at all, in the second place. I wish to stress this heavily. *Except as an implicate in the righteousness and love of God, immortality is not a religious interest at all.* It has an interest for us as beings who cling to life, but there is nothing religious about that. It has an interest for us as social beings who love our friends and desire to meet again those who have died before us; that is an interest capable of religious value, but even this is not religious in itself. No; the centre of all true religious interest is God, and self comes into it not as a primary concern which God must serve, but as that one thing which each can offer for the glory of God. And if it were so, that His Glory could best be served by my annihilation—so be it.

But in fact God is known to us through His dealings with us. And if He left us to perish with hopes frustrated and purposes unaccomplished, He could scarcely be—certainly we could not know Him to be—perfect love. Thus the hope of immortality is of quite primary importance when regarded both doctrinally and emotionally as a part of, because a necessary consequence of, faith in God. There is here a stupendous paradox; but it is the paradox which is characteristic of all true religion. We must spiritually renounce all other loves for the love of God or at least so hold them in subordination to this that we are ready to forgo them for its sake; yet when we find God, or, rather, when we know ourselves as found of Him, we find in and with Him all the loves which for His sake we had forgone. If my desire is first for future life for myself, or even first for reunion with those whom I have loved and lost, then the doctrine of immortality may do me positive harm by fixing me in that self-concern or in concern for my own joy in my friends. But if my desire is first for God's glory, and for myself that I may be used to promote it, then the doctrine of immortality will give me new heart in the assurance that what here must be a very imperfect service may be made perfect hereafter, that my love of friends may be one more manifestation of the overflowing Love Divine, and God may be seen as perfect Love in the eternal fellowship of love to which he calls us.

For these reasons it seems to me, so far as I can judge, positively undesirable that there should be experimental proof of man's survival of death. For this would bring the hope of immortality into the area of purely intellectual apprehension. It might or might not encourage the belief that God exists; it would certainly, as I think, make very much harder the essential business of faith, which is the transference of the centre of interest and concern from self to God. If such knowledge comes, it must be accepted, and we must try to use it for good and not for evil. And I could never urge the cessation of enquiry in any direction; I cannot ask that so-called Psychical Research should cease. But I confess I hope that such research will continue to issue in such dubious results as are all that I can trace to it up to date.

William Temple, ***Nature, Man and God*****, Macmillan & Co., 1934, page 457**

INFLUENCE

Influence—affecting character and destiny of person; action insensibly exercised upon, ascendancy, moral power (over, with, persons, etc.); thing, person, exercising power

There are certainly some very important institutional influences at work in our lives—home, school, higher education, state, Church, work, marriage, the media, and so on. Looking back over my life so far, I can see there have been many institutional forces at work which have helped to mould and fashion me. These institutions, however, are made up of vast numbers of individual people, and I know that thousands of men, women and children, have influenced me at various stages of my life. Practically everyone I meet still influences me to a certain extent. As a college chaplain for over twenty years I've been exposed to the influences of young people from all over the world. Adjustments have not been easy to make, but the result is a richness and variety of life.

Books have exerted an incalculable influence on me, so have the difficulties and tragedies I've been through. Other people's experiences of life have been invaluable. If someone was to ask me what has been the greatest single influence in my life I would have to say something of 'the Divine presence' I feel to have experienced in the depths of my being. This sometimes comes to the surface in the quiet times of reflection and exercises an influence over the whole of life.

The Lord our God be with us, as he was with our fathers; may he not leave us or forsake us; that he may incline our hearts to him, to walk in all his ways, and to keep his commandments, his statutes, and his ordinances, which he commanded our fathers.

1 Kings 8:57–58

O Lord, the God of Abraham, Isaac, and Israel, our fathers, keep for ever such purposes and thoughts in the hearts of thy people, and direct their hearts towards thee.

1 Chronicles 29:18

One who heard us was a woman named Lydia, from the city of Thyatira, a seller of purple goods, who was a worshipper of God. The Lord opened her heart to give heed to what was said by Paul.

Acts 16:14

. . . he being dead yet speaketh.

Hebrews 11:4 (AV)

In every relationship lies a possibility of influence.

André Gide, *The Journals of André Gide*, translated by Justin O'Brien, Secker & Warburg, 1947, page 42

Your influence, your life, your all, depends on prayer.

Forbes Robinson, *Letters to his Friends*, Spottiswoode & Co. Ltd, 1904, page 165

Except by the personal influence of God's nature on ours, we cannot reach our higher manhood.

Henry Ward Beecher, *Proverbs from Plymouth Pulpit*, Charles Burnet & Co., 1887, page 153

Every throb of our spirit that answers to spiritual things is caused by the influence of God.

Henry Ward Beecher, *Proverbs from Plymouth Pulpit*, Charles Burnet & Co., 1887, page 153

The very point of power in the church of Christ is the personal influence of Christian lives.

Henry Ward Beecher, *Proverbs from Plymouth Pulpit*, Charles Burnet & Co., 1877, page 161

It would be difficult to exaggerate the degree to which we are influenced by those we influence.

Eric Hoffer, *The Passionate State of Mind*, Secker & Warburg, 1956, page 63

It is certain, that either wise bearing or ignorant carriage is caught, as men take diseases, one of another, therefore, let men take heed of their company.

William Shakespeare, *II King Henry IV*, V. ii. 76

Our thoughts, our tastes, our emotions, our partialities, our prejudices, and finally our conduct and habits, are insensibly changed by the influence of men who never once directly tempted us, or even knew the effect which they produced.

Henry Ward Beecher, *Proverbs from Plymouth Pulpit*, Charles Burnet & Co., 1887, page 13

The secret of his influence lay in a self-discipline that was as habitual as most men's habits are, an inner culture of mind and heart and will that gave his life a poise, so that he could not be untrue either to himself or his fellow-men.

Said of Edward Wilson, in George Seaver, *Edward Wilson of the Antarctic*, John Murray, 1935, page 104

When we think about the people who have given us hope and have increased the strength of our soul, we might discover that they were not the advice givers, warners or moralists, but the few who were able to articulate in words and actions the human condition in which we participate and who encouraged us to face the realities of life.

Henri J.M. Nouwen, *Reaching Out*, William Collins Sons & Co., 1980, page 59

The older we grow, the more we understand our own lives and histories, the more we shall see that the spirit of wisdom is the spirit of love; that the true way to gain influence over our fellow-men is to have charity towards them. That is a hard lesson to learn; and all those who learn it generally learn it late; almost... too late!

Charles Kingsley, *Daily Thoughts*, Macmillan & Co., 1884, page 37

... the driving force behind the process of our history is the impact of Christianity upon Europe, and the slow penetration of the Christian spirit through its habits of life and thought. For in spite of temporary appearances, I am convinced that the influence of Christianity, properly understood, was never more widespread nor more effective than it is to-day.

John Macmurray, *Conditions of Freedom*, Faber and Faber, 1950, page 35

'Tis the same with human beings as with books. All of us encounter, at least once in our life, some individual who utters words that make us think for ever. There are men whose phrases are oracles; who condense in a sentence the secrets of life; who blurt out an aphorism that forms a character or illustrates an existence. A great thing is a great book; but greater than all is the talk of a great man.

Benjamin Disraeli, *Coningsby*, Peter Davies, 1927, page 129

Whatever influence the Holy Spirit exercises on the subconscious and unconscious, no question becomes a question of religion or duty until it meets us in the conscious mind, and even the most sudden conversion does not leap like the genie of the lamp out of nothing, but has at its heart some dazzling conscious insight of the true relation of the soul and God.

W.E. Sangster, *The Path to Perfection*, Hodder and Stoughton, 1943, page 122

Certainly religion has lost its extensive control over other fields: it has less and less direct influence—on science, education, politics, law, medicine, social service. But can we conclude from all this that the influence of religion on the life of the individual and of society as a whole has declined? Instead of the former extensive control and guardianship, it may now have a more extensive and indirect moral influence.

Hans Küng, *On Being a Christian*, translated by Edward Quinn, William Collins Sons & Co., 1977, page 63

The odd thing, when speaking of *influence*, is that one almost never considers any but direct influences. Influence through protest is, in certain natures, at least as important; sometimes it is much more so, though most often very hard to recognize. It is by no means always through affection, weakness, and need of imitation that our characters are bent. A somewhat strong nature yields more to reaction than to direct action.

André Gide, *The Journals of André Gide*, translated by Justin O'Brien, Secker & Warburg, 1947, page 33

If this sublime fire of infused love burns in your soul, it will inevitably send forth throughout the Church and the world an influence more tremendous than could be estimated by the radius reached by words or by example. St. John of the Cross writes: 'A very little of this pure love is more precious in the sight of God and of greater profit to the Church, even though the soul appear to be doing nothing, than are all other works put together.'

Thomas Merton, *Elected Silence*, Hollis and Carter, 1949, page 371

Any man or woman, in any age and under any circumstances, who will, can live the heroic life and exercise heroic influences.

It is of the essence of self-sacrifice, and therefore of heroism, that it should be voluntary; a work of supererogation, at least, towards society and man; an act to which the hero or heroine is not bound by duty, but which is above though not against duty.

Charles Kingsley, *Daily Thoughts*, Macmillan & Co., 1884, page 71

The influences we never speak of; the strongest ones, it so happens, are the secret ones. That of women, of the public, of our juniors. It is possible to escape one or two of them, but it is very difficult, very rare, to escape all three. We let ourselves be influenced by a woman or by those whom we want to please, whose regard or esteem we want to win. The artist who is after success always lets himself be influenced by the public. Generally such an artist contributes nothing new, for the public acclaims only what it already knows, what it recognizes.

André Gide, *Pretexts, Reflections on Literature and Morality*, selected by Justin O'Brien, Secker & Warburg, 1960, page 303

There are two sides to the influence of love, because the world is full of very unpleasant and even very dreadful things, and things which seem as if they could not possibly have emanated from anything affectionate or sympathetic. The effect of evil catastrophes on one's mind is so much more powerful to obliterate happy thoughts, than happy thoughts are to obliterate painful thoughts, that one cannot help feeling that there one has got down to the truth at last.

A.C. Benson, *Extracts from the Letters of Dr. A.C. Benson to M.E.A.*, Jarrold Publishing, 1927, page 8

Thelwell thought it very unfair to influence a child's mind by inculcating any opinions before it should have come to years of discretion, and be able to choose for itself. I showed him my garden, and told him it was my botanical garden. 'How so?' said he, 'it is covered with weeds'.—

'Oh,' I replied, '*that* is only because it has not yet come to its age of discretion and choice. The weeds, you see, have taken the liberty to grow, and I thought it unfair of me to prejudice the soil towards roses and strawberries.'

Samuel Taylor Coleridge, *The Table Talk and Omniana of Samuel Taylor Coleridge*, Oxford University Press, 1917, page 122

I have found that things unknown have a secret influence on the soul, and, like the centre of the earth unseen violently attract it. We love we know not what, and therefore everything allures us. As iron at a distance is drawn by the loadstone, there being some invisible communications between them, so is there in us a world of Love to somewhat, though we know not what in the world that should be. There are invisible ways of conveyance by which some great thing doth touch our souls, and by which we tend to it. Do you not feel yourself drawn with the expectation and desire of some Great Thing?

Thomas Traherne, *Centuries*, The Faith Press, 1969, page 3

What was the secret of such an one's power? what had she done? Absolutely nothing; but radiant smiles, beaming good humour, the tact of divining what every one felt, and every one wanted, told that she had got out of self and learned to think for others; so that at one time it showed itself in deprecating the quarrel, which lowering brows and raised tones already showed to be impending, by sweet words; at another, by smoothing an invalid's pillow; at another, by soothing a sobbing child; at another, by humouring and softening a father who had returned weary and ill-tempered from the irritating cares of business. None but she saw those things. None but a loving heart could see them. That was the secret of her heavenly power.

F.W. Robertson, *Sermons*, Kegan Paul, Trench, Trubner & Co., 1907, First Series, page 241

INSPIRATION

Inspiration—drawing in of breath; divine influence, sudden happy idea; inspiring principle

Inspiration takes me back to my most original belief. In the Genesis story of the creation of man, God is depicted as fashioning and shaping man in his own image and likeness, and the last thing he does is breathe into man and man becomes a living being—that is, man is fundamentally 'inspired.'

If we want to see this fully worked out in a life, we go to the person of Christ, 'the image of the invisible God'. After his baptism he found something of the presence of the 'Father' in the depths of his being, the source of his 'inspiration'. It turned out to be rich and many-sided—Holy Spirit, life, light, truth, joy, grace, love and so on. At the end of his life, to complete the circuit for others, He 'breathed on' his disciples with the words, 'Receive the Holy Spirit.' What followed was a generous dispersion of inspiration and lives were transformed.

Consider for a moment the people we usually think of having been inspired—William Shakespeare. What was the source of his inspiration? The composers, Mozart, Beethoven and Bach. What about their inspiration? Where did their melodies come from? Could they have come from within their souls? The artists, Michelangelo and Leonardo da Vinci. Was this divine influence or merely genes?—or possibly a combination of both? The poets, Shelley, Wordsworth and Keats. What was the source of their inspiration? Was it environment and hereditary, or something deeper? The scientist, Marie Curie. Where did her inspiration come from?

We might all have seeds of 'inspiration' in us, and be unaware of them. We might have been caught up in material necessity, and never realized our divine inheritance. Reflecting on this section might prove to be a source of hope for the future.

Now therefore go, and I will be with your mouth and teach you what you shall speak.

Exodus 4:12

The Lord has given me the tongue of those who are taught, that I may know how to sustain with a word him that is weary. Morning by morning he wakens, he wakens my ear to hear as those who are taught.

Isaiah 50:4

And when they bring you before the synagogues and the rulers and the authorities, do not be anxious how or what you are to answer or what you are to say; for the Holy Spirit will teach you in that hour what you ought to say.

Luke 12:11–12

Now we have received not the spirit of the world, but the Spirit which is from God, that we might understand the gifts bestowed on us by God. And we impart this in words not taught by human wisdom but taught by the Spirit, interpreting spiritual truths to those who possess the Spirit.

1 Corinthians 2:12–13

Inspiration will always sing; inspiration will never explain.

Kahlil Gibran, *Sand and Foam*, William Heinemann, 1927, page 21

The soul may be so inspired by the Divine Spirit as to be certified of its relationship to God.

Henry Ward Beecher, *Proverbs from Plymouth Pulpit*, Charles Burnet & Co., 1887, page 168

An inspiration—a long deep breath of the pure air of thought—could alone give health to the heart.

Richard Jefferies, *The Story of My Heart*, Macmillan & Co., 1968, page 1

Spirit gives meaning to his [man's] life, and the possibility of the greatest development.

C.G. Jung, *Psychological Reflections*, selected and edited by Jolande Jacobi, Routledge & Kegan Paul, 1953, page 239

When a man has given up the one fact of the inspiration of the Scriptures, he has given up the whole foundation of revealed religion.

Henry Ward Beecher, *Proverbs from Plymouth Pulpit*, Charles Burnet & Co., 1887, page 132

Grace only visits them in moments of inspiration, and then it is of a noble character, enhanced as it is by the ever-present gift of strength.

S. de Madariaga in Miguel de Unamuno, *The Tragic Sense of Life*, Macmillan and Co., 1921, page xxii

People in whom... God has awakened the enjoyment of music, painting, poetry, drama, should use these tastes deliberately in their fostering of their religious life.

J. Neville Ward, *The Use of Praying*, Epworth Press, 1967, page 112

Christ reformed man by inspiring the love of goodness, as well as by hatred of evil. He controlled the passions by the inspiration of the moral sentiments.

Henry Ward Beecher, *Proverbs from Plymouth Pulpit*, Charles Burnet & Co., 1887, page 150

It is the man who puts the vigour and enthusiasm which God inspires into the life that now is who will be fitted for the world that is to come. 'Having done all, stand.'

Henry Ward Beecher, *Proverbs from Plymouth Pulpit*, Charles Burnet & Co., 1887, page 23

Goodness rather than talent had given her a wisdom, and goodness rather than courage a power of using that wisdom, which to those simple folk seemed almost an inspiration.

Charles Kingsley, *Daily Thoughts*, Macmillan & Co., 1884, page 105

Every good deed comes from God. His is the idea, His the inspiration, and His its fulfilment in time, and therefore no good deed but lives and grows with the everlasting life of God Himself.

Charles Kingsley, *Daily Thoughts*, Macmillan & Co., 1884, page 187

There is in human life very little spiritual inspiration; very little that men can get from each other; very little that they can get from society; very little that they can get from laws and institutions. Its source is above us.

Henry Ward Beecher, *Proverbs from Plymouth Pulpit*, Charles Burnet & Co., 1887, page 54

And do we not all agree to call rapid thought and noble impulse by the name of inspiration? After our subtlest analysis of the mental process, we will still say... that our highest thoughts and our best deeds are all given to us.

George Eliot, *Adam Bede*, Virtue & Co., 1908, volume I, page 168

Oh may some spark of your celestial fire,
The last, the meanest of your sons inspire...
To teach vain wits a science little known,
T'admire superior sense, and doubt their own!

Alexander Pope, 'An Essay on Criticism', in *The Poems of Alexander Pope*, Methuen & Co., 1961, volume I, page 263

The authority of the inspired scriptures resides, not in an intrusive control of the writing process, nor in an error-free presentation, but in a reliable expression of the faith in the unique period of its earliest gestation.

James Tunstead Burtchaell, CSC, in Alan Richardson and John Bowden, editors, *A New Dictionary of Christian Theology*, SCM Press, 1985, page 304

God should be in the Christian's soul, in his living consciousness, vital, active, fiery. He should inspire him and fill him with admiration. His God should be one that loves him, inspires him, rebukes him, punishes him, wounds him, heals him, and rejoices him—one whose arms and whose bosom he feels.

Henry Ward Beecher, *Proverbs from Plymouth Pulpit*, Charles Burnet & Co., 1887, page 170

To dare to listen to that inspiration from within which voices the ultimate reality of one's own being requires an act of faith which is rare indeed. When the conviction is borne in upon one that anything which is put together, or made up, has no ultimate reality and so is certain to disintegrate, one turns to one's own final reality in the faith that it and it alone can have any virtue or any value.

Esther Harding, *Women's Mysteries*, Pantheon Books Inc., 1955, page 232

The artist's inspiration may be either a human or a spiritual grace, or a mixture of both. High artistic achievement is impossible without at least those forms of intellectual, emotional and physical mortification appropriate to the kind of art which is being practised. Over and above this course of what may be called professional mortification, some artists have practised the kind of self-naughting which is the indispensable pre-condition of the unitive knowledge of the divine

Ground. Fra Angelico, for example, prepared himself for his work by means of prayer and meditation.

Aldous Huxley, *The Perennial Philosophy,* Chatto & Windus, 1974, page 196

The uninitiated imagine one must await inspiration in order to create. That is a mistake. I am far from saying that there is no such thing as inspiration; quite the opposite. It is found as a driving force in every kind of human activity, and is in no wise peculiar to artists. But that force is only brought into action by an effort, and that effort is work. Just as appetite comes by eating, so work brings inspiration, if inspiration is not discernible at the beginning. But it is not simply inspiration that counts; it is the result of inspiration—that is, the composition.

Igor Stravinsky, *An Autobiography,* Calder & Boyars, 1975, page 174

How can my muse want subject to invent
While thou dost breathe that pour'st into my verse,
Thine own sweet argument, too excellent,
For every vulgar paper to rehearse?
O give thy self the thanks if aught in me,
Worthy perusal stand against thy sight,
For who's so dumb that cannot write to thee,
When thou thy self dost give invention light?
Be thou the tenth Muse, ten times more in worth
Than those old nine which rhymers invocate,
And he that calls on thee, let him bring forth
Eternal numbers to outlive long date.
If my slight muse do please these curious days,
The pain be mine, but thine shall be the praise.

William Shakespeare, Sonnet 38

What sacred instinct did inspire
My soul in childhood with a hope so strong?
What secret force moved my desire,
To expect my joys beyond the seas, so young?
Felicity I knew
Was out of view:
And being here alone,
I saw that happiness was gone
From me! For this
I thirsted absent bliss,
And thought that sure beyond the seas,
Or else in something near at hand
I knew not yet (since nature did please
I knew,) my bliss did stand.

But little did the Infant dream
That all the treasures of the World were by:
And that himself was so the cream
And crown of all, which round about did lie:
Yet thus it was. The gem,
The diadem,
The ring enclosing all

That stood upon this earthy ball;
The heavenly eye,
Much wider than the sky,
Wherein they all included were
The glorious soul that was the king
Made to possess them, did appear
A small and little thing!

Thomas Traherne, *Centuries*, The Faith Press, 1969, page 124

INTEGRITY

Integrity—wholeness; soundness; uprightness, honesty, purity

Shortly after returning from our expedition to Nepal, one of the members, David Bloomer, put me in touch with a book entitled *Edward Wilson of the Antarctic* by George Seaver. (You may already have come across extracts from this book in *Visions of Love* and possibly *Visions of Hope*). Edward Wilson was the doctor on Scott's expedition to the Antarctic in 1910. He was a man of deep religious convictions, and at an early age, during his medical studies, spent time in the slums of Battersea teaching aspects of faith to young children. He had an intense love of the countryside and developed into a sensitive artist, committing to paper what he observed in nature. In the pages of this book I was confronted with the finest character I have ever come across. Throughout his life he was solid and dependable. Scott wrote of him that he was shrewdly practical, intensely loyal and quite unselfish. He knew and understood people, more deeply than most. He had a quiet sense of humour and was modest and unassuming in his relationships. Always discreet and tactful, he was given over to kindness and friendship. He was a man of many parts—a skilful doctor as well as a zoologist. Some members of the expedition thought of him as the real leader, but he was staunchly loyal to Scott. His courage and bravery were outstanding features of his character and personality. In short, he was a man of integrity and absolutely trustworthy.

He who walks blamelessly, and does what is right, and speaks truth from his heart; who does not slander with his tongue, and does no evil to his friend, nor takes up a reproach against his neighbour; in whose eyes a reprobate is despised, but who honours those who fear the Lord; who swears to his own hurt and does not change; who does not put out his money at interest, and does not take a bribe against the innocent. He who does these things shall never be moved.

Psalm 15:2–5

The integrity of the upright guides them.

Proverbs 11:3

...by purity, knowledge, forbearance, kindness, the Holy Spirit, genuine love, truthful speech, and the power of God; with the weapons of righteousness for the right hand and for the left, in honour and dishonour, in ill repute and good repute. We are treated as impostors, and yet are true.

2 Corinthians 6:6–8

For a bishop, as God's steward, must be blameless; he must not be arrogant, or quick-tempered or a drunkard or violent or greedy for gain, but hospitable, a lover of goodness, master of himself, upright, holy, and self-controlled.

Titus 1:7–8

What stronger breastplate than a heart untainted!

William Shakespeare, *II King Henry VI*, III. ii. 232

The only drama that really interests me and that I should always be willing to depict anew is the debate of the individual with whatever keeps him from being authentic, with whatever is opposed to his integrity, to his integration. Most often the obstacle is within him. And all the rest is merely accidental.

André Gide, *The Journals of André Gide*, translated by Justin O'Brien, Secker & Warburg, 1947, page 116

One person with integrity, even living the most private life, affects the entire behaviour of the universe. That is God's promise, and it is among modern psychology's great lessons. But the converse is also true. So with each of us empowered with this awesome ability, will we dare be less than as fully Christians as we can?

Harry James Cargas, *Encountering Myself*, SPCK, 1978, page 67

By integrity I do not mean simply sincerity or honesty; integrity rather according to the meaning of the word as its derivation interprets it—entireness—wholeness—soundness: that which Christ means when He says, 'If thine eye be single or sound, thy whole body shall be full of light.'

This integrity extends through the entireness or wholeness of the character. It is found in small matters as well as great; for the allegiance of the soul to truth is tested by small things rather than by those which are more important.

F.W. Robertson, *Sermons*, Kegan Paul, Trench, Trubner & Co., 1907, First Series, page 286

If we could adapt ourselves more to the life of God within us we would be more able to adapt ourselves to the will of God as expressed all about us. We are unyielding in outward things only because we have not fully yielded to inward ones. The integrated soul, the man who has broken down the barriers of selfishness and is detached from his own will, is ready to meet every circumstance however suddenly presented and however apparently destructive, fortuitous, unreasonable, and mad.

Hubert van Zeller, *Leave Your Life Alone*, Sheed and Ward, 1973, page 109

Let your actions speak; your face ought to vouch for your speech. I would have virtue look out of the eye, no less apparently than love does in the sight of the beloved. I would have honesty and sincerity so incorporated with the constitution, that it should be discoverable by the senses, and as easily distinguished as a strong breath, so that a man must be forced to find it out whether he would or no... In short, a man of integrity, sincerity, and good-nature can never be concealed, for his character is wrought into his countenance.

Marcus Aurelius, *The Meditations of Marcus Aurelius*, translated by Jeremy Collier, Walter Scott, page 186

The integrated man, who looks at the world with adult eyes, is able to say: 'This is where I belong, and this is the time which belongs to me to use or misuse. I am a member of a clan which has grown up with me and from which I have much to learn. I have need primarily to lean on God but I shall need, too, the support of my fellow men. If I think myself to be above others in experience and maturity, I am, in fact, below them and have not even begun to live. There is no fulness of life without humility, and there is no humility that is not taught of God.'

Hubert van Zeller, *Leave Your Life Alone*, Sheed and Ward, 1973, page 102

Who is the honest man?
He that doth still and strongly good pursue,
To God, his neighbour, and himself most true:
Whom neither force nor fawning can
Unpinne, or wrench from giving all their due...
Who rides his sure and even trot,
While the world now rides by, now lags behinde...
All being wrought into a summe,
What place or person calls for,—he doth pay...
Who, when he is to treat
With sick folks, women, those whom passions sway,
Allows for that, and keeps his constant way:
Whom others faults do not defeat;
But though men fail him, yet his part doth play.
Whom nothing can procure,
When the wide world runs bias from his will,
To writhe his limbes, and share, not mend the ill.
This is the Mark-man, safe and sure,
Who still is right, and prays to be so still.

George Herbert, 'The Church, Constancie', in *The Poems of George Herbert*, Oxford University Press, 1979, page 63

People must be able to trust their leaders. They want to feel that their interests are safe in the leader's hands—that he will not betray them, or sell out, or get tired of serving them. They want to be confident that he is not going to offend them or their sense of the fitness of things by conduct unbecoming to the position he holds or inconsistent with the esteem in which he is held. They want to feel a sense of solidity, of honesty, of reliability. 'We can trust him' and 'he keeps his promises' are tributes he must have earned...

In short, they want their leader to possess integrity. Integrity orginally means wholeness. The leader who can attain within himself a unity or wholeness of drive and outlook will possess integrity. The acquiring of this quality is thus no little thing, and the process requires no minor adjustments. It is a major problem of the whole life philosophy and character of the individual. It is a question of the leader's capacity to be loyal to the basic demand for loyalty itself.

Ordway Tead, *The Art of Leadership*, McGraw-Hill Book Company, 1935, page 111

The least to be required of those who judge a particular set of doctrines, is that they should accept them in the sense in which they were understood by the teacher. But he understood his teaching, not as a far-fetched ideal of humanity, the fulfilment of which was impossible, not as a visionary poetical fancy with which to captivate the simple-minded folk of Galilee. To him, his teaching meant life; actual work which should save the life of man. It was no dreamer who hung on the Cross, to suffer, to die for his teaching. In the same way many others have died and still will die. It cannot be said of such teaching that it is a dream of the fancy.

All teaching of the truth is fanciful to those who stray from it. We have come to this, that many (and I myself was of their number) say, 'This teaching is visionary because it is unsuited to man's nature. It is against man's nature,' they say, 'when he is beaten on one cheek to turn the other, unnatural to work not for ourselves but for others. It belongs to a man,' they say, 'to take care of himself, of his own safety and of that of his family, to defend his property; in other words, it is natural for a man to fight for his existence. Learned jurists logically prove that the most sacred duty of man is to defend his rights; that is to say, to fight.'

The moment, however, we dismiss the thought that the existing conditions of society as made by men are the best and most sacred of which human life is capable, the objection—that the teaching of Jesus is opposed to man's nature immediately becomes an argument against the objectors. Who will dispute that to torture a dog, to kill a hen or a calf, much more to torture and kill a man, is contrary and painful to man's nature? I have known men to abstain from meat because they had themselves to kill the animals. Meanwhile human society is so constituted, that not a single personal good is obtained without the sufferings of others, and these sufferings are repugnant to our human nature.

The whole system of our social life, the complicated mechanism of our varied institutions, which all have violence for their aim, bear witness to the degree to which violence is contrary to human nature. Not a single judge will consent to strangle with a rope the man he has condemned to death in his court. No one of high rank will consent to snatch a peasant from his weeping family and shut him up in prison. No general, nor soldier, save in obedience to discipline, to his oath, and in time of war, would kill hundreds of Turks or Germans and destroy their villages; he could not so much as wound one of them.

These things are due to that complicated machinery of Society and the State, which makes it its first business to destroy the feeling of responsibility for such deeds, so that no man shall feel them to be as unnatural as they are. Some make laws, others apply them. Others again train men and educate them in the habit of discipline, in the habit, that is to say, of senseless and irresponsible obedience. Again others, and these are the best trained of all, practise every kind of violence, even to the slaying of men, without the slightest knowledge of the why and wherefore. We need only clear our minds for an instant from the network of human institutions in which we are entangled, to feel how adverse it all is to our true nature.

Leo Tolstoy, *What I Believe ('My Religion')*, C.W. Daniel, 1922, page 45

INTELLECT

Intellect—faculty of knowing and reasoning; understanding; persons collectively, of good understanding

I remember a boy at school. He was extremely clever but odd and eccentric. He spent his days studying hard, reading books, getting excellent exam results, but was hopeless at everything else. He had a particular problem in relating to people. As regards religion he adopted the typical stance of the intellectual: unless he was let into all the secrets of the Creator, he would not believe. Hence he was an agnostic.

In contrast, I know a professor whose intellect puts him at the very top of his field. He is a stimulating teacher and in the forefront of research. A marked characteristic, however, is his humility. He is modest, unassuming, and relates well with people. Although well versed in his particular discipline he is more concerned with the areas of his subject as yet unknown. He is good with his hands and has a practical bent. As regards the universe as a whole, many years ago he made an act of faith, and from that perspective, has used his intellect as far as it will go. He is thoughtful and kindly, a man of integrity and of good understanding. He is a genuine intellectual.

Look carefully at the final quotation in this section. I'm afraid it is very long, but I've included it in totality as I think it is extremely important.

A wise man is mightier than a strong man, and a man of knowledge than he who has strength.

Proverbs 24:5

For wisdom is a loving spirit.

Wisdom of Solomon 1:6 (AV)

Behold, I send you out as sheep in the midst of wolves; so be wise as serpents and innocent as doves.

Matthew 10:16

... gird up your minds.

1 Peter 1:13

But only to our intellect is he incomprehensible: not to our love.

The Cloud of Unknowing, translated by Clifton Wolters, Penguin Books, 1961, page 55

Logic does not help you to appreciate York Minster, or Botticelli's Primavera, and mathematics give no useful hints for lovers.

W. Macneile Dixon, *The Human Situation*, Edward Arnold & Co., 1937, page 64

It is always the task of the intellectual to 'think otherwise.' This is not just a perverse idiosyncrasy. It is an absolutely essential feature of a society.

Harvey Cox, *The Secular City*, SCM Press, 1967, page 228

There is a moral faith which is a virtue—faith in a friend, for example. Is there not an intellectual faith which is a virtue, which holds fast when proof fails? I believe there is such an intellectual faith and that it is a sign of strength.

Mark Rutherford, *Last Pages From a Journal*, Oxford University Press, 1915, page 311

To cultivate the man of intellect is not enough, for stillness is a quality of the whole man... Each man must discover the perfect tension of his being—in action or solitude, in love or asceticism, in philosophy or faith—by continual adjustments of thought and experience.

Charles Morgan, *The Fountain*, Macmillan & Co., 1932, page 58

But intellectual acceptance even of correct doctrine is not by itself vital religion; orthodoxy is not identical with the fear or the love of God. This fact of the inadequacy of the truest doctrine is a warning that to argue syllogistically from doctrinal formulae is to court disaster. The formula may be the best possible; yet it is only a label used to designate a living thing.

William Temple, *Nature, Man and God*, Macmillan & Co., 1934, page 379

The intellectual is constantly betrayed by his own vanity. God-like, he blandly assumes that he can express everything in words; whereas the things one loves, lives, and dies for are not, in the last analysis, completely expressible in words. To write or to speak is almost inevitably to lie a little. It is an attempt to clothe an intangible in a tangible form; to compress an immeasurable into a mold. And in the act of compression, how Truth is mangled and torn!

Anne Morrow Lindbergh, *The Wave of the Future*, Harcourt, Brace and Company, 1940, page 6

Robbing your life of charm and variety
the taste of adventure, of space, spontaneity.

How cramped are your notions, formulas, judgements,
always condensing yet hungry for content.
Don't break down my defences, accept the human lot;
each road must take the direction of thought.

Karol Wojtyla, 'Man of Intellect', in *Easter Vigil and Other Poems*, translated by Jerzy Peterkiewicz, Hutchinson & Co. (Publishers), 1979, page 43

Western civilization is distinguished by its worship of the intellect. Yet there is no reason to give intellect pride of place over feeling. It is obviously wrong to classify young people by examinations in which the moral and organic values have no place. To make thought itself the goal of thought is a kind of mental perversion. Intellect and sexual activity alike should be exercised in a natural way. The function of the intellect is not to satisfy itself but to contribute, along with the other organic and mental functions, to the satisfaction of the individual's total needs.

Alexis Carrel, *Reflections on Life*, Hamish Hamilton, 1952, page 33

Faith is first of all an intellectual assent. It perfects the mind, it does not destroy it. It puts the intellect in possession of Truth which reason cannot grasp by itself. It gives us certitude concerning God as He is in Himself; faith is the way to a vital contact with a God who is alive, and not to the view of an abstract First Principle worked out by syllogisms from the evidence of created things...

Faith is not expected to give complete satisfaction to the intellect. It leaves the intellect suspended in obscurity, without a light proper to its own mode of knowing. Yet it does not frustrate the intellect, or deny it, or destroy it. It pacifies it with a conviction which it knows it can accept quite rationally under the guidance of love. For the act of faith is an act in which the intellect is content to know God by *loving* Him and accepting His statements about Himself on His own terms. And this assent is quite rational because it is based on the realization that our reason can tell us nothing about God as He actually is in Himself, and on the fact that God Himself is infinite actuality and therefore infinite Truth, Wisdom, Power and Providence, and can reveal Himself with absolute certitude in any manner He pleases, and can certify His own revelation of Himself by external signs.

Faith is primarily an intellectual assent. But if it were that and nothing more, if it were only the 'argument of what does not appear,' it would not be complete. It has to be something more than an assent of the mind. It is also a grasp, a contact, a communion of wills, 'the substance of things to be hoped for.' By faith one not only attains to truth in a way that intelligence and reason alone cannot do, but one assents to God Himself. One *receives* God. One says 'yes' not merely to a statement *about* God, but to the Invisible, Infinite God Himself. One fully accepts the statement not only for its own content, but for the sake of Him who made it.

Thomas Merton, *New Seeds of Contemplation*, Burns & Oates, 1962, page 98

Dr James Martineau, the great Unitarian divine, used to tell a story of a young American, cultivated, intelligent and prosperous, who had come to Europe expressly to ask his advice. The American had no beliefs, except the belief that religion was a mischievous illusion; and for ten years he had steadily and publicly attacked religion with considerable success. But after a time he had somehow got uneasy. He had begun to feel that perhaps after all something was left out of his reading of life; that one could not be sure that all the side of existence which religion represents was mere delusion. And so he had given up his work and come to Europe; because he felt that he must find out whether there was something in religion after all. And now the question was: How was he going to find out?

Here was Dr Martineau's prescription. He said: 'You must give yourself a year; and you must spend that year in the same country, and with people of the same race. Live for the first six months among simple, slow-minded, narrow, even superstitious peasants, brought up in and practising a rigid traditional faith. Share their lives as intimately as you can. And then go for the second six months to alert, cultured, modern intellectuals, who have given up and despise all Church and all religion. And then ask yourself: which of these two groups of people—if either—has got that mysterious thing, a hold on the secret of life? Which knows best how to meet the deepest, most crucial realities of life—birth—suffering—joy—passion—sin—failure—loneliness—death?'

So the American went to Germany for a year, and then returned to report. He had spent six months in the home of a Westphalian peasant family; devout, narrow, ignorant, slow-minded and prejudiced people, full of superstitions, always treading on his toes, always offending his taste. 'And what,' said Dr Martineau, 'did they know of how to meet the deep realities of birth and death, love, suffering, sin?' The American said, 'Everything.' They seemed to have a sure touch, a wonderful conviction that went far beyond the crude way in which it was expressed. Their lives were entirely grasped and penetrated by something greater than themselves. And then he had spent six months in the student world of Berlin; among delightful, intelligent, keen-witted people, entirely emancipated from all moral and religious prejudices, with whom he had felt most sympathetic and thoroughly at home. 'And what about these?' said Dr Martineau. 'How did they meet the dread and unescapable realities of life?' The American said, 'They were helpless.' No clue, no inwardness.

Now I think that this story expresses with peculiar vividness the real cause of the so-called modern dilemma, in so far as it concerns religion. The cause, I believe, is the contrast, the opposition which modern life and modern culture tend to set up between breadth and depth; between the sharply focused scientific truth which quickened the students' minds, and the dim, deep, spiritual truth which nourished the peasants' souls. I suppose what the American had learned from his experience was this: that the life of those peasants, however rough and uncultured, had an invisible aim running through it which ennobled it. God and the soul mattered more to them than anything else. Their being was rooted in eternal realities. And this attitude of reverence towards the fundamental mysteries of our existence gave them in life's deepest moments an immense advantage over mere cleverness. The life of the Berlin intellectuals, so free, keen, alert and delightful, had no aim or significance beyond itself, no reverence. Confronted by the awful mysteries within which we move, they were without guidance or defence. They had no root in anything that endures. And those two groups of people, one rather dull and slow and faithful, the other very quick, critical, progressive; these exhibit, each in an exclusive way, the two great movements which are possible to the human spirit—the one inwards, the other outwards. And both these movements are needed for a full, deep, and real human life. Because we are twofold creatures, we are not happy, we are not secure, we are not fully alive, until our life has an inside as well as an outside. We need the deeps of the world of spirit, as well as the wide and varied outer world of knowledge and of sense.

And here is where our modern dilemma comes in. Our generation has made such immense discoveries, has achieved such undreamed enrichments of the outside of life, that it has rather lost touch, I think, with the inside of life. It has forgotten the true riches and beauties of its spiritual inheritance: riches and beauties that go far beyond our modern chatter about values and ideals. The human mind's thirst for more and more breadth has obscured the human heart's craving for more and more depth. Not for the first time in human history, we are just now—at least many of us are—the dupes of our own cleverness. And because, in spite of this remarkable cleverness, it is very difficult for us to attend to more than a few things at a time, we leave out a great range of experience which comes in by another route and tells us of another kind of life. Our interest rushes out to the furthest limits of the universe, but we seldom take a sounding of the ocean beneath our restless keels. And then, like the American in the story, we get a queer feeling that we are leaving something out. Knowledge has grown. But wisdom, savouring the deep wonder and mystery of life: that lingers far behind. And so the life of the human spirit, which ought to maintain a delicate balance between the world visible and the world invisible, is thrown out of gear...

Because the outer world and outer life are changing so much and so quickly, always showing us new possibilities, adding more and more new powers and experiences to our natural life, we feel that the inner world and its experiences have somehow become discredited and old-fashioned; that they have got to change too. We need a new heaven to match the new earth. But does that really follow?...

As a matter of fact, those remarkable changes that strike us so much when we observe the modern scene are mostly on life's surface. There are very few changes at life's heart. That is why great literature, however ancient, always moves us and is always understood. It has to do with the unchanging heart of life. And it is in the heart, not on the surface, that the world of religion makes itself known. 'With Thee is the well of life, and in Thy light we see light.' Does the theory of relativity really make any difference to that? I do not think so. We do not, after all, reconstruct our married life every time we move into a new and larger flat. The old, sacred intimacies remain. So too, the move-out of the human mind into a new and larger physical world, which is, I suppose, the great fact of our time, does not make any real difference to the soul's relation to God; even though it may make some difference to the language in which we describe Him. And the reason in both cases is surely the same.

The reason is that the deepest and most sacred relationships between human creatures—man and wife, parent and child, teacher and disciple, friend and friend—and the yet deeper relationship between the human creature and its Keeper and Creator, God: these are real facts, which go on and will go on, quite independently of what we think about them, or the degree in which we understand or feel them. If we treat these deep things with contempt, we merely cheapen our own lives. We do not make any difference to truth. If we leave them out, then we get a very incomplete picture of reality; the picture of a world which has an outside but no inside. But we do not alter reality. Clever as we are, we cannot manage that. Just so, if we choose to shut all our own windows, the room certainly gets stuffy; but we do not alter the quality of the fresh air outside. So the reality of God, the living atmosphere of Spirit, maintains its unalterable pressure; whether we acknowledge it or not...

I am sure it is of the very essence of the modern dilemma to find a reading of reality which will give wonder and love—both together, not one alone—full value and full scope. And it is here that organized religion, so distasteful in many ways to the modern mind, so often criticized and condemned, comes in—or ought to come in—to wake up and feed our poor dim sense of the beauty and aliveness of God. For the real business of the Church is not just what is sometimes called 'surplice work.' Its business is to bind us together—the learned and simple, the strong and the weak—in a great social act of love and worship: to provide a home for the nurturing of the spiritual life. For we cannot get on alone, in religion or anything else. Our spiritual life must be a social life too. We can each only manage a bit of it—it is far too big and various in its richness for any one soul. We must be content to pool our contributions, to learn from the past and learn from each other; humbly receive, and generously give. Wonder and love are caught, not taught: and to catch them we must be in an atmosphere where we are sure to find the germs. A living Church ought to be full of the germs of wonder and love.

I think that failure of the churches which we are always hearing about comes mainly from forgetting these facts. On the one hand, we forget what the real function of a church is, and expect the wrong things from it. On the other hand, the Church in its anxiety for custom, and to meet, as it says, the needs of the present day, has often tried to give us the wrong things. It has forgotten its true business—the production of holiness. Holiness; not just consolation, moral uplift or social reform. Its real job is to weave up men's love and wonder into worship; teach us that 'holy marvelling delight in God.' Its real stock-in-trade is the pearl of great price. It is not a general store. All its symbols and sacraments, all those services which ought to be great corporate works of art—all these are meant to train the souls of men to look up.

And surely modern men, gazing at the inconceivable vastness and splendour of the universe which science has disclosed to us, should be ready for this...

Adoration is the unchanging heart of religion, and the only key to its mysterious truths. There is no dilemma for the adoring soul, 'Be still, and know!' 'Those that wait upon the Lord shall renew their strength.' The Church which teaches, nourishes and practises that adoring attention to God will never lose her hold on the hearts of men. That alone can make public worship the wonderful thing which it ought to be, and usually fails to be. But there is so much to do, there really is not time for all this, is there? Martha is busy with the cooking—she can't sit down and look. So many organizations, committees and practical questions of every sort and kind. And the poor Church is expected to attend to them all. Only lately, a London church advertised a sermon on the text, 'Buy British'; excellent practical advice, of course, but hardly the sort of sermon we should have heard on the Mount, driving its shaft into the hidden deeps of life, and disclosing the real nature of our link with God. And the business of religion is with that relation, and with those hidden deeps. Its aim is to give men eternity, and make them give themselves to eternity—that so, by this resort to the centre, they may integrate their whole existence, and learn how to make the practical surface of life significant and real. There is no other way of doing it. That is what those slow, uncultured, narrow peasants knew; and what the quick, charming, cultured, wide-minded students had missed.

Here, then, is the conclusion of the matter. We are called to live in two directions, not in one; and to obey two commandments, not one. We are not fully human until we do. For we are compound creatures, of sense and of spirit, of mind and of soul—dwellers in time, yet capable of eternity. Therefore nature alone is not going to content us; nor are the greatest triumphs of the intellect ever going to teach us the secret of life.

Reason has moons, but moons not hers
Lie mirror'd on her sea,
Confounding her astronomers,
But O! delighting me.

Evelyn Underhill, *Collected Papers*, edited by Lucy Menzies, Longmans, Green and Co., 1946, page 94

JUSTICE

Justice—just conduct; fairness; exercise of authority in maintenance of right

Every year in the college chapel we have a confirmation service. I had not been at University College, Oxford very long before a post-graduate mathematician came to see me. He wanted to be prepared for confirmation.

We began our informal classes—a slightly varied form of a reflection group. On one occasion he chose the topic 'justice'. After our half-hour period of silent reflecting on the topic, I asked him if there was any particular reason for choosing 'justice'. 'Yes,' he said, 'I'm thinking about what to do in life. My plans are to complete my doctorate, work in the City, make some money, and then set up my own business. I'm wondering if I can justify this as a Christian.'

I asked him if he had found anything helpful in the section. Yes, it had given him plenty to think about. He felt that justice was indeed the key word. He would have to be careful in his choice of product which his company would be producing. It would have to be meeting a genuine need for customers, and not just a want stimulated by clever advertising. He would also have to be fair to his work force—give them a decent wage—and make every effort to provide them with good working conditions. This would require careful forethought. He would like to reduce boredom and monotony to a minimum, and make jobs in his firm as interesting as possible. As for marketing, he wondered if he had an important responsibility to the customer—that the product be well made.

Justice is important in all walks of life, and if lived out to the full, gives hope for the future.

Justice, and only justice, you shall follow, that you may live and inherit the land which the Lord your God gives you.

Deuteronomy 16:20

He has showed you, O man, what is good; and what does the Lord require of you but to do justice, and to love kindness, and to walk humbly with your God?

Micah 6:8

Set your mind on God's kingdom and his justice before everything else, and all the rest will come to you as well.

Matthew 6:33 (NEB)

Man is unjust, but God is just; and finally justice
Triumphs.

Henry Wadsworth Longfellow, 'Evangeline', in *The Poetical Works of Longfellow*, Oxford University Press, 1913, page 149

True peace is not merely the absence of tension; it is the presence of justice.

Martin Luther King, *The Words of Martin Luther King*, selected by Coretta Scott King, William Collins Sons & Co., 1986, page 83

It is compassion rather than the principle of justice which can guard us against being unjust to our fellow men.

Eric Hoffer, *The Passionate State of Mind*, Secker & Warburg, 1956, page 69

For no human actions ever were intended by the Maker of men to be guided by balances of expediency, but by balances of justice.

John Ruskin, *Unto This Last*, George Allen, 1906, page 7

The profound and thrilling vibration of justice, sense of ultimate justice
makes the heart suddenly quiver with love.

D.H. Lawrence, 'Vibration of Justice', in Vivian de Sola Pinto and Warren Roberts, editors, *The Complete Poems of D.H. Lawrence*, William Heinemann, 1967, volume II, page 653

Is it not the fact that in problems concerning the relations of corporate groups of men, the way of love lies through justice?

William Temple, *Citizen and Churchman*, Eyre and Spottiswoode, 1941, page 78

Believe nothing against another, but upon good authority; nor report what may hurt another, unless it be a greater hurt to others to conceal it.

William Penn, *Fruits of Solitude*, A.W. Bennett, 1863, page 28

Now, if these men have defeated the law and outrun
native punishment, though they can outstrip men they
have no wings to fly from God.

William Shakespeare, *King Henry V*, IV. i. 170

Who shall put his finger on the work of justice, and say 'It is there'? Justice is like the Kingdom of God—it is not without us as a fact, it is within us as a great yearning.

George Eliot, *Romola*, Virtue & Co., 1908, volume II, page 396

Liberty, equality,—bad principles! The only true principle for humanity is justice, and justice towards the feeble becomes necessarily protection or kindness.

Henri Frédéric Amiel, *Amiel's Journal*, translated by Mrs Humphry Ward, Macmillan & Co., 1918, page 96

While the Church exists to preach love, and the State to maintain justice, the Christian citizen draws on the inspiration of love to establish a closer approximation to real justice.

William Temple, *Citizen and Churchman*, Eyre and Spottiswoode, 1941, page 80

Justice does not the less exist, because her laws are neglected... A sense of what she commands lives in our breasts; and when we fail to obey that sense, it is to weakness, not to virtue, that we yield.

Ann Radcliffe, *The Italian*, Oxford University Press, 1968, page 168

Justice means much more than the sort of thing that goes on in law courts. It is the old name for everything we should now call 'fairness'; it includes honesty, give and take, truthfulness, keeping promises, and all that side of life.

C.S. Lewis, *Mere Christianity*, William Collins Sons & Co., 1961, page 72

I am convinced that one reason why the Church has counted for comparatively little in the public affairs of recent times is that its spokesmen have talked a great deal too much about love and not nearly enough about justice.

William Temple, *Citizen and Churchman*, Eyre and Spottiswoode, 1941, page 77

I am firmly convinced that the passionate will for justice and truth has done more to improve man's condition than calculating political shrewdness which in the long run only breeds general distrust.

Albert Einstein, *Out of my Later Years*, Thames and Hudson, 1950, page 10

In the corrupted currents of this world
Offence's gilded hand may shove by justice;
And oft 'tis seen the wicked prize itself
Buys out the law, but 'tis not so above!

William Shakespeare, *Hamlet*, III. iii. 57

. . . Jesus came to bring men *justice.* The Greeks defined *justice* as *giving to God and to men that which is their due.* Jesus showed men how to live in such a way that both God and men receive their proper place in our lives. He showed us how to behave both towards God and towards men.

William Barclay, *The Gospel of Matthew*, The Saint Andrew Press, 1975, volume II, page 37

Our hope for creative living in this world house that we have inherited lies in our ability to reestablish the moral ends of our lives in personal character and social justice. Without this spiritual and moral reawakening we shall destroy ourselves in the misuse of our own instruments.

Martin Luther King, *The Words of Martin Luther King*, selected by Coretta Scott King, William Collins Sons & Co., 1986, page 58

Justice without might is helpless, might without justice is tyrannical. Justice without might is gainsaid, because there are always offenders; might without justice is condemned. We must then combine justice and might, and for this end make what is just strong, or what is strong, just.

Blaise Pascal, *Pensées*, translated by W.F. Trotter, Random House, 1941, page 103

The mistake of the best men through generation after generation, has been that great one of thinking to help the poor by almsgiving, and by preaching of patience, or of hope, and by every other means, emollient or consolatory, except the one thing which God orders for them, justice.

John Ruskin, *Unto This Last*, George Allen, 1906, page 72

It often falls in course of common life,
That right long time is overborne of wrong,
Through avarice, or power, or guile, or strife,
That weakens her, and makes her party strong:
But Justice though her doom she do prolong,
Yet at the last will make her own cause right.

Edmund Spenser, 'The Faerie Queene', Book Five, XI. i. 1, in *The Works of Edmund Spenser*, The Johns Hopkins Press, 1936, page 125

In the struggle against injustice, the Christian suffers a serious handicap, which, at least in the short term, can reduce his effectiveness. He doesn't have the right, at any time, to walk over his adversary or destroy him. He doesn't have the right to 'sacrifice' one single person today (let alone a generation) to save a thousand tomorrow.

Michel Quoist, *With Open Heart*, translated by Colette Copeland, Gill and Macmillan, 1983, page 123

Justice. To be ever ready to admit that another person is something quite different from what we read when he is there, (or when we think about him). Or rather, to read in him that he is certainly something different, perhaps something completely different, from what we read in him. Every being cries out silently, to be read differently.

Simone Weil, *Gravity and Grace*, Routledge and Kegan Paul, 1972, page 121

Justice is the right to the maximum of individual independence compatible with the same liberty for others;—in other words, it is respect for man, for the immature, the small, the feeble; it is the guarantee of those human collectivities, associations, states, nationalities—those voluntary or involuntary unions—the object of which is to increase the sum of happiness, and to satisfy the aspiration of the individual. That some should make use of others for their own purposes is an injury to justice.

Henri Frédéric Amiel, *Amiel's Journal*, translated by Mrs Humphry Ward, Macmillan & Co., 1918, page 245

Justice is a virtue which, if it be not developed in youth, has little chance of ever being developed. It depends on a peculiarly sensitive reaction to good and evil, and it is only in youth that those reactions are keen and disinterested. Real justice is always a sign of great innocence; it cannot exist side by side with interested motives or a trace of self-seeking. And a sense of justice is hard to develop in this great industrial world where the relations of men are so out of joint and where such flaunting anomalies assail one at every turn.

Randolph Bourne, *Youth and Life*, Constable & Co., 1913, page 84

It is strange to see how completely justice is forgotten in the presence of great international struggles. Even the great majority of the spectators are no longer capable of judging except as their own personal tastes, dislikes, fears, desires, interests, or passions may dictate,—that is to say, their judgment is not a judgment at all. How many people are capable of delivering a fair verdict on the struggle now going on? Very few! This horror of equity, this antipathy to justice, this rage against a merciful neutrality, represents a kind of eruption of animal passion in man, a blind fierce passion, which is absurd enough to call itself a reason, whereas it is nothing but a force.

Henri Frédéric Amiel, *Amiel's Journal*, translated by Mrs Humphry Ward, Macmillan & Co., 1918, page 178

1. Every child should find itself a member of a family housed with decency and dignity, so that it may grow up as a member of that basic community in a happy fellowship unspoilt by under-feeding or over-crowding, by dirty and drab surroundings or by mechanical monotony of environment.

2. Every child should have the opportunity of an education till years of maturity, so planned as to allow for his peculiar aptitudes and make possible their full development. This education should throughout be inspired by faith in God and find its focus in worship.

3. Every citizen should be secure in possession of such income as will enable him to maintain a home and bring up children in such conditions as are described in paragraph 1 above.

4. Every citizen should have a voice in the conduct of the business or industry which is carried on by means of his labour, and the satisfaction of knowing that his labour is directed to the well-being of the community.

5. Every citizen should have sufficient daily leisure, with two days of rest in seven, and, if an employee, an annual holiday with pay, to enable him to enjoy a full personal life with such interests and activities as his tasks and talents may direct.

6. Every citizen should have assured liberty in the forms of freedom of worship, of speech, of assembly, and of association for special purposes.

William Temple, *Christianity and Social Order*, Penguin Books, 1942, page 73

LEADERSHIP

Leadership—direction given by going in front, example; encourage by doing thing

During my time of National Service in Singapore, the brigadier decided to give a talk to the officers under his command on leadership. We were all summoned to appear at a certain location on a given day. The essence of his talk was the words of his motto: 'It all depends on me.' He explained that when we were alone in the jungle with our men, and things were verging on the impossible, the words we had to remember were: 'It all depends on me.' This would jolt us into action and we would get something done.

This worked in well with our original training on leadership at Mons Officer Cadet School in Aldershot. Here we had been given a technique for making decisions in the field. First of all we had to 'make an appreciation of the situation'. This meant we had to identify our aim and objective. We then had to work out our strategy; how we were going to achieve our aim and objective. This meant in turn a consideration of factors to be taken into account. Having made an appreciation of the situation, identified our aim and objective, and worked out our strategy, we would then be in a position to give clear, concise orders, and take group action. We were then able to exercise effective practical leadership.

This might all sound simplistic, especially when compared with the leadership of Jesus as revealed in the Gospels, but it has helped me in practical ways since leaving the army, and might be of value to others. Leadership skills are increasingly needed in modern society.

Choose able men from all the people, such as fear God, men who are trustworthy and who hate a bribe.

Exodus 18:21

The Lord hath wrought great glory by them through his great power from the beginning. Such as did bear rule in their kingdoms, men renowned for their power, giving counsel by their understanding, and declaring prophecies: Leaders of the people by their counsels, and by their knowledge of learning meet for the people, wise and eloquent in their instructions.

Ecclesiasticus 44:2–4 (AV)

Let the greatest among you become as the youngest, and the leader as one who serves. For which is the greater, one who sits at table, or one who serves? Is it not the one who sits at table? But I am among you as one who serves.

Luke 22:26–27

Remember your leaders, those who spoke to you the word of God; consider the outcome of their life, and imitate their faith.

Hebrews 13:7

You taught me how to know the face of right.

William Shakespeare, *King John*, V. ii. 88

A leader must have but one passion: for his work and his profession.

André Maurois, *The Art of Living*, The English Universities Press, 1940, page 160

The noblest mind he carries
That ever govern'd man.

William Shakespeare, *Timon of Athens*, I. i. 283

People think of leaders as men devoted to service, and by service they mean that these men serve their followers... The real leader serves truth, not people.

J.B. Yeats, *Letters to his son, W.B. Yeats and others*, Faber and Faber, 1944, page 218

Good leaders are aware of both their strengths and weaknesses. They are not afraid to admit to the latter. They know how to find support and are humble enough to ask for it. There is no perfect leader who has all the gifts necessary for good leadership.

Jean Vanier, *Community and Growth*, Darton, Longman and Todd, 1991, page 220

Leaders must take great care of those who have been given responsibility in the community and who for one reason or another (health, tiredness, lack of certain qualities, etc.) cannot exercise it well. Sometimes they must be relieved of their responsibility; in other cases, the leader must be more demanding and encourage them to do better. Much wisdom is needed here.

Jean Vanier, *Community and Growth*, Darton, Longman and Todd, 1991, page 219

After so much stress on the necessity of a leader to prevent his own personal feelings and attitudes from interfering in a helping relationship, it seems necessary to re-establish the basic principle that no one can help anyone without becoming involved, without entering with his whole person into the painful situation, without taking the risk of becoming hurt, wounded or even destroyed in the process. The beginning and end of all Christian leadership is to give your lives for others.

Henri J.M. Nouwen, *The Wounded Healer*, Doubleday, 1979, page 72

Organizations tend to put a premium upon a display of sheer activity or busyness and upon constant physical presence on the job. Yet the values which leadership peculiarly demands are not cultivated by a flurry of constant action. More thoughtfulness, more chance for meditation, for serenity, for using one's imagination, for developing one's total personal effectiveness and poise, for being more straightforwardly human with one's associates—these are required. And these values flourish where there is physical well-being. People who are going to lead have to be rested and fresh; they need time to think about the aims and the problems of their organization. And their working schedules should allow for this.

Ordway Tead, *The Art of Leadership*, McGraw-Hill Book Company, 1935, page 87

The leader is one who knows with greater than average strength of intuition what he wants to get done and where he wants to go. 'The world stands aside to let pass the man who knows whither he is going.'

This means that he possesses clarity and precision as to the objectives, purposes or aims that he desires for himself and his group, and that he holds these deeply enough and permanently enough to see them well on the way to being realized. Purposefulness to be effective requires that the aims are: (1) definite; (2) readily communicable to others; (3) potentially attractive to others; and (4) vigorously, persistently and enthusiastically sustained by the leader.

Ordawy Tead, *The Art of Leadership*, McGraw-Hill Book Company, 1935, page 94

The mere presence of a sound purpose is obviously not enough. It must be *felt* to be sound by all. In other words it must be surcharged with a dynamic emotion, with a hopefulness, with a will to win and an abounding, robust sense of joy in the job. It is something like this which is meant by enthusiasm. And this too is an essential attribute. It is important because it is contagious. Beyond a limited point it cannot be faked. Its genuineness is quickly sensed.

Where the leader has real vigour on the physical side and definiteness of objective on the mental side, enthusiasm is the normal offspring. This does not mean that enthusiasm cannot be deliberately increased. It means that its creation is a derived fact and that out from the springs of great energy and of deep intellectual conviction will pour that emotional exhilaration which is essential for arousing others.

Ordway Tead, *The Art of Leadership*, McGraw-Hill Book Company, 1935, page 98

Many leaders are in the first instance executives whose primary duty is to direct some enterprise or one of its departments or sub-units...

It remains true that in every leadership situation the leader has to possess enough grasp of the ways and means, the technology and processes by means of which the purposes are being realized, to give wise guidance to the directive effort *as a whole*...

In general the principle underlying success at the coordinative task has been found to be that *every special and different point of view in the group affected* by the major executive decisions should be *fully represented by its own exponents when decisions are being reached.* These special points of view are inevitably created by the differing outlooks which different jobs or functions inevitably foster. The more the leader can know at first hand about the technique employed by all his group, the wiser will be his grasp of all his problems...

But more and more the key to leadership lies in other directions. It lies in ability to make a team out of a group of individual workers, to foster a team spirit, to bring their efforts together into a unified total result, to make them see the significance of the particular task each one is doing in relation to the whole.

Ordway Tead, *The Art of Leadership*, McGraw-Hill Book Company, 1935, page 115

It is easy to be sentimental and rhetorical about the part which friendliness and affection play in the task of leadership. But it is hard to convey by mere written utterance how true it is that the good leader feels deeply and affectionately for those he leads...

One should be quite clear as to what affection is and why it is so potent a force. It is here taken to mean a state of sympathetic warmth of feeling, friendliness of attitude and conscious solicitude for the well-being and happiness of others. It is an attitude which gives sensitiveness to one's awareness as to the desires of others and the good of others, and creates an eagerness to help realize these.

The one who loves is incited by it to greater efforts to divine the wishes and aspirations of those loved and to behaviour which is at once considerate and discerning. Affection heightens sympathetic insight—or at least the effort in that direction.

Affection is therefore essential for the leader because *it predisposes people toward being influenced.* On the whole, individuals prefer to do and to be what they believe those who care for them want them to do and be. They then have something to live up to. They have at last a definite idea as to what is expected of them by someone who cares. And it brings them happiness to try to fulfil those expectations and to have the sense of communion which that brings. People thus get a sense that they are needed and everyone wants the support of feeling themselves necessary to someone or to some cause.

Ordway Tead, *The Art of Leadership*, McGraw-Hill Book Company, 1935, page 102

Almost every study of the secret of the successful leader has agreed that the possession of a generous and unusual endowment of physical and nervous energy is essential to personal ascendancy. Those who rise in any marked way above the mass of men have conspicuously more drive, more sheer endurance, greater vigour of body and mind than the average person. The leader's effectiveness is in the first instance dependent upon his basic constitutional strength and robustness.

The subtle ways in which one person vitalizes another are closely related to the possession of this endowment. Energy seems to be imparted and to be drawn out of others by an effective show of energy. The leader's energy begets energy in the followers. The existence of abounding vigour goes far toward making the leader crave to work for significant purposes, and toward producing that total mobilized zeal we call enthusiasm. Each of us knows in our day-to-day life how our working effectiveness and ability to expend effort fluctuate with our physical and nervous condition. Sluggishness, apathy, chronic fatigue, routine execution—these are foes of good leadership which only abounding energy can keep at bay.

The leader also must recognize that his job is more demanding than the average. Strength literally goes out from him. Leading is hard work. It usually requires more average working hours than are given by others. It often requires sustained, concentrated effort; it requires occasional emergency demands which must be able to draw on physical reserves of strength and endurance. By his enthusiasm the leader makes unusual demands upon himself. Leading means a generous lavishing of energy which is abnormally taxing.

Ordway Tead, *The Art of Leadership*, McGraw-Hill Book Company, 1935, page 83

LEISURE

Leisure—opportunity to do, afforded by free time, time at one's disposal, not occupied, also deliberately without hurry

In our theological training we were told it was important to take a day off a week in our ministry. This is often difficult to do in a hectic term, so at Christmas, when college is closed, I make up for this by going to Switzerland to look after a church in Mürren, near Interlaken.

Mürren is situated in a delightful spot 4,000 feet up in the mountains of the Bernese Oberland. Inaccessible by road, there are no cars in the village, so it is quiet and peaceful, and scenically beautiful. It is the home of down-hill skiing, and very popular with members of the Kandahar Ski Club, who have a training programme during the Christmas and New Year period. On Christmas Eve, the church is almost full for the midnight Communion service, and on Christmas Day, at the evening festival of nine lessons and carols, standing room only.

When Christmas duties have been completed, 'leisure' begins and I take to the slopes. Mürren faces east and being at a high altitude enjoys long hours of sunshine. Most of the slopes are steep, so skiing is both challenging and demanding. The air is crystal clear and the views of the mountains breathtaking. I like to take things at a leisurely pace and unwind after a term in college. It's an excellent place for contemplation and for re-charging one's batteries. In addition to excellent skiing facilities, Mürren boasts a modern sports centre for ice-skating, curling, indoor swimming, squash, and a large well-equipped gym for many indoor sports. No wonder people come back to Mürren year after year. It is a perfect place for leisure.

Six days you shall do your work, but on the seventh day you shall rest.

Exodus 23:12

The wisdom of a learned man cometh by opportunity of leisure; and he that hath little business shall become wise.

Ecclesiasticus 38:24 (AV)

Come to me, all who labour and are heavy laden, and I will give you rest.

Matthew 11:28

Come away by yourselves to a lonely place, and rest a while. For many were coming and going, and they had no leisure even to eat.

Mark 6:31

Rest belongs to the work as the eyelids to the eyes.

Rabindranath Tagore, 'Stray Birds', XXIV, in *Collected Poems & Plays of Rabindranath Tagore*, Macmillan & Co., 1936, page 290

There is an appetite of the eye, of the ear, and of every sense, for which God has provided the material.

Henry Ward Beecher, *Proverbs from Plymouth Pulpit*, Charles Burnet & Co., 1887, page 78

Devoting our whole life to make preparation for its security, we have no leisure to profit by life itself.

Leo Tolstoy, *What I Believe ('My Religion')*, C.W. Daniel, 1922, page 172

A sound schooling should have a dual aim—to equip a man for hours of work and for hours of leisure. They interact; if the leisure is misspent, the work will suffer.

Norman Douglas, *An Almanac*, Chatto & Windus in association with Secker & Warburg, 1945, page 2

Let my doing nothing when I have nothing to do become untroubled in its depth of peace like the evening in the seashore when the water is silent.

Rabindranath Tagore, 'Stray Birds', CCVII, in *Collected Poems & Plays of Rabindranath Tagore*, Macmillan & Co., 1936, page 314

Life consists of much more than work; it includes, for instance, love, the sense of beauty or aesthetic enjoyment, worship, philanthropy and social, physical, and other pleasures of many kinds. A day is not necessarily 'lost,' because it is entirely spent in leisure or enjoyment.

J.T. Hackett, *My Commonplace Book*, Macmillan and Co., 1923, page 152

Leisure is pain; take off our chariot wheels;
How heavily we drag the load of life!
Blest leisure is our curse; like that of Cain,
It makes us wander, wander earth around
To fly that tyrant, Thought.

Edward Young, 'Night Thoughts', xi. 125, in *Young's Complete Poems*, William Tegg and Co., 1854, volume I, page 17

All too often modern man becomes the plaything of his circumstances because he no longer has any leisure time, or rather, he doesn't know how to provide himself with the leisure he needs to stop for a moment and take a good look at himself. He hasn't time to become aware of himself as a person.

Michel Quoist, *The Christian Response*, Gill and Macmillan, 1965, page 73

Idleness and the incapacity for leisure correspond with one another; leisure is the contrary of both. Leisure is only possible to a man who is at one with himself and also at one with the world. These are the presuppositions of leisure, for leisure is an affirmation. Idleness on the other hand, is rooted in the omission of these two affirmations.

Josef Pieper, in W.H. Auden and Louis Kronemberger, editors, *The Faber Book of Aphorisms*, Faber and Faber, 1978, page 47

Would that I could loiter! Everything I do I hurry, and in the midst of pleasure press forward to the end. I swallow and never taste. This vice infects very high up and prevents the enjoyments of anything beautiful, for I have not the patience to stay long enough with it. It drives me from life to the consideration of death.

Mark Rutherford, *Last Pages From a Journal*, Oxford University Press, 1915, page 287

The more intense and difficult community life becomes, and the more tension and struggles it produces, then the more we need times of relaxation. When we feel strung up, tense and incapable of praying or listening, then we should take some rest—or even get away for a few days.

Some people don't know what to do with free time. They spend hours just sitting about and talking. It is sad if people have no interest outside the community, if they have given up reading, if they don't enjoy simple pleasures like walking and listening to music. We have to help each other keep alive the personal interests which help us relax and re-create us.

Jean Vanier, *Community and Growth*, Darton, Longman and Todd, 1991, page 180

Compared with the exclusive ideal of work as activity, leisure implies (in the first place) an attitude of non-activity, of inward calm, of silence; it means not being 'busy,' but letting things happen.

Leisure is a form of silence, of that silence which is the prerequisite of the apprehension of reality: only the silent hear and those who do not remain silent do not hear. Silence, as it is used in this context, does not mean 'dumbness' or 'noiselessness'; it means more nearly that the soul's power to 'answer' to the reality of the world is left undisturbed. For leisure is a receptive attitude of mind, a contemplative attitude, and it is not only the occasion but also the capacity for steeping oneself in the whole of creation.

Josef Pieper, *Leisure, the Basis of Culture*, translated by Alexander Dru, Faber and Faber, 1952, page 52

A new element of relaxation and of education for leisure is important in senior education. This element, present in good primary schools, is lamentably lost in the upper reaches of school life. All this means a new stress upon creativity, therapeutic drama, art and writing, much more work in small groups; and timetabled time for these things. The arts must be rescued and put to their proper use as enrichments of the human spirit: these attitudes will then carry over into life outside school. Just now the vandalism on buses, the scrawling on walls, the drunkenness and the vulgarity and basic poverty of ideas for spending leisure are as much our failure as those of the young people who will not only enjoy their parties and their occasional sowings of wild oats, but also walking, mountaineering, painting, writing, making music, undertaking social and political research even. And these things could be enjoyed as much as the bashing up of property.

Roy Stevens, *Education and the Death of Love*, Epworth Press, 1978, page 144

Celebrations certainly have a role in helping people to accept the sufferings of everyday life by offering them a chance to relax and let go. But to see them as nothing but a form of escape or drug, is to fail to understand human nature. We all live a daily life which brings its own weariness: we make things dirty, we clean them, we plough, sow, and harvest. We have long hours to travel to work, which is frustrating; and at work there is discipline, efficiency and a programme to be respected, and then there is the stress. In family life there are sometimes barriers and lack of communication between people; we may close ourselves off from others in television, books or other things, feeling guilty and making others feel guilty; inside us there is a lot of inner pain. As we need the day for work, activity, prayer, rejoicing and the night for sleep and, as we need the four seasons with their different climates, so too we need the drudgery of dailiness and the joys of celebration; we need the work day and the sabbath. Our human hearts need something beyond the limitations and frustrations of the daily grind. We thirst for a happiness which seems unattainable on earth. We crave the infinite, the universal, the eternal—something which gives a sense to human life and its irksome daily routines. A festival is a sign of heaven. It symbolizes our deepest aspiration—an experience of total communion.

Jean Vanier, *Community and Growth*, Darton, Longman and Todd, 1991, page 314

I often hear talk of people committed to social action or in communities who are 'burned-out'. These people have been too generous; they have thrown themselves into activity which has finally destroyed them emotionally. They have not known how to relax and to be refreshed. Those in responsibility must teach such people the discipline of physical rest and relaxation, and the need for spiritual nourishment and for fixing clear priorities. They must also set an example.

Many people get burned out because, perhaps unconsciously, some part of them is rejecting the need to relax and find a harmonious rhythm of life for themselves. In their over-activity they are fleeing from something, sometimes because of deep unconscious guilt feelings. Maybe they do not really want to put down roots in the community and stay for the long haul. They may be too attached to their function, perhaps even identified with it. They want to control everything, and perhaps also want to appear to be perfect, or at least a perfect hero! They have not yet learned how to live; they are not yet free inside themselves; they have not yet discovered the wisdom of the present moment, which can frequently mean saying 'no' to people.

These people need a spiritual guide to help them look at themselves and discover why they have not the freedom to stop, and what is the cause of their compulsive need to do things. They need someone who can help them stand back and relax enough to clarify their own motives and become people living with other people, children among other children. God has given each of us an intelligence. It may not be very great, but it is great enough for us to reflect on what we need to order to live what we are called to live—community. These over-active people, it seems, can be fleeing from their own cry for friendship and love, from their own sensitivity and maybe from their inner anguish and agitation. They may be afraid of their emotions, of their own sexuality. They need to reflect on their own deep needs and to refind the child in themselves which is crying because it feels alone. Our bodies need to relax, but so do our hearts, in secure and unthreatening relationships.

Jean Vanier, *Community and Growth*, Darton, Longman and Todd, 1991, page 177

LISTENING

Listening—make effort to hear something, hear person speaking with attention; give ear to or now usually to (person or sound or story)

I was prepared for confirmation by our school chaplain. As part of our preparation we were taught how to say our prayers. He suggested we start with thanksgiving, thanking God for all the blessings of the day, and then move on to confession, owning up to all we had done wrong during the day—in thought, word, deed and omission. This was to be followed by absolution—accepting God's forgiveness, and freedom for a fresh start. We were then to say the Lord's Prayer, and move on to intercession—praying for people whom we knew to be in need. We were to end in praying for ourselves and our own particular needs.

I used this simple method for several years, until I gradually became aware of the importance of *listening*. I realized that in my prayer-life I was doing all the talking, almost telling God what to do. If God was indeed, in some mysterious way, in the depths of my being, then perhaps I ought to be taking a much more humble approach and listening to him instead of speaking. It was just possible he might have something important to say to me.

So I started *listening*. At first I found it very difficult. I would sit down in my room in a comfortable chair and try to listen. Soon I would get very restless and fidgety. A breakthrough came when I took up a pen and paper, and started writing—eventually leading to keeping a spiritual diary. I used Victor Gollancz's *A Year of Grace*, and slowly went through the contents, *listening* carefully, and recording insights which came to me in times of quiet. This form of *listening prayer* has become a vital source of guidance and is strongly recommended. *Visions of Hope* can be used in this way.

He who listens to me will dwell secure and will be at ease, without dread of evil.

Proverbs 1:33

Incline your ear, and come to me; hear, that your soul may live.

Isaiah 55:3

And a cloud overshadowed them, and a voice came out of the cloud, 'This is my beloved Son; listen to him.'

Mark 9:7

Behold, I stand at the door and knock; if any one hears my voice and opens the door, I will come in to him and eat with him, and he with me.

Revelation 3:20

He [God] cannot be seen, but he can be listened to.

Martin Buber, *I and Thou*, translated by Walter Kaufman, T. & T. Clark, 1971, page 26

Listen for the meaning beneath the words.

Anon.

Listen, my heart, to the whispers of the world with which it makes love to you.

Rabindranath Tagore, 'Stray Birds', XIII, in *Collected Poems & Plays of Rabindranath Tagore*, Macmillan & Co., 1936, page 288

The more faithfully you listen to the voice within you, the better you will hear what is sounding outside.

Dag Hammarskjöld, *Markings*, translated by W.H. Auden & Leif Sjoberg, with a foreword by W.H. Auden, Faber and Faber, 1964, page 35

How can you expect to keep your powers of hearing when you never want to listen? That God should have time for you, you seem to take as much for granted as that you cannot have time for Him.

Dag Hammarskjöld, *Markings*, translated by W.H. Auden & Leif Sjoberg, with a foreword by W.H. Auden, Faber and Faber, 1964, page 34

I'm become, re-become, a sceptic: with however a deepened spiritual sense, more of a Listener, a deeper sense of the possibilities of something stirring, emerging, from There Back-of-things.

Stephen MacKenna, *Journal and Letters*, Constable and Company, 1936, page 260

Before we can hear the Divine Voice we must shut out all other voices, so that we may be able to listen, to discern its faintest whisper. The most precious messages are those which are whispered.

Mark Rutherford, *More Pages From a Journal*, Oxford University Press, 1910, page 223

And when, as happens more and more here, people bring their problems to me, I know that that is no compliment to my learning. It is better than that. It is a recognition on their part that I am free to listen to them, that I am open to them, that I am in some sort a free man.

Dan Billany and David Dowie, *The Cage*, Longmans, Green and Co., 1949, page 158

We listen in our own hearts, individually, in prayer and experience. We listen also as a people, gathered together by the Spirit. There are three special 'places' for listening which in some way give the key to all the rest: the word comes to us through Scripture, through people and the human condition, and in personal prayer.

Marcia Boulding, *The Coming of God*, SPCK, 1982, page 77

There are different kinds of listening. There is the listening of criticism; there is the listening of resentment. There is the listening of superiority; there is the listening of indifference. There is the listening of the man who only listens because for the moment he cannot get the chance to speak. The only listening that is worth while is the listening which listens and learns. There is no other way to listen to God.

William Barclay, *The Gospel of John*, The Saint Andrew Press, 1974, volume I, page 225

If he didn't tell you what was on his mind it was because he didn't feel he could.

You think he was afraid. In a way that's true, but if he was afraid, it was because you weren't really inviting, you weren't 'empty' enough, loving enough, to receive him. Listening isn't easy! And yet, I'm fairly sure that people are overflowing with words, and in allowing them to express themselves, we allow them a measure of release, and a chance to become themselves again.

Michel Quoist, *With Open Heart*, translated by Colette Copeland, Gill and Macmillan Ltd, 1983, page 159

Whenever a man listens to what another says, the more significant the utterance, the more complete the listener's response, and the greater his difficulty in realizing what is happening to him. He will be aware of an intensification of his feelings as well as a multiplicity of thoughts which he cannot force into a pattern. The greater the sermon the less listeners will be inclined to talk about its exact effects on them. People are generally bored by sermons they understand too easily and are moved by those they do not fully understand.

R.E.C. Browne, *The Ministry of the Word*, SCM Press, 1958, page 66

... many people are looking for an ear that will listen. They do not find it among Christians, because these Christians are talking where they should be listening. He who can no longer listen to his brother will soon be no longer listening to God either; he will be doing nothing but prattle in the presence of God too. This is the beginning of the death of the spiritual life, and in the end there is nothing left but spiritual chatter and clerical condescension arrayed in pious words. One who cannot listen long and patiently will presently be talking beside the point and be never really speaking to others, albeit he be not conscious of it. Anyone who thinks that his time is too valuable to spend keeping quiet will eventually have no time for God and his brother, but only for himself and for his own follies.

Dietrich Bonhoeffer, *Life Together*, SCM Press, 1955, page 87

The most difficult and decisive part of prayer is acquiring this ability to listen. Listening is no passive affair, a space when we happen not to be doing or speaking. Inactivity and superficial silence do not necessarily mean that we are in a position to listen. Listening is a conscious, willed action, requiring alertness and vigilance, by which our whole attention is focused and controlled. Listening is in this sense a difficult thing. And it is decisive because it is the beginning of our entry into a personal and unique relationship with God, in which we hear the call of our own special responsibilities for which God has intended us. Listening is the aspect of silence in which we receive the commission of God.

Mother Mary Clare, SLG., *Encountering the Depths*, Darton, Longman and Todd, 1981, page 33

It is to Jesus Christ that we must listen. Men must not be heard or believed, but inasmuch as they speak with the truth and from the authority of Jesus. He spoke and acted, that we might attend to and study the details of his life. Mistaken creatures that we are! we follow our own fancies, and neglect the words of eternal life.

We often say, that we desire to know what we must do to become more virtuous; but when the word of God teaches us, our courage fails us in the execution. We are conscious that we are not what we ought to be. We see our own wretchedness; it increases every day and we think we have done a great deal in saying that we desire to be delivered from it. But we must count for nothing, any resolution that falls short of absolute determination to sacrifice whatever arrests us in our progress to perfection. Let us listen to what God inspires, prove the spirit so as to know if it comes from him, and then follow where they may lead us.

François de la M. Fénelon, *Selections from the Writings of Fénelon*, 'Mrs. Follen', Edward T. Whitfield, 1850, page 229

To listen to a living word flowing from the heart of someone is not the same thing as to read the same message from a book. As we listen to a person, it is a life and a spirit that are communicated. And God uses this living word to give life.

Those who announce the Word must remember this. They are called not to give good ideas to people but communicate life and reveal communion.

Sometimes it is said that for people with a handicap words should be replaced by music, pictures and mime. It is true that many cannot understand abstract ideas. But many are sensitive to loving words flowing from the heart. I am touched as I watch their attentive faces as they listen to the words of Father Thomas during the Eucharist.

Words can truly become a sacrament bringing the light and the presence of Jesus. Didier, who has a quite serious mental handicap, told me 'when Father Gilbert was talking, my heart was burning'.

Jean Vanier, *Growth and Community*, Darton, Longman and Todd, 1991, page 175

There is also a grace of kind listening, as well as a grace of kind speaking. Some men listen with an abstracted air, which shows that their thoughts are elsewhere. Or they seem to listen, but by wide answers and irrelevant questions show that they have been occupied with their own thoughts, as being more interesting, at least in their own estimation, than what you have been saying. Some listen with a kind of importunate ferocity, which makes you feel, that you are being put upon your trial, and that your auditor expects beforehand that you are going to tell him a lie, or to be inaccurate, or to say something which he will disapprove, and that you must mind your expressions. Some interrupt, and will not hear you to the end. Some hear you to the end, and then forthwith begin to talk to you about a similar experience which has befallen themselves, making your case only an illustration of their own. Some, meaning to be kind, listen with such a determined, lively, violent attention, that you are at once made uncomfortable, and the charm of conversation is at an end. Many persons, whose manners will stand the test of speaking, break down under the trial of listening. But all these things should be brought under the sweet influences of religion. Kind listening is often an act of the most delicate interior mortification, and is a great assistance towards kind speaking.

F.W. Faber, *Spiritual Conferences*, Thomas Richardson and Son, 1859, page 40

LITERATURE

Literature—literary culture; realm of letters, writings of country or period; writings whose value lies in beauty of form or emotional effect

E.M. Forster, in his book *Anonymity. An Enquiry*, wrote that each human mind has two personalities, one on the surface, the other deeper down. The upper personality has a name. It is called S.T. Coleridge, or William Shakespeare, or Mrs Humphry Ward. It is conscious and alert, it does things like dining out, answering letters, and so on, but differs vividly and amusingly from other personalities. The lower personality, he thought, was a very queer affair. In many ways it is a perfect fool, but without it there is no literature, because, unless a man dips a bucket down into it occasionally he cannot produce first class work. There is something general about it. Although it is in S.T. Coleridge, it cannot be labelled with his name. It has something in common with all other deeper personalities, and the mystic will assert that the common quality is God, and that here, in the obscure recesses of our being, we near the gates of the Divine.

You can imagine how excited I was to read this as it fits in closely with what I believe about *being made in the image and likeness of God* and of *the divine inbreathing.* I wonder if all great literature is inspired in this way, and that everyone, in theory at least, has the capacity to appreciate and understand it. I would go even further than E.M. Forster, and include such things as art, music, science, philosophy, and so on, but also to all activities of human life. There is abundant evidence of this in the pages of *Visions of Hope.*

For whatever was written in former days was written for our instruction.

Romans 15:4

... continue in what you have learned and have firmly believed, knowing from whom you learned it, and how from childhood you have been acquainted with the sacred writings which are able to instruct you for salvation through faith in Christ Jesus.

2 Timothy 3:14–15

... something that was greater than Jefferies's books—the spirit that led Jefferies to write them.

E.M. Forster, *Howards End,* Penguin Books, 1981, page 127

Great literature is simply language charged with meaning to the utmost possible degree.

Ezra Pound, *How to Read,* Desmond Harmsworth, 1931, page 21

Works of fiction are just as wholesome as anything else, if they are read wholesomely.

Henry Ward Beecher, *Proverbs from Plymouth Pulpit,* Charles Burnet & Co., 1887, page 102

The Bible stands alone in human literature in its elevated conception of manhood, in character and conduct.

Henry Ward Beecher, *Proverbs from Plymouth Pulpit,* Charles Burnet & Co., 1887, page 129

Can anything be called a book unless it forces the reader by one method or another, by contrast or sympathy, to discover himself?

Norman Douglas, *An Almanac,* Chatto & Windus in association with Secker & Warburg, 1945, page 31

... a true work of art... is an analysis of experience and a synthesis of the findings into a unity that excites the reader.

Rebecca West, *Ending in Earnest,* Doubleday, Doran & Company, 1931, page 77

Literature is rather an image of the spiritual world, than of the physical, is it not?—of the internal, rather than the external.

Henry Wadsworth Longfellow, 'Kavanagh', in *The Writings of Henry Wadsworth Longfellow,* George Routledge and Sons, volume II, page 366

I tell him prose and verse are alike in one thing—the best is that to which went the hardest thoughts. This also is the secret of originality, also the secret of sincerity.

J.B. Yeats, *Letters to his son, W.B. Yeats and others*, Faber and Faber, 1944, page 53

Those writers are to be valued above all others who lay hold of us and gently transform us into a new world, closing communication with the world in which we live.

Mark Rutherford, *Last Pages From a Journal*, Oxford University Press, 1915, page 280

Dreams, books, are each a world; and books, we know,
Are a substantial world, both pure and good:
Round these, with tendrils strong as flesh and blood,
Our pastime and our happiness will grow.

William Wordsworth, 'Personal Talk', in E. de Selincourt, editor, *The Poetical Works of William Wordsworth*, Oxford at the Clarendon Press, 1947, volume IV, page 74

It is a marvel of literature that the most profound conceptions of the sin and guilt of mankind are the subject-matters of a sacred literature more cheerful and hopeful, more invigorating and comforting, than any that has ever existed.

Henry Ward Beecher, *Proverbs from Plymouth Pulpit*, Charles Burnet & Co., 1887, page 128

There is, first, the literature of knowledge; and, secondly, the literature of power. The function of the first is—to teach; the function of the second is—to move: the first is a rudder; the second, an oar or a sail. The first speaks to the mere discursive understanding; the second speaks ultimately, as it may happen, to the higher understanding or reason, but always through affections of pleasure and sympathy.

Thomas de Quincey, 'The Poetry of Pope', in *De Quincey's Works*, A. & C. Black, 1897, volume XI, page 54

The peoples of the West no longer share a literature and a system of ancient wisdom. All that they now have in common is science and information. Now, science is knowledge, not wisdom; deals with quantities, not with the qualities of which we are immediately aware. In so far as we are enjoying and suffering beings, its words seem to us mostly irrelevant and beside the point. Moreover, these words are arranged without art; therefore possess no magical power and are incapable of propping or moulding the mind of the reader.

Aldous Huxley, *The Olive Tree*, Chatto & Windus, 1936, page 42

'To write well' means far more than choosing the apt word or the telling arrangement of syllables, though it means these things as well; it is a matter of feeling and living at the required depth, fending off the continual temptation to be glib and shallow, to appeal to the easily aroused response, to be evasive and shirk the hard issues. It is a matter of training oneself to live with reality, and, as our greatest living poet has warned us: 'Human kind cannot bear very much reality'. But, if one is to write well, one *must* bear it: increasing the dose, perhaps, until one can absorb it in quantities that would unhinge the ordinary person.

John Wain, *Sprightly Running*, Macmillan & Co., 1962, page 263

Tolstoi comes before us as a man who has himself lived deeply, a man who has had an intense thirst for life, and who has satisfied that thirst. He has craved to know life, to know women, the joy of wine, the fury of battle, the taste of the ploughman's sweat in the field. He has known all these things, not as material to make books, but as the slaking of instinctive personal passions. And in knowing them he has stored up a wealth of experiences from which he drew as he came to make books, and which bear about them that peculiar haunting fragrance only yielded by the things which have been lived through, personally, in the far past.

Havelock Ellis, *Affirmations*, Constable and Company, 1915, page 140

This is the age of *books*. And we should reverence books. Consider! except a living man there is nothing more wonderful than a book—a message to us from the dead, from human souls whom we never saw, who lived perhaps thousands of miles away, and yet in those little sheets of paper speak to us, amuse us, terrify us, teach us, comfort us, open their hearts to us as brothers!

We ought to reverence books, to look at them as awful and mighty things. If they are good and true, whether they are about religion or politics, trade or medicine, they are messengers of Christ, the Maker of all things, the Teacher of all truth, which He has put into the heart of some men to speak.

Charles Kingsley, *Daily Thoughts*, Macmillan and Co., 1884, page 57

There are some books, when we close them; one or two in the course of our life, difficult as it may be to analyse or ascertain the cause: our minds seem to have made a great leap. A thousand obscure things receive light; a multitude of indefinite feelings are determined. Our intellect grasps and grapples with all subjects with a capacity, a flexibility and a vigour before unknown to us. It masters questions hitherto perplexing, which are not even touched or referred to in the volume just closed. What is this magic? It is the spirit of the supreme author, by a magnetic influence blending with our sympathising intelligence, that directs and inspires it. By that mysterious sensibility we extend to questions which he has not treated the same intellectual force which he has exercised over those which he has expounded. His genius for a time remains in us.

Benjamin Disraeli, *Coningsby*, Peter Davies, 1927, page 129

Reading ought to be an act of homage to the God of all truth. We open our hearts to words that reflect the reality he has created or the greater reality which he is. It is also an act of humility and reverence towards other men who are instruments by which God communicated his truth to us. Reading gives God more glory when we get more out of it, when it is a more deeply vital act not only of our intelligence but of our whole personality, absorbed and refreshed in thought, meditation, prayer, or even in the contemplation of God.

Books can speak to us like God, like men or like the noise of the city we live in. They speak to us like God when they bring us light and peace and fill us with silence. They speak to us like God when we desire never to leave them. They speak to us like men when we desire to hear them again. They speak to us like the noise of the city when they hold us captive by a weariness that tells us nothing, give us no peace and support, nothing to remember, and yet will not let us escape. Books that speak like God speak with too much authority to entertain us. Those that speak like good men hold us by their human charm; we grow by finding ourselves in them. They teach us to know ourselves better by recognizing ourselves in another.

Books that speak like the noise of multitudes reduce us to despair by the sheer weight of their emptiness. They entertain us like the lights of the city streets at night, by hopes they cannot fulfil.

Great though books may be, friends though they may be to us, they are no substitute for persons, they are only means of contact with great persons, with men who had more than their own share of humanity, men who were persons for the whole world and not for themselves alone.

Ideas and words are not the food of the intelligence, but truth. And not an abstract truth that feeds the mind alone. The Truth that a spiritual man seeks is the whole Truth, reality, existence and essence together, something that can be embraced and loved, something that can sustain the homage and the service of our actions: more than a thing: persons, or a Person. Him above all whose essence is to exist. God, Christ, the Incarnate Word, is the Book of Life in whom we read God.

Thomas Merton, *Thoughts in Solitude*, Burns & Oates, 1958, page 52

LONGING

Longing—yearn, wish vehemently, for thing or to do

I find I'm surrounded by people with longings. I remember a fifteen-year-old boy in our youth fellowship at Bradford Cathedral confiding in me that he would do anything for money. In London, we used to joke about the longing for greatness seen in one of our chaplains. We reckoned he wanted to be Pope. In working amongst young people there has been abundant evidence of longing in the whole realm of sexuality. The large number of weddings at which I've officiated suggest a deep longing for relationships. In college a longing for distinction can be seen in academic endeavour, whether this be in the arts or in the sciences. Recently two of our old members have been in the public eye for sporting achievements—one playing rugby for Australia in the World Cup (which they won), and the other competing in the Olympics. If we were to examine the careers chosen by our graduates we would find evidence of a multiplicity of longings. Can a longing for power, for instance, be detected in the fact that Clement Attlee, Harold Wilson, Bob Hawke (Prime Minister of Australia) and Bill Clinton, President of the United States, have all passed through the portals of University College, Oxford? Perhaps Sir Stephen Spender and C.S. Lewis (old members of Univ.) were moved by literary longings, and Stephen Hawking by scientific longings, in wanting to solve some of the mysteries of the universe.

All of us have longings of one sort or another. I sometimes wonder if our longing for God and quest for ultimate reality is the deepest longing of all.

As a hart longs for flowing streams, so longs my soul for thee, O God.

Psalm 42:1

My soul longs, yea, faints for the courts of the Lord; my heart and flesh sing for joy to the living God.

Psalm 84:2

For the creation waits with eager longing for the revealing of the sons of God.

Romans 8:19

Here indeed we groan, and long to put on our heavenly dwelling.

2 Corinthians 5:2

In every man's bosom there is that which at times longs for something better and purer than he is.

Henry Ward Beecher, *Proverbs from Plymouth Pulpit*, Charles Burnet & Co., 1887, page 116

This longing is for the one who is felt in the dark, but not seen in the day.

Rabindranath Tagore, 'Stray Birds', LXXXVIII, in *Collected Poems & Plays of Rabindranath Tagore*, Macmillan & Co., 1936, page 298

There is such a longing for religion among the people in the large cities. Many a labourer in a factory or shop has had a pious childhood. But city life sometimes takes away the 'early dew of morning.' Still the longing for the 'old, old story' remains; whatever is in the bottom of the heart, stays there.

Vincent van Gogh, *Dear Theo: an autobiography of Vincent van Gogh*, edited by Irving Stone, Constable & Company, 1937, page 7

Your whole life now must be one of longing, if you are to achieve perfection. And this longing must be in the depths of your will, put there by God, with your consent. But a word of warning: he is a jealous lover, and will brook no rival; he will not work in your will if he has not sole charge; he does not ask for help, he asks for you.

The Cloud of Unknowing, translated by Clifton Wolters, Penguin Books, 1978, page 60

He found God in solitude, 'the source and reason of all joy,' but he still felt, even after he had found God, an unfulfilled longing for intimacy. It was an undifferentiated longing that did not know whether it longed for God or for a human being. It was dark and unknowing like the heart of a leopard, fierce and violent like the heart of a lion, cold and unloving like the heart of a wolf.

John S. Dunne, *The Reasons of the Heart*, SCM Press, 1978, page 112

Once the longing for money comes, the longing also comes for what money can give: superfluities, nice rooms, luxuries at table, more clothes, fans and so on. Our needs will increase, for one thing brings another, and the result will be endless dissatisfaction. This is how it comes. If you ever happen to have to get things, remember that the superiors have to depend on you. As a religious you must buy things of cheaper quality and your good example in saving will keep up the spirit of poverty.

Mother Teresa, *Jesus, the Word to be Spoken*, compiled by Brother Angelo Devananda, William Collins Sons & Co., 1990, page 92

This longing, this love has, we believe, undoubtedly been implanted in us by God; and as the eye naturally demands light and vision and our body by its nature desires food and drink, so our mind cherishes a natural and appropriate longing to know God's truth and to learn the causes of things.

Now we have not received this longing from God on the condition that it should not or could not ever be satisfied; for in that case the 'love of truth' would appear to have been implanted in our mind by God the Creator to no purpose, if its gratification is never to be accomplished.

Origen, in G.W. Butterworth, *Origen on First Principles*, SPCK, 1936, page 149

For just as there is in God the quality of sympathy and pity, so too in him is there that of thirst and longing. And in virtue of this longing which is in Christ we in turn long for him too. No soul comes to heaven without it. This quality of longing and thirst springs from God's eternal goodness just as pity does. Though, to my mind, longing and pity are quite distinct, it is the same goodness that gives point to the spiritual thirst; a thirst which persists in him as long as we are in need, and which draws us up to his blessedness. All this was seen in the revelation of his compassion.

Julian of Norwich, *Revelations of Divine Love*, translated by Clifton Wolters, Penguin Books, 1976, page 109

In saying: 'I know who I am' Don Quixote said only: 'I know what I will be!' That is the hinge of all human life: to know what one wills to be. Little ought you to care who you are; the urgent thing is what you will to be. The being that you are is but an unstable, perishable being, which eats of the earth and which the earth some day will eat; what you will to be is the idea of you in God, the Consciousness of the universe; it is the divine idea of which you are the manifestation in time and space. And your longing impulse toward the one you will to be is only homesickness drawing toward your divine home. Man is complete and upstanding only when he would be more than man.

Miguel de Cervantes Saavedra, *The Life of Don Quixote and Sancho*, translated by Homer P. Earle, Alfred A. Knopf, 1927, page 33

We see a Christian who desires God very much. He finds it hard to meditate and think with the mind about God because the mind is feeble and scatterbrained. He may find it hard to pray intelligently for this or that person or for this or that cause, and is very conscious of weakness and inadequacy. But in the very acknowledgement of weakness, inadequacy, and inability to pray, there is a deep longing for God. He wants God very much; he is hungry and thirsty for God, and perhaps all he is able to tell God is that he has a hunger and thirst for him, though even that is very feeble, but he wishes that the hunger and thirst were more.

And this longing for God, when released in simplicity, appears to be, not something that the brain is doing, but rather something in the depths of the person—call it personality, or the self, or the soul: call it what you will. A writer, Father Augustine Baker, spoke of this longing as the prayer that comes 'from the ground of the soul'. Well, this hungry longing for God leads on to an experience in which the self—emptying itself of its own capacities—finds itself filled by God.

Michael Ramsey, in Margaret Duggan, editor, *Through the Year with Michael Ramsey*, Hodder and Stoughton, 1975, page 153

Have you never cried in your hearts with longing, almost with impatience, 'Surely, surely, there is an ideal Holy One somewhere—or else, how could have arisen in my mind the conception, however faint, of an ideal holiness? But where? oh, where? Not in the world around strewn with unholiness. Not in myself, unholy too, without and within. Is there a Holy One, whom I may contemplate with utter delight? and if so, where is He? oh, that I might behold, if but for a moment, His perfect beauty, even though, as in the fable of Semele of old, "the lightning of His glance were death."' . . . And then, oh, then—has there not come that for which our spirit was athirst—the very breath of pure air, the very gleam of pure light, the very strain of pure music for it is the very music of the spheres—in those words, 'Holy, holy, holy, Lord God Almighty, which was, and is, and is to come'? Yes, whatever else is unholy, there is a Holy One—spotless and undefiled, serene and self-contained. Whatever else I cannot trust, there is One whom I can trust utterly. Whatever else I am dissatisfied with, there is One whom I can contemplate with utter satisfaction and bathe my stained soul in that eternal fount of purity. And who is He? Who, save the Cause and Maker and Ruler of all things past, present, and to come?

Charles Kingsley, *Daily Thoughts*, Macmillan & Co., 1884, page 73

All our spirits are born of God's Spirit; the likeness of God's own nature is planted in every one of us; and therefore our spirits can never be at rest till they reach the heavenly fountain from which they came. Unhappily we do not understand our own selves: we feel the thirst within us, but we are long before we learn what alone will quench it.

The thirst of the spirit is chiefly of two kinds, the desire of light and the desire of love. No one surely is without the desire of light. We all are constantly meeting with things which provoke us to ask within ourselves, What is this? how is this? why is this? If we are not curious about such things as books might tell us, we still are troubled with much greater questions. We cannot help seeing what is going on around us among our friends and neighbours, and then we ask how it is that this or that event happens to them. We are still more troubled by thoughts about ourselves and our present and future life. We wonder how a world so full of evil and sorrow can be the work of a good God. This is a longing for light. It is partly satisfied every time that a word spoken by any one else, or a verse from the Bible, or any other cause gives us a hint which throws light upon what was dark before. And the more we know, the more we desire to know, and then we soon find that there is no teaching like God's own; and all His words and works seem to give forth ever fresh light so long as we remember that they do indeed proceed from Him. At last we find that nothing less can satisfy us than God Himself to shew us all truth, and we fall on our knees before Him, and pray Him to scatter all our darkness, and fill us wholly with His own light.

The desire of love is a still deeper thirst of the spirit. There is to us a delight in the presence and affection of those who are dear to us, which we would not exchange for any thing that men could give us, whether it be child, or father, or mother, or husband, or wife, or brother, or sister that we love. They partly satisfy the thirst of our hearts, as God meant that they should. But they are not always the same to us; sometimes, it may be, fretful, sometimes cold: and then, it may be, they die from among us, and our eyes can behold them no more. The more tenderly we love them, the more we shall feel that they cannot exhaust our love, that there is something within us which longs after One who cannot change like poor weak mortals, whose love is as deep and constant as the everlasting heavens, from whose presence death itself cannot cut us off. Our love is therefore never fulfilled till it lays hold upon God Himself, and renews itself from that never-failing source.

F.J.A. Hort, *Village Sermons*, Macmillan and Co., Second Series, 1905, page 198

MATERIALISM

Materialism—opinion that nothing exists but matter and its movements and modifications; that consciousness and will are wholly due to material agency; tendency to lay stress on material aspect of objects

Our expedition to Nepal in 1963 was an eye-opener. We spent the first two months completing our scientific project, and then went on a trek to a remote part of Nepal. We eventually pitched our tents between two villages at 10,000 feet on the slopes of Annapurna. Here we made a film of village life, which was later shown on TV.

Life was very simple in the villages. There were no shops, no telephones, no vehicles, no electricity, no newspapers, and in the houses, very little furniture. The nearest doctor was several days' walk away, in Pokhara. Most of the able-bodied inhabitants were involved in subsistence farming, with crops of rice and maize, and if the harvest failed, there were big problems. A few of the inhabitants had primitive looms and wove blankets, and we saw at least one elderly man making baskets. Life was primitive and hard, particularly as regards health. However, an atmosphere of peace prevailed in the villages, and the surrounding mountains made it a place of great beauty. We became aware of that unusual quality in the lives of local inhabitants—contentment. We were impressed with the quality of family relationships, especially the love and care expressed for children and the elderly.

What a contrast when we returned to Britain. I for one was hard hit by the impact of materialism. It's true there have been enormous benefits from the findings of science and technology, but at a cost. We can see this in the environment, and in the whole realm of personal relationships, and in the breakdown of traditional beliefs. We are now in danger of destroying ourselves, as materialism more and more becomes the order of the day.

Man does not live by bread alone, but... by everything that proceeds out of the mouth of the Lord.

Deuteronomy 8:3

Surely every man stands as a mere breath! Surely man goes about as a shadow! Surely for nought are they in turmoil; man heaps up, and knows not who will gather!

Psalm 39:5–6

As for what was sown among thorns, this is he who hears the word, but the cares of the world and the delight in riches choke the word, and it proves unfruitful.

Matthew 13:22

Take heed, and beware of all covetousness; for a man's life does not consist in the abundance of his possessions.

Luke 12:15

How amazing are those moments when we really possess our possessions!

Logan Pearsall Smith, *Afterthoughts*, Constable & Company, 1931, page 60

Set the bird's wings with gold and it will never again soar in the sky.

Rabindranath Tagore, 'Stray Birds', CCXXXI, in *Collected Poems & Plays of Rabindranath Tagore*, Macmillan & Co., 1936, page 316

Those who have everything but thee, O God, laugh at those who have nothing but thyself.

Rabindranath Tagore, 'Stray Birds', CCXXVI, in *Collected Poems & Plays of Rabindranath Tagore*, Macmillan & Co., 1936, page 316

... there is a hunger of the heart which it is not in material things to satisfy.

William Barclay, *The Gospel of Matthew*, The Saint Andrew Press, 1987, volume I, page 68

To the covetous man life is a nightmare, and God lets him wrestle with it as best he may.

Henry Ward Beecher, *Proverbs from Plymouth Pulpit*, Charles Burnet & Co., 1887, page 42

The world continues to offer glittering prizes to those who have stout hearts and sharp swords.

Lord Birkenhead, in Ephesian, editor, *The Pocket Birkenhead*, Mills & Boon, 1927, page 76

Convincing man that happiness lies in consumerism is making him dependent, and indeed enslaving him, to material goods.

Michel Quoist, *With Open Heart*, translated by Colette Copeland, Gill and Macmillan, 1983, page 217

The newer people, of this modern age, are more eager to amass than to realize. They are in their generation, wiser than the children of light.

Rabindranath Tagore, 'The Cycle of Spring', in *Collected Poems & Plays of Rabindranath Tagore*, Macmillan & Co., 1936, page 35

The splash of wealth can distract the rich from the needs of the poor and make them forget their humanity. Wealth also seems to be a source of perpetual anxiety.

Christopher Bryant, SSJE., *The Heart in Pilgrimage*, Darton, Longman and Todd, 1980, page 41

What gives a man lasting significance is not the accumulation he leaves behind, but rather the activity and zest that permeates his life and passes itself on to others.

Johann Wolfgang von Goethe, *Wisdom and Experience*, selected by Ludwig Curtius, translated and edited by Hermann J. Weigand, Routledge & Kegan Paul, 1949, page 146

There must be reasonable men everywhere; men who refuse to wear away their faculties in a degrading effort to plunder one another, men who are tired of hustle and strife.

Norman Douglas, *An Almanac*, Chatto & Windus in association with Secker & Warburg, 1945, page 39

There is peril when men assess prosperity by material things, when civilization is assessed in terms of money and material goods. It is to be remembered that it is always true that a man may lose his soul far more easily in prosperity than in adversity; and he is on the way to losing his soul when he assesses the value of life by the number of things which he possesses.

William Barclay, *The Letters to Timothy and Titus*, The Saint Andrew Press, 1965, page 212

No amount of technological progress will cure the hatred that eats away the vitals of materialistic society like a spiritual cancer. The only cure is, and must always be, spiritual. There is not much use talking to men about God and love if they are not able to listen. The ears with which one hears the message of the Gospel are hidden in man's heart, and these ears do not hear anything unless they are favoured with a certain interior solitude and silence.

Thomas Merton, *Thoughts in Solitude*, Burns & Oates, 1958, page 13

Our generation has made such immense discoveries, has achieved such undreamed enrichments of the outside of life, that it has rather lost touch, I think, with the inside of life. It has forgotten the true riches and beauties of its spiritual inheritance: riches and beauties that go far beyond our modern chatter about values and ideals. The human mind's thirst for more and more breadth has obscured the human heart's craving for more and more depth.

Evelyn Underhill, in John Stobbart, editor, *The Wisdom of Evelyn Underhill*, A.R. Mowbray & Co., 1951, page 19

Read the first chapter of Genesis without prejudice, and you will be convinced at once. After the narrative of the Creation of the earth and brute animals, Moses seems to pause, and says: 'And God said, Let us make man in *our image*, after *our* likeness.' And in the next chapter, he repeats the narrative: 'And the Lord God formed man of the dust of the ground, and breathed into his nostrils the breath of life;' and then he adds these words—'*and man became a living soul.*' Materialism will never explain those last words.

Samuel Taylor Coleridge, *Table Talk and Omniana of Samuel Taylor Coleridge*, Oxford University Press, 1917, page 39

Communities which live simply and without waste, and which do not use television all the time, help people to discover a whole new way of life, which demands fewer financial resources but more commitment to relationships and to celebration. Is there a better way to bridge the gulf which widens daily between rich and poor countries? It is not simply a question of generous people going to work in developing countries. Rich countries themselves have to be awakened to the fact that happiness is not to be found in a frantic search for material goods, but in simple and loving relationships, lived and celebrated in communities which have renounced that search.

Jean Vanier, *Community and Growth*, Darton, Longman and Todd, 1991, page 309

Mammoth productive facilities with computer minds, cities that engulf the landscape and pierce the clouds, planes that almost outrace time—these are awesome, but they cannot be spiritually inspiring. Nothing in our glittering technology can raise man to new heights, because material growth has been made an end in itself, and, in the absence of moral purpose, man himself becomes smaller as the works of man become bigger. Gargantuan industry and government, woven into an intricate, computerized mechanism, leave the person outside. The sense of participation is lost, the feeling that ordinary individuals influence important decisions vanishes, and man becomes separated and diminished.

When an individual is no longer a true participant, when he no longer feels a sense of responsibility to his society, the content of democracy is emptied. When culture is degraded and vulgarity enthroned, when the social system does not build security but induces peril, inexorably the individual is impelled to pull away from a soulless society. This process produces alienation—perhaps the most pervasive and insiduous development in contemporary society.

Martin Luther King, *The Words of Martin Luther King*, selected by Coretta Scott King, William Collins Sons & Co., 1986, page 19

It is stupidity and madness to want always that which can neither satisfy nor even diminish your desire. While enjoying those riches, you strive for what is missing and are dissatisfied, longing for what you lack. Thus the restless mind, running to and fro among the pleasures of life, is tired out but never satisfied; like the starving man who thinks whatever he stuffs down his throat is not enough, for his eyes see what remains to be eaten. Thus man craves continually for what is missing with no less fear than he possesses with joy what is in front of him. Who can have everything? A man clings to the fruits of his work (however small they may be), never knowing when he will have the sorrow of losing them, yet he is certain to lose them some day. In like manner a perverted will contends for what is best, and hastens in a straight line toward what will afford it the most satisfaction. Rather vanity makes sport of it in those tortuous ways, and evil deceives itself. If you wish to accomplish in this way what you desire, to gain hold of that which leaves nothing further to be desired, why bother about the rest? You are running on crooked roads and will die long before you reach the end you are seeking.

The wicked, therefore, walk round in circles, naturally wanting whatever will satisfy their desires, yet foolishly rejecting that which would lead them to their true end, which is not in consumption but in consummation. Hence they exhaust themselves in vain instead of perfecting their lives by a blessed end. They take more pleasure in the appearance of things than in their Creator, examining all and wanting to test them one by one before trying to reach the Lord of the universe. They might even succeed in doing so if they could ever gain hold of what they wish for; that is, if any one man could take possession of all things without him who is their Principle. By the very law of man's desire which makes him want what he lacks in place of what he has or grow weary of what he has in preference to what he lacks, once he has obtained and despised all in heaven and on earth, he will hasten toward the only one who is missing, the God of all. There he will rest, for just as there is no rest this side of eternity, so there will be no restlessness to bother him on the other side. Then he will say for sure: 'It is good for me to adhere to God.' He will even add to that: 'What is there for me in heaven and what have I desired on earth, if you?' And, also: 'God of my heart, God, my lot forever.' Therefore, as I said, whoever desires the greatest good can succeed in reaching it, if he can first gain possession of all he desires short of that good itself.

This is altogether impossible because life is too short, strength too weak, competition too keen, men too fatigued by the long road and vain efforts; wishing to attain all they desire, yet unable to reach the end of all their wants. If they could only be content with reaching all in thought and not in deed.

Bernard of Clairvaux, 'On Loving God', in *Treatises II*, Cistercian Publications, 1980, page 111

MATURITY

Maturity—complete in natural development; with fully developed powers of body and mind

Someone once asked me what I was trying to do in my anthologies and reflection groups. I had difficulty at first in giving a clear answer. In the end I settled for *maturity*, and went on to outline three areas in which people might benefit from using these books in the practice of reflection. The first is in developing the mind and the capacity to think. Ever since reading Harry Blamires' book, *The Christian Mind*, I have been convinced of the importance of educating the Christian mind. A common reaction to *Visions of Hope* is: 'It makes me think.' Once people start thinking for themselves about the deeper things in life, they are on their way to maturity.

The second is in educating the feelings. So often the emphasis of modern education is on getting people through exams. I can understand this, for in a competitive world qualifications are important. However I do hope there is still room in our schools and universities for an education of the feelings. How often have I seen people come to grief, particularly in the realm of personal relationships, because feelings and emotions are in a primitive state. *Visions of Hope* and the practice of reflection can be used to rectify this and educate our feelings.

The third is to foster 'the daily increase' in the Holy Spirit, and so lead on to maturity in the spiritual dimension. The Swiss psychologist C.G. Jung warned us of the dangers of the superficial nature of Christian faith in so many people in modern times. *Visions of Hope* brings together an important part of our spiritual heritage to foster spiritual maturity through the practice of reflection. Let us hope that the pages of this book will lead to greater maturity in the areas mentioned.

... do not be children in your thinking; be babes in evil, but in thinking be mature.

1 Corinthians 14:20

... until we all attain to the unity of the faith and of the knowledge of the Son of God.

Ephesians 4:13

But solid food is for the mature, for those who have their faculties trained by practice to distinguish good from evil.

Hebrews 5:14

Therefore let us leave the elementary doctrine of Christ and go on to maturity.

Hebrews 6:1

God instructs the heart, not by means of ideas, but by pains and contradictions.

Jean Pierre de Caussade, S.J., *Self Abandonment to Divine Providence*, translated by Algar Thorold, William Collins Sons & Co., 1972, page 100

And man matures through work
which inspires him to difficult good.

Karol Wojtyla, 'The Quarry', 11, 'Inspiration', in *Easter Vigil and Other Poems*, translated by Jerzy Peterkiewicz, Hutchinson & Co. (Publishers), 1979, page 28

Maturity: among other things, the unclouded happiness of the child at play, who takes it for granted that he is at one with his play-mates.

Dag Hammarskjöld, *Markings*, translated by W.H. Auden & Leif Sjoberg, foreword by W.H. Auden, Faber and Faber, 1964, page 89

It may almost be a question whether such wisdom as many of us have in our mature years has not come from the dying out of the power of temptation, rather than as the results of thought and resolution.

Anthony Trollope, *The Small House at Allington*, The Zodiac Press, 1963, page 133

What our civilization needs today, as a condition for increasing human maturity and for an inner renewal, is the cultivation of an exquisite sensibility and an incomparable tenderness.

Lewis Mumford, *The Conduct of Life*, Secker & Warburg, 1952, page 153

It is more important for the old to maintain serenity and self-respect than to recapture enthusiasm and emotion. Plato held that 'if a man is moderate and tolerant, then age need be no burden to him; and if he is not then even youth is full of cares.'

Hubert van Zeller, *Considerations*, Sheed and Ward, 1974, page 62

Reaching maturity is painful chiefly because so many conclusions have to be reappraised—if not altogether scrapped. Not that in maturity one is ever quite sure of one's conclusions, but at least one does not have to be forever changing them.

Hubert van Zeller, *Considerations*, Sheed and Ward, 1974, page 64

Poverty of mind as a spiritual attitude is a growing willingness to recognise the incomprehensibility of the mystery of life. The more mature we become the more we will be able to give up our inclination to grasp, catch, and comprehend the fullness of life and the more we will be ready to let life enter into us.

Henri J.M. Nouwen, *Reaching Out*, William Collins Sons & Co., 1980, page 96

The mark of the spiritually mature man is that he can endure sorrow without bitterness, bewilderment without fuss, loss without envy or recrimination or self-pity. Above all, whatever the set-backs and misunderstandings, public and private, that he maintains a belief in the essential goodness of mankind.

Hubert van Zeller, *Considerations*, Sheed and Ward, 1974, page 122

There can be confusion of thought in this matter of maturity. Maturity need not necessarily go with being a man or woman of the world. The saints are the mature people, and they are certainly not men and women of the world. There is this about maturity—that it does not go with putting on an act. The moment a person pretends to be what he is not, he is nothing. The saints did not pretend; so they were simple, so they were mature.

Hubert van Zeller, *Leave Your Life Alone*, Sheed and Ward, 1973, page 100

... there seems to be some consensus among those in the psychological field... concerning the characteristics such self-actualized or mature people will display. They will be, for instance, accepting, spontaneous, able to enjoy privacy, 'peak-experienced', and humour, and to relate to others irrespective of race, class, education or religion, having some few relationships which are able to go deep.

Frank Wright, *The Pastoral Nature of the Ministry*, SCM Press, 1980, page 25

Man, having come into the full possession of his sphere of action, his strength, his maturity and his unity, will at last have become an adult being; and having reached this apogee of his responsibility and freedom, holding in his hands all his future and all his past, will make the choice between arrogant autonomy and loving excentration.

This will be the final choice: whether a world is to revolt or to adore.

Pierre Teilhard de Chardin, *The Future of Man*, translated by Norman Denny, William Collins Sons & Co., 1982, page 19

A mature religion is integral in nature—that means that it is flexible enough to integrate all new knowledge within its frame of reference and keep pace with all the new discoveries of the human mind. It indeed takes the cross into the spacecraft. Going to school means starting on the road to science, and if religion does not follow the same road with an open and critical eye, the grown adult who flies the ocean in superjets might be religiously still content with a tricyle. Essential for mature religion is the constant willingness to shift gears, to integrate new insights, and to revise our positions.

Henri J.M. Nouwen, in Robert Durbach, editor, *Seeds of Hope*, Darton, Longman and Todd, 1989, page 46

The mature person is not the 'ideal person', the one who from a particular moral standpoint has reached perfection. The gospel injunction, 'Be ye perfect' which has caused such feelings of guilt and inadequacy in so many people should really be translated, 'be rounded, complete, mature'; and maturity cannot be seen as a fixed, predictable goal or static point. Rather it is a road, a direction of movement. 'Each growth stage has its new opportunities and hazards, with fresh frustrations and unexpected open doors. Whatever else the future is, it is always a surprise.' It is important to recognize that maturity and moral perfection are not synonymous since any fullness of vision will have to include the dark side of our being, the almost cosmic battle that we all know within ourselves, even when we find it hard to admit.

Frank Wright, *The Pastoral Nature of the Ministry*, SCM Press, 1980, page 27

A maturity check-up

1. A mature person does not take himself too seriously—his job, yes!
2. A mature person keeps himself alert in mind.
3. A mature person does not always 'view with alarm' every adverse situation that arises.
4. A mature person is too big to be little.
5. A mature person has faith in himself which becomes stronger as it is fortified by his faith in God.
6. A mature person never feels too great to do the little things and never too proud to do the humble things.
7. A mature person never accepts either success or failure in themselves as permanent.
8. A mature person never accepts any one of his moods as permanent.
9. A mature person is one who is able to control his impulses.
10. A mature person is not afraid to make mistakes.

Leonard Wedel, source unknown

Essential to maturity... is a sufficient rising above pose which enables a man spontaneously to express his own nature to the full. It is frank perception of the person he really is and of his ability, by God's grace, to maintain his identity. It is not... the man's 'moulding of his own life into completeness' but rather the handing of his own life over to the life of God for moulding. Since the life of God is expressed for us in the life of Christ, the moulding to which the mature Christian submits himself will assume, on a major part of the process, the cross. The element of suffering in the Christian's growing up is not a fortuitous circumstance. It is not accidental but essential. The serious Christian does not opt for suffering or leave it out according to temperament and attraction: it will be there in his life whether he feels spiritually drawn to it or not. It is not only an ideal but a datum. For Christian perfection it is a sine qua non, and one ventures to think that even as regards psychological stature the bitter experience of sorrow and rejection must be part of the training. Outward defeat, inward sense of failure: maturity is the phoenix.

Hubert van Zeller, *Leave Your Life Alone*, Sheed and Ward, 1973, page 101

MIND

Mind—direction of thoughts or desires; way of thinking and feeling, seat of consciousness; thought, volition, and feeling; person as embodying mental qualities

I was delighted with my rooms in Balliol. They were old and had a medieval feel about them. Sadly, they no longer exist. I had only been in residence a few days when I learnt they had once been occupied by a famous person—William Temple, an outstanding Archbishop of Canterbury. What an atmosphere in which to carry out one's undergraduate studies. I was intrigued and immediately went out and bought his biography, *William Temple* by F.A. Iremonger.

Here was a man who impressed me with the sheer quality of his mind. He went on to be a lecturer in philosophy at Queen's College, Oxford, and wrote a major work—*The Creative Mind*. Later he combined his philosophy with theology, and became one of the most influential thinkers in the Church of England in recent times. I've included many of his insights in this and the other anthologies, *Visions of Love* and *Visions of Faith*.

'You shall love the Lord your God . . . with all your mind.' What a challenge for us to use our minds. 'Have this mind among yourselves, which is yours in Christ Jesus.' What a command. 'Be transformed by the renewal of your mind.' What potential.

The quotations which make up *Visions of Hope* have been gathered from the great minds of earlier generations. The practice of reflection is a way to develop our minds on these lines.

Prove me, O Lord, and try me; test my heart and my mind. For thy steadfast love is before my eyes, and I walk in faithfulness to thee.

Psalm 26:2–3

For the inward mind and heart of a man are deep!

Psalm 64:6

You shall love the Lord your God . . . with all your mind.

Mark 12:30

Have this mind among yourselves, which is yours in Christ Jesus.

Philippians 2:5

It is the mind that maketh good or ill,
That maketh wretch or happy, rich or poor.

Edmund Spenser, 'The Faerie Queene', Book VI, XI. xxx. 1, in *The Works of Edmund Spenser*, The Johns Hopkins Press, 1961, page 109

But the essential thing is to put oneself in a frame of mind which is close to that of prayer.

Henri Matisse, in Françoise Gilot and Carlton Lake, *Life with Picasso*, Thomas Nelson and Sons, 1965, page 245

The centre of nature is in the human mind. The meaning of the outward world is not in itself but in us.

Henry Ward Beecher, *Proverbs from Plymouth Pulpit*, Charles Burnet & Co., 1887, page 26

The Divine Mind does not think for us, or in spite of us, but works in us to think, and to will, and to do.

Henry Ward Beecher, ***Proverbs from Plymouth Pulpit*****, Charles Burnet & Co., 1887, page 153**

Thinkers sometimes look on doers with pity. Things are always easier and more attractive in the mind....

Michel Quoist, ***With Open Heart*****, translated by Colette Copeland, Gill and Macmillan, 1983, page 135**

Few of us... make the most of our minds. The body ceases to grow in a few years; but the mind, if we will let it, may grow almost as long as life lasts.

Sir John Lubbock, ***The Pleasures of Life*****, Macmillan & Co., 1904, part II, page 250**

Christ presents to the mind a better, wider, deeper, and more correct theory and conception of what God is than can be derived from nature or philosophy or any of the analogies of human life or human experience.

Henry Ward Beecher, ***Proverbs from Plymouth Pulpit*****, Charles Burnet & Co., 1887, page 147**

The truth of things is what they are in the mind of God, and it is only when we act according to the mind of God that we are acting in accordance with the truth, in accordance with reality. Everything else is making a mistake.

William Temple, ***Basic Convictions*****, Hamish Hamilton, 1937, page 78**

No man is changed till his mind is changed. We do most of our living within. Our deeds express our thoughts. It is into our minds that Christ must come if He is to come into our lives. From our minds, He will shape our character, discipline our will and control our bodies.

W.E. Sangster, ***The Secret of Radiant Life*****, Hodder and Stoughton, 1957, page 174**

It is a hard thing for a man to take such an instrument as the human mind and keep it in tune with itself, and also keep it in accord with other minds, with their different temperaments, and in all their varying moods, and under all their trials and swayings, and warpings and biasings.

Henry Ward Beecher, ***Proverbs from Plymouth Pulpit*****, Charles Burnet & Co., 1887, page 30**

There is a certain paradox in the human situation. God gave man a mind, and it is man's duty to use that mind to think to the very limits of human thought. But it is also true that there are times when that mind can only go so far, and, when that limit is reached, all that is left is to accept and to adore.

William Barclay, ***The Letter to the Romans*****, The Saint Andrew Press, 1969, page 167**

By use of its capacity for free ideas, it [the mind] conceives situations for its organism which do not exist, and directs the energies of the organism towards bringing these into existence. Thus are initiated moral action and responsibility, art, science and every form of deliberate progress.

William Temple, ***Nature, Man and God*****, Macmillan & Co., 1934, page 504**

This is a plea for the use of the whole mind, intellectual and emotional, detached and involved; for only when the whole mind is alive can imagination work and creatively operate. And the trouble is that so many institutions formally connected with education and with morality behave as if they had, at best, only half a mind.

Roy Stevens, ***Education and the Death of Love*****, Epworth Press, 1978, page 138**

How can we attain to the blessed and noble state of mind—the mind of Christ, who must needs be about His Father's business, which is doing good? Only by prayer and practice. There is no more use in praying without practising than there is in practising without praying. You cannot learn to walk without walking; no more than you learn to do good without trying to do good.

Charles Kingsley, *Daily Thoughts*, Macmillan & Co., 1884, page 267

In studying the history of the human mind one is impressed again and again by the fact that the growth of the mind is the widening of the range of consciousness, and that each step forward has been a most painful and laborious achievement. One could almost say that nothing is more hateful to man than to give up even a particle of his unconsciousness. Ask those who have tried to introduce a new idea!

C.G. Jung, *Psychological Reflections*, selected and edited by Jolande Jacobi, Routledge & Kegan Paul, 1953, page 30

... the mind may experience the infinite in itself; that in the human individual there arises sometimes the divine spark which reveals to him the existence of the original, fundamental, principal Being, within which all is contained like a series within its generating formula. The universe is but a radiation of mind; and the radiations of the Divine mind are for us more than mere appearances; they have a reality parallel to our own.

Henri Frédéric Amiel, *Amiel's Journal*, translated by Mrs Humphry Ward, Macmillan & Co., 1918, page 256

We, by the exercise of our own intelligence, are able to penetrate the secrets of nature, and always discover an order more exquisite in the perfection of each detail, more immense in the scope of its range, than our minds can begin to compass. We cannot any longer hesitate in supposing that behind the world of nature there is at work a power, guided by principles such as those which appear also in our own minds. The two things correspond.

William Temple, *Basic Convictions*, Hamish Hamilton, 1937, page 12

There is deep, deep within us the irrational as well. It is our motor energy, our creative demon. You think we know the world only on the basis of what we observe or can deduce logically? No, my good friend. As you grew up, did you meet no one who spoke of his experiences through the use of images rather than logic, who spoke of things that did not correspond to any reality we can observe? The irrational completes us.

Professor Malkuson, in Chaim Potok, *The Book of Lights*, William Heinemann, 1982, page 26

We must love... with all our *mind*... The mind is that which seeks, that which guesses, that which discerns. It is the sword of charity.

It is the mind that distinguishes good from evil; it is the mind that sees the difference between one man and another man. It is the mind that examines and explores, that probes the hidden depths of things. To love with all one's mind is to add justice to one's charity. To love with all one's mind is to pardon superficial imperfections, and to attach oneself to the nobility concealed beneath them. To love with one's mind—with all one's mind—is to understand the needs of other minds, other souls. To love with all one's mind is to detect, wherever they exist, the hunger and thirst of the intellect, and to fly to their relief. To love with all one's mind is to go to the assistance of mind, wherever it lives, wherever it suffers. 'Blessed is he that understandeth concerning the needy and poor,' says Holy Scripture.

Now there are many kinds of poverty.
I repeat of set purpose the sacred words:
'I was hungry, and you gave Me not to eat.'
He loves with all his mind, who has been able to divine the needs of others.

Ernest Hello, *Life, Science, and Art*, R. & T. Washbourne, 1913, page 44

It is certain that He read much. Unlike some of His followers, whose boast it is that the Bible is all they need, Jesus read outside the sacred Canon. For the Hebrew people did not cease to write noble books when the Old Testament was complete. There were works which would be accounted modern in the youth of Jesus, authentic traces of which may be seen in His teaching. I mean especially, *Enoch*, *Sirach*, *The Wisdom of Solomon*, and *The Testaments of the Twelve Patriarchs*. He read, for He had an open mind. But His mind's openness was not like a door that ever stands open to the street, admitting all the litter and odds and ends careless passers-by may cast away and the winds blow in. The open mind should be an active mind. And His was a mind that could sift and divide, taking in all the truths He could attest and use in the upbuilding of Himself, and casting away, like the shavings of His joinery, the mere fancies and wildness of the age. This is wisdom. It is the working of the Spirit of God. And it comes to him who prays.

A.D. Martin, *Aspects of the Way*, Cambridge at the University Press, 1925, page 26

MISSION

Mission—body sent by religious community to convert heathen; field of missionary activity; missionary post; organization in a district for conversion of the people

I was impressed with the work of a missionary society in Nepal. They had been forbidden to proselytize by word of mouth so instead they built a hospital, near Pokhara, in the heart of western Nepal. The quality of their healing work and compassionate care spoke for itself, so something of the Gospel was proclaimed to those who used the hospital. It was well patronized.

There was also an interesting development as regards outreach. The local Nepalese officials would only allow the mission to build a temporary hospital. This consisted of a number of nissen huts. These reflected the light of the sun, so the Gurkhas in the remote hills many miles away, suddenly became aware of a bright light shining in their midst and were curious to know what it was. They soon found out, and came in droves to the hospital with their sick. The 'Shining Hospital', as it came to be called, spoke well of 'Christ, the Light of the World.'

In our own country we tend to think of mission in terms of a massive rally, sometimes conducted in Earl's Court. In college I carry out an ongoing mission using *Visions of Love* and *Visions of Hope* in reflection groups. Sometimes the message gets home swiftly, but on the whole it is a slow steady method with long-term effects. A number of undergraduates have told me it is their most valuable hour of the week.

Sing to the Lord, all the earth! Tell of his salvation from day to day. Declare his glory among the nations, his marvellous works among all the peoples!

1 Chronicles 16:23–24

I heard the voice of the Lord saying, 'Whom shall I send, and who will go for us?' Then I said, 'Here I am! Send me.'

Isaiah 6:8

Go therefore and make disciples of all nations, baptizing them in the name of the Father and of the Son and of the Holy Spirit.

Matthew 28:19

Jesus said to them again, 'Peace be with you. As the Father has sent me, even so I send you.'

John 20:21

In the end the only all-conquering argument is the argument of a Christian life.

William Barclay, *The Gospel of Matthew*, The Saint Andrew Press, 1987, volume I, page 269

Zeal in proselytizing is often due to an uneasy suspicion that we only half-believe.

Mark Rutherford, *More Pages From a Journal*, Oxford University Press, 1910, page 244

We cannot make a man a Christian, but we can do everything possible to bring him into Christ's presence.

William Barclay, *The Gospel of Matthew*, The Saint Andrew Press, 1987, volume I, page 326

The goal of Mission is nothing less than a New Creation, and the Church's renewal occurs only at the same time and to the same extent as the renewal of the world.

Colin Morris, *The Hammer of the Lord*, Epworth Press, 1973, page 33

People resist those whose approaches to them are too intense but always tend to be moved by those who respect them; the apologist must respect the integrity of others as much as he respects his own.

R.E.C. Browne, *The Ministry of the Word*, SCM Press, 1958, page 108

This is the true sequence of mission: a surpassing awareness of the reality of Christ, corporately shared, expressing itself in thankfulness and wonder, causing the world to ask questions to which an answer must be given in a form that every hearer can understand.

John V. Taylor, *The Go-Between God*, SCM Press, 1973, page 112

We cannot cease to be missionary; we have to want the number of Christians to increase, to want their influence, their importance, the concrete realization of a Christian spirit in public affairs and social institutions to grow; we have to try to diminish the contrary of these things.

Karl Rahner, S.J., *Mission and Grace*, translated by Cecily Hastings, Sheed and Ward, 1963, volume I, page 39

If you knew a place where the world's biggest treasure was buried, if you knew that anyone who knew the way could go and help himself to it, and if you knew that the treasure was life and constant love and joy, could you possibly keep it all a secret?

Michel Quoist, *With Open Heart*, translated by Colette Copeland, Gill and Macmillan, 1983, page 33

True intercession in the service of the Christian mission is the purest acknowledgement that the mission is God's not ours. For this reason it is far more significant that a church or a particular missionary fellowship should be, and be seen to be, a community to which God is a burning, joyful reality, than that it should bury itself with vigils of intercession and lists of names.

John V. Taylor, *The Go-Between God*, SCM Press, 1973, page 234

Had he had more of the wisdom of the serpent, he would not have carried them the New Testament as an ending of strife, the words of the Lord as an enlightening law; he would perhaps have known that to try too hard to make people good, is one way to make them worse; that the only way to make them good is to be good—remembering well the beam and the mote; that the time for speaking comes rarely, the time for being never departs.

George Macdonald, *Sir Gibbie*, J.M. Dent & Sons, 1914, page 335

The farther I go the more convinced I am of the futility of religious discussions with unbelievers. The intellectual and historical standpoint to which they confine themselves is not sufficient in view of the phenomena of the spiritual life. All that is living and profound and subtle in the soul is unknown to them,—their soul itself is unknown. Let us rather try to arouse in these people a sense of eternal things, showing them the path to God without barriers or obstacles. That will be enough. Then let us ardently pray, and Providence will do the rest.

Elizabeth Leseur, *A Wife's Story*, Burns & Oates, 1919, page 196

... there are some people who cannot receive Christian truth. It may be that their minds are shut; it may be that their minds are brutalised and covered over with a film of filth; it may be that they have lived a life which has obscured their ability to see the truth; it may be that they are constitutional mockers of all things holy; it may be, as sometimes happens, that we and they have absolutely no common ground on which we can argue. A man can only understand what he is fit to understand. It is not to everyone we can lay bare the secrets of our hearts. There are always those to whom the preaching of Christ will be foolishness, and in whose minds the truth, when expressed in words, will meet an insuperable barrier.

William Barclay, *The Gospel of Matthew*, The Saint Andrew Press, 1987, volume I, page 269

The mission of the church... is to live the ordinary life of men in that extraordinary *awareness* of the other and *self-sacrifice* for the other which the Spirit gives. Christian activity will be very largely the same as the world's activity—earning a living, bringing up a family, making friends, having fun, celebrating occasions, farming, manufacturing, trading, building cities, healing sickness, alleviating distress, mourning, studying, exploring, making music, and so on. Christians will try to do these things to the glory of God, which is to say that they will try to perceive what God is up to in each of these manifold activities and will seek to do it with him by bearing responsibility for the selves of other men.

John V. Taylor, *The Go-Between God*, SCM Press, 1973, page 135

The Gospel is true for all, if it is true at all; and, if so, then upon whomever has received it lies the inescapable obligation to impart it to others. And so here alone is the foundation on which to build a world civilisation. There has been much discussion, naturally and rightly in these days, about the new world order that we want to see. On what principle is it going to be built? Are we going to make it by an extraordinary complex calculation of the various desires and passions and aspirations of the different countries of the world? Certainly these are factors in the situation; we must not ignore them; but is that going to be all? What more shifting sand than that could there be on which to build any great structure? If there is ever to be a world civilisation, it must be built upon some truth which affects the bases of human life. If we are truly Christians, we believe that the Gospel is that truth. It is the one possible foundation on which a world civilisation can be reared.

William Temple, *Basic Convictions*, Hamish Hamilton, 1937, page 82

... a new theology of mission and a new exegesis of the Bible are now emerging through the shared life of growing numbers of small, often poor or persecuted groups of Christians, many of them in the heart of hitherto Islamic, Hindu or Buddhist worlds, in Communist China, Russia and its satellites, in the shanty towns and rural areas of Africa, Asia and South America, or in the inner cities of the West.

The members of these groups are close in spirit to the first Christians. Like them they come out of frameworks of faith and culture which have been shaken apart. They have sensed a new breaking-open of a gulf always latent in human experience: a gulf between heaven and earth, ideal and reality, between a spiritual depth on the one hand and on the other the hard inconsequential surface of mundane life. Faiths and ideologies have sought to span this gulf by varied means by manipulating the world into harmony through ritual cleansing and spirit possession; by moralizing the world, pressing it into conformity with a divinely revealed law; or by attributing to some members of society a special purity, empowering them to spiritualize the world into some ultimate underlying unity.

But now these people have been attracted by the sense of an actual divine presence in this world, in the figure of a wounded man alongside them, and the release, through him, of a new love, bringing together justice and mercy, ideal and real, heaven and earth. They would claim that the Divine Spirit flows out through the life and above all the death of that wounded man, Jesus the Christ, sent forth from God and in turn sending out others (John 20:21). As they apply his cross, in shared repentance, to their corporate life, they sense the movement of the Spirit empowering and equipping them to be channels in the new Love, integrating divine and human, community and social structure, spiritual and material, with a new redemptive energy.

This also happened in New Testament times.

Simon Barrington-Ward, in John Macquarrie and John Bowden, editors, *A New Dictionary of Christian Theology*, SCM Press, 1985, page 372

MONEY

Money—current coin; property viewed as convertible into money; coin in reference to its purchasing power

About thirty years ago I remember reading a book called *Miracle on the River Kwai*. It was a grim account of life in a prisoner of war camp in the Second World War. When the POWs were dying (of wounds, fever, dysentery, malnutrition and the like) they were moved to a special hut and left to die. There were hardly any survivors.

As I remember it, a Scottish minister, the author of the book, rounded up some able-bodied men and began to care for the sick and dying. With the help of prayer, nursing and friendship, there was soon a noticeable change of atmosphere. Morale improved. Prisoners started to get well again. A few were discharged and returned to the main compound. Lives were saved. For those caught up in this healing work this was the miracle of the River Kwai—evidence of the healing power of the gospel at work. Eventually when the war was over the survivors returned home and dispersed.

The author, encouraged by what he had experienced, went home with high hopes for the future. Sadly he soon saw a return to the conditions which had existed before the war. He felt that men were set apart from each other by *economic competition.* The love of money was indeed the root of all evil. I feel this is still true today.

He who loves money will not be satisfied with money; nor he who loves wealth, with gain: this also is vanity.

Ecclesiastes 5:10

Like the partridge that gathers a brood which she did not hatch, so is he who gets riches but not by right; in the midst of his days they will leave him, and at his end he will be a fool.

Jeremiah 17:11

It will be hard for a rich man to enter the kingdom of heaven ... it is easier for a camel to go through the eye of a needle than for a rich man to enter the kingdom of God.

Matthew 19:23–24

But those who desire to be rich fall into temptation, into a snare, into many senseless and hurtful desires that plunge men into ruin and destruction. For the love of money is the root of all evils; it is through this craving that some have wandered away from the faith and pierced their hearts with many pangs.

1 Timothy 6:9–10

To have money is a fear, not to have it a grief.

George Herbert, 'Outlandish Proverbs', number 591, in F.E. Hutchinson, editor, *The Works of George Herbert,* Oxford at the Clarendon Press, 1945, page 341

The dangers gather as the treasures rise.

Samuel Johnson, 'The Vanity of Human Wishes', in *The Yale Edition of the Works of Samuel Johnson,* Yale University Press, 1964, volume VI, 'Poems', page 92

He who multiplies Riches multiplies Cares.

Benjamin Franklin, *Poor Richard's Almanack,* Taurus Press, 1962, page 4

Riches are gotten with pain, kept with care, and lost with grief.

Thomas Fuller, *Gnomologia,* Stearne Brock, 1733, page 172

There is nothing that makes men rich and strong but that which they carry inside of them.

Henry Ward Beecher, *Proverbs from Plymouth Pulpit,* Charles Burnet & Co., 1887, page 8

The commerce of the world is conducted by the strong; and usually it operates against the weak.

Henry Ward Beecher, *Proverbs from Plymouth Pulpit,* Charles Burnet & Co., 1887, page 36

Is there no prosperity other than commercial? It is surely time to have done with this utilitarian nonsense.

Norman Douglas, *An Almanac*, Chatto & Windus in association with Secker & Warburg, 1945, page 2

Whenever money is the principal object of life with either man or nation, it is both got ill, and spent ill; and does harm both in the getting and spending.

John Ruskin, *The Crown of Wild Olive*, George Allen & Sons, 1910, page 46

We are prone to judge success by the index of our salaries or the size of our automobiles, rather than by the quality of our service and our relationship to humanity.

Martin Luther King, *The Words of Martin Luther King*, selected by Coretta Scott King, William Collins Sons & Co., 1986, page 21

We can hardly respect money enough for the blood and toil it represents.
Money is frightening. It can serve or destroy man.

Michel Quoist, *Prayers of Life*, translated by Anne Marie de Commaile and Agnes Mitchell Forsyth, Gill and Macmillan, 1963, page 23

... money-getting men, men that spend all their time first in getting, and next in anxious care to keep it; men that are condemned to be rich, and then always busy or discontented.

Izaak Walton, *The Compleat Angler*, The Nonesuch Press, 1929, page 17

I saw that... where the heart was set on greatness, success in business did not satisfy the craving; but that commonly with an increase of wealth, the desire of wealth increased.

John Woolman, *The Journal of John Woolman*, Edward Marsh, 1857, page 16

Strong as is money and invincible, yet, in the long run, ideas are mightier than money. Tyrannies are overthrown by ideas. Armies are defeated by ideas. Nations, and Time itself, are overmatched by ideas.

Henry Ward Beecher, *Proverbs from Plymouth Pulpit*, Charles Burnet & Co., 1887, page 27

Riches are a slow poison, which strikes almost imperceptibly, paralyzing the soul at the moment when it seems healthiest. They are thorns which grow with the grain and suffocate it right at the moment when corn is beginning to shoot up.

Carlo Carretto, *Letters from the Desert*, translated by Rose Mary Hancock, Darton, Longman and Todd, 1972, page 81

For forty years he had fought against economic fatality. It was the central ill of humanity, the cancer which was eating into its entrails. It was there that one must operate; the rest of the healing process would follow.

Arthur Koestler, *Darkness at Noon*, translated by Daphne Hardy, Jonathan Cape, 1980, page 257

Money as money is not evil. It speeds on errands of mercy, and lends itself to a thousand philanthropies. It feeds the hungry, clothes the naked, and succours men who are tempted to suicide. It is the insensate love of riches which is the perilous thing.

W.E. Sangster, *He is Able*, Hodder and Stoughton, 1936, page 124

The profit motive in industry and in finance, when given such freedom and prominence as it now has, becomes a profoundly and pervasively disturbing factor.

The one thing that has become international in our world is Finance; it is arguable that it ought to have been the last.

William Temple, *The Hope of a New World*, SCM Press, 1940, page 103

Broadly speaking, there are three basic benefits from wealth. First is the satisfaction in the power with which it endows the individual. Second is the physical possession of the things which money can buy. Third is the distinction or esteem that accrues to the rich man as the result of his wealth.

J.K. Galbraith, *The Affluent Society*, Hamish Hamilton, 1958, page 68

Have money-worshippers really considered it, that the Living God is not dead metal, and yet that He is, strictly speaking, the only *human gold*? Rich men are the men who carry God in their souls, and these are the only men who have true human gold to give. The receiver of this gold, receives an unmingled blessing; and the giver becomes rich by giving.

John Pulsford, *Quiet Hours*, James Nisbet & Co., 1857, page 31

'My other piece of advice, Copperfield,' said Mr. Micawber, 'you know. Annual income twenty pounds, annual expenditure nineteen nineteen six, result happiness. Annual income twenty pounds, annual expenditure twenty pounds ought and six, result misery. The blossom is blighted, the leaf is withered, the God of day goes down upon the dreary scene, and—and in short, you are for ever floored. As I am!'

Charles Dickens, *David Copperfield*, Oxford at the Clarendon Press, 1981, page 150

It is clear that, in the natural order of things, God's order, the object of all industry is the supply of men's wants; in the language of the economist, the consumer is the person whose interest should be supreme in determining the whole process; for his sake goods are produced; and finance comes in as the servant of production. But in our world, goods are produced, not primarily to satisfy the consumer, but to enrich the producer.

William Temple, *The Hope of a New World*, SCM Press, 1940, page 17

The principle that money should function as a means of exchange, and that those who have the handling of it should receive no doubt a perfectly reasonable remuneration for their integrity and their honesty in dealing with it, but not have the opportunity by that mere manipulation of creating new values for themselves which do not correspond to any useful services offered by them to the community—that is, I think, an undoubtedly sound principle.

William Temple, *The Church Looks Forward*, Macmillan & Co., 1944, page 148

In the mental climate... the idea of profit has invaded our whole field of consciousness. Wealth appears as the supreme good; success is measured in units of money. Business affairs are sacred. The search for material gain has spread from banking, industry and commerce to all other human activities. The mainspring of our actions is the desire to gain some personal and, above all, pecuniary advantage. Equally, we want to satisfy our vanity by promotions, titles, decorations and social positions.

Alexis Carrel, *Reflections on Life*, Hamish Hamilton, 1952, page 31

Money is in its own nature a medium of exchange, and, therefore, if you use it as a commodity in the sense of trying to profit yourself by variations in its value over against goods, you are destroying it for its proper social purpose; and there are some kinds of activity in that direction which I think public opinion is tending to think ought undoubtedly to be prohibited, as for example, speculation in foreign currencies. This is not a crime of the Banks, which never, I believe, indulge in this evil practice. It is a crime of the private fortune-hunter. If it can be stopped, it ought to be stopped.

William Temple, *The Church Looks Forward*, Macmillan & Co., 1944, page 148

The social struggle, in varying forms, runs through all classes except the very highest and the very lowest. For this purpose men and women make great moral efforts, and show amazing powers of self-control; but all their efforts and all their self-control, being not used for any creative end, serve merely to dry up the well-spring of life within them, to make them feeble, listless, and trivial. It is not in such a soil that the passion which produces genius can be nourished. Men's souls have exchanged the wilderness for the drawing-room: they have become cramped and petty and deformed, like Chinese women's feet. Even the horrors of war have hardly awakened them from the smug somnambulism of respectability. And it is chiefly the worship of money that has brought about this death-like slumber of all that makes men great.

Bertrand Russell, *The Principles of Social Reconstruction*, George Allen & Unwin, 1971, page 81

Given the enormity of the problem, it would be foolish to suggest that the only way forward would be for Britain as a nation to get poorer. If the national standard of living is to grow, the process of wealth creation must be supported wholeheartedly. The pursuit of efficiency in industry is to follow the biblical insistence on the proper stewardship of resources—providing, that is, such a pursuit does not become a short-sighted and selfish exploitation of human and material resources, and that... it is accompanied by the fair distribution of the wealth created. To affirm the importance of wealth creation... is not enough. Economic policy should be as concerned with the distribution of income and wealth as with its creation. What seems to be lacking at present is an adequate appreciation of the importance of the distributive consequences—for cities and regions, and for groups of people—of national economic policies.

'Is Wealth Creation the Answer?', from *Faith in the City*, Church House Publishing, 1985, page 204

The main assumption on which present economic policies are based is that prosperity can be restored if individuals are set free to pursue their own economic salvation. The appeal is to economic self-interest and individualism, and freeing market mechanisms through the removal of 'unnecessary' governmental interference and restrictive trade union practice.

Individual responsibility and self-reliance are excellent objectives. The nation cannot do without them. But pursuit of them must not damage a collective obligation for those who have no choice, or whose choices are at best forced ones. We believe that at present too much emphasis is being given to individualism, and not enough to collective obligation. In the absence of a spirit of collective obligation, or the political will to foster it, there is no guarantee that the pursuit of innumerable individual self-interests will add up to an improvement in the common good.

***Faith in the City*, Church House Publishing, 1985, page 208**

MUSIC

Music—art of combining sounds with a view to beauty of form and expression of emotion; sounds so produced

I wonder if in *music* we can see another variant and consequence of what it means to be made in the image and likeness of God, and of the divine inbreathing. A seed or a spark of God is planted in the depths of our being. Some people, with a sensitive and intuitive ear for sound, might experience this as music. Take, for instance, a composer such as Beethoven. In the depths of the night, or out for a walk in the forest he becomes aware of a tune or harmony. It grows, develops and expands in moments when he is quiet. Slowly a symphony takes form, he can feel it all in the depths of his being. He decides to go one stage further and commits it to note form. A conductor comes along—a gifted musician—also made in the image and likeness of God. With his intuitive feel for music he examines the score and recognizes a great work. He gets the members of his orchestra together (also made in the image and likeness of God) and they rehearse the work. Communication takes place within the members of the orchestra. Together they get the 'feel' of the work. A concert is arranged. Along comes an audience (also made in the image and likeness of God, with an intuitive feel for music) and the orchestra and audience both experience communication and a beauty of form and harmony. Rapturous applause follows. Dare we say it—that in this concert something of a divine performance has taken place? It is no accident that music plays such an important part in worship in a church, but why restrict it to a church building? Music is everywhere.

Sing to God, sing praises to his name.

Psalm 68:4

It is good to give thanks to the Lord, to sing praises to thy name, O Most High; to declare thy steadfast love in the morning, and thy faithfulness by night, to the music of the lute and the harp, to the melody of the lyre.

Psalm 92:1–3

I will sing with the spirit and I will sing with the mind also.

1 Corinthians 14:15

Be filled with the Spirit, addressing one another in psalms and hymns and spiritual songs, singing and making melody to the Lord with all your heart.

Ephesians 5:19

When music sounds, gone is the earth I know,
And all her lovely things even lovelier grow.

Walter de la Mare, 'Music', in *The Complete Poems of Walter de la Mare*, Faber and Faber, 1969, page 199

The song feels the infinite in the air, the picture in the earth, the poem in the air and the earth.

Rabindranath Tagore, 'Stray Birds', CCIV, in *Collected Poems & Plays of Rabindranath Tagore*, Macmillan & Co., 1936, page 313

... music is a higher revelation than all wisdom and philosophy, the wine which inspires one to new generative processes.

Ludwig von Beethoven, in *Thayer's Life of Beethoven*, revised and edited by Elliot Forbes, Princeton University Press, 1970, page 494

God makes every man happy who knows how to play upon himself. Every man is full of music; but it is not every man who knows how to bring it out.

Henry Ward Beecher, *Proverbs from Plymouth Pulpit*, Charles Burnet & Co., 1887, page 11

Music resembles Poetry, in each
Are nameless Graces which no Methods teach,
And which a Master-Hand alone can reach.

Alexander Pope, 'Pastoral Poetry and an Essay on Criticism', in *The Poems of Alexander Pope*, Methuen & Co., 1961, Volume I, page 256

There was no instrument that was ever struck that has such music as every faculty of the human soul has in it. God never makes anything else so beautiful as man.

Henry Ward Beecher, *Proverbs from Plymouth Pulpit*, Charles Burnet & Co., 1887, page 28

Music religious heats inspires,
It wakes the soul, and lifts it high,
And wings it with sublime desires,
And fits it to bespeak the Deity.

Joseph Addison, 'A Song for St Cecilia's Day', iv. 1, in A.C. Guthkelch, editor, *The Miscellaneous Works of Joseph Addison*, G. Bell and Sons, 1914, volume I, page 22

The more nearly the performer on a musical instrument approaches perfection, the larger is that part of his execution which is unconscious. Consciousness arises with defect, or sense of something to be overcome. How conscious we are when striving to think and work in ill-health!

Mark Rutherford, *More Pages From a Journal*, Oxford University Press, 1910, page 220

... I came gradually to see that music and poetry were perhaps closer kin than I had at first realized. I came gradually to see that beyond the music of both arts there is an essence that joins them—an area where the meanings behind the notes and the meaning beyond the words spring from some common source.

Aaron Copland, *Music and Imagination*, Harvard University Press, 1977, page 1

For his part, Henri Bergson was interested in Casals' subjective reactions to music—what did he feel when he was playing the music of Bach or Beethoven? Casals tried to explain that if he was satisfied after a good performance... he had a special feeling, an almost physical sensation that could be likened to carrying inside himself a weight of gold.

H.L. Kirk, *Pablo Casals, A Biography*, Hutchinson & Co. (Publishers), 1974, page 187

Music the fiercest Grief can charm,
And Fate's severest Rage disarm:
Music can soften Pain to Ease,
And make Despair and Madness please:
Our Joys below it can improve,
And antedate the Bliss above.

Alexander Pope, 'Ode for Musick on St Cecilia's Day', from 'Minor Poems', in *The Poems of Alexander Pope*, Methuen & Co., 1964, page 34

A patient once said to S., 'I sometimes have the feeling that God is right inside me, for instance when I hear the St Matthew Passion.' And S. said something like: 'At such moments you are completely at one with the creative and cosmic forces that are at work in every human being.' And these creative forces are ultimately part of God, but you need courage to put that into words.

Etty Hillesum, *A Diary, 1941–43*, translated by Arnold J. Pomerans, Jonathan Cape, 1983, page 62

Everything is music for the born musician. Everything that throbs, or moves, or stirs, or palpitates—sunlit summer days, nights when the wind howls, flickering light, the twinkling of the stars, storms, the song of birds, the buzzing of insects, the murmuring of trees, voices, loved or loathed, familiar fireside sounds, a creaking door, blood moving in the veins in the silence of the night—everything that is in music; all that is needed is that it should be heard.

Romain Rolland, 'Storm and Stress', in *John Christopher*, translated by Gilbert Cannan, William Heinemann, 1910, volume II, page 105

I pant for the music which is divine,
My heart in its thirst is a dying flower;
Pour forth the sound like enchanted wine,
Loosen the notes in a silver shower;
Like the herbless plain, for the gentle rain,
I gasp, I faint, till they wake again.

Let me drink of the spirit of that sweet sound,
More, oh more,—I am thirsting yet;
It loosens the serpent which care has bound
Upon my heart to stifle it;
The dissolving strain, through every vein,
Passes into my heart and brain.

Percy Bysshe Shelley, 'Music', in Thomas Hutchinson, editor, *The Complete Poetical Works of Percy Bysshe Shelley*, Oxford University Press, 1935, page 651

Music—there is something very wonderful in music. Words are wonderful enough, but music is more wonderful. It speaks not to our thoughts as words do, it speaks straight to our hearts and spirits, to the very core and root of our souls. Music soothes us, stirs us up; it puts noble feelings into us; it melts us to tears, we know not how; it is a language by itself, just as perfect, in its way, as speech, as words; just as divine, just as blessed. Music has been called the speech of angels; I will go farther, and call it the speech of God Himself.

The old Greeks, the wisest of all the heathen, made a point of teaching their children music, because, they said, it taught them not to be self-willed and fanciful, but to see the beauty of order, the usefulness of rule, the divineness of law.

Charles Kingsley, *Daily Thoughts*, Macmillan & Co., 1884, page 107

Music is given us with our existence. An infant cries or crows or talks with his own voice and goes one step beyond to sing. Above other arts, music can be possessed without knowledge; being an expression largely of the subconscious, it has its direct routes from whatever is in our guts, minds and spirits, without need of a detour through the classroom. That direct route I knew, thank God. I learned to love music before I learned to say so; I was given the raw material when I could scarcely read or write; I early felt the wonder of taking up a violin and making it speak, communicate with others, express the thoughts and feelings of great composers. No doubt I had great aptitude which enabled me to excel my teachers in specific performances, but this phenomenon is generally accounted more mysterious than it is. Violin in hand, a talented youngster with music in his heart, an inspiring master, and the capacity to play by 'feel' and imitation can hurdle obstacles apparently insuperable to the adult mind, which would erect barriers of qualification to be surmounted before one wins the right to self-expression.

Yehudi Menuhin, *Unfinished Journey*, Macdonald and Jane's Publishers, 1977, page 88

I carry my thoughts about with me for a long time, sometimes a very long time, before I set them down... At the same time my memory is so faithful to me that I am sure not to forget a theme which I have once conceived, even after years have passed. I make many changes, reject and reattempt until I am satisfied. Then the working-out in breadth, length, height and depth begins in my head, and since I am conscious of what I want, the basic idea never leaves me. It rises, grows upward, and I hear and see the picture as a whole take shape and stand forth before me as though cast in a single piece, so that all that is left is the work of writing it down. This goes quickly, according as I have the time, for sometimes I have several compositions in labor at once, though I am sure never to confuse one with the other. You will ask me whence I take my ideas? That I cannot say with any degree of certainty: they come to me uninvited, directly or indirectly. I could almost grasp them in my hands, out in Nature's open, in the woods, during my promenades, in the silence of the night, at the earliest dawn. They are roused by moods which in the poet's case are transmuted into words, and in mine into tones, that sound, roar and storm until at last they take shape for me as notes.

Ludwig von Beethoven, in *Thayer's Life of Beethoven*, revised and edited by Elliot Forbes, Princeton University Press, 1970, page 851

NATURE

Nature—physical power causing phenomena of material world, these phenomena as a whole

The Bible opens with the words—'In the beginning God created the heavens and the earth... and the Spirit of God was moving over the face of the waters.'

The Creator—the Spirit of God—was at work in his creation. Can we not expect to see something of the Creator in his creation? I've been greatly helped by such people as William Wordsworth who in one of his poems wrote of 'a presence... whose dwelling is the light of setting suns'. This was an eye-opener. I had experienced something of the glory of the setting sun. I knew what he was writing about. Equally glorious is the dawn. I shall never forget a certain dawn when I was high up on Mount Kenya. When the sun came up it was possible to look down on a sea of cloud and to see Mount Kilimanjaro, two hundred miles away. I have often experienced the beauty of mountains, not just in Africa, but in the Himalayas and the Alps, and felt a sense of awe and reverence. Recently I've walked through the Samaria Gorge in Crete—the largest gorge in Europe—and it made me wonder. Sometimes a sunset in Mürren, Switzerland, is breathtakingly beautiful—the Jungfrau bathed in an orange red purple glow. I have found visits to the sea equally uplifting. Here one is faced with something vast and profound. Numerous visits to the Yorkshire Dales and the Lake District confront me with 'a presence'. Even the desert in North Yemen has a beauty and a wonder all of its own and the whispering sands in the gentle breeze gave me an eerie feeling I was not alone. Like Moses before the burning bush, I had an awareness of the numinous.

God blessed them, and God said to them, 'Be fruitful and multiply, and fill the earth and subdue it; and have dominion over the fish of the sea and over the birds of the air and over every living thing that moves upon the earth.' And God said, 'Behold, I have given you every plant yielding seed which is upon the face of all the earth, and every tree with seed in its fruit; you shall have them for food. And to every beast of the earth, and to every bird of the air, and to everything that creeps on the earth, everything that has the breath of life, I have given every green plant for food.' And it was so. And God saw everything that he had made, and behold, it was very good.

Genesis 1:28–31

Thou visitest the earth and waterest it, thou greatly enrichest it; the river of God is full of water; thou providest their grain, for so thou hast prepared it. Thou waterest its furrows abundantly, settling its ridges, softening it with showers.

Psalm 65:9–10

He did not leave himself without witness, for he did good and gave you from heaven rains and fruitful seasons, satisfying your hearts with food and gladness.

Acts 14:17

Ever since the creation of the world his invisible nature, namely, his eternal power and deity, has been clearly perceived in the things that have been made.

Romans 1:20

There is in those workes of nature, which seeme to puzle reason, something Divine, and [that] hath more in it than the eye of a common spectator doth discover.

Sir Thomas Browne, 'Religio Medici', part 1, section 39, in Geoffrey Keynes, editor, *The Works of Sir Thomas Browne*, Faber & Faber, 1964, volume I, page 50

It is a happy world after all. The air, the earth, the water, teem with delighted existence. In a spring noon or a summer evening, on whichever side I turn my eyes, myriads of happy beings crowd upon my view.

William Paley, *Natural Theology*, Ward, Lock & Co., 1879, page 230

The laws, the life, and the joy of beauty in the material world of God, are as eternal and sacred parts of His creation as, in the world of spirits, virtue; and in the world of angels, praise.

John Ruskin, *Modern Painters*, George Allen & Sons, 1910, volume V, page 390

Nature responds so beautifully.
Roses are only once-wild roses, that were given an extra chance,
So they bloomed out and filled themselves with coloured fulness.
Out of sheer desire to be splendid, and more splendid.

D.H. Lawrence, 'Roses', in Vivian de Sola Pinto and Warren Roberts, editors, *The Complete Poems of D.H. Lawrence*, William Heinemann, 1967, volume II, page 831

I remember perfectly well thinking to myself as I trod this path through Waringore, that, whatever was happening to me in life, just to be able to stare at this green moss, at these fallen twigs, at these blood-stained funguses, was sufficient reward for having been born upon this cruelty-blasted planet!

John Cowper Powys, *Autobiography*, Macdonald & Co. (Publishers), 1967, page 292

He is made one with Nature: there is heard
His voice in all her music, from the moan
Of thunder, to the song of night's sweet bird;
He is a presence to be felt and known
In darkness and in light, from herb and stone,
Spreading itself where'er that Power may move
Which has withdrawn his being to its own;
Which wields the world with never-wearied love,
Sustains it from beneath, and kindles it above.

Percy Bysshe Shelley, 'Adonais', xlii. 370, in Thomas Hutchinson, editor, *The Complete Poetical Works of Percy Bysshe Shelley*, Oxford University Press, 1935, page 436

Of all the blessings which the study of Nature brings to the patient observer, let one, perhaps, be classed higher than this, that the farther he enters into those fairy gardens of life and birth, which Spenser saw and described in his great poem, the more he learns the awful and yet comfortable truth, that they do not belong to him, but to the One greater, wiser, lovelier than he; and as he stands silent with awe, amid the pomp of Nature's ever-busy rest, hears as of old, The Word of the 'Lord God walking among the trees of the garden in the cool of the day.'

Charles Kingsley, *Daily Thoughts*, Macmillan & Co., 1884, page 7

God is the God of Nature as well as the God of Grace. For ever he looks down on all things which He has made; and behold they are very good. And therefore we dare to offer to Him in our churches the most perfect works of naturalistic art, and shape them into copies of whatever beauty He has shown us in man or woman, in cave or mountain-peak, in tree or flower, even in bird or butterfly. But Himself? Who can see Him except the humble and the contrite heart, to whom He reveals Himself as a Spirit to be worshipped in spirit and in truth, and not in bread nor wood, nor stone nor gold, nor quintessential diamond?

Charles Kingsley, *Daily Thoughts*, Macmillan & Co., 1884, page 151

'Bathe, O disciple, thy thirsty soul in the dew of the dawn!' says Faust to us, and he is right. The morning air breathes a new and laughing energy into veins and marrow. If every day is a repetition of life, every dawn signs as it were a new contract with existence. At dawn everything is fresh, light, simple, as it is for children. At dawn spiritual truth, like the atmosphere, is more transparent, and our organs, like the young leaves, drink in the light more eagerly, breathe in more ether, and less of things earthly. If night and the starry sky speak to the meditative soul of God, of eternity and the infinite, the dawn is the time for projects, for resolutions, for the birth of action. While the silence and the 'sad serenity of the azure vault' incline the soul to self-recollection, the vigour and gaiety of nature spread into the heart and make it eager for life and living.

Henri Frédéric Amiel, *Amiel's Journal*, translated by Mrs Humphry Ward, Macmillan & Co., 1918, page 19

When I came into the country, and being seated among the silent trees, and meads and hills, had all my time in mine own hands, I resolved to spend it all, whatever it cost me, in the search of happiness, and to satiate that burning thirst which Nature had enkindled in me from my youth. In which I was so resolute, that I chose rather to live upon ten pounds a year, and to go in leather clothes, and feed upon bread and water, so that I might have all my time clearly to myself, than to keep many thousands per annum in an estate of life where my time would be devoured in care and labour. And God was so pleased to accept of that desire, that from that time to this, I have had all things plentifully provided for me, without any care at all, my very study of Felicity making me more to prosper, than all the care in the whole world. So that through His blessing I live a free and kingly life as if the world were turned again into Eden, or much more, as it is at this day.

Thomas Traherne, *Centuries*, The Faith Press, 1969, page 134

How beautiful this dome of sky;
And the vast hills, in fluctuation fixed
At Thy command, how awful! Shall the Soul,
Human and rational, report of thee
Even less than these!—Be mute who will, who can,
Yet I will praise thee with impassioned voice:
My lips, that may forget thee in a crowd,
Cannot forget thee here; where thou hast built,
For thy own glory, in the wilderness! . . .
—Come, labour, when the worn-out frame requires
Perpetual sabbath; come, disease and want;
And sad exclusion through decay of sense;
But leave my unabated trust in thee—
And let thy favour, to the end of life,

Inspire me with ability to seek
Repose and hope among eternal things—
Father of heaven and earth! and I am rich,
And will possess my portion in content!

William Wordsworth, 'The Excursion', iv. 34, in E. de Selincourt and Helen Darbishire, editors, *The Poetical Works of William Wordsworth*, Oxford at the Clarendon Press, 1959, page 111

To speak truly, few adult persons can see nature. Most persons do not see the sun. At least they have a very superficial seeing. The sun illuminates only the eye of the man, but shines into the eye and the heart of the child. The lover of nature is he whose inward and outward senses are still truly adjusted to each other; who has retained the spirit of infancy even into the era of manhood. His intercourse with heaven and earth becomes part of his daily food. In the presence of nature a wild delight runs through the man, in spite of real sorrows. Nature says,—he is my creature, and maugre all his impertinent griefs, he shall be glad with me. Not the sun or the summer alone, but every hour and season yields its tribute of delight; for every hour and change corresponds to and authorizes a different state of the mind, from breathless noon to grimmest midnight. Nature is a setting that fits equally well a comic or a mourning piece. In good health, the air is a cordial of incredible virtue. Crossing a bare common, in snow puddles, at twilight, under a clouded sky, without having in my thoughts any occurrence of special good fortune, I have enjoyed a perfect exhilaration. I am glad to the brink of fear. In the woods, too, a man casts off his years, as the snake his slough, and at what period soever of life is always a child. In the woods is perpetual youth. Within these plantations of God, a decorum and sanctity reign, a perennial festival is dressed, and the guest sees not how he should tire of them in a thousand years. In the woods, we return to reason and faith. There I feel that nothing can befall me in life,—no disgrace, no calamity (leaving me my eyes), which nature cannot repair. Standing on the bare ground,—my head bathed by the blithe air and uplifted into infinite space,—all mean egotism vanishes. I become a transparent eyeball; I am nothing; I see all; the currents of the Universal Being circulate through me; I am part or parcel of God. The name of the nearest friend sounds then foreign and accidental: to be brothers, to be acquaintances, master or servant, is then a trifle and a disturbance. I am the lover of uncontained and immortal beauty. In the wilderness, I find something more dear and connate than in streets or villages. In the tranquil landscape, and especially in the distant line of the horizon, man beholds somewhat as beautiful as his own nature.

The greatest delight which the fields and woods minister is the suggestion of an occult relation between man and the vegetable. I am not alone and unacknowledged. They nod to me, and I to them. The waving of the boughs in the storm is new to me and old. It takes me by surprise, and yet is not unknown. Its effect is like that of a higher thought or a better emotion coming over me, when I deemed I was thinking justly or doing right.

Yet it is certain that the power to produce this delight does not reside in nature, but in man, or in a harmony of both. It is necessary to use these pleasures with great temperance. For nature is not always tricked in holiday attire, but the same scene which yesterday breathed perfume and glittered as for the frolic of the nymphs is overspread with melancholy to-day. Nature always wears the colours of the spirit. To a man labouring under calamity, the heat of his own fire hath sadness in it. Then there is a kind of contempt of the landscape felt by him who has just lost by death a dear friend. The sky is less grand as it shuts down over less worth in the population.

Ralph Waldo Emerson, in Edward L. Ericson, editor, *Emerson on Transcendentalism*, The Ungar Publishing Company, 1986, page 5

NEW CREATION

New Creation—renewed, fresh; further, additional; one converted to Christianity, put on the 'new man', show conversion by amendment

Just when I left school a brown envelope arrived, requiring me to report for National Service. Two years later I was demobbed and went up to Balliol with two main aims in mind: to get as good a law degree as possible, and a golf blue. On arrival I was bombarded with a mass of literature, including invitations to go to this church and that church. Having been a rum-drinking Gurkha Officer I decided this was kid's stuff, and threw the lot into the waste-paper basket. A week or so later a friend persuaded me to go and hear a certain preacher who was reputed to be outstanding. I went along, somewhat reluctantly. I can't remember a thing the preacher said now, but I was impressed. He was radiantly alive, and seemed to possess the very thing I was looking for. An inner struggle and dialogue went something like this. 'I know you exist now, God, but I don't want to commit myself to you just yet. I'm young. Life is pretty good at the moment and you might spoil the fun. I'll come to you when I'm an old dodderer...'. Another voice seemed to say, 'Come on, Bill. If you don't commit yourself now, you never will.' I knew that was true, and that I must go forward. What followed was the most momentous decision of my life. Everything changed from that moment, and I experienced something of a new creation. It was as if I had been born again, and I felt a great sense of joy and peace.

After a few weeks I noticed my aims were gently challenged, and found wanting. They were, in essence, selfish. I really had to think out my life afresh, and work out some new priorities. It took me nearly two years to sort out, but happily the 'new creation' still continues, day by day.

For behold, I create new heavens and a new earth.

Isaiah 65:17

Cast away from you all the transgressions which you have committed against me, and get yourselves a new heart and a new spirit!

Ezekiel 18:31

Truly, truly, I say to you, unless one is born anew, he cannot see the kingdom of God... Unless one is born of water and the Spirit, he cannot enter the kingdom of God. That which is born of the flesh is flesh, and that which is born of the Spirit is spirit. Do not marvel that I said to you, 'You must be born anew.' The wind blows where it wills, and you hear the sound of it, but you do not know whence it comes or whither it goes; so it is with every one who is born of the Spirit.

John 3:3, 5–8

Therefore, if any one is in Christ, he is a new creation; the old has passed away, behold, the new has come.

2 Corinthians 5:17

It is true in a sense to say that a Christian is a new creature. But he is a creature for which all the old material has been used.

Evelyn Underhill, in John Stobbart, editor, *The Wisdom of Evelyn Underhill*, A.R. Mowbray & Co., 1951, page 30

The adult population of the world are knotted and warted by bad habits, and it would seem impossible to get a man clean of them. But Christ says, 'Go, wash!' and they return clean.

Henry Ward Beecher, *Proverbs from Plymouth Pulpit*, Charles Burnet & Co., 1887, page 21

The Spirit of God can recreate us. When the Spirit of God enters into a man the disorder of human nature becomes the order of God; our dishevelled, disorderly, uncontrolled lives are moulded by the Spirit into the harmony of God.

William Barclay, *The Gospel of Matthew*, The Saint Andrew Press, 1987, volume I, page 49

If we are to be in Christ new creatures, we must show that we are so, by having new ways of living in the world. If we are to follow Christ, it must be in our common way of spending every day.

William Law, *A Serious Call to a Devout and Holy Life*, J.M. Dent and Co., 1898, page 8

Everything that is born of God is truly no shadowy work, but a true life work. God will not bring forth a dead fruit, a lifeless and powerless work, but a living, new man must be born from the living God.

Johann Arndt, *True Christianity*, translated by Peter Erb, SPCK, 1979, page 46

A new life begins for us with every second. Let us go forward joyously to meet it. We must press on, whether we will or no, and we shall walk better with our eyes before us than with them ever cast behind.

Jerome K. Jerome, *Idle Thoughts of an Idle Fellow*, J.M. Dent & Sons, 1983, page 165

It was a neo-Marxist philosopher, Herbert Marcuse, who declared that changes in social structures and political institutions are not enough and that what we need is 'a new type of man, with new needs, capable of finding a qualitatively different way of life'.

John Macquarrie, *The Humility of God*, SCM Press, 1978, page 23

We must create in ourselves a 'new spirit', the spirit of intelligence and strength; we must renew ourselves and live with intensity our interior life. We must pray and act. Every day of our life must carry us nearer to the supreme Good and Intelligence—that is, nearer to God.

Elizabeth Leseur, *A Wife's Story*, Burns & Oates, 1919, page 43

And now in age I bud again,
After so many deaths I live and write;
I once more smell the dew and rain,
And relish versing: O, my onely light,
It cannot be
That I am he
On whom thy tempests fell at night.
These are thy wonders, Lord of love.

George Herbert, 'The Church, The Flower', in *The Poems of George Herbert*, Oxford University Press, 1979, page 157

When a man becomes a Christian, there ought to be a complete change in his personality. He puts off his old self, and puts on a new self, just as the candidate for baptism puts off his old clothes and puts on the new white robe. We very often evade the truth on which the New Testament insists, the truth that a Christianity which does not change a man is a most imperfect Christianity. Further, this change is a progressive change. This new creation is a continual renewal. It makes a man grow continually in grace and knowledge until he reaches that which he was meant to be—manhood in the image of God. Christianity is not really Christianity unless it recreates a man into what he was meant to be.

William Barclay, ***The Letters to the Philippians, Colossians and Thessalonians,*** **The Saint Andrew Press, 1971, page 185**

... Christ had to become man and be grasped by the Holy Spirit, become sanctified with the Holy Spirit beyond all measure. For indeed, the spirit of the Lord rested upon him, the spirit of wisdom and understanding, the spirit of counsel and might, the spirit of knowledge and the fear of the Lord (Isaiah 11:2) so that in him and through him human nature might be renewed and we in him, out of him, and through him might be born again and become new creatures so that we might inherit from him the spirit of wisdom and understanding for the spirit of foolishness, the spirit of knowledge for our inherited blindness, the spirit of the fear of God for the spirit of opposition to God. This is the new life and the new birth in us.

Johann Arndt, ***True Christianity,*** **translated by Peter Erb, SPCK, 1979, page 38**

If someone commits himself to Jesus as the standard, if he lets himself be determined by the person of Jesus Christ as the *basic model for a view of life and a practice of life,* this means in fact the transformation of the whole man. For Jesus Christ is not only an external goal, a vague dimension, a universal rule of conduct, a timeless ideal. He determines and influences man's life and conduct, not only externally, but from within. Following Christ means not only information, but formation: not merely a superficial change, but a change of heart and therefore the change of the whole man. It amounts to the fashioning of a *new man*: a new creation within the always diverse, individually and socially conditioned context of each one's own life in its particularity and singularity, without any attempt to impose uniformity.

Hans Küng, ***On Being a Christian,*** **translated by Edward Quinn, William Collins Sons & Co., 1977, page 551**

A wind has blown across the world
And tremors shake its frame;
New things are struggling to their birth
And naught shall be the same.
The earth is weary of its past,
Of folly, hate and fear;
Beyond a dark and stormy sky
The dawn of God is near.

A wind is blowing through the earth,
A tempest fierce and strong;
The trumpets of the Christ, the King,
Thunder the skies along;
The summons to a high crusade
Calling the brave and true
To find a new Jerusalem
And make the world anew.

F.C. Happold, ***The Journey Inwards,*** **Darton, Longman and Todd, 1974, page 17**

In this renewal in the Church today we have a new awareness of the full spectrum of the gifts of the Holy Spirit. We must not be afraid to accept the Spirit with all its manifestations, just as we find them in the gospels and in the writings of St. Paul. We must not be afraid of accepting that the Holy Spirit is manifesting himself in the same ways today. We must open our faith to that. What is needed from each of us today is what I should call an 'expectant faith.' In order to receive the gifts of God, we must *expect* them, be open to them. And in the measure that we are 'expectantly' open to him, the Holy Spirit can accomplish all those wonders that we read about at the beginning of the Church. Each one of us needs that expectant faith. Come, Holy Spirit! I do not ask of you any special gift but neither do I refuse any gift either, because we receive those manifestations not for ourselves but for the kingdom of God, for the building up of His church. One person will receive a certain manifestation of the Spirit, another a different one, but all will use their particular gifts to share in the upbuilding of the Church.

Michael Ramsey, Leon Joseph Cardinal Suenens, *Come Holy Spirit*, Darton, Longman and Todd, 1977, page 55

In this age of ours, the Church sees a human society that is seriously disturbed and looking towards a complete change. And while human society is being carried along toward a new order, far-reaching tasks remain for the Church; as we have learned, this has been the case in every period of great distress. The Church is now called upon to take the perennial, vital divine power of the Gospel and inject it into the veins of the human society of today, which glories in its recent scientific and technological advances, at the same time that it is suffering damage to its social order, which some people have tried to repair without God's assistance...

These causes of sorrow and anxiety that come to mind should point up the need for vigilance and make every individual aware of his own responsibilities. We know that the over-all picture of these evils has disturbed some people to such an extent that they can see nothing but darkness and shadows, and feel that the world has been completely covered by them. But we prefer to place our unshakeable trust in the divine saviour of the human race, who has not deserted the human beings whom he has redeemed. As a matter of fact, in keeping with the advice of Christ the Lord who urged us to recognize the 'signs... of the times,' we can, in the midst of all the hideous clouds and darkness, perceive a number of things that seem to be omens portending a better day for the Church and for mankind.

Pope John XXIII, in Vincent A. Yzermans, editor, *Readings from Pope John*, A.R. Mowbray & Co., 1968, page 34

OPPORTUNITY

Opportunity—favourable juncture, good chance, opening (of doing, to do, for action, find, make, get, seize, give, afford an opportunity)

The telephone rang one evening. It was one of our old members who had left college some years ago. As an undergraduate he had read modern languages, concentrating on Russian, and was a keen musician—a talented pianist. As a way of supplementing his grant he had acted as a courier on the continent in summer vacations, taking groups of American tourists around Europe. He greatly enjoyed this and it was good experience and lucrative in tips. When he graduated he was undecided what to do in life so he joined the parent travel company in the States on a temporary basis. He returned to London a few months later and became a ship-broker. A bonus of this was the opportunity of going to concerts.

He wanted me to listen to him on the phone whilst he talked through a possible change of career. He had noticed a job advertised in the newspapers to do with the Aldeburgh Festival. He would dearly love to get this job, but it would mean a big drop in salary, and a drastic change of career. He would miss life in London, the theatre and concerts. Would he be able to cope on his own in a remote part of Suffolk? What should he do? I passed the questions back to him, and continued to listen. Eventually he thought through this possible change of career and successfully applied for the job. He worked there for several years, and then recently branched out on his own in St Petersburg. He has set up an agency to arrange for Russian musicians to give concerts in Britain and vice versa. He has managed to combine all his qualifications, language skills, and music in one job. I think of him as one of those people who have 'observed the opportunity'.

The place on which you are standing is holy ground.

Exodus 3:5

Observe the opportunity.

Ecclesiasticus 4:20 (AV)

So then, as we have opportunity, let us do good to all men, and especially to those who are of the household of faith.

Galatians 6:10

Behold, I have set before you an open door, which no one is able to shut.

Revelation 3:8

But the man who loses his opportunity, loses himself.

George Moore, *The Bending of the Bough*, Act V, T. Fisher Unwin, 1900, page 121

For the highest task of intelligence is to grasp and realize genuine opportunity, possibility.

John Dewey, *Human Nature and Conduct*, George Allen & Unwin, 1922, page 234

A door that seems to stand open must be of a man's size, or it is not the door that Providence means for him.

Henry Ward Beecher, *Proverbs from Plymouth Pulpit*, Charles Burnet & Co., 1887, page 54

To become expert in some field, to acquire mastery in some specific activity to a degree not easily shared by anyone else near by—that is what counts.

Johann Wolfgang von Goethe, *Wisdom and Experience*, selected by Ludwig Curtius, translated and edited by Hermann J. Weigand, Routledge & Kegan Paul, 1949, page 215

To keep in the rear of opportunity in matters of indulgence is as valuable a habit as to keep abreast of opportunity in matters of enterprises.

Thomas Hardy, *The Mayor of Casterbridge*, Macmillan & Co., 1916, page 104

I find my zenith doth depend upon
A most auspicious star, whose influence
If now I court not, but omit, my fortunes
Will ever after droop.

William Shakespeare, *The Tempest*, I. ii. 181

Human nature is frail. We shall shrink as [opportunities] come, from disappointment, from bereavement, from disabilities, sickness and failing powers, but they have a ministry: to those who dwell in Christ, and in whom Christ dwells, they are golden opportunities to make something worthy to endure.

W.E. Sangster, *Why Jesus Never Wrote a Book*, The Epworth Press, 1932, page 59

This art of seizing opportunities and turning even accidents to account, bending them to some purpose, is a great secret of success. Dr. Johnson has defined genius to be 'a mind of large general powers accidentally determined in some particular direction.' Men who are resolved to find a way for themselves, will always find opportunities enough; and if they do not lie ready to their hand, they will make them.

Samuel Smiles, *Self Help*, S.W. Partridge & Co., 1912, page 74

It is not accident... that help a man in the world, but purpose and persistent industry. These make a man sharp to discern opportunities, and to turn them to account. To the feeble, the sluggish and purposeless, the happiest opportunities avail nothing—they pass them by, seeing no meaning in them. But if we are prompt to seize and improve even the shortest intervals of possible action and effort, it is astonishing how much can be accomplished.

Samuel Smiles, *Self Help*, S.W. Partridge & Co., 1912, page 79

The greatest results in life are usually attained by simple means and the exercise of ordinary qualities. The common life of every day, with its cares, necessities and duties, afford ample opportunity for acquiring experience of the best kind; and its most beaten paths provide the true worker with abundant scope for effort and room for self-improvement. The great high-road of human welfare lies in the old highway of steadfast well-doing; and they who are most persistent and work in the truest spirit will invariably be the most successful.

Samuel Smiles, *Self Help*, S.W. Partridge & Co., 1912, page 49

Men can be as original now as ever, if they had but the courage, even the insight. Heroic souls in old times had no more opportunities than we have; but they used them. There were daring deeds to be done then—are there none now? Sacrifices to be made—are there none now? Wrongs to be redrest—are there none now? Let any one set his heart in these days to do what is right, and nothing else; and it will not be long ere his brow is stamped with all that goes to make up the heroical expression—with noble indignation, noble self-restraint, great hopes, great sorrows; perhaps even with the print of the martyr's crown of thorns.

Charles Kingsley, *Daily Thoughts*, Macmillan & Co., 1884, page 239

There are often great opportunities in the little things of life. An ordinary life may be quite extraordinarily romantic, because beneath the conventional clothes of the local tailor, and the daily progress along the pavement of the same dull streets, is going on all the while the spiritual movement of a soul, accepting or rejecting the beckoning of the Divine Ideal, following in one way or another the romance and adventure of a spiritual destiny.

When the greatest of all created beings, the Blessed Virgin Mary, first looked upon the Face of God, what she saw was just a little Child, born of her own pure travail; when the boys and girls came down the street of Nazareth on their way home from school, and passed the carpenter's shop, the Divine Life was there amongst the sawdust and the shavings; and when the thief on the gallows turned an eye of admiration upon the courage and undefeated love of his fellow-sufferer, there, in the very place of common execution, was the grandest of all sacrifices being enacted.

Little things bring great opportunities for a great love, and have been the steps of a heavenly ladder to the greatest of lives. A convent comes into being because some good women see how wonderful a thing silence can be; a children's home grows about the idea of the joy of guiding developing lives. All quiet housework and care and arrangement of the garden may have their inspiration from Nazareth, ministry to the sick and courage in growing old find their hallowing and help from Calvary, and the patience of prayer its radiant fortitude from the vision of the Saviour on the Holy Mount.

Father Andrew, SDC, *Meditations for Every Day*, A.R. Mowbray & Co., 1941, page 255

PAIN

Pain—suffering, distress, of body or mind

Whilst chaplain to University College, London, I lived in a student house in Gower Street for three years. One of the occupants was a post-graduate student from Egypt. Whilst she was with us she went through a very painful mental illness. Apparently as a young girl she had been sexually abused by her uncle, and the psychological damage of this experience now began to emerge. She was treated by a psychiatrist. From time to time she was admitted to a hospital in Queen's Square, and I would go to visit her. Progress was extremely slow. At the end of the year she was no better and had to move on to other accommodation. I kept in touch with her but she was still suffering acutely from mental pain, and nothing seemed to alleviate it. Eventually she had had enough and threw herself out of a third storey window in an attempt to end it all. She was terribly disappointed to find she was still alive after impact and even more so when she felt the physical pain of her injuries. She had broken her pelvis and several other major bones in her body and was confined in an orthopaedic ward of a hospital in South London. I went to visit her. There was a freak storm and I found the way to the hospital barred with flood waters. Unperturbed I took off my shoes and socks, and rolled up my trousers as far as they would go and waded through the flooded area to complete the visit. Eventually she was discharged, but succeeded in the next attempt. The psychological pain had just been too much for her to bear. The quotes are designed to give hope to people in pain.

Turn thou to me, and be gracious to me; for I am lonely and afflicted. Relieve the trouble of my heart, and bring me out of my distresses. Consider my affliction and my trouble.

Psalm 25:16–18

My soul cleaves to the dust;
revive me according to thy word!

Psalm 119:25

We know that the whole creation has been groaning in travail together until now; and not only the creation, but we ourselves, who have the first fruits of the Spirit, groan inwardly as we wait for adoption as sons, the redemption of our bodies.

Romans 8:22–23

Although he was a Son, he learned obedience through what he suffered.

Hebrews 5:8

It is not true that all pain is evil.

J. Neville Ward, *The Use of Praying*, Epworth Press, 1967, page 75

The world has kissed my soul with its pain, asking for its return in songs.

Rabindranath Tagore, 'Stray Birds' CLXVII, in *Collected Poems & Plays of Rabindranath Tagore*, Macmillan & Co., 1936, page 308

A painless life, in time, would be a curse not a blessing, it would be a life outside the movement of all that matters.

J. Neville Ward, *Five for Sorrow, Ten for Joy*, Epworth Press, 1971, page 34

Behind joy and laughter there may be a temperament, coarse, hard and callous. But behind sorrow there is always sorrow. Pain, unlike pleasure, wears no mask.

Oscar Wilde, *The Works of Oscar Wilde*, William Collins Sons & Co., 1948, page 864

Once you have experienced the pain of your own infirmity (and to feel the pain is the first step on the way to a cure) you soon learn compassion and a corresponding tenderness toward other people.

Thomas Merton, *The Waters of Silence*, Hollis & Carter, 1950, page 20

The survivors [from concentration camps] showed me another possibility: that one could live with pain precisely by not fighting it; by not denying its existence, by taking it into oneself, seeing it for what it was, using it, going beyond it.

Mary Craig, *Blessings*, Hodder and Stoughton, 1979, page 49

Sometimes, our pain is very deep and real, and we stand before her very silent, because there is no language for our pain, only a moan. Night's heart is full of pity for us: she cannot ease our aching; she takes our hand in hers, and the little world grows very small and very far beneath us, and, borne on her dark wings, we pass for a moment into a mightier Presence than her own, and in the wondrous light of that great Presence, all human life lies like a book before us, and we know that Pain and Sorrow are but the angels of God.

Jerome K. Jerome, *Three Men in a Boat*, J.M. Dent & Sons, 1964, page 102

The saints believe that no sorrow met in God is sterile of good. Suffering buys something, they believe, worthy of the price which pain has paid. Woe need never be wasted. Their thought of God will not allow the saints to trifle with the idea that His tender heart is indifferent to their *long*-suffering. Good will come of it. Love will find a way... In the dark, these brave souls hold still to the skirts of God. He will vindicate them some day. If not on earth, in heaven. With this longsuffering, they confidently believe that He will purchase something worthy of the price which pain has paid.

W.E. Sangster, *The Pure in Heart*, The Epworth Press, 1954, page 130

Following the tragic death of a friend of mine, I needed to talk to someone about it. I discovered once again how compelling our need to talk about such things and not just painful events but happy ones as well. It just bursts inside and can't be contained in the narrow, deep solitude of our being.

I looked for someone who had known my friend well, or even a little, to tell them the terrible news; but, in reality, I was just looking for someone with whom to share the pain. This is our profound need—to call out to another and share the burden. Shared suffering always brings a little relief. Again I told myself: Help others to talk. Listen to them quietly, don't worry about saying the right things or saying anything at all. Just be welcoming, people need your support in carrying their pain.

Michel Quoist, *With Open Heart*, translated by Colette Copeland, Gill and Macmillan, 1983, page 127

The cry of man's anguish went up unto God—
'Lord, take away pain—
The shadow that darkens the world Thou hast made,
The close-coiling chain
That strangles the heart—the burden that weighs
On the wing that would soar—
Lord, take away pain from the world
Thou hast made,
That it loves Thee the more.'

Then answered the Lord to the cry of the world:
'Shall I take away pain,
And with it the power of the soul to endure,
Made strong by the strain?
Shall I take away pity, that knits heart to heart,
And sacrifice high?
Will ye lose all your heroes that lift from the fire
White brows to the sky?
Shall I take away love, that redeems with a price
And smiles at its loss?
Can ye spare from the lives, that would climb unto Mine
The Christ on His Cross?

C.L. Drawbridge, *Common Objections to Christianity*, Robert Scott, 1914, page 77

It is a hard matter to reconcile the fact of pain with belief in a God of love. The atheist has met the difficulty by dismissing God; the Christian Scientist has met the difficulty by dismissing pain. But there are people who are quite sure of both, who know God and who know pain—such are certain saints and martyrs of the Catholic Church. Can they give us a clue to a reconciling thought? We think they can...

We do believe that we can say surely with the saints and martyrs of the Church of Christ that the reconciling thought that explains how there can be pain in a world created by a God of love is *the thought of holiness.*

It is not possible that an all-holy God should create a world in which sin would result in anything else but catastrophe; it is also impossible to think that an all-loving God should be content that the sorrow and suffering that sin causes should be nothing more than catastrophe. And so the love of God has captured pain that He may make pain the servant of holiness. That has been the discovery of holy people.

Father Andrew, SDC, *The Melody of Life*, A.R. Mowbray & Co., 1929, page 48

And a woman spoke, saying, Tell us of Pain.
And he said:
Your pain is the breaking of the shell that encloses your understanding.
Even as the stone of the fruit must break, that its heart may stand in the sun, so must you know pain.
And could you keep your heart in wonder at the daily miracles of your life, your pain would not seem less wondrous than your joy;
And you would accept the seasons of your heart, even as you have always accepted the seasons that pass over your fields.
And you would watch with serenity through the winters of your grief.
Much of your pain is self-chosen.
It is the bitter potion by which the physician within you heals your sick self.

Therefore trust the physician, and drink his remedy in silence and tranquillity:
For his hand, though heavy and hard, is guided by the tender hand of the Unseen,
And the cup he brings, though it burn your lips, has been fashioned of the clay which the Potter has moistened with His own sacred tears.

Kahlil Gibran, *The Prophet*, William Heinemann, 1970, page 61

PANIC

Panic—unreasoning, excessive terror, infectious fright, sudden alarm leading to hasty measures

I worked in Nigeria for six months in 1968, standing in for the regular priest, who was on long leave in England. It was at the height of the Nigerian Civil War, and the church I was looking after was just outside Ibadan, three hundred miles away from the war-front, on the Federal side. There was talk of starvation in 'Biafra' so I discussed this with our church members with a view to doing something about it. We rounded up some relief supplies which I took to Enugu—the capital city of the Eastern state. This lovely garden city had recently been relieved by Federal troops. It was rather frightening—a ghost town. Many buildings had been destroyed, water supplies cut off and there was no electricity. Troops were prowling around, and the villages surrounding the city were deserted apart from a few elderly people. The local population had either been killed or had fled to the bush. The relief supplies were handed over to the elderly people who managed to get them to their families hiding in the bush.

When I returned to Ibadan, I described what had happened in a sermon in our church the following Sunday. I happened to mention the Federal troops had been looting. In retrospect this was a mistake, for shortly after the service ended a police landrover drew up and I was arrested. Someone must have reported me. Panic! What could I do? Best stay calm. I was taken off to the police station for questioning. They wanted a copy of the text of the sermon. Fortunately there was no such text. I had preached without a script. After a couple of hours they released me and that was the last I heard of it.

Panic hits us all from time to time. The following quotes give us some ideas how best to cope with it.

And there was a panic in the camp, in the field, and among all the people; the garrison and even the raiders trembled; the earth quaked; and it became a very great panic.

1 Samuel 14:15

Do not be afraid of sudden panic, or of the ruin of the wicked, when it comes; for the Lord will be your confidence and will keep your foot from being caught.

Proverbs 3:25–26

'Can *you* keep from crying by considering things?' she [Alice] asked.
'That's the way it's done,' the Queen said with great decision.

Lewis Carroll, *Through the Looking-Glass*, Oxford University Press, 1971, page 177

Let things around you all go to pieces. Let your body bear the cross and pain and weariness. Let your soul be sorrowful and barren. But let the spirit be untouched by all these things, still and glad, dwelling above the clouds and mists of lower things, satisfied and at peace with God within, and His will without.

Gerhard Tersteegen, in Frances Bevan, *Sketches of the Quiet in the Land*, John F. Shaw and Co., 1891, page 401

Severed ties create anguish. Think how a spider panics when one of the strands of its cobweb is broken. In the same way people panic and suffer when their ties with nature, with other people, with God, are broken. They lose their sense of security. They're cut off from their lifeline. Hurt and frightened, they lose their self control. Like ship-wrecked people they frantically search for something to hold on to—but there's nothing strong enough to carry their weight, so they drown.

Michel Quoist, *With Open Heart*, translated by Colette Copeland, Gill and Macmillan, 1983, page 133

Once he has gone some distance on the inward journey, a man will know that there is one thing above all he needs to do. On every occasion that presents itself, from facing death in the dark to waiting for the bus, from being caught in a sterile patch to being carried away by panic fear, he... should consciously, deliberately, with all his strength, centre.

How best to do this each must find his own way. To anyone who knows what it is for a Quaker Meeting to 'centre down', then it is to do like that, to hold a meeting of one. To anyone who has said to himself in a life-or-death emergency, 'I must pull myself together and face this', it is such a pulling together. For the man of responsibility it is, as it were, to follow that responsibility down to its ultimate roots in the depths of his physical and moral being. It is the deep convulsive breath with which, in an agony of fear, we seek and find ourselves. And the injunction that goes with this is, pray; especially that form of prayer which consists in a wordless, imageless, lifting of the soul—the 'naked intent directed unto God' as *The Cloud of Unknowing* puts it. For it is by this means that the 'different spiritual dimension' becomes manifest, interpenetrating and transcending the space-time cause-effect world in which our bodies exist.

Especially is it necessary to centre and to pray in the 'Infirm glory of the positive hour'. In disaster one naturally has recourse to these means. In success it is otherwise: and success, notoriously, can be far more dangerous than disaster. And not in a time of outward success only but also, and particularly, of inward success, is it necessary to 'give the glory to God'. Whenever we feel we have come through to something vital... seen for the first time what we have been getting wrong, traced down what it was that has been separating us from those we love, that is the time to centre and pray. For it is then that inflation threatens; and the unclean spirit gathers his seven companions for the counter-attack.

Above all is it vital to centre and pray whenever, as from time to time will happen, the whole pattern of life breaks up: sometimes the outer life, sometimes the inner life, sometimes both at once. Then a man is in mortal peril: and the further he has gone in the experiment, the greater the danger. In such straits it is well to remember that individuation necessarily consists of such periods of flux: that for the wider integration to be made, some measure of disintegration is essential. But intellectual considerations at such a time mean relatively little. What is needed is that the integrative and consolidating process shall come into operation no less swiftly and no less powerfully than the disintegrative. And for this, centre and pray, *descendite ut ascendatis*, is the effective means.

P.W. Martin, *Experiment in Depth*, Routledge & Kegan Paul, 1967, page 244

Let me give you three images, all of which have helped me on along 'many a minty furlong.' . . . I would be climbing a mountain where, off and on, I might be enveloped in mist for days on end, unable to see a foot before me. Had I noticed how mountaineers climb mountains? how they have a quiet, regular, short step—on the level it looks petty; but then this step they keep up, on and on, as they ascend, whilst the inexperienced townsman hurries along, and soon has to stop, dead beat with the climb. That such an expert mountaineer, when the thick mists come, halts and camps out under some slight cover brought with him, quietly smoking his pipe, and moving on only when the mist has cleared away...

How I was taking a long journey on board ship, with great storms pretty sure ahead of me; and how I must now select, and fix in my little cabin, some few but entirely appropriate things—a small trunk fixed up at one end, a chair that would keep its position, tumbler and glass that would do ditto: all this, simple, strong, and selected throughout in view of stormy weather. So would my spirituality have to be chosen and cultivated especially in view of 'dirty' weather...

I am travelling on a camel across a huge desert. Windless days occur, and then all is well. But hurricanes of wind will come, unforeseen, tremendous. What to do then? It is very simple, but it takes such practice to do well at all. Dismount from the camel, fall prostrate face downwards on the sand, covering your head with your cloak. And lie thus, an hour, three hours, half a day: the sandstorm will go, and you will arise, and continue your journey as if nothing had happened...

You see, whether it be great cloud-mists on the mountain-side, or huge, mountain-high waves on the ocean, or blinding sandstorms in the desert: there is each time one crucial point—to form no conclusions, to take no decisions, to change nothing during such crises, and especially at such times, not to force any particular religious mood or idea in oneself. To turn gently to other things, to maintain a vague, general attitude of resignation—to be very meek, with oneself and with others: the crisis goes by, thus, with great fruit.

Baron Friedrich von Hügel, *Letters to a Niece*, J.M. Dent & Co., 1929, page 85

Approaching Broad Street, I suddenly became aware that something peculiar was happening to me. Inexplicably, my heart had started to race, my palms to moisten with sweat, my head to swim. I realized I was terribly afraid. But afraid of what? What was there to be so afraid of on this soft blue afternoon? Dazed, barely able to maintain my balance, barely able to breathe, I huddled against the wall of Balliol. The summer sky, so benign, so unthreatening, was transformed into a wheeling amphitheatre of undefined menace—a maelstrom of annihilating vacuity. As I stared at it, wave upon wave of raw fear swept through me. I imagined myself a body: a nameless corpse to be picked up from the street. It was as if all the secret terrors accumulated from birth had broken loose and come upon me in one overwhelming, retributive flood. How long I remained huddled against that wall I cannot say. Maybe no more than a minute or two.

The worst of the panic receded. In its place came exhaustion—a sensation of such utter weariness and debilitation that for an interval I could do nothing at all, lacking even the small amount of strength required to lift my arms and dry my sweat-soaked forehead. Shoulders hunched, I remained half collapsed against the wall, staring at the passersby, who—although they moved close enough for me to touch them, although I could hear the soft snatches of their laughter and talk—seemed remote and enigmatic creatures, holographic projections from an external world that had lost its solidity. When some semblance of strength was restored to my muscles, I made my way to a nearby pub and swiftly, unthinkingly, drank three pints of beer. I returned to my room, stretched myself out in front of the electric fire, and, stupefied by the beer, went to sleep.

All the same, that night I found myself wide awake in the small hours, staring blankly into the darkness. For the first time, I properly understood the meaning of the word 'desolation;' for the first time I felt myself to be entirely alone and helpless. Lying there, I noted with a start of dread the creeping onset of a fresh rush of the terror that had already become my familiar. It was too much for me. Throwing on my dressing gown, I fled from the room out into the empty quad and hammered on a friend's door. I cannot imagine what he must have made of the trembling apparition standing on his threshold. 'I think I'm dying,' I said to him—or words to that effect. 'You must help me. I'm dying.' He reacted with commendable calm to the news. He made tea, and we talked (what could we have talked about?) until the sky began to lighten. With the coming of the day, my agitation waned and I became gradually less afraid.

The calamity that had befallen me—at first sight so gratuitous an assault—was, I quickly realized, linked to an event I had tried to banish from my consciousness. Earlier that summer, I had had a bad shock. Just before the start of the term, a friend of mine, a fellow-student from Trinidad, had been found dead in his rooms at Balliol.

Shiva Naipaul, an excerpt from *A Trinidad Childhood*

PERFECTION

Perfection—completion; making perfect; full development; faultlessness; comparative excellence; perfect person or thing; highest pitch, perfect specimen or manifestation

I used to sing in the choir of the University Church of Christ the King, in London. During a summer vacation we went to sing the services in Llandaff Cathedral for a week, and this was followed by a short tour in Germany. Our singing improved as we went from church to church. Having sung together for a fortnight we were beginning to sing quite well.

We came to our final Service in a church in Cologne. I shall never forget this service. The anthem was Byrd's *Ave Verum Corpus.* Something strange happened to us whilst singing this anthem. It was as though everything suddenly clicked into place. We were conscious of being on a higher plane. There was a glorious feeling of absolute and utter harmony. We felt we were singing as one person. The conductor only had to move his little finger and there was an instant reaction. It was a thrilling experience. At the end of the anthem we all gasped in amazement. This was the closest we had come to perfection, and it was a wonderful sensation.

I used to think of perfection in terms of ethics and behaviour. I no longer think in these terms, since the experience in Cologne. I now tend to think of perfection as wholeness, harmony, as a unity, as a oneness with God. I see my role as a priest primarily as exercising a cure of souls—enabling people to come to wholeness through releasing the divine that is already within them. This surely must be the source of our perfection.

For I will proclaim the name of the Lord. Ascribe greatness to our God! The Rock, his work is perfect; for all his ways are justice. A God of faithfulness and without iniquity, just and right is he.

Deuteronomy 32:3–4

This God—his way is perfect; the promise of the Lord proves true.

2 Samuel 22:31

If you would be perfect, go, sell what you possess and give to the poor, and you will have treasure in heaven; and come, follow me.

Matthew 19:21

And let steadfastness have its full effect, that you may be perfect and complete, lacking in nothing.

James 1:4

Every heart contains perfection's germ.

Percy Bysshe Shelley, 'Queen Mab', v. 146, in Thomas Hutchinson, editor, *The Complete Poetical Works of Percy Bysshe Shelley*, Oxford University Press, 1935, page 772

Perfection is always to be measured, by its nearness to the pattern of perfection.

Benjamin Whichcote, *Moral and Religious Aphorisms*, century xii, number 1129, Elkin Mathews & Marrot, 1930, page 132

Nature, in her productions slow, aspires
By just degrees to reach perfection's height.

William Somervile, *The Chase*, George Redway, 1896, first book, page 3

The great question, therefore, which each religion must be asked is, how far it produces permanent and profound incentives to the inward perfecting of personality and to ethical activity.

Albert Schweitzer, *Christianity and the Religions of the World*, George Allen & Unwin, 1923, page 37

But Jesus did not offer life a little more bearable, he promised life more abundant; neither did he exhort his disciples to aim at a respectable mediocrity but to perfection.

Martin Thornton, *Spiritual Direction*, SPCK, 1984, page 10

In trying to do everything for the best, we do not avoid all mistakes. So the Christian life is not a huge effort to do good, but abdication and a prayer that God will guide us through all the reefs.

Paul Tournier, *The Person Reborn*, SCM Press, William Heinemann, 1967, page 90

Thy life is dear, for all that life can rate
Worth name of life in thee hath estimate:
Youth, beauty, wisdom, courage, all
That happiness and pride can happy call.

William Shakespeare, *All's Well That Ends Well*, II. i. 175

Only the best matters, in man especially.
True, you can't produce the best without attending to the whole
but that which is secondary is only important
in so far as it goes to the bringing forth of the best.

D.H. Lawrence, 'The Best Matters', in Vivian de Sola Pinto and Warren Roberts, editors, *The Complete Poems of D.H. Lawrence*, William Heinemann, 1967, volume II, page 668

We cannot offer to God the service of Angels; we cannot obey Him as man in a state of perfection could; but fallen men can do their best, and this is the perfection that is required of us; it is only the perfection of our best endeavours, a careful labour to be as perfect as we can.

William Law, *A Serious Call to a Devout and Holy Life*, J.M. Dent and Co., 1898, page 27

In philosophical ethics the original Latin sense of *perfectio*, completeness, persists: it indicates the full development of one's distinctively human capacities, cognitive, aesthetic, moral, religious. In this wide sense the notion comes from the Greeks, who included health and bodily perfection.

T.E. Jessop, in James F. Childress and John Macquarrie, editors, *A New Dictionary of Christian Ethics*, SCM Press, 1985, page 464

That men should perfectly love God and worthily magnify his holy name is the goal of the Christian life. Christian perfection is defined in terms of the Great Commandment (Matthew 22:37–39)—of love of God and man. Absolute perfection lies beyond this life, in the vision of God, when faith and hope have passed away, but the love of God endures (Aquinas).

E.G. Rupp, in Alan Richardson and John Bowden, editors, *A New Dictionary of Christian Theology*, SCM Press, 1985, page 440

It is good for a man, when he makes his debut in the world, to regard himself highly, to aim at perfecting himself in a great number of ways, to take the broadest view of his possibilities. But after he has arrived at a certain degree of self-perfection it is of advantage for him to learn to lose himself in a crowd, to live for the sake of others, and to forget himself in activity prescribed by duty. Only then does he begin to know himself; for it is in what we do that we truly measure ourselves against others.

Johann Wolfgang von Goethe, *Wisdom and Experience*, selected by Ludwig Curtius, translated and edited by Hermann J. Weigand, Routledge & Kegan Paul, 1949, page 204

He [Jesus] was 'perfect' at every stage, as infant, as boy, as youth, as man; but it is evident that there is a height and depth of 'perfection' in the man's obedience to God which has no place in the boy's and no meaning for the infant. 'Perfect' at every stage, He 'yet learned obedience by the things which He suffered, and having been made perfect (or full grown) became to all them that obey Him the cause of eternal salvation' (Hebrews 5:9).

William Temple, *Readings in St. John's Gospel* (First and Second Series), Macmillan & Co., 1947, page 208

Every day the choice between good and evil is presented to us in simple ways. When we choose the higher, we fashion our character in harmony with our future environment, and, when we prefer the lower, we are making ourselves less capable of life where Christ reigns. God's laws work on immutably. 'We are not punished for our sins, but by our sins.' Yet God is at hand to aid the most helpless who will turn to Him for help. Devout souls are not made perfect in the instant of death by some stroke of power. Perfection can never be given: it can only be co-operatively attained. But that is God's ambition for us all, and the end He will pursue through all eternity.

W.E. Sangster, *These Things Abide*, Hodder and Stoughton, 1939, page 185

Everything that is perfect in this life has some imperfection bound up with it, and there is nothing we investigate that is without its darkness. Humble recognition of what your nature is will lead more surely to God than profound searching for knowledge. Learning or the simple knowledge of facts can be good and instituted by God, and then there is no fault to be found with it, but a good conscience and a holy life must always be preferred...

When the day of judgment comes, we shall not be asked what we have read, but what we have done, not if we made fine speeches, but if we lived religious lives.

Thomas à Kempis, *The Imitation of Christ*, translated by Betty I. Knott, William Collins Sons & Co., 1977, page 41

... I evidently saw that the way to become rich and blessed was not by heaping accidental and devised riches to make ourselves great in the vulgar manner, but to approach more near, or to see more clearly with the eye of our understanding, the beauties and glories of the whole world: and to have communion with the Deity in the riches of God and Nature.

I saw moreover that it did not so much concern us what objects were before us, as with what eyes we beheld them, with what affections we esteemed them, and what apprehensions we had about them. All men see the same objects, but do not equally understand them. Intelligence is the tongue that discerns and tastes them, Knowledge is the Light of Heaven, Love is the Wisdom and Glory of God, Life extended to all objects is the sense that enjoys them. So that Knowledge, Life, and Love are the very means of all enjoyment, which above all things we must seek for and labour after. All objects are in God Eternal: which we by perfecting our faculties are made to enjoy. Which then are turned into Act, when they are desolate and idle; or discontented and forlorn. Whereby I perceived the meaning of the definition wherein Aristotle describeth Felicity, when he saith, *Felicity is the perfect exercise of perfect virtue in a perfect Life.* For that life is perfect when it is perfectly extended to all objects, and perfectly sees them, and perfectly loves them: which is done by a perfect exercise of virtue about them.

Thomas Traherne, *Centuries*, The Faith Press, 1969, page 146

PERSEVERANCE

Perseverance—a steadfast pursuit of an aim, constant persistence

I met a young disabled woman. She had come to University College, London, to do a post-graduate diploma in librarianship. After a week or so she told me about herself. She had been born with cerebral palsy. Her father left home when she was very young and had not been seen by her since. She decided to get stuck into life, and got through her O and A levels at school. She made a successful application to Exeter University and managed to get an honours degree. Disaster struck again. In her early twenties she was involved in a serious car accident, which left her more disabled than ever. Life then became a constant struggle to survive. She had now arrived in London to get a further qualification for a career as a librarian.

She was not finding it easy. London provided her with peculiar problems of its own. The course was academic and demanding. It required all her powers of perseverance. She had another car crash in which she was not hurt, but her car was damaged. This was an added complication and frustration, especially as she was living some distance from the college. Her persistence was rewarded when she got her diploma, and a job as a librarian.

After a year or two she made a brave decision to have major surgery on her legs to remedy some of the damage resulting from the original car accident. She was admitted to St George's Hospital, and was in and out of the orthopaedic wards for two years. Eventually a splint was found which enabled her to walk on her badly-damaged limb. She returned to work, and has persisted in her job ever since, but recently has had to take early retirement. She is barely fifty years old and is faced with an uncertain future. With the odds against her she has managed to find a part-time job. There are some people you just have to admire.

Seek the Lord and his strength, seek his presence continually!

1 Chronicles 16:11

Yet the righteous holds to his way, and he that has clean hands grows stronger and stronger.

Job 17:9

As for that in the good soil, they are those who, hearing the word, hold it fast in an honest and good heart, and bring forth fruit with patience.

Luke 8:15

Pray at all times in the Spirit, with all prayer and supplication. To that end keep alert with all perseverance.

Ephesians 6:18

Perseverance, dear my lord,
Keeps honour bright.

William Shakespeare, *Troilus and Cressida*, III. iii. 150

Attempt the end, and never stand to doubt;
Nothing's so hard, but search will find it out.

Robert Herrick, 'Hesperides: Seek and Find', in *The Poetical Works of Robert Herrick*, Oxford University Press, 1915, page 311

No great cause is ever lost or ever won. The battle must always be renewed and the creed restated.

John Buchan, *Montrose*, Oxford University Press, 1957, page 423

For me at least there came moments when faith wavered. But there is the great lesson and the great triumph if you keep the fire burning until, by and by, out of the mass of sordid details there comes some result, be it some new generalization or be it a transcending spiritual repose.

Oliver Wendell Holmes, in Max Lerner, editor, *The Mind and Faith of Justice Holmes*, Little, Brown and Company, 1945, page 425

Exasperation at not being able to do a thing *uninterruptedly*; and I am more and more convinced that nothing good is achieved without a long perseverance, without applying one's effort for some time in the same direction. It is a matter of patient selection, analogous to that exercised by good horticulturalists.

André Gide, *The Journals of André Gide*, translated by Justin O'Brien, Secker & Warburg, 1929, volume IV, page 71

We live in a very beautiful world; but few good things are to be had in it without hard work. It is not a world in which any one can expect to be prosperous if he is easily discouraged. Perseverance—earnest, steady perseverance—is necessary to success. This is no drawback. Good, solid work is as necessary to peace of mind as it is for the health of the body; in fact the two are inseparable.

Right Hon. Lord Avebury, *Essays and Addresses*, Macmillan and Co., 1903, page 276

There is nothing that so much develops faith as to persevere in asking through disappointment. If you always get the blessing you seek at once, or something you recognise as corresponding with it, your faith will remain at about the level at which you started. The reason why God calls for perseverance is not, of course, that He wishes to test our faith. He knows exactly what it is worth. But He may wish to deepen it. The thing that will most deepen it is to persist with faith through disappointment.

William Temple, *Christian Faith and Life*, SCM Press, 1963, page 116

Disraeli the elder held that the secret of all success consisted in being master of your subject, such mastery being attainable only through continuous application and study. Hence it happens that the men who have most moved the world have been not so much men of genius, strictly so called, as men of intense mediocre abilities, untiring workers, persevering, self-reliant and indefatigable; not so often the gifted, of naturally bright and shining qualities, as those who have applied themselves diligently to their work, in whatever line that might lie.

Samuel Smiles, *Self Help*, S.W. Partridge & Co., 1912, page 53

Another important value in an abundance of energy should be mentioned. The *ability to persevere* in the face of discouragement and disappointment and the possession of *courage* to face strong opposition are both qualities which mark successful leaders. And both of these qualities are fed at their roots by an endowment of energy. Probably no single corroding influence eats away perseverance and courage so much as fatigue and bodily unfitness. Both the buoyancy of the outlook and the constancy of the effort of all of us derive from forces not primarily of the mind but of the body. When the leader begins to question whether 'what I am trying to do is worth doing,' the chances are that he needs a rest.

Ordway Tead, *The Art of Leadership*, McGraw-Hill Book Company, 1935, page 92

The prayer of *perseverance* keeps us following and suffering, not triumphing consciously but just weathering the storm, learning our weakness more and more, being grounded in humility more and more. The fruit of this prayer will be a very humble constancy in the following of our Lord. Supplication and perseverance will bring about in the soul at last a condition of silent contemplation, as the development of the life of prayer issues increasingly in the death of self, the passing from the thought of self, all selfish wants, irritations, resentments, vanities, to the thought of God, His kingdom, His righteousness, His interests. By the way of meditation we are led at last to this prayer, and this is the prayer without ceasing about which S. Paul the Apostle speaks.

Father Andrew, SDC., *In the Silence*, A.R. Mowbray & Co., 1947, page 84

Perseverance is not merely the crown and stamp of perfection, it must accompany every step in the growth of every grace; just as the texture of the tree must be woven firm in every stage of its growth, so perseverance has to watch over the growth of each virtue day by day; every day in which it fails, the graces which are under its care begin to droop and lose their bloom.

Thus perseverance is not only a virtue in itself, but it is one without whose constant presence and assistance no other virtue can develop one step in its growth. If charity, then, be the soil into which all must spread their roots, perseverance is the cohesive force that gives form and consistency to all over whose development it presides. And thus temptation will often leave all the graces that the soul is trying to form unassailed, and attack the one grace of perseverance; for it knows well that if it can destroy or weaken this, all else must fail with it. We often meet with people with very high aspirations and the beginnings of many graces and with great possibilities, but nothing in them matures, nothing attains its full bloom, for they are lacking in the one grace which is the guardian and protector of all—they have no perseverance.

Now perseverance having so great a work to do, having to watch over every good thing that the soul would develop, cannot work alone—it has not only to keep everything under its protection, but it must live both in the present and future; it must look forward, but it must not for a moment forget the present. It knows indeed that many a promising virtue has died because its possessor was living in the future and neglecting it in the present, and virtues are too delicate to grow untended for a day; and it knows also that many a virtue has been killed because the soul in which it was trying to grow could not look forward and wait and hope, recognising the law of its organic growth and rejoicing, as it saw the blade, in the thought of the full-grown ear.

Therefore perseverance needs the aid of two fellow-workers: it needs, as it were, eyes with which to look forward, and hands with which to toil. It must keep ever before it the ideal towards which it presses, and it must never cease to work towards that ideal. Perseverance is not a mere dogged plodding on toward an unseen end, it is full of inspiration and enthusiasm; in all its endeavours, therefore, it is assisted by the two fellow-workers, hope and patience.

B.W. Maturin, *Some Principles and Practices of The Spiritual Life*, Longmans, Green, and Co., 1899, page 195

PERSONALITY

Personality—being a person; personal existence or identity; distinctive personal character

I was very hard hit by some words of the Swiss psychologist, Carl Gustav Jung, on 'personality'. In one of his books he wrote that the achievement of personality means nothing less than the optimum development of the whole individual human being. I could see in an instant he was pinpointing our great aim in life, namely, to grow a personality which is us at our highest level of development and expression. Linking this with the Genesis story of the creation of man—of man made in the image and likeness of God, and of the divine inbreathing—I could discern a way in which this could be done. We can see this fully worked out in the life (and personality) of Jesus Christ. He found 'the Father' in the depths of himself and, following on from this, discovered attributes of the Father: light, life, truth, joy, love, hope and so on. In the pages of the Gospels we catch a glimpse of the personality of God, in a human life. Christ was the pioneer, the prototype, of personality. He knew what it meant to be made in the image and likeness of God. The Apostle Paul made the discovery that what Christ had experienced we can all in some measure also experience. We, too, are made 'in the image and likeness of God,' we are 'sons and daughters of God,' i.e., there is something divine in us. This might come alive in us in a dramatic way, through baptism and confirmation, the cross, or any other way which God might choose. Perhaps the time has come for the 'daily increase' to be put on not just by prayer and by partaking in Holy Communion, but by a disciplined form of reflection, meditation and contemplation. A start could be made by using the contents of this anthology. We might then see many more instances of the optimum development of the whole individual human being in our midst, and more fulfilment and contentment.

So God created man in his own image, in the image of God he created him; male and female he created them.

Genesis 1:27

A good name is to be chosen rather than great riches, and favour is better than silver or gold.

Proverbs 22:1

Do you not believe that I am in the Father and the Father is in me?

John 14:11

I have been crucified with Christ; it is no longer I who live, but Christ who lives in me; and the life I now live in the flesh, I live by faith in the Son of God, who loved and gave himself for me.

Galatians 2:20

Each [man] needs to develop the sides of his personality which he has neglected.

Alexis Carrel, *Reflections on Life*, Hamish Hamilton, 1952, page 183

Truth before God is essence; 'truth' before man is personality.

A.R. Orage, *On Love*, The Janus Press, 1957, page 59

It never will be altogether well with us until we see that religion at its best is a great emancipator of personality.

Harry Emerson Fosdick, *Twelve Tests of Character*, Hodder and Stoughton, 1924, page 85

His life was gentle, and the elements
So mixed in him that nature might stand up
And say to all the world 'This was a man.'

William Shakespeare, *Julius Caesar*, V. v. 72

All personality has a radiation. The radiations of those in whom God dwells are mighty beyond measurement. Much experience lies behind the common assertion that 'religion is caught, not taught'.

W.E. Sangster, *The Pure in Heart*, The Epworth Press, 1954, page 30

A cultivation of the powers of one's own personality is one of the greatest needs of life, too little realized even in these assertive days, and the exercise of the personality makes for its most durable satisfactions.

Randolph Bourne, *Youth and Life*, Constable & Co., 1913, page 181

Physical fitness, temperament, and circumstances are not prime causes and do not of themselves explain radiant personality.

For the secret spring of that, we must look elsewhere.

W.E. Sangster, *The Secret of Radiant Life*, Hodder and Stoughton, 1957, page 16

... the individual needs to be in constant struggle with his environment if he is to develop to his highest capacity. Hard conditions of life are indispensable to bringing out the best in human personality.

Alexis Carrel, *Reflections on Life*, Hamish Hamilton, 1952, page 41

They carp at personality,
The wise folk, shamelessly,
Yet what can make you glad and free
But your own personality,
Whatever it may be?

Johann Wolfgang von Goethe, 'Gentle Reminders', 3, in *The Practical Wisdom of Goethe*, chosen by Emil Ludwig, George Allen & Unwin, 1933, page 20

Personality is the greatest work of God, and it is a very wonderful thing to consider that you and I, each one of us, is a personality, and that personality rises to its full stature when it says deliberately to the God to Whom it owes its creation, 'In all things direct and rule my heart.'

Father Andrew, SDC., *The Good Shepherd*, A.R. Mowbray & Co., 1949, page 22

The south-west wind is roaring round the house, bringing up from the sea a storm of rain, splashing against the windows and streaming down them. How much better to be a breath of that south-west wind than to be a pitiful *personality* like myself, crouching over a fire.

Mark Rutherford, *Last Pages From a Journal*, Oxford University Press, 1915, page 288

I am now trying to write on personality. *Personality is neither right nor wrong*—for it is divine—it transcends intellect and morality, and while it keeps to being pure personality we love it for it is *one with our very selves, and with the all pervasive Divine*—at least this I believe and contend.

J.B. Yeats, *Letters to his son, W.B. Yeats and others*, Faber and Faber, 1944, page 150

The impact of one personality on another can indeed produce the most wonderful effects. Very often a man has been launched on a career of scholarship by the impact of the personality of a great teacher upon him; many a man has been moved to the Christian way and to a life of Christian service by the impact of a great Christian personality on his life. Preaching itself has been described and defined as 'truth through personality.'

William Barclay, *The Gospel of Matthew*, The Saint Andrew Press, 1987, volume I, page 312

When I find it hard to believe in a Personal God who can be called 'Father'—and who doesn't sometimes?—I always find myself pulled up short by the fact of human personality. I can't for the life of me see how personality could have been produced by a process that was merely mechanistic and impersonal. Could a being capable of love and reason and imagination somehow come from a machine which could not think or feel? Could man have emerged from the evolutionary process as the result of 'a chance accident in a backwater'? Men far more able than I have believed it possible, but it stretches my credulity too far. Because I believe in God my mind sometimes twists itself into the shape of a question mark, but if I threw belief overboard I am sure I should not be able to make sense of anything.

Leslie J. Tizard, *Facing Life and Death*, George Allen and Unwin, 1959, page 151

Every normal person would like to be a radiant personality: to be respected, attractive and, indeed, loved: to be at peace within, useful, happy and sought after—not just for the things they might be able to give, but for themselves alone.

If there are people who deny all this, and say that they do not care a bit what others think of them, and even seem to enjoy being disagreeable, that is only a proof that they are odd. Some mishandling in childhood, or some major defeat in later life, has given them a kink, and it is not less a kink because they have come to take pride in it. We are so made that we cannot hate our kind and be happy ourselves, and people who seem to get pleasure from being unpleasant are twisted in their thinking and emotionally immature.

W.E. Sangster, *The Secret of Radiant Life*, Hodder and Stoughton, 1957, page 13

If the inmost secret of the moral life is that it is a life of 'making the best' of ourselves, of achieving, out of the crude and conflicting stresses and tensions with which we start, a genuine personality which is free and its own master, and if the price which has to be paid for every advance towards such freedom is surrender, then, as it seems to me, we can think of such a life as not condemned in principle to futility only on one condition. The condition is that we anticipate the completion of the process as found in the winning of a personality absolutely above circumstance and mutability by a supreme surrender of the whole realm of merely temporal values, as dying out of time into a real eternity. What such an eternal life would be like is, of course, more than we can imagine, since all our imaginations are borrowed from the temporal. What we imagine is a tissue of 'events', though some of the events may be 'slow-moving'.

Still, imaginable or not, and the human imagination is no criterion of the real—that dying out of the temporal into the eternal which writers like Suso spoke of as 'passing away into the high godhead' must be real, and must be no mere negation, but the final affirmation of the moral self, if morality itself is to be, in the end, more than a futility. What is put off in such an achievement of the moral end must be not personality or individuality, but that inner division of the soul against itself which makes the tragedy of life and leaves us here mere imperfect fragments of persons.

A.E. Taylor, *The Faith of a Moralist*, Macmillan & Co., 1930, volume 1, page 311

We find then, that Jesus Christ, as depicted in the pages of the New Testament, threw a totally new light upon the personality of man. He took love as His point of departure, the central principle in our nature, which gathers all its other faculties and functions into one; our absolutely fundamental and universal characteristic. He taught us that virtues and graces are only thorough when they flow from love; and further, that love alone can reconcile the opposite phases of our life—action and passion, doing and suffering, energy and pain, since love inevitably leads to sacrifice, and perfect sacrifice is perfect love. It may be granted that previous teachers had said somewhat kindred things. But Jesus Christ carried His precepts home by practice, as none had ever done before. He lived and died the life and death of love; and men saw, as they had never seen, what human nature meant. Here at last was its true ideal, and its true ideal realized. Now the content of man's own personality is, as we have seen, the necessary standard by which he judges all things, human or divine; his final court of critical appeal.

Consequently one effect of the life of Christ upon our race was to provide us, if the phrase may be allowed, with a new criterion of God. Man had learned that love was the one thing needful, and had looked into the depths of love, as he had never looked before. And thenceforth love became the only category under which he could be content to think of God.

J.R. Illingworth, *Personality Human and Divine*, Macmillan and Co., 1984, page 200

PETITION

Petition—asking, supplication, request; ask humbly (for thing, to be allowed to do, etc.)

I had only been ordained a short time when the senior curate in the clergy house stopped me one morning outside his room, and said, 'Bill, come into my room for a moment. I've made an exciting discovery.' I went in and he told me he'd been reading the Old Testament story of Naaman the leper. Naaman was the commander of the army of the king of Syria, a mighty man of valour. Naturally he wanted to be cured of his leprosy, so he went to see the prophet Elisha. He was told to wash himself in the Jordan seven times and he would be healed. Naaman was angry. He declined to take Elisha's advice, and his leprosy remained. Eventually he went and dipped himself seven times in the Jordan, and was healed. 'Do you see what really happened Bill? Naaman wanted something dramatic to happen—perhaps a great victory so he would have earned his healing. In the end it was a simple act of faith that did it. That's what healed him.' He looked at me excitedly.

I'm afraid I wasn't as impressed as I should have been, but that afternoon I was hospital visiting and came across a man reading his Bible. That was unusual. He was reading about Naaman the leper. He needed help with the passage. I proudly shared with him my newly-acquired knowledge. He was impressed and it did the trick. 'Now listen,' he said, 'you won't believe this but yesterday I was in Austria. I had a terrific pain in my side. Stones in the kidneys were diagnosed by the doctor. I came straight back to England. Here I am, just about to go down for an X-ray, prior to an operation. Please lay hands on me and pray that I may be healed.' I did as requested.

Next week he was not on the ward. The Charge Nurse said there was no trace of the stones on the X-ray and no need for an operation. Had these passed through his system naturally, or was this an answer to petitionary prayer? The coincidence of Naaman the leper leads me to believe that when we engage in this form of prayer 'things happen'.

Answer me when I call, O God of my right! Thou hast given me room when I was in distress. Be gracious to me, and hear my prayer.

Psalm 4:1

The Lord is just in all his ways, and kind in all his doings. The Lord is near to all who call upon him, to all who call upon him in truth. He fulfills the desire of all who fear him, he also hears their cry, and saves them.

Psalm 145:17–19

Ask, and it will be given you; seek, and you will find; knock, and it will be opened to you. For every one who asks receives, and he who seeks finds, and to him who knocks it will be opened. Or what man of you, if his son asks him for bread, will give him a stone? Or if he asks for a fish, will give him a serpent? If you then, who are evil, know how to give good gifts to your children, how much more will your Father who is in heaven give good things to those who ask him!

Matthew 7:7–11

If two of you agree on earth about anything they ask, it will be done for them by my Father in heaven. For where two or three are gathered in my name, there am I in the midst of them.

Matthew 18:19–20

Prayer is properly not petition, but simply an attention to God which is a form of love. With it goes the idea of grace, of a supernatural assistance to human endeavour which overcomes empirical limitations of personality.

Iris Murdoch, *The Sovereignty of Good*, Routledge & Kegan Paul, 1970, page 55

The prayer of *petition* is the reaction of a love that is needing and needy to the revelation of a love that is all-sufficing. The vocation of life is always making demands upon us which we cannot possibly meet in our own strength. We look up to God, as the poor man by the pool looked up to Jesus. Our need, the needs of others, our spiritual conflicts, our troubles, our temptations, all these form the prayer of petition that silently or vocally we bring to the presence of our God. It is a comfort to think we may know S. Paul's experience, and that as we find our weakness in ourselves so we may find our strength in our Lord.

Father Andrew, SDC, *In the Silence*, A.R. Mowbray & Co., 1947, page 84

Prayer is speaking to God; so the first necessity is that you should be directing your mind towards God. That is the best part and the most important part of prayer anyhow, and without it all the rest is useless... Our Lord says that when you come into the presence of God you should forget all about yourself and your needs, even your sins; you should be so filled with the thought of God that what you want above all things is that God's Name may be hallowed—reverenced—throughout the world. You are to ask for that first, because you ought to want it most. And next, that He may be effectively King of the world He has made, so that all men obey His law; and then, that His whole purpose of love shall be carried out unspoiled by the selfishness of men.

William Temple, *Christian Faith and Life*, SCM Press, 1963, page 113

Many of our prayers are prayers of petition, and people seem to think that petition is the lowest level of prayer; then comes gratitude, then praise. But in fact it is gratitude and praise that are expressions of a lower relationship. On our level of half-belief it is easier to sing hymns of praise or to thank God than to trust him enough to ask something with faith. Even people who believe half-heartedly can turn to thank God when something nice comes their way; and there are moments of elation when everyone can sing to God. But it is much more difficult to have such undivided faith as to ask with one's whole heart and whole mind with complete confidence. No one should look askance at petition, because the ability to say prayers of petition is a test of the reality of our faith.

Anthony Bloom, *The Essence of Prayer*, Darton, Longman and Todd, 1989, page 80

The prayers of petition and intercession give voice to the confident trust in the power and willingness of God to intervene helpfully in human life. There is a naïvety, a childlike quality, about petition which is apt to shock the sophisticated. But below the level of adult consciousness there exists a well of primitive feeling which resembles a child. Petitionary prayer awakens this childlike thing and involves it in prayer. Further, it seems that there are healing forces at work within us which the doubt and mistrust fostered by a sceptical society repress. Confident petition helps to break down the imprisoning wall of mistrust and so enables the life-renewing energy to flow out. The mysterious fact of telepathy which seems to imply that mind unconsciously touches and flows into mind independently of spacial proximity illuminates the corporate nature of private prayer. For it seems probable that the confident petition which opens the personality to its depths causes either distress signals or impulses of healing and encouragement to be sent out below the level of consciousness. This would shed light on some of the extraordinarily detailed answers to prayer which those who pray with confidence sometimes record.

Christopher Bryant, SSJE., in Gordon S. Wakefield, editor, *The Dictionary of Christian Spirituality*, SCM Press, 1986, page 318

Petition is the prayer of asking. It is often regarded as a 'low level' of prayer like the mewing of a cat for milk, and it may be selfish. Some spiritual writers feel that we should grow out of petition and not expect answers, that if we do we may become frantic with disappointment and torture ourselves with guilt like the prophets of Baal cutting themselves with knives to call down fire from heaven. We have to learn that prayer is communion with God, perhaps even a support for him in his cause against evil, rather than a demand for ourselves and the satisfaction of our wants.

Those who take this view are embarrassed by the teaching of Jesus—'Ask and it shall be given you. Seek and you shall find; Knock and it shall be opened unto you' (Luke 11:9). The Lord's Prayer is petitionary and Jesus holds before his hearers human importunity, persistent and discourteous, as an example of prayer (Luke 11:5ff.; 18:1–8).

Petition means that we recognize our entire dependence on God and that the earth is his and we should ask his permission before we take anything, even a crust of bread. It demands the recognition that we are not lone individuals but members of a family and that my request may have to be denied for the sake of others. It is the prayer of faith and may not be the simplest and easiest stage of prayer, but one which requires great spiritual maturity. Fundamental is the belief that God waits for us to ask not only to try our faith, but because he wants the whole of our life to be in relation to him, every need, hope and fear binding us to himself. We must not become absorbed in our own needs but in God and his unbounded mercy, love and generosity.

Jesus promised that God would do for us all that we ask in Christ's name. This means more than adding 'through Jesus Christ' at the end of each prayer. It means praying as Christ himself would pray, asking only for the things for which he would pray. In John 15 Jesus puts it in another way: 'If you abide in me and I in you, ask what you will and it shall be done unto you.' This is an even stiffer condition, if we allow him to pray in us in our name. Yet with our asking there is the assurance that God is always more ready to hear than we deserve or desire. It is easy enough to believe that God gives more than we desire. Jesus assured us that God our Father is more generous than human parents: 'If you then who are evil know how to give good gifts to your children, how much more will your Father in heaven give good things to those who ask him?' (Matthew 7:11). Luke in his version in 11:13 has 'How much more will the heavenly Father give the Holy Spirit to those who ask him?' Our greatest need, perhaps our ultimate need, is as Luke suggests, God; so our fundamental prayer should be, 'O God, give us Yourself.'...

The distinction between petition and intercession—which is petition for others—is not always easy to draw. But the two should be kept separate. Petition concerns our straight course to God; intercession our placing of ourselves between him and the world.

George Appleton, in Gordon S. Wakefield, editor, *A Dictionary of Christian Spirituality*, SCM Press, 1986, page 311

PHILOSOPHY

Philosophy—love of wisdom or knowledge, especially that which deals with ultimate reality, or with the most general causes—principles of things, study of principles of human action or conduct; system of conduct of life

At university the study of philosophy has become a very exacting academic discipline, far removed from the ordinary person. I have been greatly helped by some words of Lord Byron in which he wrote in his poem, *Childe Harold's Pilgrimage*, of *that untaught innate philosophy.* This was fortified in turn by some words of a former Dean of St Paul's—W.R. Inge. In his book *Outspoken Essays* he wrote that *philosophy means thinking things out for oneself.* I wonder if we can make yet another link here with the Genesis story of the creation of man and of the divine inbreathing; that as a natural consequence of this we have inside us something of *that untaught innate philosophy.* If ordinary people can get hold of this, then they may be given confidence to go one stage further and *think out things for themselves.* We might then get an increase in the 'love of wisdom or knowledge,' and an enrichment of our corporate life.

I mentioned in *Visions of Love* a certain medical student who got hold of this. He was weary of taking in vast quantities of factual knowledge of anatomy, physiology and biochemistry, and had become depressed. After a short period of reflection, he became excited and had 'his first thoughts ever'. He discovered something of *that untaught innate philosophy* and started the process of *thinking things out for himself.*

Visions of Hope provides us with some thought-provoking material and the practice of reflection, whether in groups or on an individual basis, a way in which we too can think things out for ourselves.

Can you find out the deep things of God? Can you find out the limit of the Almighty?

Job 11:7

It is the glory of God to conceal things, but the glory of kings is to search things out.

Proverbs 25:2

... and my speech and my message were not in plausible words of wisdom, but in demonstration of the Spirit and of power.

1 Corinthians 2:4

See to it that no one makes a prey of you by philosophy and empty deceit, according to human tradition, according to the elemental spirits of the universe, and not according to Christ.

Colossians 2:8

The philosopher aspires to explain away all mysteries, to dissolve them into light.

Henri Frédéric Amiel, *Amiel's Journal*, translated by Mrs Humphry Ward, Macmillan & Co., 1918, page 171

People often complain that philosophy is useless. This, however, is merely to vilify our own minds. Philosophy is nothing but men's thinking.

W. Macneile Dixon, *The Human Situation*, Edward Arnold & Co., 1937, page 19

The Philosopher is Nature's pilot. And there you have our difference: to be in hell is to drift: to be in heaven is to steer.

George Bernard Shaw, *Man and Superman*, Act III, The Bodley Head, 1971, page 685

The maxims and statements of Christ were the very roots of philosophy. We have never, under any moral philosophy, come up to the maxims and root-teachings of the Lord Jesus.

Henry Ward Beecher, *Proverbs from Plymouth Pulpit*, Charles Burnet & Co., 1887, page 152

For me philosophy is a manner of apprehending things, a mode of perception of reality. It does not create nature, man or God, but it finds them and seeks to understand them.

Henri Frédéric Amiel, *Amiel's Journal*, translated by Mrs Humphry Ward, Macmillan & Co., 1918, page 34

No man can form a philosophical conception of God which is perfect, which he can round out and present to the world, and of which he can say, 'That is God—just that, and no more.'

Henry Ward Beecher, *Proverbs from Plymouth Pulpit*, Charles Burnet & Co., 1887, page 139

For philosophy is the study of wisdom, and wisdom is the knowledge of things divine and human; and their causes. Wisdom is therefore queen of philosophy.

Clement of Alexandria, 'The Miscellanies', in *The Writings of Clement of Alexandria*, translated by the Rev. William Wilson, T. & T. Clark, 1867, page 368

The philosophy of six thousand years has not searched the chambers and magazines of the soul. In its experiments, there has always remained, in the last analysis, a residium it could not resolve.

Ralph Waldo Emerson, 'Essay on the Over Soul', from 'Essays and Representative Men', in *The Works of Ralph Waldo Emerson*, George Bell & Sons, 1906, volume I, page 143

I do not call to mind any passages in the Bible commending the temperate philosophic life, though it would be strange if so large a miscellany did not contain a few sound reflections.

Norman Douglas, *An Almanac*, Chatto & Windus in association with Martin Secker & Warburg, 1945, page 76

I do not myself believe that philosophy can either prove or disprove the truth of religious dogmas, but ever since Plato most philosophers have considered it part of their business to produce 'proofs' of immortality and the existence of God.

Bertrand Russell, *History of Western Philosophy*, George Allen & Unwin, 1967, page 789

In modern philosophy... it is its outer ring that is obviously artistic and emancipated; its despair is within. And its despair is this, that it does not really believe that there is any meaning in the universe.

G.K. Chesterton, *Orthodoxy*, The Bodley Head, 1935, page 290

The strength of an argument in favour of a philosophy or religion is proportionate to the applicability of the philosophy or religion to life. If in all situations we find it ready, it is true.

Mark Rutherford, *More Pages From a Journal*, Oxford University Press, 1915, page 253

This is that mystical Philosophy, from whence no true Scholar becomes an Atheist, but from the visible effects of nature, grows up a real Divine, and beholds not in a dream, as Ezekiel, but in an ocular and visible object the types of his resurrection.

Sir Thomas Browne, 'Religio Medici', in Geoffrey Keynes, editor, *The Works of Sir Thomas Browne*, Faber and Faber, 1964, volume I, page 59

How charming is divine philosophy!
Not harsh and crabbed, as dull fools suppose,
But musical as in Apollo's lute,
And a perpetual feast of nectar'd sweets
Where no crude surfeit reigns.

John Milton, 'Comus', in F.T. Prince, editor, *Comus and other Poems*, Oxford University Press, 1968, page 60

Theology, which is the science of Religion, starts from the Supreme Spirit and explains the world by reference to Him. Philosophy starts from the detailed experience of men, and seeks to build up its understanding of that experience by reference to that experience alone.

William Temple, *Nature, Man and God*, Macmillan & Co., 1934, page 45

'The business of philosophy,' says Landor (*Pericles and Aspasia*, Letter CLXXVI), 'is to examine and estimate all those things which come within the cognizance of the understanding.' But the conception of an Infinite which actually exists is one with which the understanding can do nothing and is nevertheless more influential than any truth which the understanding can define.

Mark Rutherford, *Last Pages From a Journal*, Oxford University Press, 1915, page 293

I touch here upon what is to me one of the profoundest philosophical mysteries: I mean the power of the individual mind to create its own world, not in complete independence of what is called 'the objective world,' but in a steadily growing independence of the attitude of other minds *towards* this world. For what people call the objective world is really a most fluid, flexible, malleable thing.

John Cowper Powys, *Autobiography*, Macdonald & Co. (Publishers), 1967, page 62

Most people in England think of a philosopher as one who talks in a difficult language about matters which are of interest only to philosophers. But Philosophy is concerned with what must interest every human being, with the nature of man and the nature of the universe. Every man is born a philosopher, but often the philosopher is suppressed in him by the hand-to-mouth thinking needed for the struggle for life.

A. Clutton Brock, *The Ultimate Belief*, Constable and Company, 1916, page 9

Do not all charms fly
At the mere touch of cold philosophy?
There was an awful rainbow once in heaven:
We know her woof, her texture; she is given
In the dull catalogue of common things.
Philosophy will clip an Angel's wings,
Conquer all mysteries by rule and line,
Empty the haunted air and gnomed mine—
Unweave a rainbow, as it erewhile made
The tender-personed Lamia melt into a shade.

John Keats, 'Lamia', xi. 229, in Miriam Allott, editor, *The Poems of John Keats*, Longman, 1986, page 645

... before the advent of the Lord, philosophy was necessary to Greeks for righteousness. And now it becomes conducive to piety; being a kind of preparatory training to those who attain to faith through demonstration. 'For thy foot,' it is said, 'will not stumble, if thou refer what is good, whether belonging to the Greeks or to us, to Providence.' For God is the cause of all good things; but of some primarily, as of the Old and New Testament; and of others by consequence, as of philosophy. Perchance, too, philosophy was given primarily to the Greeks, directly and primarily, till the Lord should call the Greeks. For this was a schoolmaster to bring 'the Hellenic mind,' as the law, the Hebrews, 'to Christ.' Philosophy, therefore, was a preparation, paving the way for him who is perfected in Christ...

The way of truth is therefore one. But into it, as into a perennial river, streams flow from all sides.

Clement of Alexandria, 'The Miscellanies', in *The Writings of Clement of Alexandria*, translated by The Revd William Wilson, T. & T. Clark, 1867, page 366

Philosophies of life, when they are widely believed, also have a very great influence on the vitality of a community. The most widely accepted philosophy of life at present is that what matters most to a man's happiness is his income. This philosophy, apart from other demerits, is harmful because it leads men to aim at a result rather than an activity, an enjoyment of material goods in which men are not differentiated, rather than a creative impulse which embodies each man's individuality...

The world has need of a philosophy, or a religion, which will promote life. But in order to promote life it is necessary to value something other than mere life. Life devoted only to life is animal, without any real human value, incapable of preserving men permanently from weariness and the feeling that all is vanity. If life is to be fully human it must serve some end which seems, in some sense, outside human life, some end which is impersonal and above mankind, such as God or truth or beauty. Those who best promote life do not have life for their purpose. They aim rather at what seems like a gradual incarnation, a bringing into our human existence of something eternal, something that appears to imagination to live in a heaven remote from strife and failure and the devouring jaws of Time. Contact with this eternal world—even if it be only a world of our imagining—brings a strength and a fundamental peace which cannot be wholly destroyed by the struggles and apparent failures of our temporal life. It is this happy contemplation of what is eternal that Spinoza calls the intellectual love of God. To those who have once known it, it is the key of wisdom.

Bertrand Russell, *Principles of Social Reconstruction*, George Allen & Unwin Ltd., 1971, page 168

POETRY

Poetry—art, work, of the poet; elevated expression of elevated thought or feeling in metrical form; quality (in any thing) that calls for poetical expression

I was intrigued to see a young poet in action. He was a student at University College, London, and lived in our chaplaincy house. In this environment I was able to observe him at close hand.

From time to time he would stay up late at night. This was when he was feeling lucid and receptive. He found his best poems came in the early hours of the morning, when it was quiet and there were no distractions. It seemed as though the source of his inspiration was in the deep centre of his being, though he did have a finely-tuned mind and a vivid imagination. All these faculties were used in the writing of his poems. In this he seemed to have much in common with the great poets, Shelley, Wordsworth, Browning, Coleridge, Keats, and so on.

The cost was great. I would see him the following morning, ashen white, haggard, and exhausted, though there was usually a twinkle in his eye. He would maintain over breakfast that the quality of what had emerged made it well worthwhile. Still, his appearance was cause for concern. His fellow students had no such qualms. They would strip him semi-naked, put him in a wheelbarrow, and trundle him round the campus as an advert for Oxfam lunches. With his ribs sticking out and his tired look, he was effective in this role too.

I think the poet taps into the same reservoir of 'inspiration' as the artist, musician, novelist, playwright and so on, but it comes out in a different form of expression. How fortunate we are to have this wide variety of choice—a great source of hope for the future.

Yet he is not far from each one of us, for 'In him we live and move and have our being'; as even some of your poets have said, 'For we are indeed his offspring.'

Acts 17:27–28

The true poet is a solitary, as is man in his great moments.

J.B. Yeats, *Letters to his son, W.B. Yeats and others*, Faber and Faber, 1944, page 105

Poets deal with what I call ultimate human nature—descending into the depths.

J.B. Yeats, *Letters to his son, W.B. Yeats and others*, Faber and Faber, 1944, page 212

Let us therefore deem the glorious art of Poetry a kind of medicine divinely bestowed upon man.

John Keble, *Lectures on Poetry*, lecture 1, Oxford at the Clarendon Press, volume I, page 22

All that is best in the great poets of all countries is not what is national in them, but what is universal.

Henry Wadsworth Longfellow, 'Kavanagh', in *The Writings of Henry Wadsworth Longfellow*, George Routledge and Sons, volume II, page 367

Poetry is divine because it is the voice of the personality—this poor captive caged behind the bars.

J.B. Yeats, *Letters to his son, W.B. Yeats and others*, Faber and Faber, 1944, page 150

The poet enters into himself in order to create. The contemplative enters into God in order to be created.

Thomas Merton, *New Seeds of Contemplation*, Burns & Oates, 1962, page 85

I had said of Christ that he ranks with the poets. That is true. Shelley and Sophocles are his company. But his entire life also is the most wonderful of poems.

Oscar Wilde, 'De Profundis', in *The Works of Oscar Wilde*, William Collins Sons & Co., 1948, page 868

Poetry, as the result of imagination, involves a certain amount of mysticism, for mysticism seems to shadow a higher truth than is known to the intellect.

J.T. Hackett, *My Commonplace Book*, Macmillan and Co., 1923, page 100

Verse comes from Heav'n, like inward Light;
Meer human Pains can ne'er come by't:
The God, not We, the Poem makes:
We only tell Folks what He speaks.

Matthew Prior, 'An Epistle to Fleetwood Shephard, Esq.', in A.R. Waller, editor, *Poems on Several Occasions*, Cambridge at the University Press, 1941, page 11

The touchstone of genuine poetry is that it has the ability, as a secular gospel, to liberate us from the weight of our earthly burden by an inner serenity and an outward sense of well-being.

Johann Wolfgang von Goethe, *Wisdom and Experience*, selected by Ludwig Curtius, translated and edited by Hermann J. Weigand, Routledge & Kegan Paul, 1949, page 246

Blessings be with them—and eternal praise,
Who gave us nobler loves, and nobler cares—
The Poets, who on earth have made us heirs
Of truth and pure delight by heavenly lays!

William Wordsworth, 'Personal Talk', x. 51, in *The Poems*, Penguin Books, 1977, volume I, page 568

For poesie being itself a thing divine of God
Who made his prophets poets, and the more
We feel of poesie we become like God,
In love and power creative.

Philip James Bailey, 'Proem', in *Festus*, George Routledge and Sons, 1889, page 11

Poetry is faith. To the poet the world is virgin soil: all is practicable; the men are ready for virtue; it is always time to do right... The test of the poet is the power to take the passing day, with its news, its cares, its fears, as he shares them, and hold it up to a divine reason... Poetry is the consolation of mortal men.

Ralph Waldo Emerson, 'Society and Solitude, Letters and Social Aims, Addresses', in *The Works of Ralph Waldo Emerson*, George Bell & Sons, 1905, volume III, page 197

Fervency, freedom, fluency of thought,
Harmony, strength, words exquisitely sought;
Fancy, that from the bow that spans the sky
Brings colours dipp'd in heav'n, that never die;
A soul exalted above earth, a mind
Skill'd in the characters that form mankind.

William Cowper, 'Table Talk', in H.S. Milford, editor, *Poetical Works*, Oxford University Press, 1967, page 15

The poet is not primarily a thinker, but incidentally he is a thinker and a stern thinker, since the source of his magic is his personal sincerity. What he says, he believes, and from this it follows that he must have few beliefs and those of the *simplest*, for time will not allow him to be travelling over the whole world of thought—that is, for the professional thinker.

J.B. Yeats, *Letters to his son, W.B. Yeats and others*, Faber and Faber, 1944, page 210

The cultivation of those sciences which have enlarged the limits of the empire of man over the external world, has, for want of the poetical faculty, proportionately circumscribed those of the internal world; and man, having enslaved the elements, remains himself a slave. To what but a cultivation of the mechanical arts in a degree disproportioned to the presence of the creative faculty, which is the basis of all knowledge, is to be attributed the abuse of all invention for abridging and combining labour, to the exasperation of the inequality of mankind.

Percy Bysshe Shelley, 'Prose, A Defence of Poetry', in Roger Ingpen and Walter E. Peck, editors, *The Works of Percy Bysshe Shelley*, Ernest Benn, 1930, volume VII, page 134

A poem is the image of life expressed in its eternal truth. There is this difference between a story and a poem, that a story is a catalogue of detached facts, which have no other bond of connexion than time, place, circumstance, cause and effect; the other is the creation of actions according to the unchangeable forms of human nature, as existing in the mind of the creator, which is itself the image of all other minds. The one is partial, and applies only to a definite period of time, and a certain combination of events which can never again recur, the other is universal, and contains within itself the germ of a relation to whatever motives or actions have place in the possible varieties of human nature.

Percy Bysshe Shelley, 'Prose, A Defence of Poetry', in Roger Ingpen and Walter E. Peck, editors, *The Works of Percy Bysshe Shelley*, Ernest Benn, 1930, volume VII, page 115

Christ's place indeed is with the poets. His whole conception of Humanity sprang right out of the imagination and can only be realised by it. What God was to the pantheist, man was to Him. He was the first to conceive the divided races as a unity. Before his time there had been gods and men, and feeling through the mysticism of sympathy that in himself each had been made incarnate, he calls himself the Son of the one or the Son of the other, according to his mood. More than anyone else in history he wakes in us that temper of wonder to which romance always appeals. There is still something to me almost incredible in the idea of a young Galilean peasant imagining that he could bear on his own shoulders the burden of the entire world; all that had already been done and suffered, and all that was yet to be done and suffered: the sins of Nero, of Caesar Borgia, of Alexander VI., and of him who was Emperor of Rome and Priest of the Sun: the sufferings of those whose names are legion and whose dwelling is among the tombs: oppressed nationalities, factory children, thieves, people in prison, outcasts, those who are dumb under oppression and whose silence is heard only of God; and not merely imagining this, but actually achieving it, so that at the present moment all who come in contact with his personality, even though they may neither bow to his altar nor kneel before his priest, in some way find that the ugliness of their sin is taken away and the beauty of their sorrow revealed to them.

Oscar Wilde, 'De Profundis', in *The Works of Oscar Wilde*, William Collins Sons & Co., 1948, page 868

Poetry is indeed some thing divine. It is at once the centre and circumference of knowledge; it is that which comprehends all science, and that to which all science must be referred. It is at the same time the root and blossom of all other systems of thought; it is that from which all spring, and that which adorns all; and that which, if blighted, denies the fruit and the seed, and withholds from the barren world the nourishment and the succession of the scions of the tree of life. It is the perfect and consummate surface and bloom of things; it is as the odour and the colour of the rose to the texture of the elements which compose it, as the form and the splendour of unfaded beauty to the secrets of anatomy and corruption. What were Virtue, Love, Patriotism, Friendship—which were the scenery of this beautiful Universe which we inhabit; what were our consolations on this side of the grave, and what were our aspirations beyond it, if Poetry did not ascend to bring light and fire from those eternal regions where the owl-winged faculty of calculation dare not ever soar?

Poetry is not like reasoning, a power to be exerted according to the determination of the will. A man cannot say, 'I will compose poetry.' The greatest poet even cannot say it: for the mind in creation is as a fading coal, which some invisible influence, like an inconstant mind, awakens to transitory brightness: this power arises from within, like the colour of a flower which fades and changes as it is developed, and the conscious portions of our natures are unprophetic either of its approach or its departure. Could this influence be durable in its original purity and force, it is impossible to predict the greatness of the results; but when composition begins, inspiration is already on the decline—and the most glorious poetry that has ever been communicated to the world is probably a feeble shadow of the original conception of the Poet.

Percy Bysshe Shelley, 'Prose, A Defence of Poetry', in Roger Ingpen and Walter E. Peck, editors, *The Works of Percy Bysshe Shelley*, Ernest Benn, 1930, volume VII, page 135

And now, when all is said, the question will still recur, though now in quite another sense, What does poetry mean? This unique expression, which cannot be replaced by any other, still seems to be trying to express something beyond itself. And this, we feel, is also what the other arts, and religion, and philosophy are trying to express: and that is what impels us to seek in vain to translate the one into the other. About the best poetry, and not only the best, there floats an atmosphere of infinite suggestion. The poet speaks to us of one thing, but in this one thing there seems to lurk the secret of all. He said what he meant, but his meaning seems to beckon away beyond itself, or rather to expand into something boundless which is only focussed in it; something also which, we feel, would satisfy not only the imagination, but the whole of us; that something within us, and without, and which everywhere

makes us seem
To patch up fragments of a dream,
Part of which comes true, and part
Beats and trembles in the heart.

Those who are susceptible to this effect of poetry find it not only, perhaps not most, in the ideals which she has sometimes described, but in a child's song by Christina Rossetti about a mere crown of wind-flowers, and in tragedies like Lear, where the sun seems to have set for ever. They hear this spirit murmuring its undertone through the Aeneid, and catch its voice in the song of Keats' nightingale, and its light upon the figures on the Urn, and it pierces them no less in Shelley's hopeless lament, *O world, O life, O time*, than in the rapturous ecstasy of his *Life of Life*. This all-embracing perfection cannot be expressed in poetic words or words of any kind, nor yet in music or in colour, but the suggestion of it is in much poetry, if not all, and poetry has in this suggestion, this 'meaning,' a great part of its value. We do it wrong, and we defeat our own purposes when we try to bend it to them:

We do it wrong, being so majestical,
To offer it the show of violence;
For it is as the air invulnerable,
And our vain blows malicious mockery.

It is a spirit. It comes we know not whence. It will not speak at our bidding, nor answer in our language. It is not our servant; it is our master.

A.C. Bradley, *Oxford Lectures on Poetry*, Macmillan and Co., 1909, page 26

POLITICS

Politics—science and art of government, political affairs of life, political principles

James Martineau reckoned there were at least two methods which aimed at human improvement. One was politics, which was institutional and worked on a large scale. The other was religion, which was personal and moral, the influence of soul on soul, life creating life. In reflection groups I've seen the seeds of both methods at work.

Some years ago we had a gifted post-graduate, studying for a doctorate in international relations. He was a lively, energetic person, capable of getting several blues. He had an engaging personality and a pleasant disposition, and was toying with the idea of going into politics later on in life. He used to refer to his reflection group as 'the Hour of Power'. He was aware of a 'source of power' within himself and other members of the group. He was thinking through how best this could be harnessed in the outworking of a political career, learning all he could from the other members of the group. It was a stimulating group. I shall be interested to see if he makes it to the top. We have had a number of eminent politicians through Univ.—Clement Attlee, Harold Wilson, Bob Hawke, former Prime Minister of Australia, and Bill Clinton, President of the United States of America. I have a feeling we shall be adding at least one other name to that list before long. I wonder if the practice of reflection has something to contribute to politicians of the future, possibly even a vision of hope.

Beware lest you say in your heart, 'My power and the might of my hand have got me this wealth.' You shall remember the Lord your God, for it is he who gives you power to get wealth.

Deuteronomy 8:17–18

Thine, O Lord, is the greatness, and the power, and the glory, and the victory, and the majesty; for all that is in the heavens and in the earth is thine; thine is the kingdom, O Lord, and thou art exalted as head above all. Both riches and honour come from thee, and thou rulest over all. In thy hand are power and might; and in thy hand it is to make great and to give strength to all. And now we thank thee, our God, and praise thy glorious name.

1 Chronicles 29:11–13

... teaching them to observe all that I have commanded you; and lo, I am with you always, to the close of the age.

Matthew 28:20

Let every person be subject to the governing authorities. For there is no authority except from God, and those that exist have been instituted by God.

Romans 13:1

It is a maxim of wise government to deal with men not as they ought to be but as they really are.

Johann Wolfgang von Goethe, *Wisdom and Experience*, selected by Ludwig Curtius, translated and edited by Hermann J. Weigand, Routledge & Kegan Paul, 1949, page 265

That vulnerable blunder: to think that in changing the form of government you change the heart of man.

Norman Douglas, *An Almanac*, Chatto & Windus in association with Martin Secker & Warburg, 1945, page 15

Disbelief in Christianity is not so much to be dreaded as its acceptance with a complete denial of it in society and politics.

Mark Rutherford, *More Pages From a Journal*, Oxford University Press, 1910, page 246

The changed circumstances of our present situation make it urgent to take seriously the politics of a kingdom of heaven as a way of handling a technologically conditioned world.

John Fenton and Michael Hare Duke, *Good News*, SCM Press, 1976, page 85

The only index by which to judge a government or a way of life is by the quality of the people it acts upon. No matter how noble the objectives of a government, if it blurs decency and kindness, cheapens human life, and breeds ill will and suspicion—it is an evil government.

Eric Hoffer, *The Passionate State of Mind*, Secker & Warburg, 1956, page 72

Truth, honour, purity, reverence, fidelity, industry, frugality, temperance, moderation, charity, and kindliness are political elements, without which politics and national life cannot exist, and the state by schools should educate its citizens in fundamental morality.

Henry Ward Beecher, *Proverbs from Plymouth Pulpit*, Charles Burnet & Co., 1887, page 56

The aim of politics is to put certain structures in place to ensure that respect for man, his development, responsibilities and freedom can grow in an environment of justice and peace. His final aim shall be to create a world in which it would be possible to love without having to be a hero. But this love can never be released by a politician—he simply doesn't have the key.

Michel Quoist, *With Open Heart*, translated by Colette Copeland, Gill and Macmillan, 1983, page 185

Politics, divorced from religion, has absolutely no meaning... Politics are a part of our being; we ought to understand our national institutions. We may do this from our infancy... But we want also the steady light, the infallible light of religious faith; not a faith which merely appeals to the intelligence, but a faith which is indelibly inscribed on the heart. First we want to realize our religious consciousness, and immediately we have done that the whole department of life is open to us; and it should then be a sacred privilege of all, so that when young men grow to manhood they may do so properly equipped to battle with life.

Mohandas K. Gandhi, in C.F. Andrews, *Mahatma Gandhi's Ideas*, George Allen & Unwin, 1929, page 110

A revolution is supposed to be a change that turns everything completely around. But the ideology of political revolution will never change anything except appearances. There will be violence, and power will pass from one party to another, but when the smoke clears and the bodies of all the dead men are underground, the situation will be essentially the same as it was before: there will be a minority of strong men in power exploiting all the others for their own ends. There will be the same greed and cruelty and lust and ambition and avarice and hypocrisy as before.

For the revolutions of men change nothing. The only influence that can really upset the injustice and iniquity of men is the power that breathes in Christian tradition, renewing our participation in the Life that is the Light of men.

Thomas Merton, *New Seeds of Contemplation*, Burns & Oates, 1962, page 112

We are coming to see more and more clearly in these anxious days that all our political problems are, in the last resort, moral and religious. Types of government, social reforms, economic adjustments will of themselves help us little. What is needed is some change in the minds of men. We must understand the real ends of life. We must learn to think differently of ourselves and of our fellow-men, and acknowledge some moral authority which is above all laws. Almost daily some new project for a better society is put before us, but always with the proviso that on both sides there must be a spirit of goodwill. As a rule this is thrown in incidentally, but it is the one thing that really matters. No plan will ever succeed when the goodwill is wanting, and when it is present the right plan comes usually of its own accord.

E.F. Scott, D.D., *Paul's Epistle to the Romans*, J.M. Dent & Co., 1909, page 24

Some Christians are very taken up by politics. They can be terribly anti-communist, forming rather fascist organisations to fight the 'red devil'. Or they can be fiercely anti-capitalistic, fighting for the new structures and redistribution of resources. Both these tendencies can lead to a centralisation—whether to protect the free-market economy or to further wholesale nationalisation.

I sometimes wonder whether these fighting Christians wouldn't do better to put their energies into creating communities which live as far as they can by the charter of the Beatitudes. If they did this, they would be able to live by, and measure progress by, values other than those of material success, acquisition of wealth and political struggle. They could become the yeast in the dough of society. They would not change political structures at first. But they would change the hearts and spirits of the people around them, by offering them a glimpse of a new dimension in human life—that of inwardness, love, contemplation, wonderment and sharing. They would introduce people to a place where the weak and poor, far from being pushed aside, are central to their society. My personal hope is that, if this spirit of community really spreads, structures will change. Structures are—tyrannies excepted—the mirrors of hearts. But if change is to come, some people should be working now on the political level towards a society which is more just, true and sharing, in which communities can take root and shine, and where human beings can be truly human.

Something similar could be said about people who throw themselves militantly into *causes*. Some people struggling for peace are terribly aggressive, even with 'rival' peace movements. To struggle for a cause it is best for people to be rooted in a community where they are learning reconciliation, acceptance of difference and of their own darkness, and how to celebrate. Isn't there a danger when groups with noble humanitarian causes develop very aggressive attitudes and divide the world into 'goodies' and 'baddies'? This type of elitism can be dangerous and continues a form of apartheid and oppression towards those who do not share the same ideas.

Jean Vanier, *Community and Growth*, Darton, Longman and Todd, 1991, page 308

... the ultimate doctrinal basis of Christian personal life and social action is that rich conception of God as both transcendent and immanent in his world, which is the very business of... worship to express in its intensest form. That the conception of God when it becomes to us a living, all-penetrating reality and not a theological statement, is found to require from us a life which spends itself in love and service to the world, whilst ever in its best expressions and aspirations, pointing beyond it. A life in fact moving towards a goal where work and prayer become one thing, since in both the human instrument is completely surrendered to the creative purposes of God, and seeks more and more to incarnate the Eternal. Since what is true to us one by one must surely become true of us in groups, we have here a principle which might at last become operative in our international, political and civic relationships. As corporate Christians we cannot be satisfied with a merely individual application of our faith. We must set as our goal such an expansion—through, in, and with us—of creative redeeming love as shall embrace the whole world and be operative on every level of our many-graded life.

What would the acceptance of such principles mean? It would mean that every Christian must work for a social order in which the outward would become ever more and more the true sacramental expression of the inward. And as an essential preliminary to this, much faithful purification of that outward—the disharmonies, atavisms, sterile passions and disguised self-seekings which the individual Christian is obliged to face and conquer on his way towards union with God, must also be identified and conquered by the group. Penitence has its social aspect—there, too, humanity is surely called upon to recognise a wrongness that can become a rightness?

But the social order which should emerge would not be distinguished by a tiresome uniformity or any oppressive and Puritanical goodness. It would possess a rich and inexhaustible variety in unity; for it is called to reflect a facet of the Mind of that God Who loves children as well as students, and has created tomtits as well as saints. It would be a social order in which energy would not be wasted in mere conflict; in which every talent and vocation had its chance. It would give a great place to the contribution which those who seek truth and beauty make to our knowledge of God; it would recognize this world as a theatre of the spirit. Whilst acknowledging and encouraging all innocent and legitimate fields of action, it would yet leave room for, and point to, a life beyond the world; gives fullest opportunity for the growth of those spiritual personalities in whom eternal values are incarnated, and through and by whom holiness is glimpsed by us. A world order, in fact, obedient to the God of Supernature and of Nature; and permitting the fullest development, interplay and mutual support of the active and contemplative lives. For this, and only this, perpetuates within history the full and balanced Christian ideal. Only this permits man to incarnate according to his measure—and even under the simplest, most homely accidents—the eternal in human life.

Evelyn Underhill, 'The Spiritual and the Secular', in Maurice B. Reckitt, editor, *Politics and the Faith*, Church Literature Association, 1953, page 22

POVERTY

Poverty—indigence, want; scarcity, deficiency; inferiority; poorness; meanness

I first came across poverty on a large scale in the streets of Calcutta. On our expedition to Nepal, we had managed to get an indulgence flight to Singapore, followed by a scheduled flight to Calcutta. In our short time in Calcutta we were besieged by beggars at every turn. Some were blind, others badly disabled, and many were destitute. It was difficult to know what to do for the best. If we gave them something we were immediately surrounded by a whole host of poverty-stricken people, demanding money. We gave where we could and kept on the move. In Nepal the atmosphere was entirely different, especially in the hills. Here the people were poor, but they were hardy and cheerful. They lived close to nature and worked hard as farmers to get sufficient food to eat. They were hospitable and friendly and there was every evidence of real community spirit. It was a delight to be in their company. The real difficulties of their poverty came with illness.

Today I'm horrified by the scenes shown on TV depicting poverty, famine and drought in Ethiopia and the Sudan. I feel we must do what we can to help. In addition I wonder if we ought to take a good hard look at ourselves. I'm very much in sympathy with Basil Hume's words—that the worst poverty today is the poverty of not having spiritual values in life. I sometimes observe people's faces in the streets of Oxford, and feel saddened. They look to be spiritually bankrupt and have an air of desperation about them. What a contrast with those early Christians, of having nothing, yet feeling they possessed everything.

Blessed is he who considers the poor! The Lord delivers him in the day of trouble; the Lord protects him and keeps him alive; he is called blessed in the land.

Psalm 41:1–2

Better is a poor man who walks in his integrity than a rich man who is perverse in his ways.

Proverbs 28:6

Blessed are you poor, for yours is the kingdom of God.

Luke 6:20

Only they would have us remember the poor, which very thing I was eager to do.

Galatians 2:10

The greatest man in history was the poorest.

Ralph Waldo Emerson, 'Domestic Life', in *Society and Solitude*, J.M. Dent & Sons, 1912, page 54

The spirit of poverty is to live in the gladness of today.

'The Rule of Taizé', in James F. Childress and John Macquarrie, editors, *A New Dictionary of Christian Ethics*, SCM Press, 1986, page 488

The worst poverty today is the poverty of not having spiritual values in life.

Basil Hume, OSB., *To be a Pilgrim*, St Paul's Publications, 1984, page 47

Poverty is not rooted in what we have or have not, but in the degrees to which we long for what is out of reach.

Anthony Bloom, *The Essence of Prayer*, Darton, Longman and Todd, 1989, page 21

To stand poor beside the brother I love means being his equal in terms of cultural values, intelligence and human dignity far more than in terms of money.

Carlo Carretto, *In Search of the Beyond*, translated by Sarah Fawcett, Darton, Longman and Todd, 1975, page 129

Poverty—the poverty of spirit of the Sermon on the Mount—is a total detachment from the material world. It is to recognize that everything comes from God—our bodies, our breath, our very existence.

Bede Griffiths, *Return to the Centre*, William Collins Sons & Co., 1976, page 12

We are the servants of the poor. We give wholehearted, free service to the poor. In the world the people are paid for their work. We are paid by God. We are bound by a vow to love and serve the poor, and to live as the poor with the poor.

Mother Teresa, *Jesus, the Word to be Spoken*, compiled by Brother Angelo Devananda, William Collins Sons & Co., 1990, page 18

You will not find happiness in multiplying external possessions, but in despising them and rooting them out of the heart. This applies not only to wealth and riches, but to ambition for honours and desire for empty praise, which all pass away with the world.

Thomas à Kempis, *The Imitation of Christ*, translated by Betty I. Knott, William Collins Sons & Co., 1979, page 154

Poverty is not only about shortage of money. It is about rights and relationships; about how people are treated and how they regard themselves; about powerlessness, exclusion, and loss of dignity. Yet the lack of an adequate income is at its heart.

Faith in the City, Church House Publishing, 1985, page 195

Look to your own poverty
welcome it
cherish it
don't be afraid
share your death
because thus you will share your love and your life.

Jean Vanier, *Community and Growth*, Darton, Longman and Todd, 1991, page 156

What is better and nobler than true poorness in spirit? Yet when that is held up before us, we will have none of it, but are always seeking ourselves, and our own things, that we may have in ourselves a lively taste of pleasure and sweetness...

This is a great error and a bad sign.

Theologia Germanica, translated by Susanna Winkworth, Stuart & Watkins, 1966, page 49

You in the West have the spiritually poorest of the poor much more than you have physically poor people. Very often among the rich there are very, very spiritually poor people. I find it not difficult to give a plate of rice to a hungry person, to furnish a bed to a person who has no bed, but to console or to remove that bitterness, to remove that anger, to remove that loneliness takes a very long time.

Mother Teresa, *Jesus, the Word to be Spoken*, compiled by Brother Angelo Devananda, William Collins Sons & Co., 1990, page 70

... Christ was shown to us poor and naked. But the poverty of his birth, the poverty of his public ministry, and the poverty of his death are, all of them, outward signs of an absolute *poverty of spirit*; that poverty of spirit of which he had spoken in one of the Beatitudes in the 'Sermon on the Mount'—'blessed are the poor in spirit, for theirs is the Kingdom of heaven'; an absolute poverty of spirit which claims nothing for itself, depends on God to provide, and does not depend upon creatures...

Poor Jesus might be, poor materially, and with a perfect poverty of spirit. But how rich! How indescribably rich! Rich towards God, rich in his own unique perfections and graces, rich in the love of the Holy Spirit, rich in his total absence of self-seeking.

Eric Symes Abbott, *The Compassion of God and the Passion of Christ*, Geoffrey Bles, 1963, page 76

For most Christians who talk about renewal in the Church, the word 'poor' means the beggar, the shabbily dressed, the underpaid, the man who is starving in Latin America, the children who are dying of hunger in Africa or India. That is to say, the poor are synonymous with the destitute...

The poor man in the biblical sense is not the beggar, the starving or the unemployed; he is the average man, who has a house, children and work, who dresses like everyone else, does the shopping and goes to the office, who buys an overcoat when he is cold and goes to the doctor when he is ill. He is the average human being—the minister, the bishop, the peasant, the craftsman, the old man, the boy, the mother, the poet, the worker.

He is everyman!

Carlo Carretto, *In Search of the Beyond*, translated by Sarah Fawcett, Darton, Longman and Todd, 1975, page 122

Poverty indeed is the strenuous life... Among us English-speaking peoples especially do the praises of poverty need once more to be boldly sung. We have grown literally afraid to be poor. We despise any one who elects to be poor in order to simplify and save his inner life. If he does not join the general scramble and pant with the money-making street, we deem him spiritless and lacking in ambition. We have lost the power even of imagining what the ancient idealization of poverty could have meant: the liberation from material attachments, the unbribed soul, the manlier indifference, the paying our way by what we are or do and not by what we have, the right to fling away our life at any moment irresponsibly...

William James, *The Varieties of Religious Experience*, William Collins Sons & Co., 1974, page 356

We know nothing, or practically nothing, about our eternal destiny, and we cling so tenaciously to what we believe is for our good. Affluent and overfed ourselves, we think that the only evil in the world is hunger; because we get upset by pain and privation, we think that the only problem to be resolved is that of providing bread and better hygienic conditions for the Third World. Of course these are serious problems for which solutions must be found, but what we fail to recognize is the far greater wretchedness of some rich people who die of boredom and drugs in comfortable bourgeois houses, and who stifle their personalities beneath their accumulated wealth and their self-centredness.

What we lack is true perspective, and this distorts the whole picture of our lives.

Carlo Carretto, *In Search of the Beyond*, translated by Sarah Fawcett, Darton, Longman and Todd, 1975, page 41

In more recent decades analysis of the causes of poverty was followed eventually by legislation to provide pensions, social insurance, unemployment relief, and health care, more so in Europe than in the USA. Christians and others have recognized that it is important to address poverty as relative deprivation in addition to eliminating poverty as absolute deprivation. Awareness of absolute poverty and gross inequality on a world scale has produced voluntary associations, directly or indirectly promoted by Christians, and proposals for fairer regulations of basic commodity prices. In Latin America liberation theologians have again, though sometimes in a more political manner, voiced the sharp criticism of oppressive inequality to be found in the Bible, and the theme of hope for the poor to be found in the Gospels.

David L. Mealand, in James F. Childress and John Macquarrie, editors, *A New Dictionary of Christian Ethics*, SCM Press, 1986, page 489

Village people in African and other poor countries have a quality of life. They know how to live in families and communities, even though they don't always know how to act efficiently. I sometimes meet missionaries who know how to do all sorts of things: build schools and hospitals, teach, and take care of people. They sometimes even know how to play an effective part in political struggles. But they often do not know how to live together. Their house doesn't feel joyful or alive; it doesn't feel like a community where everyone is relaxed, bound together in deep relationship. That is sad, because Christians should, above all, bear witness by their lives. That is as important today, when African countries are torn between village traditions and a taste for money and progress, as it has ever been. Missionaries often seem to be saying that successful living depends on being able to use machinery and costly techniques, on having a refrigerator and a car. I always marvel at the Little Sisters of Jesus, the sisters of Mother Teresa and others who live among their people and bear witness by their lives.

Jean Vanier, *Community and Growth*, Darton, Longman and Todd, 1991, page 311

PROGRESS

Progress—forward or onward movement in space, advance, development

The last thirty years have seen enormous developments in science and technology and on the material side of life. I remember being in the jungle in 1960, and the Gurkhas asking me what I thought of this 'thing' watching them as they ate their *bhat* (curry). I asked them what they meant. They were referring, of course, to the Sputnik which had recently gone into space. They had read somewhere it could be used for observing troop movements and were concerned. Should they change their camouflage?

We have come a long way since then but have we made overall progress? We are aware now of the enormous cost to the environment and the dangers of running out of certain resources. We know how easily we can be destroyed at the press of a button. The media continue to feed us with horror-stories from all over the world. There are vast areas in our lives where we have made no progress at all but have regressed.

This really came home to me a few months ago. I had a visit from a former student, now in her thirties. She is currently working in London. She was walking home in the early evening after work in a busy well-lit street. Suddenly without warning she was brutally attacked from behind and her handbag snatched. She was then hurled down a long flight of stone steps, and could have been killed. She is struggling to get back to normal life.

I wonder if we have progressed outwardly, but regressed inwardly. It seems as though in our material affluence we are morally and spiritually wanting.

Now the boy Samuel continued to grow both in stature and in favour with the Lord and with men.

1 Samuel 2:26

I press on toward the goal for the prize of the upward call of God in Christ Jesus.

Philippians 3:14

And so, from the day when we heard of it, we have not ceased to pray for you, asking that you may be filled with the knowledge of his will in all spiritual wisdom and understanding, to lead a life worthy of the Lord, fully pleasing to him, bearing fruit in every good work and increasing in the knowledge of God.

Colossians 1:9–10

Progress is often ruin...

Stephen MacKenna, *Journal and Letters*, Constable and Company, 1936, page 305

There's a back'ard current in the world, and we must do our utmost to advance in order just to bide where we be.

Thomas Hardy, *Desperate Remedies*, Macmillan & Co., 1918, page 450

Progress in the spiritual life comes from climbing a ladder of which the rungs are made alternatively of belief and doubt.

Edward Patey, *Christian Life Style*, A.R. Mowbray & Co., 1976, page 113

His test of progress—of the moral worth of his own or any other age—was the *men* it produced. He admired most of all things in this world single-minded and sincere people, who believed honestly what they professed to believe, and lived it out in their actions.

James A. Froude, *Thomas Carlyle*, Longmans, Green, & Co., 1884, volume II, page 77

The whole process of social and civic development is the parallel growth of two things: richness of individual personality with completeness of social intercourse. The development of personality in fellowship is no bad definition of what we mean by progress.

William Temple, *Christian Faith and Life*, SCM Press, 1963, page 96

Life has lost its controlling unity. The idea of progress has been dissociated from the inspiration of faith. The subsidence of the ancient frame-work has brought down the over-arching roof of certainty that God is regnant in the universe which, for the men of an earlier generation, gave life shelter and significance.

F.R. Barry, *The Relevance of Christianity*, Nisbet & Co., 1932, page 14

... the heart of moral improvement, the heart of moral progress, therefore also of social progress, and the amelioration of this world's bitter condition, is always to be found in worship, worship which is the opening of the heart to the love of God and the exposure of the conscience to be quickened by it.

William Temple, *The Preacher's Theme Today*, SPCK, 1936, page 60

Progress, however, of the best kind, is comparatively slow. Great results cannot be achieved at once; and we must be satisfied to advance in life as we walk, step by step... 'to know *how to wait* is the great secret of success.' We must sow before we can reap, and often have to wait long, content meanwhile to look patiently forward in hope; the fruit best worth waiting for often ripening the slowest. But 'time and patience,' says the Eastern proverb, 'change the mulberry leaf to satin.'

Samuel Smiles, *Self Help*, S.W. Partridge & Co., 1912, page 54

If our plans are not for time but for eternity, our knowledge, and therefore our love to God, to each other, to everything, will progress for ever. And the attainment of this heavenly wisdom requires neither ecstacy nor revelation, but prayer and watchfulness, and observation, and deep and solemn thought.

Two great rules, for its attainment are simple enough—Never forget what and where you are, and grieve not the Holy Spirit, for 'If a man will do God's will he shall know of the doctrine.'

Charles Kingsley, *Daily Thoughts*, Macmillan & Co., 1884, page 163

Human progress is neither automatic nor inevitable. Even a superficial look at history reveals that no social advance rolls in on the wheels of inevitability. Every step toward the goal of justice requires sacrifice, suffering, and struggle; the tireless exertions and passionate concern of dedicated individuals. Without persistent effort, time itself becomes an ally of the insurgent and primitive forces of irrational emotionalism and social destruction. This is no time for apathy or complacency. This is a time for vigorous and positive action.

Martin Luther King, *The Words of Martin Luther King*, selected by Coretta Scott King, William Collins Sons & Co., 1986, page 59

Just as it was thought that developing science and technology would bring happiness and progress, there are people today who think that building just, social, economic and political structures will bring happiness and progress.

It is true that better conditions help, but it's illusory to believe that they alone are sufficient. Man doesn't change anything—unless *man himself takes part in these changes* for himself and his brothers. What changes him then is his commitment, his dedication to others. It becomes a spiritual mission at the core of which the believer recognises the presence of God.

Michel Quoist, *With Open Heart*, translated by Colette Copeland, Gill and Macmillan, 1983, page 186

It has been observed... that if the last 50,000 years of man's existence were divided into lifetimes of approximately sixty-two years each, there have been about 800 such lifetimes. Of these 800, fully 650 were spent in caves.

Only during the last seventy lifetimes has it been possible to communicate effectively from one lifetime to another—as writing made it possible to do. Only during the last six lifetimes did masses of men ever see a printed word. Only during the last four has it been possible to measure time with any precision. Only in the last two has anyone anywhere used an electric motor. And the overwhelming majority of all the material goods we use in daily life today have been developed within the present, the 800th, lifetime.

Alvin Toffler, *Future Shock*, Pan Books, 1970, page 22

We must work passionately and indefatigably to bridge the gulf between our scientific progress and our moral progress. One of the great problems of mankind is that we suffer from a poverty of the spirit which stands in glaring contrast to our scientific and technological abundance. The richer we have become materially, the poorer we have become morally and spiritually.

Every man lives in two realms, the internal and the external. The internal is that realm of spiritual ends expressed in art, literature, morals, and religion. The external is that complex of devices, techniques, mechanisms, and instrumentalities by means of which we live. Our problem today is that we have allowed the internal to become lost in the external. We have allowed the means by which we live to outdistance the ends for which we live.

Martin Luther King, *The Words of Martin Luther King*, selected by Coretta Scott King, William Collins Sons & Co., 1986, page 67

According to Paul's teaching, you have to keep on the move, go forward: 'Walk on' is the strong command. We want to make this clear to young people in particular, for at times they may be tempted to look upon obedience to the laws of the Lord and of his Church as an obstacle, something that holds them in check and clips their wings in their flight towards a free assertion of their own personalities. No, dear children, it is not true: a true Christian who has made the teaching and the example of St. Paul his own does not know the meaning of the word 'stop' or, even worse, 'go back.'

Instead he is full of joyful hopes and a desire to improve himself and the world, and he moves ahead confidently in his relentless search for what is good: in his steady deepening of his own sublime dignity as one who lives in Christ and who aims at making his thoughts and desires and actions and work worthy of him. You must move ahead in the constant perfecting of yourselves, in seeking to do good, in peace with God and with your neighbour, and you must have a firm conviction that this is the only way to be modern, completely rounded, up to date, with an outlook that joins time with eternity, creatures and God....

Pope John XXIII, in Vincent A. Yzermans, editor, *Readings from Pope John*, A.R. Mowbray & Co., 1968, page 5

If we believe in the wisdom of God we must believe that creation moves according to a providential plan and that the end of the world can come about only when mankind has developed to a point of maturity preordained by God. If nature's movement towards maturity is purposeful and not arbitrary, Christianity is no less so. Nor is this a matter for the world seen in terms of the human race, or for the church seen as all believers: the pull towards maturity is designed by God to attract every single member of the human race, every separate single soul made in the image of God. When the time comes for the Eternal Father to lock all doors save the one at the entrance of heaven, he may find that charity on earth has grown cold and that the faith is being held by only a few, but as far as you and I are concerned the summons of the perfections of charity and faith remains the same. The thought that the human race has a long way to go is daunting enough, the thought that we as individuals have got to climb our way to the degree of perfection God is demanding of us is even less encouraging. At the present rate of progress there would seem to be no hope, but this is exactly where trust must be brought to bear.

Hubert van Zeller, *Leave Your Life Alone*, Sheed and Ward, 1973, page 96

Believers in progress, along with believers in democracy, usually emphasize the increasing domination of matter by mind (Peirce) and the guidance of the mind by ever higher ends. As a consequence, there is little if any debate about what is usually called 'outward progress'—control over environment, communication, relief of pain, and growth in health. Argument exists chiefly, if not solely, about the fact and degree of so-called 'inward progress'—that is, the human being's capacity to become a free and responsible person in a world of free and responsible nations. Thus, from Will Durant to J.B. Bury, contemporary observers, while placing serious strictures on evolutionary naturalism's belief in the inevitability of progress, soundly reaffirm belief in the idea of progress, either within the naturalistic and humanistic context or within the framework of Christian theology. The latter emphasizes the possibilities of individuals' personal and collective growth when they are under the guidance of God. Indeed there is *a contemporary reassessment* of the whole doctrine of nature and grace which, employing both philosophical and biblical insights, stresses, though cautiously and critically, the redemptive and therefore improving character of a life under God.

With particular reference to religion, the last decades of the 20th century witness the appearance, at least among scholars, of efforts to develop, after centuries of conflict, a progressive spirit of mutual understanding and cooperation among the major religions of the world, with a cautious metaphysical thrust; it is argued that the deity will bring about an ultimate redemption of all human life.

Charles W. Kegley, in James F. Childress and John Macquarrie, editors, *A New Dictionary of Christian Ethics*, SCM Press, 1986, page 505

PROPHETS

Prophets—inspired teachers, revealers or interpreters of God's will

It was Charles Parkhurst who told us that prophecy consists in catching the best of God's thoughts and in telling them. We can discern this in the utterances of the great Old Testament prophets: Elijah, Elisha, Isaiah, Jeremiah and Ezekiel. We catch more of a glimpse of this in the pages of the Gospels in the preaching and teaching of our Lord, in whom the best of God's thoughts were made manifest. After the resurrection there was a burst of activity. The prophetic legacy, culminating in Christ, was shed abroad by the apostles and bore fruit in the lives of those early Christians. Excellent, but what has happened to prophecy in the last two thousand years? Have we become too set in our ways? Do we expect to hear the prophetic voice? Have we become too institutionalized in our church life and ended up as God's frozen people? Has the study of theology become too introverted and academic, so that it no longer speaks to ordinary men and women? Have we restricted the best of God's thoughts to Scripture, and missed 'that still small voice' over the last two thousand years?

Visions of Hope is a small attempt to bring together some of the best of God's thoughts down the ages and in telling them. In the pages of this topic, and throughout the anthology, there is a rich vein of prophecy. My own hope is that towards the end of the twentieth century the prophetic voice may be heard again, enabling people once more to live in hope.

If there is a prophet among you, I the Lord make myself known to him in a vision, I speak with him in a dream.

Numbers 12:6

Where there is no prophecy the people cast off restraint.

Proverbs 29:18

A prophet is not without honour except in his own country and in his own house.

Matthew 13:57

Make love your aim, and earnestly desire the spiritual gifts, especially that you may prophesy.

1 Corinthians 14:1

The true prophet is not he who peers into the future but he who reads and reveals the present.

Eric Hoffer, *The Passionate State of Mind*, Secker & Warburg, 1956, page 105

The prophet is the forth-teller of the will of God, the man who has lived so close to God that he knows the mind and the purposes of God.

William Barclay, *The Gospel of John*, The Saint Andrew Press, 1974, volume I, page 245

The prophet must live the life so that others may know the doctrine: he hands down the idea in a form deeper than words to his followers and successors; and they, in turn, must dramatically install themselves in his role.

Lewis Mumford, *The Conduct of Life*, Secker & Warburg, 1952, page 101

Prophecy can be defined as human utterance believed to be inspired by a divine or transcendent source... Its expressions may be words, signs, actions, way of life or sacrifice of life.

R.P.R. Murray, in Alan Richardson and John Bowden, editors, *A New Dictionary of Christian Theology*, SCM Press, 1985, page 473

It is the prophetic interpretation of historical events which is the vehicle of special revelation in the sense in which the biblical and Christian tradition understands that conception. Where there are no prophets, there can be no special revelation.

Alan Richardson, *Christian Apologetics*, SCM Press, 1947, page 140

Someone has said that prophecy is criticism based on hope. A prophet points out to a man or a nation what is wrong; but he does so, not to push the man or the nation into despair; he does so to point the way to cure and to amendment and to rightness of life.

William Barclay, *The Gospel of John*, The Saint Andrew Press, 1974, volume I, page 149

When, tempted by immediate and concrete action, the prophet turns into a politician, he fails in his mission, because if there are no prophets to keep the politicians on their toes, the latter will end up working only for themselves and their party—not for other people.

Michel Quoist, *With Open Heart*, translated by Colette Copeland, Gill and Macmillan, 1983, page 123

[Every prophet's] ... appeal is not to a new principle, but to a new application of an old principle, so that he often presents himself as urging a return to the better ways of past generations. Few radical reformers can hope for great success who are unable to present themselves with perfect honesty as the only true conservatives.

William Temple, *Nature, Man and God*, Macmillan & Co., 1934, page 176

There is a history in all men's lives
Figuring the natures of the times deceased;
The which observed, a man may prophesy,
With a near aim, of the main chance of things
As yet not come to life, which in their seeds
And weak beginnings, lie intreasured.

William Shakespeare, *II Henry IV*, III. i. 75

... The minister of the Word must wait in what seems to be darkness, for prophecy and eloquence are not according to the will of man. They are born in integrity; the moments come when the prophet sees the dim outlines of truth and his eloquence is the ambiguity which points to the many-sidedness of truth, not vaguely but with the precision of one who also knows the single-centredness of truth.

R.E.C. Browne, *The Ministry of the Word*, SCM Press, 1958, page 75

The poor are always prophetic. As true prophets always point out, they reveal God's design. That is why we should take time to listen to them. And that means staying near them, because they speak quietly and infrequently; they are afraid to speak out, they lack confidence in themselves because they have been broken and oppressed. But if we listen to them, they will bring us back to the things that are essential.

Jean Vanier, *Community and Growth*, Darton, Longman and Todd, 1991, page 186

We need politicians although, heaven knows, we have more than enough. We need prophets, but there's a desperate shortage of them. For a prophet is not someone with ideas, shouting them all over the place; a prophet is one whose very life is *word, cry, shout.* A prophet can't help speaking, you'd have to kill him to muzzle him. And even in death, his voice would echo throughout the world.

Michel Quoist, *With Open Heart*, translated by Colette Copeland, Gill and Macmillan, 1983, page 122

Every great religious prophet has been the harbinger of a more universal way of life, which unites his fellows into a wider community that ideally encompasses all mankind. In that sense, the new leader is the individual embodiment of a whole society; and from his personality, his new attitudes, his fresh aims, his daily practices, not least from little hints he drops by the way without developing them, the complex activities of a higher society will take form.

Lewis Mumford, *The Conduct of Life*, Secker & Warburg, 1952, page 99

Jesus Christ belonged to the true race of prophets. He saw with open eye the mystery of the soul. Drawn by its severe harmony, ravished with its beauty, he lived in it, and had his being there. Alone in all history, he estimated the greatness of man. One man was true to what is in you and me. He saw that God incarnates himself in man, and evermore goes forth anew to take possession of his world. He said, in this jubilee of sublime emotion, 'I am divine. Through me, God acts; through me, speaks. Would you see God, see me; or see thee, when thou also thinkest as I now think.'

Ralph Waldo Emerson, 'Society and Solitude, Letters and Social Aims, Addresses, Divinity College Address', in *The Works of Ralph Waldo Emerson*, George Bell & Sons, 1906, volume III, page 397

I have tried to say that mysticism, the core of all religious experience, has led to the most dynamic and revolutionary action the world has known. I believe that the great prophets were mystics in action—their inner eye was awakened so that they saw not only the glory of God but also the suffering, the injustice, the inequality, the sin of the world. This drove them into action and often led to their death. And just as the great prophets were mystics, so the great mystics had a prophetic role—even when this was fulfilled through a solitude and a silence and a self-oblation which spoke louder than words and shook the universe.

William Johnston, *The Inner Eye of Love*, William Collins Sons & Co., 1978, page 11

The only satisfactory parallel to the prophetic experience is the phenomena of mysticism as described by writers like Teresa of Avila, John of the Cross, and others. They affirm that the immediate experience of God is ineffable; like the prophets, they must employ imagery and symbolism to describe it, with explicit warnings that these are used. They describe it as a transforming experience which moves one to speech and action beyond one's expected capacities. It grants them a profound insight not only into divine reality but into the human scene. Thus the prophet experience is such a mystical immediate experience of the reality and presence of God. The prophets disclose the nature and character of God so experienced, and they state the implications of the divine nature and character for human thought and action.

John L. McKenzie, S.J., *Dictionary of the Bible*, Geoffrey Chapman, 1965, page 697

... the Church to-day has to become determined to learn a new way of talking to the world and not less of interfering with the world. A new way of talking, because the secularized world in which we live has developed so many new, human possibilities that she can only be legitimately talked to if she is also *listened* to, and the talking has a chance of becoming real *mutual* communication. A new way of interfering, because... it is appalling to notice the smallness of the Church's significance in the welter of the dominant powers and tendencies which govern men's lives and thinking... Nothing great and new is achieved without one-sided insistence on matters of capital importance... The prophets undoubtedly were, humanely speaking, often very one-sided, but it was a one-sidedness in obedient response to a divine command. It is this prophetic one-sidedness which the Christian Church needs today, and should earnestly pray for.

Hendrik Kraemer, *A Theology of the Laity*, Lutterworth Press, 1958, pages 185 and 168

When the true prophet speaks, he gives utterance to the word of God that proceeds from his own soul but has its origin in the creative impulse that moves the whole cosmos. He is still, and enables God's word to use the experience of his life as a way of enlightening the minds of those who hear him. When the wisdom of God speaks through the human mouthpiece, that person is entrusted with adding his own contribution to the finished product. He does not alter the message, but flavours it with his own life's experience so that the supernatural wisdom is made available to the human audience through the prophet's own participation in the human condition. Without God there can be no true knowledge; without man that knowledge would remain unearthed and unformed. The human instrument brings the divine wisdom down to the capacity of his brothers. Their own souls are quickened by it, and a fresh view of reality is revealed to the people who have heard the message. From slothful apathy they are awakened to joyful commitment, so that in the end they may bear witness to an inner transfiguration of the human will that can now work in harmony and trust with God.

Martin Israel, *The Spirit of Counsel*, Hodder and Stoughton, 1983, page 11

... it is acknowledged by all students of the subject, that the Hebrew prophets made predictions concerning the fortunes of their own and other countries which were unquestionably fulfilled. It is a simple and universally recognized fact, that, filled with these Prophetic images, the whole Jewish nation—nay, at last the whole Eastern world—did look forward with longing expectation to the coming of this future Conqueror. Was this unparalleled expectation realized? And here again I speak only of facts which are acknowledged by Germans and Frenchmen, no less than by Englishmen, by critics and by sceptics, even more fully than by theologians and ecclesiastics. There did arise out of this nation a Character by universal consent as unparalleled as the expectation which has preceded Him. Jesus of Nazareth was, on the most superficial no less than on the deepest view we take of His coming, the greatest name, the most extraordinary power, that has ever crossed the stage of History. And this greatness consisted not in outward power, but precisely in those qualities in which from first to last the Prophetic order had laid the utmost stress—justice and love, goodness and truth.

Dean Stanley, *History of the Jewish Church*, John Murray, 1863, part I, page 466

PSYCHOLOGY

Psychology—science of nature; functions, and phenomena, of human soul or mind

When I started my job as chaplain to University College, London, the student world was very unsettled. There had recently been riots in Paris, violent protests in America, and sit-ins in the London School of Economics. I was sent on a course at the Tavistock Institute of Human Relations. This provided me with some valuable psychological insights of students in higher education. As a follow-up I was fortunate in having a colleague who was an expert in the psychology of C.G. Jung. He opened me up to the immense possibilities of depth psychology. When I eventually came across the book *The Choice is Always Ours*, I was well down the psychological road. No doubt you have already noticed the valuable contributions of psychologists in the pages of *Visions of Hope*.

I remember talking to a former medical student, who had qualified as a medical practitioner, and then specialized as a psychiatrist. She was currently working in one of H.M. Prisons. She had a dilemma. It was all very well listening to prisoners and using analytical skills, and drugs when necessary, but who was to put people together again at the end of the day?

We acknowledged the valuable work done by the medical profession, the social services, families, relatives and friends, but perhaps the greatest integrating factor of all is God in the depths of our being—the One who heals and makes whole. We concluded that the time was ripe for more collaboration between clergy and psychologists, but she did raise a question as to how many clergy were open and equipped to work in this area.

You will be secure, and will not fear.

Job 11:15

Keep your tongue from evil, and your lips from speaking deceit.

Psalm 34:13

I wish above all things that thou mayest prosper and be in health, even as thy soul prospereth.

3 John 2 (AV)

. . . I am he who searches mind and heart.

Revelation 2:23

The love problem is part of mankind's heavy toll of suffering, and nobody should be ashamed that he must pay his tribute.

C.G. Jung, *Psychological Reflections*, selected and edited by Jolande Jacobi, Routledge & Kegan Paul, 1953, page 90

Religions, in my opinion, with all which they are and assert, are so near to the human soul that psychology least of all can afford to overlook them.

C.G. Jung, *Psychological Reflections*, selected and edited by Jolande Jacobi, Routledge & Kegan Paul, 1953, page 299

There are many spirits, both bright and dark. One should therefore accept the view that spirit is something relative, not absolute, that calls for completion and embodiment in life.

C.G. Jung, *Psychological Reflections*, selected and edited by Jolande Jacobi, Routledge & Kegan Paul, 1953, page 239

Depth psychology has discovered the positive significance of religion for the human psyche, its self-discovery and its healing. Modern psychologists have established a significant connection between the decline in religiosity and increasing disorientation, lack of standards, loss of meaning, the typical neuroses of our time.

Hans Küng, *On Being a Christian*, translated by Edward Quinn, William Collins Sons & Co., 1977, page 59

Canst thou not minister to a mind diseas'd,
Pluck from the memory a rooted sorrow,
Raze out the written troubles of the brain,
And with some sweet oblivious antidote
Cleanse the stuff'd bosom of that perilous stuff
Which weighs upon the heart?

William Shakespeare, *Macbeth*, V. iii. 40

The great decisions of human life have as a rule far more to do with the instincts and other mysterious unconscious factors than with conscious will and well-meaning reasonableness. The shoe that fits one person pinches another; there is no recipe for living that suits all cases. Each of us carries his own life-form—an indeterminable form which cannot be superseded by any other.

C.G. Jung, *Modern Man in Search of a Soul*, Kegan Paul, Trench, Trubner & Co., 1944, page 69

There is of course a 'science' which concerns itself especially with the history of the individual: psychoanalysis... The analyst is pictured as somehow 'there', as the ultimate competent observer playing the part of the eye of God... But why should some unspecified psychoanalyst be the measure of all things? Psychoanalysis is a muddled embryonic science, and even if it were not there is no argument that I know of that can show us that we have got to treat its concepts as fundamental.

Iris Murdoch, *The Sovereignty of Good*, Routledge & Kegan Paul, 1970, page 26

Primarily however it is based upon the discovery in psychotherapy, that as the individual becomes more open to, more aware of, all aspects of his experience, he is increasingly likely to act in a manner we would term socialized. If he can be aware of his hostile impulses, but also of his desire for friendship and acceptance; aware of his expectations of his culture, but equally aware of his own purposes; aware of his selfish desires, but also aware of his tender and sensitive concern for another; then he behaves in a fashion which is harmonious, integrated, constructive.

Carl R. Rogers, *On Becoming a Person*, Constable & Company, 1977, page 353

The erotic instinct is something questionable, and will always be so whatever a future set of laws may have to say on the matter. It belongs, on the one hand, to the original animal nature of man, which will exist as long as man has an animal body. On the other hand, it is connected with the highest forms of the spirit. But it blooms only when spirit and instinct are in true harmony. If one or the other aspect is missing, then an injury occurs, or at least there is a one-sided lack of balance which easily slips into the pathological. Too much of the animal disfigures the civilized human being, too much culture makes a sick animal.

C.G. Jung, *Psychological Reflections*, selected and edited by Jolande Jacobi, Routledge & Kegan Paul, 1953, page 93

Religions are psychotherapeutic systems in the most actual meaning of the word, and in the widest measure. They express the scope of the soul's problems in mighty images. They are the acknowledgment and recognition of the soul, and at the same time the revelation and manifestation of the nature of the soul. No human soul is separated from this universal basis; only an individual consciousness which has lost the connection with the whole soul is caught in the illusion that the soul is a tiny, circumscribable region, suitable as the object of some 'scientific' theory. The loss of the wider connection is the fundamental evil of neurosis, and therefore the path of the neurotic strays into the smallest side-streets of doubtful reputation, for whoever denies the big things must look for the blame in the smallest things.

C.G. Jung, *Psychological Reflections*, selected and edited by Jolande Jacobi, Routledge & Kegan Paul, 1953, page 298

Psychologists well know that the deepest element of human happiness is embodied in the idea of movement toward something; movement in the 'right' direction; and all the devices of therapeutic psychiatry are really only shoves and pushes and suggestions intended to help a mind to find its particular right direction of movement. Continued observations of this basic dynamic nature of happiness, especially in clinical psychological practice, leads almost inevitably to the conclusion that deeper and more fundamental than sexuality, deeper than the craving for social power, deeper even than the desire for possessions, there is a still more generalized and more universal craving in the human make-up. *It is the craving for knowledge of the right direction—for orientation.*

This craving is not quite so obvious as the other patterns of human desire, because it is more general, deeper, and the positive and negative feeling-tones it engenders are not locally felt, hence come less often to a specific attention focus. Yet every system of philosophy, whether called religious or not, is at bottom a human attempt to satisfy the craving to be pointed in the right direction.

William H. Sheldon, in Dorothy Berkley Phillips, editor, *The Choice is Always Ours*, Harper & Row, Publishers, 1960, page 3

Some people need yet another kind of accompaniment. Because of severe conflicts with their parents or the indifference or absence of their parents during early childhood, they were obliged to create strong barriers around their hearts. In this way they protected themselves from the pain, anguish, loneliness, guilt, confusion and anger which could have overwhelmed and killed them if these had remained on the surface of their consciousness. In order to live and get on with life, human nature is such that children can hide all this pain away in the secret recesses of their being and forget it. But this inner pain or darkness, stored up in the shadow side of their being is a sort of inner tomb, continues to govern unconsciously many of their attitudes and actions. Sometimes, hidden in this secret place, there is too much unresolved anger, too deep a yearning to be seen and loved as unique; too much loneliness transformed into guilt and lack of self-confidence; too much ambivalence in respect to authority for them to be able to live harmoniously in community.

Some people with a lot of pain in them are able to enter community; their generosity and deep need for belonging seem to cover it up. They are able to function quite well, obey all the rules and find quite a lot of personal satisfaction and peace. Their hidden anguish can even become a drive toward greater competence and achievement. But when they are finally accepted as permanent members, and frequently at a moment of personal set-back, there can be a terrible explosion. All the mess hidden in the tomb seems to rise up into the consciousness. Living in community becomes unbearable for them.

It is then that they will need far more professional, psychological help, or some more specialised spiritual support. They will need someone to whom they can reveal all the pain, even all that their mind had forgotten but which their being had not. Then they can gradually be liberated from these deep powers that have been governing them, or at least come to a better understanding and acceptance of them. They start then on a journey towards inner healing and wholeness.

Jean Vanier, *Community and Growth*, Darton, Longman and Todd, 1991, page 250

It may easily happen, therefore, that a Christian who believes in all the sacred figures is still undeveloped and unchanged in his inmost soul because he has 'all God outside' and does not experience Him in the soul. His deciding motives, his ruling interests and impulses, do not spring from the sphere of Christianity, but from the unconscious and undeveloped psyche, which is as pagan and archaic as ever. Not the individual alone but the sum total of individual lives in a people proves the truth of this contention. The great events of our world as planned and executed by man do not breathe the spirit of Christianity, but rather of unadorned paganism. These things originate in a psychic condition that has remained archaic and has not been even remotely touched by Christianity... Christian civilization has proved hollow to a terrifying degree: it is all veneer, but the inner man has remained untouched and therefore unchanged. His soul is out of key with his external beliefs; in his soul the Christian has not kept pace with external developments. Yes, everything is to be found outside—in image and in word, in Church and Bible—but never inside. Inside reign the archaic gods, supreme as of old; that is to say the inner correspondence with the outer God-image is undeveloped for lack of psychological culture and has therefore got stuck in heathenism. Christian education has done all that is humanly possible, but it has not been enough. Too few people have experienced the divine image as the innermost possession of their own souls. Christ only meets them from without, never from within the soul; and that is why dark paganism still reigns there, a paganism which, now in a form so blatant that it can no longer be denied and now in all too threadbare disguise, is swamping the world of so-called Christian culture...

So long as religion is only faith and outward form, and the religious function is not experienced in our own souls, nothing of any importance has happened. It has yet to be understood that the *mysterium magnum* is not only an actuality but is first and foremost rooted in the human psyche. The man who does not know this from his own experience may be a most learned theologian, but he has no idea of religion and still less of education.

C.G. Jung, 'Psychology and Alchemy', in *The Collected Works of C.G. Jung*, translated by R.F.C. Hull, Routledge & Kegan Paul, 1955, volume XII, page 11

PURPOSE

Purpose—object, thing intended; fact, faculty, of resolving on something; design or intention

Louis Lavelle wrote that the object of life is the discovery (by a deepening of the self) of the centre of the self that constitutes our unique and personal essence. He went on to add that most of us miss this by remaining on the surface of things, thinking only in terms of self-aggrandisement.

In retrospect, I realize that I lived very much on the surface of things for the first twenty years of my life. At school I worked away to get through O levels, and then specialized in three subjects for A levels. In other areas of life my interest was mainly on sporting achievement. It was only later that I realized this was superficial. Self-aggrandisement was the order of the day. I would do National Service, go to university, get a well-paid job, buy a house and a car, have a family, and so on. I thought this must surely be right because everyone else was doing it.

I received a severe jolt in the army in Singapore. I was friendly with the battalion doctor, and from time to time we would go out for a drink. On one occasion he asked me what I was going to do after the army. I told him I was going to university to do a law degree. 'And then what?' he asked. 'I hope to become a solicitor in the family firm.' 'And then what?' he asked again. 'Well, I suppose I'll get married, have a family and become a partner.' 'And then what?' he persisted. 'I expect I shall work until I retire.' 'And then what?' he asked again. 'Well, die I suppose.' 'And then what?' he demanded. I couldn't answer this one, but that afternoon he had set me thinking.

In my twenties I had a change of priorities, due to an evolving Christian faith. I began to go deeper and gradually freed myself from self-aggrandisement. Through reflection and my work as a college chaplain I began to discover my unique and personal essence. Eventually I discovered a real sense of purpose, which has been with me ever since.

I cry to God Most High, to God who fulfils his purpose for me.

Psalm 57:2

The purpose in a man's mind is like deep water, but a man of understanding will draw it out.

Proverbs 20:5

We know that in everything God works for good with those who love him, who are called according to his purpose.

Romans 8:28

For he has made known to us in all wisdom and insight the mystery of his will, according to his purpose which he set forth in Christ as a plan for the fulness of time.

Ephesians 1:9–10

Make me useful, positive, appreciative, generous.
Make me live.

Norman W. Goodacre, *Layman's Lent*, A.R. Mowbray & Co., 1969, page 33

Man is never happy until his own vague striving has found and fixed its goal.

Johann Wolfgang von Goethe, 'Wilhelm Meister's Apprenticeship', in *The Practical Wisdom of Goethe*, chosen by Emil Ludwig, Secker & Warburg, 1933, page 26

God has a purpose and it is the function of normal beings to try to comprehend that purpose.

A.R. Orage, *On Love*, The Janus Press, 1957, page 54

As individuals, we should sometimes pause and ask ourselves: what is our aim in life? Have we got one at all?

William Barclay, *The Letters to Timothy and Titus*, The Saint Andrew Press, 1965, page 225

Deeply the Christian believes that beneath all the flux and change of this mortal life, God is seeking to work out a profound purpose.

W.E. Sangster, *God Does Guide Us*, Hodder and Stoughton, 1934, page 30

Decide who and what you want to be; then pursue your purpose with total concentration until you become what you wish to be.

Anon.

We need God, not in order to understand the why, but in order to feel and sustain the ultimate wherefore, to give a meaning to the Universe.

Miguel de Unamuno, *The Tragic Sense of Life*, Macmillan and Co., 1921, page 152

The end of life is not profit, amusement, philosophy, science or religion. It is not even happiness: it is life itself. Life consists in the plenitude of all the organic and mental activities of the body.

Alexis Carrel, *Reflections on Life*, Hamish Hamilton, 1952, page 131

What will be the outcome of what I do to-day? Of what I shall do to-morrow? What will be the outcome of all my life? Why should I live? Why should I do anything? Is there in life any purpose which the inevitable death which awaits me does not undo and destroy?

William James, *The Varieties of Religious Experience*, William Collins Sons & Co., 1974, page 161

This is the true joy in life, the being used for a purpose, recognized by yourself as a mighty one; the being thoroughly worn out before you are thrown on the scrap heap; the being a force of Nature instead of a feverish selfish little clod of ailments and grievances complaining that the world will not devote itself to making you happy.

George Bernard Shaw, *The Complete Bernard Shaw Prefaces*, Paul Hamlyn, 1965, page 163

But it is not the place where you are that is the important thing. It is the intensity of your presence there. It is not the situation that counts. What counts is that you are fully alive in any situation. It is this that puts down roots and then flowers in your life. Availability: that is obedience. That, and looking hard at the place where you are, instead of wanting to work wonders somewhere else.

Neville Cryer, *Michel Quoist*, Hodder and Stoughton, 1977, page 53

To accomplish anything you need an interest, a motive, a centre for your thought. You need a star to steer by, a cause, a creed, an idea, a passionate attachment. Men have followed many guiding lights. They have followed Christ, Mahomet, Napoleon. Something must beckon you or nothing is done, something about which you ask no questions. Thought needs a fulcrum for its lever, effort demands an incentive or an aim.

W. Macneile Dixon, *The Human Situation*, Edward Arnold & Co., 1937, page 34

Let us then live, speak, work and pray 'to the greater glory of God' '*ad majorem Dei gloriam*'. This will afford us the same motive as Christ our Lord had. This will direct all our work to an end beyond ourselves. This will afford us a worthy ambition—the glory of God and the Kingdom of God. It will also strengthen us when life seems to lack purpose, to lose its cogency. '*Ad majorem Dei gloriam*' will also lift us out of our self-centredness, to look beyond our own glory to God's. It will give us a simple and salutary form of self-examination—'whose is the glory I am seeking, in the things I do and say?' It will help us to see that we are *instruments only* in the hand of our Lord; to realise that we enjoy being used; but 'not unto us, not unto us, but unto thy name give the praise' (Psalm 15:1).

Eric Symes Abbott, *The Compassion of God and the Passion of Christ*, Geoffrey Bles, 1963, page 93

The removal of a loved companion renders life meaningless, at least for a considerable period, until one has regained one's bearings and begun to see the path ahead. Life that is tolerable must be imbued with purpose to give it meaning. The human mind cannot tolerate meaninglessness, for a meaningless life can assume a quality of non-existence that seems worse than death itself. For death is the great unknown experience which may conceivably open up a new vista of fulfilment, whereas the interminable misery of a mortal life that is purposeless and devoid of growth is something that can scarcely be contemplated in normal consciousness. How can one proceed with living in such circumstances? This is the valley of the shadow of death, cold and featureless, that is mentioned in Psalm 23. Until one knows its contours and extent as well as one does one's native domain, one has not tasted life fully. The end is a changed person, one who lives the transpersonal life, whose perspectives are no longer limited to human objectives but are infused with divine forebodings.

Martin Israel, *Living Alone*, SPCK, 1982, page 52

I don't know Who—or what—put the question, I don't know when it was put. I don't even remember answering. But at some moment I did answer *Yes* to Someone—or Something—and from that hour I was certain that existence is meaningful and that, therefore, my life, in self-surrender, had a goal.

From that moment I have known what it means 'not to look back', and 'to take no thought for the morrow'.

Led by the Ariadne's thread of my answer through the labyrinth of Life, I came to a time and place where I realised that the Way leads to a triumph which is a catastrophe, and to a catastrophe which is a triumph, that the price for committing one's life would be reproach, and that the only elevation possible to man lies in the depths of humiliation. After that, the word 'courage' lost its meaning, since nothing could be taken from me.

As I continued along the Way, I learned, step by step, word by word, that behind every saying in the Gospels, stands *one* man and *one* man's experience. Also behind the prayer that the cup might pass from him and his promise to drink it. Also behind each of the words from the Cross.

Dag Hammarskjöld, *Markings*, translated by W.H. Auden & Leif Sjoberg, with a foreword by W.H. Auden, Faber and Faber, 1964, page 169

Your 'personal' life cannot have a lasting intrinsic meaning. It can acquire a contingent meaning, but only by being fitted into and subordinated to something which 'lasts' and has a meaning in itself. Is this something what we attempt to identify when we speak of 'Life'? Can your life have a meaning as a tiny fragment of Life?

Does Life exist? Seek and your shall find, experience Life as a reality. Has Life a 'meaning'? Experience Life as reality and the question becomes meaningless.

Seek—? Seek by daring to take the leap into unconditional obedience. Dare this when you are challenged, for only by the light of a challenge will you be able to see the cross-roads and, in full awareness of your choice, turn your back upon your personal life—with no right ever to look back.

You will find that 'in the pattern' you are liberated from the need to live 'with the herd'.

You will find that, thus subordinated, your life will receive from Life all its meaning, irrespective of the conditions given you for its realisation.

You will find that the freedom of the continual farewell, the hourly self-surrender, gives to your experience of reality the purity and clarity which signify—self-realisation.

You will find that obedience requires an act of will which must continually be re-iterated, and that you will fail, if anything in your personal life is allowed to slip back into the centre.

Dag Hammarskjöld, *Markings*, translated by W.H. Auden & Leif Sjorberg, with a foreword by W.H. Auden, Faber and Faber, 1964, page 114

QUIETNESS

Quietness—silence, stillness; being free from disturbance or agitation or urgent tasks; rest, repose; peace of mind

Ambrose Bierce in his book, *The Devil's Dictionary*, defined noise as a 'stench in the ear'. Noise has become one of the great pollutions of modern time. I know this only too well having spent the last thirty years in the centre of cities. I'm also fond of the phrase 'oases of quiet'—those times when we can withdraw, perhaps, from the thick of things, and find moments of quiet to get a sense of perspective and proportion.

This is roughly what has happened to me. I have had a busy and active ministry, but have been able to balance this by having times of quietness. The practice started as an undergraduate. When the busy day was over, I used to retire to my bedroom, kneel by my bed, and read a passage from the Gospels. This was the start of learning how to reflect. I would simply ponder over the verses, and feed on them as best I could. Later, when I was more conversant with Scripture, I moved on and used part of what now forms the contents of *Visions of Hope* as a stimulus for keeping a spiritual diary. I regard this as the most valuable thing of my life. I have found it possible to have 'oases of quiet' on a Sunday and on holiday. I love going to an isolated part of the coast and having an extended time of reflection which sets me up for the following year. Through this practice it is possible from time to time to experience that rare commodity—peace of mind.

Stop here yourself for a while, that I may make known to you the word of God.

1 Samuel 9:27

In returning and rest you shall be saved; in quietness and in trust shall be your strength.

Isaiah 30:15

Study to be quiet.

1 Thessalonians 4:11 (AV)

... but let it be the hidden person of the heart with the imperishable jewel of a gentle and quiet spirit, which in God's sight is very precious.

1 Peter 3:4

I am come by a hard way to the quiet of God.

Alistair MacLean, *The Quiet Heart*, Allenson & Co., 1940, page 25

Think glorious thoughts of God and serve with a quiet mind.

Charles S. Duthie, *God in His World*, Independent Press, 1955, page 43

The quiet of quiet places is made quieter by natural sounds. In a wood on a still day the quiet is increased by the whisper of the trees.

Mark Rutherford, *Last Pages From a Journal*, Oxford University Press, 1915, page 273

The deepest affections are those of which we are least conscious—that is, which produce least *startling* emotion, and most easy and involuntary practice.

Charles Kingsley, *Daily Thoughts*, Macmillan & Co., 1884, page 179

Unhappy, unfulfilled people, who find it difficult to care, are going to be the people interested in wars, fast cars, consumer fads in ridiculous variety, in conflict and in competition and in all the hectic and feverish pursuit of a lost security—not in those things which make for quietness of heart and mind.

Roy Stevens, *Education and the Death of Love*, Epworth Press, 1978, page 127

Many of us are sick of our noisy cities, of the streets where you can't hear your own voice, the whole urban howl and roar which we have been brainwashed into accepting as civilized and normal. We are weary of the scream of jets in the skies as they prepare for war. To help people to be quiet, to see where they are going, is a neglected duty...

Roy Stevens, *Education and the Death of Love*, Epworth Press, 1978, page 103

It is good for a man to have holy and quiet thoughts, and at moments to see into the very deepest meaning of God's word and God's earth, and to have, as it were, heaven opened before his eyes; and it is good for a man sometimes actually to *feel* his heart over-powered with the glorious majesty of God—to *feel* it gushing out with love to his blessed Saviour; but it is not good for him to stop there any more than for the Apostles in the Mount of Transfiguration.

Charles Kingsley, *Daily Thoughts*, Macmillan & Co., 1884, page 205

Violence is not strength, noisiness is not earnestness. Noise is a sign of want of faith, and violence is a sign of weakness.

By quiet, modest, silent, private influence we shall win. 'Neither strive nor cry nor let your voice be heard in the streets,' was good advice of old, and is still. I have seen many a movement tried by other method of striving and crying and making a noise in the streets, but I have never seen one succeed thereby, and never shall.

Charles Kingsley, *Daily Thoughts*, Macmillan & Co., 1884, page 139

Drop thy still dews of quietness,
Till all our strivings cease;
Take from our souls the strain and stress,
And let our ordered lives confess
The beauty of thy peace.

Breathe through the heats of our desire
Thy coolness and thy balm;
Let sense be dumb, let flesh retire;
Speak through the earthquake, wind, and fire,
O still, small voice of calm!

John Greenleaf Whittier, 'The Brewing of Soma', in *The Poetical Works of John Greenleaf Whittier*, Macmillan and Co., 1874, page 457

Many people today look for silence, solitude and peace. They dream of places where they can rest, away from the daily hassles of living which tear them apart, exhaust them and leave them dissatisfied, wounded and bleeding—and always alone.

But they won't necessarily find peace and quiet waiting for them in other places.

There is a place within us where quiet reigns—the centre, our heart of hearts. There we can find him who is the plenitude of silence. But who will guide us there? We must learn the way.

Michel Quoist, *With Open Heart*, translated by Colette Copeland, Gill and Macmillan, 1983, page 65

God is a Being, still, and peaceful, dwelling in the still eternity. Therefore should your mind be as a still, clear mountain tarn, reflecting the glory of God as in a mirror, where the image is unbroken and perfect. Avoid, therefore, all that would needlessly disturb or confuse or stir up your natural mind, from without or from within. Nothing in the whole world is worth being disturbed about. Even the sins you have committed should humble you, but not disturb you. God is in His holy temple. Let all that is in you keep silence before Him—silence of the mouth, silence of all desires and all thoughts, silence of labour and toil. Oh, how precious and how useful is a still and quiet spirit in the eyes of God!

Gerhard Tersteegen, in Frances Bevan, *Sketches of the Quiet in the Land*, John F. Shaw and Co., 1891, page 400

... we simply need quiet time in the presence of God. Although we want to make all our time for God, we will never succeed if we do not reserve a minute, an hour, a morning, a day, a week, a month, or whatever period of time for God and God alone.

This asks for much discipline and risk-taking because we always seem to have something more urgent to do and 'just sitting there' and 'doing nothing' often disturbs us more than it helps. But there is no way around this. Being useless and silent in the presence of our God belongs to the core of all prayer. In the beginning we often hear our own unruly inner noises more loudly than God's voice. This is at times very hard to tolerate. But slowly, very slowly, we discover that the silent time makes us quiet and deepens our awareness of ourselves and God. Then, very soon, we start missing these moments when we are deprived of them, and before we are fully aware of it an inner momentum has developed that draws us more and more into silence and closer to that still point where God speaks to us.

Contemplative reading of the holy scriptures and silent time in the presence of God belong closely together. The word of God draws us into silence; silence makes us attentive to God's word...

Henri J.M. Nouwen, in Robert Durback, editor, *Seeds of Hope*, Darton, Longman and Todd, 1989, page 70

SCIENCE AND RELIGION

Science—branch of knowledge; organized body of knowledge that has been accumulated on a subject; one dealing with material phenomena and based mainly on observation, experiment, and induction, as chemistry, biology

The leader of our expedition to Nepal was a brilliant scientist. By the age of twenty-eight he had two doctorates to his name and a professorship. I remember a conversation we had in which we were discussing the relationship of science and religion. 'Bill,' he said, 'the scientific method is limited. In essence it depends on an experiment in which you have to keep everything constant and add a variant and observe what happens. It is virtually impossible to keep everything constant, so the scientific method is very limited. You must not be overawed by science.'

This fitted in well with an account I'd heard of a conversation which took place in an officers' mess. One of the officers, who had graduated in physics before being commissioned, was talking to the padre. 'You know, padre, I have a problem with religion. Whilst studying physics at university I never came across anything that convinced me of the existence of God. What have you to say about that?' The padre looked thoughtful for a moment and replied: 'It's funny you should mention that. I have a similar problem. When I was training for the ministry I made a careful study of the Bible, and do you know, I never found any evidence there for the existence of physics.' 'I see,' said the officer, after a moment's pause. 'I take your point.'

I'm very impressed with the discoveries of science, and the enormous strides that have been made in applied technology in the twentieth century, but recognize there are several avenues that lead to truth—art, science, and spirit—and each needs to be respected.

Great is Truth, and mighty above all things.

1 Esdras 4:41 (AV)

For he hath given me certain knowledge of the things that are, namely, to know how the world was made, and the operation of the elements: the beginning, ending, and midst of the times: the alteration of the turning of the sun, and the change of seasons: the circuits of years, and the positions of stars: the natures of living creatures, and the furies of wild beasts: the violence of winds, and the reasonings of men: the diversities of plants, and the virtues of roots.

Wisdom of Solomon 7:17–20 (AV)

The Lord hath created medicines out of the earth; and he that is wise will not abhor them. Was not the water made sweet with wood, that the virtue thereof might be known? And he hath given men skill, that he might be honoured in his marvellous works. With such doth he heal [men,] and taketh away their pains.

Ecclesiasticus 38:4–7 (AV)

. . . the earth is the Lord's, and everything in it.

1 Corinthians 10:26

Science without religion is lame, religion without science is blind.

Albert Einstein, *Out of my Later Years*, Thames and Hudson, 1950, page 26

Science cannot supply faith in a loving God, and a God whom we can love.

Henry Ward Beecher, *Proverbs from Plymouth Pulpit*, Charles Burnet & Co., 1887, page 118

Perhaps some day science can explain the world(?), but it can never explain its meaning.

Michel Quoist, *With Open Heart*, translated by Colette Copeland, Gill and Macmillan, 1983, page 196

[Evolution] has for many taken the place of God Himself, and bowed Him calmly out of His Own Universe.

G.A. Studdert Kennedy, *Food for the Fed-up*, Hodder and Stoughton, 1921, page 34

Science and religion are, in my opinion, two utterly different things, and neither should dictate to the other.

A Consultant Bacteriologist, in C.L. Drawbridge, *Common Objections to Christianity*, Robert Scott, 1914, page 216

Science sees everything mechanically, through part of the moving-instinctive centre. It has no answer to human needs in a crisis.

A.R. Orage, *On Love*, The Janus Press, 1957, page 57

Science has its life in mental restlessness; it asks of every fact the questions Why? or How? and of the answer it asks Why? or How? again.

William Temple, *Nature, God and Man*, Macmillan & Co., 1934, page 145

Scientists are attempting to come to God head-first. They must come to Him heart-first. Then let their heads interpret what they have found.

Henry Ward Beecher, *Proverbs from Plymouth Pulpit*, Charles Burnet & Co., 1887, page 138

Science and religion appeal to two different sides of human nature. Each speaks its own language, and their spheres of influence are separate. Any conflict between them would be undesirable and aimless.

Professor Sergius N. Winogradsky, in C.L. Drawbridge, *The Religion of Scientists*, Ernest Benn, 1932, page 126

But to the great man of science, science is an art, and he himself is an artist. And his creation is not the less a work of art because it is but a faint and imperfect copy of another—of the supreme work of art which is nature itself.

J.W.N. Sullivan, *Limitations of Science*, Chatto & Windus, 1933, page 266

It may be that in the practice of religion men have real evidence of the Being of God. If that is so, it is merely fallacious to refuse consideration of this evidence because no similar evidence is forthcoming from the study of physics, astronomy or biology.

William Temple, *Nature, God and Man*, Macmillan & Co., 1934, page 11

Hitherto science has been mainly the subjection of the external world. I dream sometimes of a science which shall be cultivated as physical science is now, but shall have for its object our own private peace and happiness; for example, the harnessing and guidance of the imagination. At present we fight naked, and are no better armed than our ancestors of 2,000 years ago.

Mark Rutherford, *Last Pages From a Journal*, Oxford University Press, 1915, page 284

There is no inevitable dichotomy between the scientific and the religious approach—for myself I feel no such 'split.' There is no reason why the facts which great and devoted men lay before us should be regarded as alien to the soul, or as 'mere facts' useful only for practical purposes or for passing examinations. They can equally well feed the imagination. The split is not real; but to suppose its existence has been easier since the coming of Newton.

John Stewart Collis, *The Vision of Glory*, Charles Knight and Co., 1972, page 53

Science investigates; religion interprets. Science gives man knowledge which is power; religion gives man wisdom which is control. Science deals mainly with facts; religion deals mainly with values. The two are not rivals. They are complementary. Science keeps religion from sinking into the valley of crippling irrationalism and paralyzing obscurantism. Religion prevents science from falling into the marsh of obsolete materialism and moral nihilism.

Martin Luther King, *The Words of Martin Luther King*, selected by Coretta Scott King, William Collins Sons & Co., 1986, page 63

... that secular science, having become a great force in the world, has, especially in the last century, investigated everything divine handed down to us in the sacred books. After a ruthless analysis the scholars of this world have left nothing of what was held sacred before. But they have only investigated the parts and overlooked the whole, so much so that one cannot help being astonished at their blindness. And so the whole remains standing before their eyes as firm as ever and the gates of hell shall not prevail against it.

Fyodor Dostoyevsky, *The Brothers Karamazov*, translated by David Magarshack, Penguin Books, 1963, volume I, page 199

The sciences which flourish within the secular world bear upon the truth concerning God and man wherever they are true in their methods and findings.

The lesson of the nineteenth century must not be forgotten. The historic Christian faith found itself confronted by the new sciences of historical criticism and evolutionary biology, and to many those sciences seemed to undermine belief in divine revelation in the Bible, and divine creation of the world and man. It took some years of trial and error to bring the realisation that the new sciences did not undermine but rather enhanced the Christian understanding of the mode of biblical revelation and the wonder of divine creation.

The moral is that God teaches his people not only through sacred theology, but also through sciences often called 'secular', and sacred theology is learner as well as mother. It is easy to grasp this moral as we survey a preceding century: it is harder to grasp its relevance to the century in which we are living.

Michael Ramsey, in Margaret Duggan, editor, *Through the Year with Michael Ramsey*, Hodder and Stoughton, 1975, page 146

No account of the scientific picture of the world and its history would be complete unless it contained a reminder of the fact, frequently forgotten by scientists themselves, that this picture does not even claim to be comprehensive. From the world we actually live in, the world that is given by our senses, our intuitions of beauty and goodness, our emotions and impulses, our moods and sentiments, the man of science abstracts a simplified private universe of things possessing only those qualities which used to be called 'primary.' Arbitrarily, because it happens to be convenient, because his methods do not allow him to deal with the immense complexity of reality, he selects from the whole of experience only those elements which can be weighed, measured, numbered, or which lend themselves in any other way to mathematical treatment. By using this technique of simplication and abstraction, the scientist has succeeded to an astonishing degree in understanding and dominating the physical environment.

The success was intoxicating and, with an illogicality which, in the circumstances, was doubtless pardonable, many scientists and philosophers came to imagine that this useful abstraction from reality was reality itself. Reality as actually experienced contains intuitions of value and significance, contains love, beauty, mystical ecstasy, intimations of godhead. Science did not and still does not possess intellectual instruments with which to deal with these aspects of reality. Consequently it ignored them and concentrated its attention upon such aspects of the world as it could deal with by means of arithmetic, geometry and the various branches of higher mathematics.

Aldous Huxley, *Collected Essays*, Chatto & Windus, 1960, page 361

In my belief, science and technology cannot serve as substitutes for religion. They cannot satisfy the spiritual needs for which religion of all kinds does try to provide, though they may discredit some of the traditional dogmas of the so-called 'higher' religions.

Historically, religion came first and science grew out of religion. Science has never superseded religion, and it is my expectation that it never will supersede it. Science demands definite, incontrovertible answers to the questions that science asks, but the questions that are of the greatest concern to human beings cannot be answered with any certainty. I think the reason why science does succeed in answering its questions is that the questions which it asks are not the most important ones. In pointing out the limits of what science can do, I am not depreciating science's achievements within its own field. Many distinguished scientists have anticipated me in expressing this opinion, and their judgement is authoritative...

How, then, can we arrive at a true, and therefore lasting peace? I do not believe that this goal can be reached without a world-wide spiritual revolution. Certainly a reformation of mankind's political organization would be required. The people of each local sovereign state will have to renounce their state's sovereignty and subordinate it to the paramount sovereignty of a literally world-wide world government. But this revolution in mankind's political organization can be brought about only as a consequence of a far more radical and more profound revolution, a revolution in our fundamental ideas and ideals. For a true and lasting peace, a religious revolution is, I am sure, a *sine qua non*. By religion... I mean the overcoming of self-centredness, in both individuals and communities, by getting into communion with the spiritual presence behind the universe and by bringing our wills into harmony with it. I think this is the only key to peace, but we are very far from picking up this key and using it, and, until we do, the survival of the human race will continue to be in doubt.

Arnold Toynbee, *Surviving the Future*, Oxford University Press, 1971, pages 44 and 66

SECULAR

Secular—concerned with the affairs of this world, worldly; not sacred, not monastic, not ecclesiastical; temporal, profane, lay; sceptical of religious truth or opposed to religious education

I remember reading a challenging book at theological college by Harry Blamires entitled *The Christian Mind.* As I remember it the author was pointing out that the Church had gradually withdrawn from the field of politics, economics, industry, education, health, and social work, and was reduced to a narrow biblicism, dogmatic theology and a private spirituality. He was critical of Church leaders, feeling they had abandoned the intellectual struggle, and were propping up an ageing edifice to maintain attendance at church services. There was now little evidence of *the Christian mind* at work in the Church as a whole and in society at large. The gap had largely been taken over by the secular mind.

There is every sign of this being so today. A considerable percentage of our undergraduate intake never darkens the door of the college chapel. They come up to university with very little religious education behind them, and are already thoroughly secularized. Someone once said that secularism has got this age by the throat. I think this is true and that there is a cost and a downside in the shape of shut minds, blighted imaginations, and stunted emotions. 'I'm bored' is a phrase I hear frequently in college, and echoes of a refrain from the Rolling Stones, 'I can't get no satisfaction.' *Visions of Hope* puts forward an alternative culture to secularism and contains material to stimulate the Christian mind through the practice of reflection. A positive critique to secularism is much needed.

Righteousness exalts a nation.
Proverbs 14:34

Remove not the ancient landmark which your fathers have set.
Proverbs 22:28

If possible, so far as it depends on you, live peaceably with all.
Romans 12:18

Pay all of them their dues, taxes to whom taxes are due, revenue to whom revenue is due, respect to whom respect is due, honour to whom honour is due. Owe no one anything, except to love one another.
Romans 13:7–8

This is at least a cultural fact: the idea of God has died out of men's minds in the secular city of today.
John Hick, *Christianity at the Centre*, Macmillan & Co., 1968, page 11

Secularization is comprehensive and not merely a partial phenomenon of the modern world. It is not a theory or plan that can be put alongside other theories and plans. It is a fact which we cannot escape by persistently ignoring it.
Hans Jürgen Schultz, *Conversions to the World*, SCM Press, 1967, page 37

The greatest intellectual challenge to faith is simply that thoroughly secularized intelligence which is now the rule rather than the exception, whether it expresses itself in science or philosophy or politics or the arts.

H.E. Root, in A.R. Vidler, editor, *Soundings*, Cambridge at the University Press, 1962, page 6

There should be no divisions in our life at all. We are accustomed to speak of certain things as sacred and other things as secular. It is a wrong distinction. If our relationship with God is true, then it affects all things in our life and all things are sacred. What we cannot consecrate we may not keep.

Father Andrew, SDC, *The Good Shepherd*, A.R. Mowbray & Co., 1949, page 24

The shift in the meaning of secularism is one of the most significant developments in modern religious thought. Traditionally the word 'secular' has been the antonym of 'religious'. It has been taken to mean a way of life pursued without reference to religious realities. Where the functions of religious institutions are taken over by the state, secularization is said to have occurred, as in programmes of education and social amelioration. Understandings of life without reference to the idea of God and his alleged intervention in the process of the world are called secular views.

Carl Michalson, in James F. Childress and John Macquarrie, editors, *A New Dictionary of Christian Ethics*, SCM Press, 1986, page 567

There has often been a wrong sort of dualism in people's minds. They have thought of here and hereafter, time and eternity, things secular and things sacred. What we want to try to get is a unifying principle that can make life really one, and bring all things into consistency. Time is only part of eternity: hereafter is really here. We have not to get somewhere to get to God. He can never be nearer to us than He is now, because in Him we live and move and have our being. It is the apprehension of that God Who is with us now that we want to get.

The art of the spiritual life is to link *all* the different happenings of our daily life on to the one golden thread of vocation. St. Paul's care was 'the care of all the churches.' Our care may be the care of a family, the care of a business, but it is just this ordinary daily task which may be for us the way of splendour and the means of union with our God.

Father Andrew, SDC, *Meditations for Every Day*, A.R. Mowbray & Co., 1941, page 81

The Christian Church with its members has the difficult but fascinating task of living in the heart of the secular world, coming alongside all the good which is there, and at the same time lovingly upholding a critique of the secular world in the light of the supernatural.

Inevitably this critique will be more lived than spoken. Christian supernaturalism will carry with it as a very part of itself the will to 'muck in' with the secular, while living the life that is 'hid with Christ in God'. In the apartness of his own contemplation of God, the Christian will be aware of the true end of both himself and those whom he is serving.

But just as Christ took upon himself the form of a servant, and the divine glory was not diminished but rather revealed, so it is with the Christian Church. 'The action of the Church,' writes Daniel Jenkins, 'is sheer worldliness however much it may be dressed up in religious garb, unless it is covered with the holiness of Christ, and the holiness of Christ is always found on earth in the form of a servant.'

Michael Ramsey, in Margaret Duggan, editor, *Through the Year with Michael Ramsey*, Hodder and Stoughton, 1975, page 85

Two motifs in particular characterize the style of the secular city. We call them *pragmatism* and *profanity*...

By *pragmatism* we mean secular man's concern with the question 'Will it work?' Secular man does not occupy himself much with mysteries. He is little interested in anything that seems resistant to the application of human energy and intelligence. He judges ideas, as the dictionary suggests in its definition of pragmatism, by the 'results they will achieve in practice.' The world is viewed not as a unified metaphysical system but as a series of problems and projects.

By *profanity* we refer to secular man's wholly terrestrial horizon, the disappearance of any supramundane reality defining his life. *Pro-fane* means literally 'outside the temple'—thus 'having to do with this world.' By calling him profane, we do not suggest that secular man is sacrilegious, but that he is unreligious. He views the world not in terms of some other world but in terms of itself. He feels that any meaning to be found in this world originates in this world itself. Profane man is simply *this*-worldly.

Harvey Cox, *The Secular City*, SCM Press, 1967, page 60

There is the widespread idea that man is competent by his own powers to organise his own progress and happiness. It is a strange idea, inasmuch as the world is deeply divided and unable to rid itself of terrible weapons of destruction. Yet the idea is there because man does not sit back and ask himself the question '*Quo tendimus?*' (in what direction are we going?) so much as press on, absorbed in the use of his powers and the fascination of them. The mind which enjoys its own creations in discovery, in technology, in the organisation of human welfare can become too busy and absorbed to question man's own competence. Hence in the middle of man's mature intellectuality there is the pride and the insensitivity to the Spirit of God which creates what we call 'modern secularism'.

Then there is the tendency for modern man to live in a whirl with his mind overcrowded. There are so many more things nowadays to think about, and so many impressions entering the mind in rapid succession, while there are still only sixty minutes in each hour, and only twenty-four hours in each day. Hence the mind of man tends to lose its freedom, and to be ruled by the flux of impressions and sensations. I sometimes think that in the circumstances of the modern world an important part of our Christian asceticism needs to be the discipline of the mind to secure its freedom, even more than the discipline of the body.

As a result of the loss of touch with God, there is a deep frustration and fear, often subconscious, and always divisive in its effects upon man's soul.

Michael Ramsey, in Margaret Duggan, editor, *Through the Year with Michael Ramsey*, Hodder and Stoughton, 1975, page 120

The changes of the last few decades have produced the phenomena known as the 'secular world' and the 'secular mind'. The word 'secular' properly means no more than 'of the age', and every generation in history is inevitably 'of the age'. But one of the marks of the new phase in our culture is the lack both of affection for past tradition and of concern for a world beyond this. There is a mentality so insulated within its own secular frontiers as not to be concerned either with the past or with eternity. It is these phenomena which give the word 'secular' its new shades of meaning.

Illustrations of the new 'secularity' come easily to mind. There is the widespread rejection of morality presented in terms of authority. There is the lack of interest in the ideas of the previous generation, and a dimming of a sense of history. There is the belief in the omnicompetence of the technological sciences to explain man and serve his needs. There is the rejection of those otherworldly undertones which affected the outlook of earlier civilisations. And, of course, religious beliefs, practices, and institutions are dismissed as devoid of relevance or meaning.

Such is the atmosphere which surrounds western Christianity today. We must of course avoid exaggeration, for secularism by no means occupies the whole scene. The lines are often blurred, and the frontiers are not rigid. Both in the United States and in Britain much from the older traditions still survives and shows creative power. In America there is still considerable practice of religion, as is seen in the habits of church-going, and in a degree of public interest in religious questions which is reminiscent of middle-class Victorian England. In England only a very few people would call themselves atheists, and while a minority have Christian convictions which they could express and defend in a meaningful way, such pattern of ethical tradition as exists is a pattern derived from an earlier Christendom.

But the ethos of secularism is strong and contagious, and the efforts of Christian evangelism often meet what can seem to be an almost impenetrable mass of secular-mindedness.

Michael Ramsey, in Margaret Duggan, editor, *Through the Year with Michael Ramsey*, Hodder and Stoughton, 1975, page 120

Religion is not now central enough to supply society with a sense of cohesion, and men conspicuously diverge widely with respect to their social and religious values: modern society depends less on cohesion, as manifested in shared consciousness among men, than on contrived and planned systems of social integration effected through bureaucratic, fiscal and technical arrangements. Individual identity is today no longer a product of religious initiation (confirmation is the pale vestige of that once important social rite) or of religious commitment. Group identity is expressed more typically in political, class or ethnic terms than in religious terms (the cases of some conspicuous minorities and politically oppressed nations notwithstanding). Modern society relies on increasingly technical arrangements for the maintenance of social control: neither supernatural after-life sanctions nor the pronouncements of moral theology are much invoked as ways of preserving social order. Explanations of natural and social phenomena no longer take God as their departure point, but rely on tested propositions of science. The church no longer seeks to justify social structure, and politicians invoke religion less and less in justification of their policies. In the matter of providing emotional support for the afflicted, religion still fulfils an extensive function for individuals, but even here secular agencies, from social work to psychotherapy, challenge the role of the clergy. A different way of documenting these associated processes of secularization might be to indicate the growth of a variety of specialist professions—teachers, civil servants, social workers and even entertainers—at least part of whose functions were once among the activities of the clergy. The process is one in which the erstwhile latent social functions of religion have been increasingly rationally planned and undertaken by more specialized departments.

Commensurate with these broad secularizing processes in society, there is a range of empirical evidences of the attendant loss of religious influence over the lives of individuals. Such are the statistics of church attendance; the decline in the proportion of live births that are followed by baptism; the diminishing proportion of those baptized who get confirmed; the decline in the numbers of the clergy; the ageing profile of that profession, and the diminution of the social reward (both in stipend and status) which the profession now commands.

Bryan Wilson, in Alan Richardson and John Bowden, editors, *A New Dictionary of Christian Theology*, SCM Press, 1985, page 534

SEEKING

Seeking—make search or inquiry for; try to be anxious to find or get; ask (thing or person) for advice

George Moore once wrote that a man travels the world over in search of what he needs and returns home to find it. I suppose in some way this sums up my own experience. At the age of twenty my pilgrimage began. I set sail in the troopship the *Empire Fowey* bound for Singapore. At one level I was going to join the 2nd Battalion of the 2nd King Edward VII's Own Gurkha Rifles for the rest of my National Service. At another level I was travelling the world over in search of something—adventure, a search for meaning, God perhaps? I didn't know.

We stopped at Gibraltar for six hours, the first foreign soil I experienced—fascinating. We sailed through the Mediterranean, past Algiers, and woke up one morning in Port Said. We had to wait our turn before entering the Suez Canal, and our next port of call was Aden (now South Yemen), for another six-hour visit. We sailed on through the Indian Ocean, with six hours in Ceylon (now Sri Lanka), and then on to Singapore, to complete the journey. Soon I was travelling round Malaya (now Malaysia), Hong Kong, and Sarawak. By the time I returned to England there certainly had been adventure, and a search for meaning, but I hadn't yet found what I was really looking for. A big step forward was taken in my first term in Oxford. I found to some extent what I was looking for in the pages of the Gospels. The pilgrimage continued. Something was still lacking. Eventually at the age of thirty, I stopped looking outside myself for God and looked within instead, aided by the book, *The Choice is Always Ours.* This was the significant breakthrough. God, I discovered, is not to be confined to the pages of a book, of a man who lived nearly 2,000 years ago, but is to be found in the depths of our being, in the present moment. One has to return 'home' to find what one has been looking for over the years. *Visions of Hope* is designed to help in this quest.

... for the Lord searches all hearts, and understands every plan and thought. If you seek him, he will be found by you.

1 Chronicles 28:9

Those who seek me diligently find me.

Proverbs 8:17

Ask, and it will be given you; seek, and you will find; knock, and it will be opened to you.

Matthew 7:7

... whoever would draw near to God must believe that he exists and that he rewards those who seek him.

Hebrews 11:6

Prayer has much more to do with God's search for us than our search for him.

Christopher Bryant, SSJE., *Jung and the Christian Way*, Darton, Longman and Todd, 1983, page 105

My only task is to be what I am, a man seeking God in silence and solitude, with deep respect for the demands and realities of his own vocation, and fully aware that others too are seeking the truth in their own way.

Thomas Merton, *Contemplation in a World of Action*, Unwin Paperbacks, 1980, page 231

The search for meaning is richly rewarded when an adolescent can find something that deeply absorbs the talents of his mind and his emotional resources. He then has a passion for life.

Arthur T. Jersild, *The Psychology of Adolescence*, The Macmillan Company, 1963, page 10

The way to know God is not by mental search, but by giving attention to Jesus Christ. The search for God can end in the contemplation of Jesus Christ, for in Him we see what God is like.

William Barclay, *The Gospel of Matthew*, The Saint Andrew Press, 1975, volume II, page 17

I veritably believe that the Religion of the future will be something like this, an awed seeking, an orientation towards the superhuman, the Power behind all; with no permanent dogma, but the use of any and every dogma, when, if only for a day that dogma appears to be either true or a bridgeway towards truth or towards spiritual value, spiritual beauty.

Stephen MacKenna, *Journal and Letters*, Constable and Company, 1936, page 206

There seem times when one can neither help oneself nor anyone else to find what we are all in search of, and it seems impossible to submit or acquiesce. I, as you know, have been in this frame of mind, and can only say that one does go on, though it seems impossible. The only way, I think, is to do whatever comes to one, as quietly and fully as one can.

A.C. Benson, *Extracts from the Letters of Dr. A.C. Benson to M.E.A.*, Jarrold Publishing, 1927, page 15

We must learn to realize that the love of God seeks us in every situation, and seeks our good. His inscrutable love seeks our awakening. True, since this awakening implies a kind of death to our exterior self, we will dread His coming in proportion as we are identified with this exterior self and attached to it. But when we understand the dialectic of life and death we will learn to take risks implied by faith, to make the choices that deliver us from the routine self and open to us the door of a new being, a new reality.

Thomas Merton, *New Seeds of Contemplation*, Burns & Oates, 1962, page 13

If we seek God earnestly, we shall find him—or—rather he will find us. If we ask God humbly to come into our lives, he will indeed come. And he will not do with us what we had expected—still less what we had 'hoped'. We shall find, to our dismay as natural men, that the God whose assistance we remotely invoked is already here, within us, speaking, even commanding; his presence manifested in an immediate and imperative revealing of duty and obligation. We asked him to advise, to help, to strengthen, from afar. He comes to indwell, command, and direct, within.

Harry Blamires, *The Will and the Way*, SPCK, 1957, page x

When is the Search ended? In one sense, it is finished when our hand, stretched out to God in the name of His anointed mediator Jesus Christ, feels the answering grasp and knows that He is there. But in another sense the searching never ends, for the first discovery is quickly followed by another, and that by another, and so it goes on....

To find *that* He is, is the mere starting-point of our search. We are lured on to explore *what* He is, and that search is never finished, and it grows more thrilling the farther one proceeds.

Isobel Kuhn, *By Searching*, Overseas Missionary Fellowship (IHQ), 1990, page 93

Have you a true desire to find Him, and to see His face? See that you do not hinder yourself by your own endeavours. God is a Spirit, and near to your spirit. You need not seek and wander far abroad, and weary yourself with the reasonings and reflections and questionings of your mind, and the straining of your head; for by these means you will wander further from God and the knowledge of His truth.

God is a Spirit, apart in the seclusion of His holiness from this coarse world, apart from the domains of the senses and of reason. And it is when your spirit, your love, your delight, and all your thoughts are withdrawn from the world, and it is as a strange land to you, that you will see His face, and hear His voice.

Gerhard Tersteegen, in Frances Bevan, *Sketches of the Quiet in the Land*, John F. Shaw and Co., 1891, page 399

... Seek God and discover Him and make Him a power in your life. Without Him all of our efforts turn to ashes and our sunrises into darker nights. Without Him, life is a meaningless drama with the decisive scenes missing. But with Him we are able to rise from the fatigue of despair to the buoyancy of hope. With Him we are able to rise from the midnight of desperation to the daybreak of joy. St. Augustine was right—we were made for God and we will be restless until we find rest in Him.

Love yourself, if that means rational, healthy, and moral self-interest. You are commanded to do that. That is the length of life. Love your neighbour as you love yourself. You are commanded to do that. That is the breadth of life. But never forget that there is a first and even greater commandment, 'Love the Lord your God with all thy heart and all thy soul and all thy mind.' This is the height of life. And when you do this you live the complete life.

Martin Luther King, *The Words of Martin Luther King*, selected by Coretta Scott King, William Collins Sons & Co., 1986, page 64

It would be well if every now and again in life, we were to ask ourselves: 'What am I looking for? What am I trying to extract from life? What's my aim and goal? If I am honest, what, in the depth of my heart, am I really trying to get out of life?' There are some who are searching for *security*. They would like a position which is safe, money enough to meet the needs of life and to put some past for the time when work is done, a material security which will take away the essential worry about material things. It is not a wrong aim, but it is a low aim, and an inadequate thing to which to direct all life; for, in the last analysis, there is no safe security in the uncertainty of the chances and the changes of this life. There are some who are searching for what they would call a *career*, for power, for prominence, for prestige, for a place to fit the talents and the abilities they believe themselves to have, for an opportunity to do the work they believe themselves capable of doing. Again it is not a bad aim. If it be directed by motives of personal ambition it can be a bad aim; if it be directed by motives of the service of our fellow men it can be a high aim. But it is not enough, for its horizon is limited by time and by the world. There are some who are searching for some kind of *peace*, for something to enable them to live at peace with themselves, and at peace with God, and at peace with men. That is the search for God; that is the aim that only Jesus Christ can meet and supply.

William Barclay, *The Gospel of John*, The Saint Andrew Press, 1974, volume I, page 70

'God is not far from each one of us, for in Him we live and move and have our being.' If ultimately only God satisfy our infinite longing, only He fill the hole in the heart, it might look as if we had to set out on a desperate search for Him. And because the words of earth can only indirectly and obliquely indicate the realities of heaven, there is a sense in which we do indeed have to search for God, to seek if we are to find, to knock if it is to be opened to us. But it is an odd sort of searching, for it ends with the discovery that God is and has been with us all the time, that He is not far off, but nearer to us than the air we breathe, and that, like the air, His presence with us is not something we have earned, but is a free gift to all. Because we can speak of God only obliquely, in our talk about Him we shall get tied up in all sorts of inconsistent spatial metaphors. That doesn't matter. What godly men try to tell us makes sense in spite of the apparent contradictions.

We discover God as our environment. In the homely image of the psalmist, He is about our path and about our bed and familiar with all our ways. It is in Him, to quote Paul again, that we live and move and have our being. But if God is around us He is also within us. And if He is within us it is not as an alien, not as Another, but as our truest selves. A human individual with a powerful personality may be said to invade us as an alien, destroying our autonomy and forcing us into his own mould so that we lose our own identity and become mere copies of his...

But unlike another human being, God is our creator, and by dwelling within us He makes us our true selves and establishes our personal identity. He negates Himself in us in order to find Himself in us. That is to say, He limits Himself so that, instead of overwhelming us, He gradually and gently calls forth into being the tender, vulnerable fragility of our true selfhood, the fragility which when made perfect is His presence, it is Himself which He discovers in us. 'God begins to live in me,' says Thomas Merton, 'not only as my creator but as my other and true self'—other and true because I spend much of my time fabricating a false self instead of allowing God to create me.

H.A. Williams, C.R., *The Joy of God*, Mitchell Beazley Publishers, 1979, page 20

SLEEP

Sleep—bodily condition, normally recurring every night and lasting several hours, in which the nervous system is inactive, eyes are closed, muscles relaxed, and consciousness nearly suspended, being immersed in sleep

I like the story of the priest who fell asleep in his own sermon. To be fair, the pulpit was high up, and he was unduly exposed to the heating system of the church, but I'm tempted to think he finally nodded off to the drone of his own voice.

Sleep is a wonderful gift. I tend to spend the last part of the day, lying down in bed, going over the day, giving thanks for all sorts of things, health, food, a roof over my head, clothes, work, people, and so on. Usually I have fallen asleep long before I get to the end of the list. I'm sure ending the day this way helps to improve the quality of sleep. To further this process I try to take some exercise during the day, either by going for a walk, or a run. Being physically tired helps to bring on sleep. There are times though when sleep is difficult. If I am troubled and anxious I tend to wake up in the early hours of the morning and find it difficult to drop off again. The mind is wide awake, struggling to find solutions to problems. This became a real difficulty some years ago, and I consulted my GP. His advice was to get up, have a cup of tea, do some reading, and go to bed again. The break tends to stop the mind racing away and going round in circles.

We spend about a third of our lives in sleep, so it is a significant feature of our lives. It is interesting to note in Old Testament times the important place given to dreams—as an arena for God's guidance. In modern times this emphasis has been regained somewhat by the Swiss psychologist C.G. Jung. He felt dreams should be taken seriously, as a time when the unconscious throws up all sorts of things to be considered by the conscious mind in the light of day. Sleep is yet another source of hope for us all.

In peace I will both lie down and sleep; for thou alone, O Lord, makest me dwell in safety.

Psalm 4:8

Into thy hand I commit my spirit.

Psalm 31:5

Sweet is the sleep of a labourer, whether he eats little or much; but the surfeit of the rich will not let him sleep.

Ecclesiastes 5:12

Besides this you know what hour it is, how it is full time now for you to wake from sleep. For salvation is nearer to us now than when we first believed.

Romans 13:11

And sleep, that sometimes shuts up sorrow's eye.

William Shakespeare, *A Midsummer Night's Dream*, III. ii. 435

O sleep, O gentle sleep, Nature's soft nurse.

William Shakespeare, *II King Henry IV*, III. i. 4

... As to sleep. I have always known only one way of procuring it—by walking exercise.

J.B. Yeats, *Letters to his son, W.B. Yeats and others*, Faber and Faber, 1944, page 208

Tired Nature's sweet restorer, balmy Sleep!
He, like the world, his ready visit pays
Where Fortune smiles; the wretched he forsakes.

Edward Young, 'Night Thoughts', in *The Complete Works of Edward Young*, William Tegg and Co., 1854, volume I, page 3

O magic sleep! O comfortable bird
That broodest o'er the troubled sea of the mind
Till it is hush'd and smooth!

John Keats, 'Endymion', i. 453, in *The Poetical Works of John Keats*, Oxford at the Clarendon Press, 1958, page 78

Sleep that knits up the ravelled sleeve of care,
The death of each day's life, sore labour's bath,
Balm of hurt minds, great nature's second course,
Chief nourisher in life's feast.

William Shakespeare, *Macbeth*, II. ii. 35

As in the world of Nature, so it is in the world of men. The night is peopled not merely with phantoms and superstitions and spirits of evil, but under its shadow all sciences, methods, social energies, are taking rest, and growing, and feeding, unknown to themselves.

Charles Kingsley, *Daily Thoughts*, Macmillan & Co., 1884, page 211

What means this heaviness that hangs upon me?
This lethargy that creeps through all my senses?
Nature oppress'd, and harass'd out with care,
Sinks down to rest. This once I'll favour her,
That my awaken'd soul may take her flight,
Renew'd in all her strength, and fresh with life,
An offering fit for heaven.

Joseph Addison, *Cato*, V. i. 32, in A.C. Guthkelch, editor, *The Miscellaneous Works of Joseph Addison*, G. Bell and Sons, 1941, volume I, 'Poems and Plays', page 412

Sleep is necessary to renew the body's strength, and to rest and refresh the mind. Most of us spend one-third of each day in sleep. For the time being we consciously forget our activities, our problems, our fears, our hopes and plans, though sometimes these are so present and vivid that we get little sleep. When we sleep, what happens during this daily period of unconsciousness? Is not the sub-conscious mind still active and the spirit at the centre of our being sending us cleverly disguised messages through dreams, telling us things we need to know, informing us of fears, hopes, unfulfilled wishes operating in the depths.

George Appleton, *Journey for a Soul*, William Collins Sons & Co., 1976, page 42

Sleep is the indispensable condition of physical health and mental sanity. It is in sleep that our body repairs the damage caused by the day's work and the day's amusements; in sleep that the *vix medicatrix naturae* overcomes our disease; in sleep that our conscious mind finds some respite from the cravings and aversions, the fears, anxieties and hatreds, the planning and calculating which drive it during waking hours to the brink of nervous exhaustion and sometimes beyond. Many of us are chronically sick and more or less far gone in neurosis. That we are not much sicker and much madder than we are is due exclusively to that most blessed of all natural graces, sleep.

Aldous Huxley, *Themes and Variations*, Chatto & Windus, 1950, page 62

'I sleep but my heart waketh.'

We sleep in peace in the arms of God, when we yield ourselves up to his providence, in a delightful consciousness of his tender mercies; no more restless uncertainties, no more anxious desires, no more impatience at the place we are in; for it is God who has put us there, and who holds us in his arms. Can we be unsafe where he has placed us, and where he watches over us as a parent watches a child? This confiding repose, in which earthly care sleeps, is the true vigilance of the heart; yielding itself up to God, with no other support than him, it thus watches while we sleep. This is the love of him, that will not sleep even in death.

François de la M. Fénelon, *Selections from the Writings of Fénelon*, 'Mrs Follen', Edward T. Whitfield, 1850, page 256

God Speaks

I don't like the man who doesn't sleep, says God.
Sleep is the friend of man.
Sleep is the friend of God.
Sleep is perhaps the most beautiful thing I have created.
And I myself rested on the seventh day.
He whose heart is pure, sleeps. And he who sleeps has a pure heart.
That is the great secret of being as indefatigable as a child.

Of having that strength in the legs that a child has.
Those new legs, those new souls,
And to begin afresh every morning, ever new,
Like young hope, new hope.

Charles Péguy, *Basic Verities*, translated by Ann and Julian Green, Kegan Paul, Trench, Trubner & Co., 1943, page 207

Sleep is the mystery of life... It was brought home to me that I was looking on at a marvellous operation of nature, and I watched it in no profane spirit. I sat silently listening, a moved and hushed spectator of this poetry of the cradle, this ancient and ever new benediction of the family, this symbol of creation sleeping under the wing of God, of our consciousness withdrawing into the shade that it may rest from the burden of thought, and of the tomb, that divine bed, where the soul in its turn rests from life.—To sleep is to strain and purify our emotions, to deposit the mud of life, to calm the fever of the soul, to return into the bosom of maternal nature, thence to re-issue, healed and strong. Sleep is a sort of innocence and purification. Blessed be He who gave it to the poor sons of men as the sure and faithful companion of life, our daily healer and consoler.

Henri Frédéric Amiel, *Amiel's Journal*, translated by Mrs Humphry Ward, Macmillan & Co., 1918, page 38

It may be said of the body in regard to sleep as well as in regard of death, 'It is sown in weakness, it is raised in power...' No one can deny the power of the wearied body to paralyse the soul; but I have a correlate theory which I love, and which I expect to find true—that, while the body wearies the mind, it is the mind that restores vigour of the body, and then, like the man who has built him a stately palace, rejoices to dwell in it. I believe that, if there be a living, conscious love at the heart of the universe, the mind, in the quiescence of its consciousness in sleep, comes into a less disturbed contact with its origin, the heart of the creation; whence gifted with calmness and strength for itself, it grows able to impart comfort and restoration to the weary frame. The cessation of labour affords but the necessary occasion; makes it possible, as it were, for the occupant of an outlying station in the wilderness to return to his Father's house for fresh supplies... The child-soul goes home at night, and returns in the morning to the labours of the school.

George Macdonald, in George Appleton, *Journey for a Soul*, William Collins Sons & Co., 1976, page 43

SOCIETY

Society—social mode of life, the customs and organization of a civilized nation—any social community

Two people—a man and a woman for whom I have the greatest respect—have spoken warmly of society today. They both feel it is an exciting time to be alive. They have jobs they find fulfilling and enjoy the fruits of applied science and technology. On the whole they feel most people are happy and content with their lot.

I have certain reservations, possibly because of the nature of the work I do, and feel a certain sympathy with the words of F.R. Barry in this section. I wonder if the source of all our troubles comes from society being undermined by endemic spiritual malnutrition. Let's just take one illustration—crime. If the statistics are correct we have, in Britain, comparatively speaking, the largest prison population in

Europe, and every indication that crime is on the increase. Law and order seem to be on the verge of breaking down. The rise of a vigilante movement suggests people have lost confidence in the police and the legal system, and are taking the law into their own hands. This seems to coincide with a lack of respect for people and property and a breakdown in morals.

I don't think we can improve this situation by patching up the framework. I think something more fundamental is needed—a spiritual revolution. I don't see this coming from the Church as constituted at present. This institution is also the victim of endemic spiritual malnutrition. Something new is needed, from the very centre of society—a spiritual rebirth.

Am I my brother's keeper?

Genesis 4:9

Honour your father and your mother, that your days may be long in the land which the Lord your God gives you.

Exodus 20:12

... as you wish that men would do to you, do so to them.

Luke 6:31

Remember those who are in prison, as though in prison with them; and those who are ill-treated, since you also are in the body.

Hebrews 13:3

Society is being undermined by endemic spiritual malnutrition.

F.R. Barry, *Secular and Supernatural*, SCM Press, 1969, page 9

Widespread dissipation is the result rather than the cause of social decadence.

Eric Hoffer, *The Passionate State of Mind*, Secker & Warburg, 1956, page 119

Life in cheap and ugly homes cannot fail to give their inmates a corresponding bent of mind.

Norman Douglas, *An Almanac*, Chatto & Windus in association with Martin Secker & Warburg, 1945, page 47

The great want of society to-day is the habit of adhering to absolute truth and reliable honesty.

Henry Ward Beecher, *Proverbs from Plymouth Pulpit*, Charles Burnet & Co., 1887, page 97

In the long run what any society is to become will depend on what it believes, or disbelieves, about the eternal things.

Charles Gore, *Jesus of Nazareth*, Thornton Butterworth, 1929, page 250

The Gospel itself loses its integrity unless it is able in significant measure to call into question the cultural context in which it is to be interpreted.

F.R. Barry, *Secular and Supernatural*, SCM Press, 1969, page 83

That which lowers the sacredness of man is the greatest evil that can visit a nation; for a nation is made rich by its manhood, and is poor when manhood is at a discount.

Henry Ward Beecher, *Proverbs from Plymouth Pulpit*, Charles Burnet & Co., 1887, page 19

Wickedness in society is all the time seeking to gain ascendency; and there is nothing to keep it down but the hatred of it which the educated conscience of society gives.

Henry Ward Beecher, *Proverbs from Plymouth Pulpit*, Charles Burnet & Co., 1887, page 191

In refusing to do our best to improve and purify the social order, we are refusing the religious obligation to make it so far as we can a fit vehicle of the Spirit of God.

Evelyn Underhill, in John Stobbart, editor, *The Wisdom of Evelyn Underhill*, A.R. Mowbray & Co., 1951, page 27

So long as society is absolutely divided as milk is, the cream being at the top and the impoverished milk at the bottom, so long will society be unbalanced, and liable to be thrown into convulsions out of which spring wars. A circulation throughout keeps it in health.

Henry Ward Beecher, *Proverbs from Plymouth Pulpit*, Charles Burnet & Co., 1887, page 47

There is no calamity that can befall the exterior fabric of society so great as benumbing the national conscience, deadening the spirit of humanity, and teaching men to be contented with the degradation of mankind.

Henry Ward Beecher, *Proverbs from Plymouth Pulpit*, Charles Burnet & Co., 1887, page 61

As the blood forever courses through the body, so for the Hebrew spiritual values were linked with what was occurring in the body politic—that is, in their ordinary ongoing history. And just as if you separate blood from body the blood dries and the body dies, so if you separate spiritual concerns from social the former become vacuous and the latter crack up. It is our failure to think in these terms that makes us imagine, quite erroneously, that you can deal with the Gospel first and that the rest will follow.

George Macleod, *Only One Way Left*, The Iona Community, 1956, page 62

Technology can elevate and improve man's life only on one condition: that it remains subservient to his *real* interests; that it respects his true being; that it remembers that the origin and goal of all being is in God. But when technology merely takes over all being for its own purposes, merely exploits and uses up all things in the pursuit of its own ends, and makes everything, including man himself, subservient to its processes, then it degrades man, despoils the world, ravages life, and leads to ruin.

Thomas Merton, *Conjectures of a Guilty Bystander*, Burns & Oates, 1968, page 230

One of the reasons, perhaps, why there has been a widespread ethical disintegration in our whole civilization is that we have created an interlocking machinery of schools, factories, newspapers, and armies that have artificially destroyed the higher centres, have impaired the power of choice, have reduced the symbol functions to an almost reflex level, and have removed the capacity to co-ordinate from the person to the machine process: the whole system powerfully re-enforced by narcotics and other drugs, from alcohol and tobacco to marijuana, cocaine, phenobarbital and aspirin. The utopia of the conditioned reflex.

Lewis Mumford, *The Conduct of Life*, Secker & Warburg, 1952, page 144

Technology is the harnessing of scientific knowledge to practical use. It can be used for great good or for great evil. It has transformed the kind of life that we lead. It has reduced drudgery, increased consumption of goods, aided health, enabled mass communication and mass transport. At the same time it is likely to reduce paid employment (by automation), cause population explosion (by reducing infant mortality and extending life expectancy) and increase war risks (by sophisticated weapons systems). It is possible for machines to dominate us, instead of us controlling machines. We need to be responsible in the ends for which we use technology and in our choice of appropriate technology. God gave to human beings power and wisdom to use aright.

Hugh Montefiore, *Confirmation Notebook*, Fifth Edition, SPCK, 1985, page 8

Society cannot exist without sacrifice.

The ethics which start from individuals try to distribute this in such a way that through the devotion of individuals as many as possible are voluntary sacrifices, and that the individuals who are most severely hit are relieved of their burden as far as possible by others. This is the doctrine of self-sacrifice.

The sociological ethics which no longer reach back to individual ethics can only lay down that the progress of society advances according to inexorable laws at the price of the freedom and prosperity of individuals and groups of individuals. This is the doctrine of being sacrificed by others.

Albert Schweitzer, in George Seaver, *Albert Schweitzer: Christian Revolutionary*, James Clarke & Co., 1944, page 96

When I am in a great city, I know that I despair.
I know there is no hope for us, death awaits, it is useless to care.
For oh the poor people, that are flesh of my flesh,
I, that am flesh of their flesh.
when I see the iron hooked into their faces
their poor, their fearful faces
I scream in my soul, for I know I cannot
take the hook out of their faces, that makes them so drawn,
nor cut the invisible wires of steel that pull them
back and forth, to work,
back and forth to work,
like fearful and corpse-like fishes hooked and being played
by some malignant fisherman on an unseen shore
where he does not choose to land them yet, hooked fishes of the factory floor.

D.H. Lawrence, 'City Life', in *The Complete Poems of D.H. Lawrence*, Vivian de Sola Pinto and Warren Roberts, editors, William Heinemann, 1967, volume II, page 632

Look at these drugs! Hard drugs—heroin, morphine, and cocaine are addictive because when used frequently life becomes unlivable without their support. Soft drugs—marihuana (pot, hemp, hashish) is less harmful but none the less narcotic in its effect. The third group consist of psychedelic drugs like mescalin and L.S.D., which bring pleasant dreams and hallucinations, but can also bring hellish experiences. The fourth group are the purple hearts and amphetamines, which play a perfectly proper part in the medical treatment of anxiety states, but can only increase dependence upon stimulants for those who use them in place of normal bodily, mental, and spiritual training. When life is demanding and difficult, as it can be today when pressures like 'getting-on', mobility, success, 'keeping up with the Joneses', passing examinations, constantly claim our attention, the weak very easily go to the wall. It is so much simpler to opt out and sit about in a pleasant half-existence, thinking 'beautiful' or 'diabolic' thoughts, as the case may be. If you have forgotten, or never learnt, that life can have a meaning—a motivation and an end, if you have never come to grips with the great Other—the numinous, the divine love, the Christ of the gospels, or realized that within you is 'the Kingdom' waiting to be discovered, then you have not yet lived and drugs may seem a quick and easy way through. A drug, as the name suggests, is something that saps a person's ability to be positive, accepting, and involved in life, in a healthy and normal way. As a healing agent it can be useful; as an addiction it is hell. The addict becomes increasingly useless in society—a parasite clinging fearfully until he drops off, dead!

Norman W. Goodacre, *Layman's Lent*, A.R. Mowbray & Co., 1969, page 19

Life in industrialised countries has become artificial, its patterns far from nature. Houses are full of electric gadgets; leisure activities are limited to television and the cinema; cities are noisy, stifling and polluted; people are exhausted by long hours of travel in subway, train and car—when they aren't equally exhausted by crawling through traffic jams. The films they watch and the news they listen to concentrate on violence. They cannot possibly integrate all that is happening over the world—earthquakes in Azerbaijan, famine in the Sahel, fighting in the Middle East, disruption in Northern Ireland, censorship of the press, tyranny, torture, people being condemned to prison without trial, or to a psychiatric hospital when they are not ill. It is overwhelming. And people are overwhelmed by it all. They are not equipped to assimilate all this dramatic information. That is why they latch on to new myths which announce the salvation of the world, or rigid sects which claim to have a monopoly of the truth. The more anguish people feel, the more they seek out new saviours—whether these are political, psychological, religious, or mystical. Or else they throw everything over in the race for instant stimulation, wealth and prestige.

Communities are a sign that it is possible to live on a human scale, even in the present world. They are a sign that we do not have to be slaves to work, to inhuman economics, or to the stimulations of artificial leisure. A community is essentially a place where we learn to live at the pace of humanity and nature. We are part of the earth and we need the heat of the sun, the water of the sea, and the air we breathe. We are part of nature and its laws are written in our flesh. That doesn't mean that scientific discoveries aren't useful too. But they have to be at the service of life, applied to create an environment in which human beings can truly grow—whether in town or country, middle-class areas or slums.

A community should be primarily not a grouping of shock-troops, commandos or heroes, but a gathering of people who want to be a sign that it is possible for people to live together, love each other, celebrate and work for a better world and a fellowship of peace. A community is a sign that love is possible in a materialistic world where people so often either ignore or fight each other. It is a sign that we don't need a lot of money to be happy—in fact, the opposite. Schumacher's *Small is Beautiful* gave us a lot to think about. In our l'Arche communities, we have to put still more thought into the quality of life. We have to learn to live each day and find our own internal and external rhythms.

Jean Vanier, *Community and Growth*, Darton, Longman and Todd, 1991, page 309

SOLITUDE

Solitude—being solitary; lonely place

P.G. Woodhouse wrote in his book *Jeeves in the Office*, that he was in rare fettle and his heart had touched a new high. He didn't know anything that braces one up like finding you don't have to get married after all.

This has roughly been my experience. I went through a phase when I would have liked to marry but now I'm grateful to be single. As the passages in this section suggest, solitude permits the mind to feel, to think and to grow. I'm extremely fortunate to live in a college community, but how I value those times when I am able to get away from everyone, and be on my own. I go to all sorts of places such as the countryside and the Lake District. I greatly enjoy the solitude of the Swiss Alps for a short time in the winter when I do some skiing. Each summer I go to a chalet in the French Alps with a group of our undergraduates on a reading/walking party. In spite of lively company there are times on the walks for moments of solitude, and an opportunity to recharge one's batteries. Holidays by the sea in remote places in Spain and Greece are a great tonic, especially when I use these primarily as a retreat for some quiet reflection. Even in the midst of our hectic eight-week terms, there are times when one can withdraw and enjoy a short time on one's own. I think there are some people who are frightened of solitude, and fear being isolated and alone. Perhaps they need to be reminded that 'alone' really means 'all one' and a state to be experienced rather than avoided. *Visions of Hope* is designed to help people make a creative use of their solitude.

Then the Lord God said, 'It is not good that the man should be alone; I will make him a helper fit for him.'

Genesis 2:18

Some wandered in desert wastes, finding no way to a city to dwell in... he led them by a straight way, till they reached a city to dwell in.... For he satisfies him who is thirsty, and the hungry he fills with good things.

Psalm 107:4, 7, 9

But when you pray, go into your room and shut the door and pray to your Father who is in secret; and your Father who sees in secret will reward you.

Matthew 6:6

And in the morning, rising up a great while before day, he went out, and departed into a solitary place, and there prayed.

Mark 1:35 (AV)

Solitude permits the mind to feel.

William Wordsworth, *The Excursion*, Book Eighth, 55

Solitude is a fine thing when one is at peace with oneself and has something definite to do.

Johann Wolfgang von Goethe, *Wisdom and Experience*, selected by Ludwig Curtius, translated and edited by Hermann J. Weigand, Routledge & Kegan Paul, 1949, page 213

The desert does not mean the absence of men, it means the presence of God.

Carlo Carretto, *The Desert in the City*, translated by Barbara Wall, William Collins Sons & Co., 1983, foreword

There is nothing more remarkable in human nature than the strength it gains from solitude.

Albion Tourgee, *Murvale Eastman*, Sampson, Low, Marston, Searle & Rivington, 1891, page 247

For solitude sometimes is best society,
And short retirement urges sweet return.

John Milton, *Paradise Lost*, ix. 249, in *The Poetical Works of John Milton*, Oxford at the Clarendon Press, 1900, page 357

It would perhaps be true to say that the more powerful and original a mind, the more it will incline towards a religion of solitude.

Aldous Huxley, *Proper Studies*, Chatto & Windus, 1927, page 178

Birth and death are solitary; thought and growth are solitary; every final reality of a man's life is his alone, incommunicable.

Charles Morgan, *The Fountain*, Macmillan & Co., 1932, page 320

Unless a man takes himself sometimes *out of* the world, by Retirement and Self-reflection; he will be in danger of losing himself *in* the world.

Benjamin Whichcote, *Moral and Religious Aphorisms*, century iv, number 302, Elkin Mathews & Marrot, 1930, page 37

I am sure of this, that by going much alone a man will get more of a noble courage in thought and word than from all the wisdom that is in books.

Ralph Waldo Emerson, *Journals*, Constable & Co., 1910, volume III, page 222

There is one means of procuring solitude which to me, and I apprehend to all men, is effectual, and that is to go to the window and look at the stars.

Ralph Waldo Emerson, *Journals*, Constable & Co., 1910, volume III, page 263

Solitude is nurse of enthusiasm, and enthusiasm is the true parent of genius. In all ages solitude has been called for—has been flown to.

Isaac Disraeli, *Literary Character of Men of Genius*, Frederick Warne and Co., 1881, page 110

Solitude has a refining and tonic influence; there we wrestle with our thoughts and set them in order; there we nurture the imagination and sow the seeds of character.

Norman Douglas, *An Almanac*, Chatto & Windus in association with Martin Secker & Warburg, 1945, page 8

But to cherish your soul; expel companions; set your habits to a life of solitude; then will the faculties rise fair and full within, like forest trees and field flowers...

Ralph Waldo Emerson, 'Society and Solitude, Letters and Social Aims, Addresses', in *The Works of Ralph Waldo Emerson*, George Bell & Sons, 1906, volume III, page 422

A man or woman who has developed this solitude of heart is no longer pulled apart by the most divergent stimuli of the surrounding world but is able to perceive and understand this world from a quiet inner centre.

Henri J.M. Nouwen, *Reaching Out*, William Collins Sons & Co., 1980, page 38

When from our better selves we have too long
Been parted by the hurrying world, and droop,
Sick of its business, of its pleasures tired,
How gracious, how benign, is Solitude.

William Wordsworth, *The Prelude*, Book Fourth, 357

Solitude is only agreeable when the power of having society is removed to a short space and can be commanded at pleasure. It is not good for man to be alone. It blunts our faculties and freezes our active virtues.

Sir Walter Scott, *The Journal of Sir Walter Scott*, Oxford University Press, 1951, page 535

Even in the most socialized community, there must always be a few who best serve it by being kept solitary and isolated. The artist, like the mystic, naturalist, mathematician or 'leader', makes his contribution out of his solitude.

Cyril Connolly, *The Unquiet Grave*, Hamish Hamilton, 1945, page 41

Sheer physical solitude can in some cases, by adroit planning, be avoided. What cannot be avoided is the solitude within oneself. The only way of not dreading either of these solitudes is to deepen one's faith in the presence of Christ.

Hubert van Zeller, *Considerations*, Sheed and Ward, 1974, page 21

The contemplatives and ascetics of all ages and religions have sought God in the silence and solitude of the desert, forest, and mountain. Jesus himself spent forty days in the desert and long hours communing with the Father in the silence of the night on the mountains.

Mother Teresa, *Jesus, the Word to be Spoken*, compiled by Brother Angelo Devananda, William Collins Sons & Co., 1990, page 116

Wisdom's self
Oft seeks to sweet retired solitude,
Where with her best nurse Contemplation
She plumes her feathers, and lets grow her wings,
That in the various bustle of resort
Were all-too ruffled and sometimes impair'd.

John Milton, *Comus and Other Poems*, Oxford University Press, 1968, 357

We must become so alone, so utterly alone, that we withdraw into our innermost self. It is a way of bitter suffering. But then our solitude is overcome, we are no longer alone, for we find that our innermost self is the spirit, that it is God, the indivisible. And suddenly we find ourselves in the midst of the world, yet undisturbed by its multiplicity, for in our innermost soul we know ourselves to be one with all being.

Hermann Hesse, in Volker Michels, *Reflections*, translated by Ralph Manheim, Jonathan Cape, 1977, page 53

Her face had the usual fulness of expression which is developed by a life of solitude. Where the eyes of a multitude continually beat like waves upon a countenance they seem to wear away its mobile power; but in the still water of privacy every feeling and sentiment unfolds in visible luxuriance, to be interpreted as readily as a printed word by an intruder.

Thomas Hardy, *The Woodlanders*, Macmillan and Co., 1920, page 8

The world is full of people who are haunted by their sense of inadequacy. The world is full of people who are haunted, and this is more serious, by their sense of guilt. The fear that they will never be reassured drives them to one of two alternatives: either they take refuge in a solitude which shows up their inadequacy all the more clearly or they try to escape into the kind of distractions which only increase their sense of guilt.

Hubert van Zeller, *Considerations*, Sheed and Ward, 1974, page 21

Later on I began to have daily pilgrimages to think these things. There was a feeling that I must go somewhere, and be alone. It was a necessity to have a few minutes of this separate life every day; my mind required to live its own life apart from other things. A great oak at a short distance was one resort, and sitting on the grass at the roots, or leaning against the trunk and looking over the quiet meadows towards the bright southern sky, I could live my own life a little while.

Richard Jefferies, *The Story of My Heart*, Macmillan & Co., 1968, page 55

Be able to be alone. Loose not the advantage of Solitude, and the Society of thy self, nor be only content, but delight to be alone and single with Omnipresency. He who is thus prepared, the Day is not uneasy nor the Night black unto him. Darkness may bound his Eyes, not his Imagination. In his Bed he may ly, like Pompey and his Sons, in all quarters of the Earth, may speculate the Universe, and enjoy the whole World in the Hermitage of himself. Thus the old Ascetick Christians found a Paradise in a Desert, and with little converse on Earth held a conversation in Heaven: thus they Astronomiz'd in Caves, and, though they beheld not the Stars, had the Glory of Heaven before them.

Sir Thomas Browne, 'Christian Morals', part III, section 9, in Geoffrey Keynes, editor, *The Works of Sir Thomas Browne*, Faber and Faber, 1964, page 276

Solitude is the furnace of transformation. Without solitude we remain victims of our society and continue to be entangled in the illusions of the false self. Jesus himself entered into this furnace. There he was tempted with the three compulsions of the world: to be relevant ('turn stones into loaves'), to be spectacular ('throw yourself down'), and to be powerful ('I will give you all these kingdoms'). There he affirmed God as the only source of his identity ('You must worship the Lord your God and serve him alone'). Solitude is the place of the great struggle and the great encounter—the struggle against the compulsions of the false self, and the encounter with the loving God who offers himself as the substance of the new self.

Henri J.M. Nouwen, *The Way of the Heart*, Darton, Longman and Todd, 1981, page 25

. . . solitude affords the occasion for the supreme battle, and the only one that can be truly decisive. All the pretences, all the false trappings of demi-virtues in which he placed his trust, now fall away in a flash. He must see himself, recognize himself for what he is. He must transfer the struggle from the superficial levels of his being, from the mirages of the world or the phantoms of the flesh, to the darkened abysses of his own will which is only a will enslaved. Then each man finds revealed to him that the strength of God is fulfilled in our weakness, that His grace is sufficient for us, that it is when we are weakest that we are strong, provided that, at this moment, faith does not weaken . . . Solitude, indeed, is the great trial of faith. It is only when a man has gone through this trial that he can say with more than his lips, 'It is no longer I who live; but it is Christ Who lives in me.'

Louis Bouyer, *Introduction to Spirituality*, Darton, Longman and Todd, 1963, page 205

THINKING

Thinking—consider; be of opinion; form conception of; exercise the mind otherwise than by passive reception of another's idea; imaging

I owe a great debt to Edward Wilson, the doctor on Scott's expedition to the Antarctic. Early on in life he adopted the practice of keeping a spiritual diary and would go through the Gospels systematically, working out in his own mind what he thought about our Lord's teaching. I adopted a variant of this practice in my early twenties, but added to the Gospels what I consider to be the great insights 'on life' in the last 2,000 years. I discovered much to my delight that I had a mind that could think. Other people's thoughts acted as a great stimulant to my thinking. I started off with *A Year of Grace*, by Victor Gollancz, which took me about six months to get through and followed this up with his other compilation *From Darkness to Light.* Aldous Huxley's *Perennial Philosophy* was the next book to stimulate my thinking and this was greatly enhanced by the book I have mentioned several times before—*The Choice is Always Ours.* Currently I'm using *Visions of Love*, *Visions of Hope*, and a manuscript copy of a new *Visions of Faith.* This thinking process is an exploration and an adventure. The more one does the more connections one makes, and somewhere in this process something akin to compound interest takes over, and thought leads to more thought. All this helps to stimulate one's vision of hope.

O Lord, what is man that thou dost regard him, or the son of man that thou dost think of him?

Psalm 144:3

The mind of the righteous ponders how to answer.

Proverbs 15:28

What do you think of the Christ?

Matthew 22:42

. . . think with sober judgment, each according to the measure of faith which God has assigned him.

Romans 12:3

A thought is a spiritual thing.

George Moore, *The Bending of the Bough*, T. Fisher Unwin, 1900, page 45

And in much of your talking, thinking is half-murdered.

Kahlil Gibran, *The Prophet*, William Heinemann, 1970, page 71

Thought feeds itself with its own words and grows.

Rabindranath Tagore, 'Stray Birds', CLXIX, in *Collected Poems & Plays of Rabindranath Tagore*, Macmillan & Co., 1936, page 308

Man is but a reed, the most feeble thing in nature; but he is a thinking reed.

Blaise Pascal, *Pensées*, translated by W.F. Trotter, Random House, 1941, page 116

It is wonderful what a breadth of life can be encompassed in a moment's thought.

O.T. Beard, *Bristling With Thorns*, The Gregg Press, 1968, page 400

... the universe begins to look more like a great thought than like a great machine.

Sir James Jeans, *The Mysterious Universe*, Cambridge at the University Press, 1930, page 148

I don't think thinking about a situation does much good. One knows by instinct what one can do.

A.C. Benson, *Extracts from the Letters of Dr. A.C. Benson to M.E.A.*, Jarrold Publishing, 1927, page 23

It is very hard to find out exactly what the best and deepest of oneself does think.

A.C. Benson, *Extracts from the Letters of Dr. A.C. Benson to M.E.A.*, Jarrold Publishing, 1927, page 76

Only think: a thousand wrongs to every right. What an opening for a man of talent....

Norman Douglas, *An Almanac*, Chatto & Windus in association with Martin Secker & Warburg, 1945, page 38

As soon as man does not take his existence for granted, but beholds it as something unfathomably mysterious, thought begins.

Albert Schweitzer, *The Teaching of Reverence for Life*, Peter Owen, 1965, page 33

A. thinks much, but it is always about something to be done. The thinking in the Old Testament and the Gospels is of this type.

Mark Rutherford, *Last Pages From a Journal*, Oxford University Press, 1915, page 272

No one can fail of the regenerative influence of optimistic thinking, pertinaciously pursued. Every man owns indefeasibly this inlet to the divine.

William James, *The Varieties of Religious Experience*, William Collins Sons & Co., 1974, page 119

Man being made a reasonable and so a thinking creature, there is nothing more worthy of his being, than the right direction and employment of his thoughts: since upon this depends both the usefulness to the public, and his own present and future benefit in all respects.

William Penn, *Fruits of Solitude*, A.W. Bennett, 1863, page 74

I began to think, and to think is one real advance from hell to heaven. All that hellish, hardened state and temper of soul, which I have said so much of before, is but a deprivation of thought; he that is restored to his power of thinking, is restored to himself.

Daniel Defoe, *Moll Flanders*, Arandar Books, 1946, page 245

Thinking gets you nowhere. It may be a fine and noble aid in academic studies, but you can't think your way out of emotional difficulties. That takes something altogether different. You have to make yourself passive then, and just listen. Re-establish contact with a slice of eternity.

Etty Hillesum, *Etty, A Diary, 1941–43*, translated by Arnold J. Pomerans, Jonathan Cape, 1983, page 38

If we examine our thoughts, we shall find them to be all set on the past and the future. Of the present we think hardly at all, and if we do, it is only that we may draw from it a light wherewith to control the future. The present is never our end; past and present are our means; the future alone is our end. Thus we never live, but we hope to live; and it is inevitable that, ever preparing to be happy, we never are so.

Blaise Pascal, *Pensées*, translated by W.F. Trotter, Random House, 1941, page 61

And, too, Jesus appeals to the mind. Again and again he challenges his hearers to think. He doesn't reveal the truth to them in a kind of tabloid packet to be swallowed whole—'Shut your eyes and swallow'. No, Jesus challenges his hearers, sowing seeds of truth in their minds and consciences, and then urging them to think out the meaning in it.

Think it out, think it out. It is in this process of thinking it out—together with the love and the will and the imagination—that Jesus and his message are made known.

Michael Ramsey, in Margaret Duggan, editor, *Through the Year with Michael Ramsey*, Hodder and Stoughton, 1975, page 24

To think well is to serve God in the interior court: To have a mind composed of Divine Thoughts, and set in frame, to be like Him within. To conceive aright and to enjoy the world, is to conceive the Holy Ghost, and to see His Love; which is the Mind of the Father. And this more pleaseth Him than many Worlds, could we create as fair and great as this. For when you are once acquainted with the world, you will find the goodness and wisdom of God so manifest therein, that it was impossible another, or better should be made. Which being made to be enjoyed, nothing can please or serve him more, than the Soul that enjoys it. For that Soul doth accomplish the end of His desire in Creating it.

Thomas Traherne, *Centuries*, The Faith Press, 1969, page 6

Thought, I love thought.
But not the jaggling and twisting of already existent ideas
I despise that self-important game.
Thought is the welling up of unknown life into consciousness,
Thought is the testing of statements on the touchstone of the conscience,
Thought is gazing on the face of life, and reading what can be read,
Thought is pondering over experience, and coming to conclusion.
Thought is not a trick, or an exercise, or a set of dodges,
Thought is a man in his wholeness wholly attending.

D.H. Lawrence, 'Thought', in Vivian de Sola Pinto and Warren Roberts, editors, *The Complete Poems of D.H. Lawrence*, William Heinemann, 1967, volume II, page 673

The world in which we live is various and astonishing: some of the things that seem plainest grow more and more difficult the more they are considered; other things, which might have been thought quite impossible to discover, have nevertheless been laid bare by genius and industry. The powers of thought, the vast regions which it can master, the much more vast regions which it can only dimly suggest to imagination, give to those whose minds have travelled beyond the daily round an amazing richness of material, an escape from the triviality and wearisomeness of familiar routine, by which the whole of life is filled with interest, and the prison walls of the commonplace are broken down. The same love of adventure which takes men to the South Pole, the same passion for a conclusive trial of strength which leads some men to welcome war, can find in creative thought an outlet which is neither wasteful nor cruel, but increases the dignity of man by incarnating in life some of that shining splendour which the human spirit is bringing down out of the unknown. To give this joy, in a greater or less measure, to all who are capable of it, is the supreme end for which the education of the mind is to be valued.

Bertrand Russell, *Principles of Social Reconstruction*, George Allen & Unwin, 1971, page 114

What can we do for the world while we live?

Many men and women would wish to serve mankind, but they are perplexed and their power seems infinitesimal. Despair seizes them; those who have the strongest passion suffer most from the sense of impotence, and are most liable to spiritual ruin through lack of hope.

So long as we think only of the immediate future, it seems that what we can do is not much.

... We must recognize that the whole world is ruled in a wrong spirit, and that a change of spirit will not come from one day to the next. Our expectations must not be for tomorrow, but for the time when what is thought now by a few shall have become the common thought of many. If we have courage and patience, we can think the thoughts and feel the hopes by which, sooner or later, men will be inspired, and weariness and discouragement will be turned into energy and ardour. For this reason, the first thing we have to do is to be clear in our own minds as to the kind of life we think good and the kind of change that we desire in the world.

The ultimate power of those whose thought is vital is far greater than it seems to men who suffer from the irrationality of contemporary politics. Religious toleration was once the solitary speculation of a few bold philosophers. Democracy, as a theory, arose among a handful of men in Cromwell's army... Socialism owes its origin to a very small number of isolated theorists... The power of thought, in the long run, is greater than any other human power. Those who have the ability to think, and the imagination to think in accordance with men's needs, are likely to achieve the good they aim at sooner or later, though probably not while they are still alive.

But those who wish to gain the world by thought must be content to lose it as a support in the present. Most men go through life without much questioning, accepting the beliefs and practices which they find current, feeling that the world will be their ally if they do not put themselves in opposition to it. New thought about the world is incompatible with this comfortable acquiescence; it requires a certain intellectual detachment, a certain solitary energy, a power of inwardly dominating the world and the outlook that the world engenders. Without some willingness to be lonely new thought cannot be achieved. And it will not be achieved to any purpose if the loneliness is accompanied by aloofness, so that the wish for union with others dies, or if intellectual detachment leads to contempt. It is because the state of mind required is subtle and difficult, because it is hard to be intellectually detached yet not aloof, that fruitful thought on human affairs is not common, and that most theorists are conventional or sterile. The right kind of thought is rare and difficult, but it is not impotent. It is not the fear of impotence that need turn us aside from thought if we have the wish to bring new hope into the world.

Bertrand Russell, *Principles of Social Reconstruction*, George Allen & Unwin, 1971, page 155

TIME

Time—duration; continued existence; progress of this viewed as affecting person or things, past, present and future

When I was at theological college I went through a minor crisis, and it was to do with 'time'. I had taken on too many commitments, and suddenly everything seemed to go wrong, and my little world collapsed. In trying to rescue the situation, I came across a book written by Max Warren, called *The Mastery of Time*, and found it helpful. According to him, the mastery of time depended on putting into practice the two main commandments, to love the Lord your God with heart, soul, mind and strength, and to love your neighbour as yourself. Easy to state, but difficult to do, even in a theological college. I put his recommendations into practice, and drastically reduced my commitments. With a little help and guidance from a member of staff, I put what was left into some order of priority. It turned out to be a valuable exercise. Even now I stand back from time to time and prune my activities. We tend to waste so much time in trivia and superficialities.

I noticed the same thing happening in the life of a post-graduate student at University College, Oxford. He was a good sportsman, with a fine mind, and a strong lively personality. He told me he kept a watchful eye on himself and his activities, and ruthlessly cut out anything that was not creative and valuable. It was interesting to see how his priorities changed during his time in college. He succeeded in getting his D.Phil., but then did a big change and ended up at medical school. He wanted to spend the rest of his life looking after people and healing them. Perhaps we should take a leaf out of his book, keep an eye on our lives, and take up the mastery of time.

Remember the sabbath day, to keep it holy. Six days you shall labour, and do all your work; but the seventh day is a sabbath to the Lord your God; in it you shall not do any work.

Exodus 20:8

For everything there is a season, and a time for every matter under heaven.

Ecclesiastes 3:1

Take heed, watch; for you do not know when the time will come.

Mark 13:33

We look not to the things that are seen but to the things that are unseen; for the things that are seen are transient, but the things that are unseen are eternal.

2 Corinthians 4:18

Let every man be master of his time.

William Shakespeare, *Macbeth*, III. i. 48

I wasted time, and now doth time waste me.

William Shakespeare, *King Richard II*, V. v. 48

He who is too busy doing good finds no time to be good.

Rabindranath Tagore, 'Stray Birds', CLXXX1V, in *Collected Poems & Plays of Rabindranath Tagore*, Macmillan & Co., 1936, page 311

The day is of infinite length for him who knows how to appreciate and use it.

Johann Wolfgang von Goethe, *Wisdom and Experience*, selected by Ludwig Curtius, translated and edited by Hermann J. Weigand, Routledge & Kegan Paul, 1949, page 216

We must use time creatively, in the knowledge that the time is always ripe to do right.

Martin Luther King, *The Words of Martin Luther King*, selected by Coretta Scott King, William Collins Sons & Co., 1986, page 33

Life must be measured rather by depth than by length, by thought and action rather than by time.

Sir John Lubbock, *The Pleasures of Life*, Macmillan & Co., 1881, page 109

If you picture Time as a straight line along which we have to travel, then you must picture God as the whole page on which the line is drawn.

C.S. Lewis, *Mere Christianity*, William Collins Sons & Co., 1961, page 143

Time is like a rapid river, and a rushing torrent of all that comes and passes. A thing is no sooner well come, but it is past; and then another is borne after it, and this too will be carried away.

Marcus Aurelius, *The Meditations of Marcus Aurelius*, translated by Jeremy Collier, Walter Scott, page 59

Love Jesus, and everything he has is yours. Because he is God, he is maker and giver of time. Because he is Man, he has given true heed to time. Because he is both God and Man he is the best judge of the spending of time.

The Cloud of Unknowing, translated by Clifton Wolters, Penguin Books, 1971, page 56

I think I have learned a new view of time—one that brings freedom from many useless anxieties, as Jesus said it would. As the horizon of the future contracts, the importance of 'now' is so much clearer than when there always seemed to be time in hand.

Leslie J. Tizard, *Facing Life and Death*, George Allen and Unwin, 1959, page 162

All men complain that they haven't enough time. It's because they look at their lives from too human a point of view. There's always time to do what God wants us to do, but we must put ourselves completely into each moment that he offers us.

Michel Quoist, *Prayers of Life*, translated by Anne Marie de Commaile and Agnes Mitchell Forsyth, Gill and Macmillan, 1963, page 76

So be very careful how you spend time. There is nothing more precious. In the twinkling of an eye heaven may be won or lost. God shows that time is precious, for he never gives two moments of time side by side, but always in succession. To do otherwise he would have to alter the whole course of creation. Time is made for man, not man for time.

The Cloud of Unknowing, translated by Clifton Wolters, Penguin Books, 1971, page 56

Love proves its spiritual origin by rising above time and space and circumstance, wealth and age, and even temporary beauty, at the same time that it alone can perfectly *use* all those material adjuncts. Being spiritual, it is the Lord of matter, and can give and receive from it glory and beauty when it will, and yet live without it.

Charles Kingsley, *Daily Thoughts*, Macmillan & Co., 1884, page 201

I don't have the time! We don't have the time!

It's not time. We don't *take* the time. We let life gnaw away at our time, stealing it from us bit by bit. We're slaves, not masters.

We must be masters of our time.

I must control my life—and the obligations it imposes on me—not the other way round.

Michel Quoist, *With Open Heart*, translated by Colette Copeland, Gill and Macmillan, 1983, page 137

Today we have no time even to look at each other, to talk to each other, to enjoy each other, and still less to be what our children expect from us, what the husband expects from the wife, what the wife expects from her husband. And so less and less we are in touch with each other. The world is lost for want of sweetness and kindness. People are starving for love because everybody is in such a great rush.

Mother Teresa of Calcutta, in *The Silence of the Heart*, compiled by Kathryn Spink, SPCK, 1983, page 42

And so all men run after time, Lord.
They pass through life running—hurried, jostled, overburdened, frantic, and they never get there. They haven't time.
In spite of all their efforts they're still short of time, of a great deal of time.
Lord, you must have made a mistake in your calculations.
There's a big mistake somewhere.
The hours are too short,
The days are too short,
Our lives are too short.

Michel Quoist, *Prayers of Life*, translated by Anne Marie de Commaile and Agnes Mitchell Forsyth, Gill and Macmillan, 1963, page 77

So many people get nervous and irritable because they are always in a hurry. Sometimes this is due to well-meant but unnecessary efforts to do more than they need. Others keep up a senseless and unbalanced activity because they dare not stop to think, others because they are ambitious and want to 'get on', to 'make a name' or to make money, or to achieve some self-centred purpose, or because they are over-anxious about the future. All these ways of living are pagan—living without God. We need to be taught how to live, how to use time aright, for it is His gift. God alone can teach us how to order our days; He alone can bring peace and order into our lives. Here no discipline is more important than the regular practice of prayer, which involves a deliberate choice of time for thought and prayer. For 'worship is the keystone of order, and therefore of peace, which is the tranquillity of order'.

Olive Wyon, *On the Way*, SCM Press, 1958, page 75

The cliché has it that time is the enemy of man. Not so—time is one of our supreme assets. It is in time that we grow, we gain experience, we learn, we mature. To fail to comprehend this may be to live on a level of immature yearning. What a tragedy it would be to actually find the fountain of youth. Imagine being young for an entire lifetime! Youth can be a wonderful period in our lives, but it is also a preparatory period. All preparation with no goal is anticipation with no climax... practicing the scales with no concert performance. Time is fulfilling. Of course, this implies not only having experiences but being able to evaluate them as well. A woman or man who has just had a fuller existence than the person with hundreds of 'events' that were lived through unanalyzed. Thus even a youth who can evaluate a single experience is more mature than an adult who has lived through all kinds of experiences that have made almost no impact on the individual. But how much more rewarding will be the life of that same youth, who has cultivated the habit of evaluating experiences, in maturity, when more experiences can be known in the light of the earlier known experiences. A forty-year-old who really wishes to be a twenty-year-old is in some important way probably a ten-year-old. Not in the sense of innocence but in the sense of ignorance. Each day fully lived guarantees that the next day will be even more fully lived. While the meaning of life is not bound up in an escape from our senses, it certainly cannot be found in an exclusive immersion in the senses. Wisdom is an attribute of true maturity and generally this maturity is arrived at through time, a time which is the great ally of human growth.

Harry James Cargas, *Encountering Myself*, SPCK, 1978, page 100

Time is precious, but we do not comprehend all its value. We shall know it only when it will no longer be of any advantage to us. Our friends make demands upon it, as if it were nothing, and we bestow it in the same way. Often it is a burthen to us. We know not what to do with it. A day will come, when a simple quarter of an hour may appear of more worth to us than the riches of the whole world. God, who is so free and liberal in his bounty to us in everything else, teaches us, by the wise economy of his providence, how careful we should be of the use of time; for he gives us but one instant, and withdraws that as he gives us a second, while he retains the third in his own hands, leaving us in entire uncertainty whether it will ever be ours.

Time is given us to prepare for eternity, and eternity will not be too long for our regrets at the loss of time, if we have misspent it. Our lives as well as our hearts belong to God; he has given them both for his service. We cannot always be doing something that belongs to our condition. To be silent, to suffer, to pray when we cannot ask, is acceptable to God. A disappointment, a contradiction, a harsh word received and endured as in his presence, is worth more than a long prayer; and we do not lose time if we bear its loss with gentleness and patience, provided the loss was inevitable, and was not caused by our own fault.

Thus let us spend our days, redeeming the time, by quitting vain amusements, useless correspondence, those weak outpourings of the heart that are only modifications of self-love, and conversations that dissipate the mind, and lead to no good. Thus we shall find time to serve God; and there is none well employed that is not devoted to him.

François de la M. Fénelon, *Selections from the Writings of Fénelon*, 'Mrs Follen', Edward T. Whitfield, 1850, page 246

TRANSFORMATION

Transformation—transforming, being transformed, as having undergone a great transformation; change of character, disposition, outward appearance

I love the story of the transfiguration—of Jesus going up the mountain with his inner core of disciples, and of being transformed before them. His face, we are told, 'shone like the sun'.

Whilst an undergraduate I was confronted with something similar. I came across someone transfigured, whose face also 'shone like the sun'. The occasion was a Sunday morning in a church in Oxford. A visiting bishop had come to preach. As soon as I saw him I was taken aback by his appearance. It was as though light was radiating from him. He was vibrantly alive, a picture of health, and full of energy. I listened carefully to what he had to say, but cannot now remember a word he said.

The important thing was him—transfigured and transformed—and I knew I wanted to be like that.

I took a step of faith, naïvely expecting to be transformed in the twinkling of an eye. It didn't work out that way at all. In the weeks that followed I was aware a fundamental change had taken place and experienced a new sense of freedom, but the process of transformation has been a long and costly process. After thirty years, I know what it is to be refined a little by fire, like silver and gold, and that there is still a long way to go, but there have been moments of transformation, which have made it all worth while.

Visions of Faith, Hope, and *Love,* have come out of my journey towards transformation. The practice of reflection is one of the gates to the source of glory.

And he was transfigured before them, and his face shone like the sun, and his garments became white as light.

Matthew 17:2

... and he was transfigured before them, and his garments became glistening, intensely white, as no fuller on earth could bleach them.

Mark 9:2

Do not be conformed to this world but be transformed by the renewal of your mind, that you may prove what is the will of God, what is good and acceptable and perfect.

Romans 12:2

And we all, with unveiled face, beholding the glory of the Lord, are being changed into his likeness from one degree of glory to another; for this comes from the Lord who is the Spirit.

2 Corinthians 3:18

Love is the only force capable of transforming an enemy into a friend.

Martin Luther King, *The Words of Martin Luther King,* selected by Coretta Scott King, William Collins Sons & Co., 1986, page 18

Human souls, transformed by the Spirit of God till they live in the highest qualities, must form a public sentiment that is to be the transforming power among men.

Henry Ward Beecher, *Proverbs from Plymouth Pulpit,* Charles Burnet & Co., 1887, page 161

The process of transforming our inner lives must be expressed in the transformation of our outer life, of the life of the individual as well as that of the community.

Martin Buber, in Aubrey Hodes, *Encounter with Martin Buber,* Allen Lane, The Penguin Press, 1972, page 83

The highest degree, which the mystics call the transformation or essential and immediate union with God, is the reality of pure love in which there is no self-interest.

François de la M. Fénelon, in B.W. Randolph, editor, *Maxims of the Mystics,* translated by W.W. Williams, A.R. Mowbray & Co., 1909, page 104

But once a man accepts Christ, he has accepted an entirely new set of standards; he is committed to an entirely new kind of life at his work, in his personal relationships, in his pleasure, in his conduct, in his speech, in the things which he allows himself to do.

William Barclay, *The Letters to Timothy and Titus,* The Saint Andrew Press, 1965, page 245

The harvest of suffering cannot be reaped until it has been eaten, burnt, digested. If the suffering is accepted and lived through, not fought against and refused, then it is completed and becomes transmuted. It is absorbed, and having accomplished its work, it ceases to exist as suffering, and becomes part of our growing self.

E. Graham Howe and L. Le Mesurier, *The Open Way*, Methuen & Co., 1939, page 180

It is one of the most moving experiences of life to watch a bewildered frightened human being, starved of friendship and hardly daring to be expectant of it, blossom out into a happy, trustful and confident personal life as the result of being so welcomed and received. It is of the essence of the Gospel that we are so received in Christ, that His Yes to men is pronounced in such directly personal terms.

Alan Ecclestone, *Yes to God*, Darton, Longman & Todd, 1975, page 116

In his love for someone he brought out that which was peculiar to a person's life, even though it lay hidden under layers of dirt; he loved it out. Therefore many who knew that he saw them and loved them became new persons and experienced the great transformation. His love was not simply a reaction to something lovable, as our love is. His love was creative. It called a 'new creature' into existence.

Helmut Thielicke, *I Believe—The Christian's Creed*, translated by John W. Doberstein and H. George Anderson, William Collins Sons & Co., 1969, page 90

A fundamental transformation is expected: something like a new birth of man himself, which can be understood only by one who actively takes part in it. It is therefore a transformation which does not come about merely through progress in right thinking for the sake of right action... or through the education of man who is fundamentally good... Nor is it a transformation through enlightenment... According to Jesus, a fundamental transformation is achieved through a man's surrender to God's will.

Hans Küng, *On Being a Christian*, translated by Edward Quinn, William Collins Sons & Co., 1977, page 249

God never does things by halves. He does not sanctify us patch upon patch... He takes our whole life and our whole being and elevates it to a supernatural level, transforms it completely from within, and leaves it exteriorly what it is: ordinary...

To love God is everything. And Love is enough. Nothing else is of any value except insofar as it is transformed and elevated by the charity of Christ. But the smallest thing, touched by charity, is immediately transfigured and becomes sublime.

Thomas Merton, *The Sign of Jonas*, Sheldon Press, 1976, page 182

When we begin to sense how far away we are from the Master of the Beatitudes, when we begin to sense how little we love our enemies, how aggressive we are, how little we are good shepherds, how little we really live in community, how little we strive to sense that we need to be healed and to be transformed, because God is calling us to something that we cannot possibly do by ourselves...

We cannot love an enemy; we flee from an enemy, we are aggressive towards him, we hurt and wound him. We disregard little people. We're frightened.

When we begin to sense all the security we have in our lives that prevents us opening ourselves to the Spirit, when we sense how comfortable we are, how we seek comfort rather than compassion and love—then we are preparing the road to transformation...

Jean Vanier, *Be Not Afraid*, Griffin House, 1975, page 106

One morning when I was in the wood something happened which was nothing less than a transformation of myself and the world, although I 'believed' nothing new. I was looking at a great, spreading, bursting oak. The first tinge from the greenish-yellow buds was just visible. It seemed to be no longer a tree away from me and apart from me. The enclosing barriers of consciousness were removed and the text came into my mind, *Thou in me and I in thee*. The distinction of self and not-self was an illusion. I could feel the rising sap; in me also sprang the fountain of life uprushing from its roots, and the joy of its outbreak at the extremity of each twig right up to the summit was my own: that which kept me apart was nothing. I do not argue; I cannot explain; it will be easy to prove me absurd, but nothing can shake me. *Thou in me and I in thee*. Death! what is death. There is no death: *in thee* it is impossible, absurd.

Mark Rutherford, *More Pages from a Journal*, Oxford University Press, 1910, page 182

'To be born again' means exactly what it says. The emphasis is still on being born: indicative of a process that is still concerned with flesh and blood, i.e., still concerned with concrete problems of this world. But it is still a complete *transformation*; we have still to deal with material things; but we see them now through the eyes of those who are born of the spirit, and not of those who are born of the will of the flesh. It is this world we are still concerned with; but we see it differently, and do different things about it. We do not deal with new things instead of old things; but with the old things in a new way: indeed all the old 'things' now take on a sacramental significance. 'If any man be in Christ Jesus, he is a new creation. The old things are passed away, *all things are become new*' (Authorised Version). The man of business, truly converted, will attend more and not less, to his business, and square up to the problems attendant on the fact that his office has now assumed something of the proportions of a holy place. If the use of a harmonium helps to make vivid for him this new vision, by all means let him buy one. The man of ambition continues to use this attribute of his character (now utterly transformed) for the things of the Kingdom. The man of humour has his humour reborn (not garrotted), and cheers up *everyone*—no longer just his self-selected clique. And all forget about halos and wings, and keep off their coats rather to get into the multifarious activities of converting humanity into Humanity again—not into an anaemic and wholly erroneous imitation of Divinity.

George Macleod, *We Shall Rebuild*, The Iona Community, 1945, page 55

We take courage from three realities which are evident to us. The first is that changes on a global scale are already upon us, as the era known as industrial society gives place to something new. The industrial city is one of the focal points of that change. In almost every sphere of life and in a brief span of time the future is being shaped by action or by default. The very assumptions of our culture are now open to debate in new ways. We do not pretend to discern clearly what is to come. We present no comprehensive political or economic analysis. That task goes beyond this Commission. At this time of immense opportunity what we can do is to pledge ourselves as citizens to do our best to engage in the daily moral confrontations of public life and personal relations.

The second evident reality is the experience of justice, love and hope in human history, focused most clearly for us in our religious tradition. We know that there is a transforming power present in human affairs which can resolve apparently intractable situations and can bring new life into the darkest places. If, as we dare to affirm, the true nature of human life is to be discerned in the life of Jesus Christ, we can take heart and pledge ourselves to a deeper commitment to create a society in which benefits and burdens are shared in a more equitable way. Any attempt to base a society or culture upon other foundations carries with it, we believe, its own nemesis of suffering, bitterness and social disintegration.

But—and this is our third evident reality—somewhere along the road which we have travelled in the past two years each of us has faced a personal challenge to our lives and life styles: a call to change our thinking and action in such a way as to help us to stand more closely alongside the risen Christ with those who are poor and powerless. We have found faith in the city.

Faith in the City, Church House Publishing, 1985, page 360

VISION

Vision—act of faculty of seeing, things seen in dream or trance; thing seen in the imagination, imaginative insight; statesmanlike foresight

I have never had a vision on the lines of Moses and the burning bush, or of Isaiah, seeing the Lord high and lifted up in the temple. My visions have been more down-to-earth, involving the imagination and imaginative insight.

I remember reading Ralph Waldo Trine's book, *In Tune with the Infinite*, in my teens, and through it coming to a belief in God, seen primarily as Creator and the power behind nature. In my early twenties I came to believe in a personal God, seen in the first instance in a living person, and confirmed in the person of Jesus Christ as portrayed in the Gospels. This vision was nurtured and sustained by a growing awareness of the Holy Spirit.

In my early thirties, my faith broke down. I was searching for a deeper and greater vision, and this came to me through reading *The Choice is Always Ours*, by Dorothy Berkley Phillips. Most of the vision came to me whilst travelling on a Greyhound bus in America with a group of students. As we journeyed through the States, I came to see what it meant to be made in the image and likeness of God, fully worked out for us in Jesus Christ. This in turn led to the emergence of a belief in the God in the depths of our being—seen primarily as Father, Son, Holy Spirit, life, light, truth, joy, love and so on. Homework had to be done. It was crucial for me to justify this position in the Scriptures. After several weeks of searching through the Old and New Testaments I was more than able to justify this radical position. The next step was to look for evidence of this vision *in the life of the last two thousand years*, and my own experience of life, and record this in *Visions of Faith, Hope* and *Love.*

Today we are acutely aware of our need for vision, and for new life.

The oracle of the man whose eye is opened,
the oracle of him who hears the words of God,
and knows the knowledge of the Most High,
who sees the vision of the Almighty.

Numbers 24:15–16

Of old thou didst speak in a vision to thy faithful one.

Psalm 89:19

And a vision appeared to Paul in the night: a man of Macedonia was standing beseeching him and saying, 'Come over to Macedonia and help us.' And when he had seen the vision, immediately we sought to go on into Macedonia.

Acts 16:9–10

I was not disobedient to the heavenly vision.

Acts 26:19

The true poet is all the time a visionary and whether with friends or not, as much alone as a man on his death bed...

J.B. Yeats, *Letters to his son, W.B. Yeats and others*, Faber and Faber, 1944, page 179

I have seen the vision,
the vision of mine own revealing itself,
coming out from within me.

Rabindranath Tagore, *The Religion of Man*, George Allen & Unwin, 1931, page 117

A mere dream, a vague hope may be more potent than certainty in a lesser matter. The faintest vision of God is more determinative of life than a gross earthly certainty.

Mark Rutherford, *More Pages From a Journal*, Oxford University Press, 1910, page 220

This truly is the vision of God: never to be satisfied in the desire to see him. But one must always, by looking at what he can see, rekindle his desire to see more.

Gregory of Nyssa, *The Life of Moses*, Paulist Press, number 239, page 116

Man has two eyes.
One only sees what moves in fleeting time,
the other
what is eternal and divine.

Angelus Silesius, *The Book of Angelus Silesius*, translated by Frederick Franck, Wildwood House, 1976, page 43

The spirit of the world, the great calm presence of the Creator, comes not forth to the sorceries of opium or of wine. The sublime vision comes to the pure and simple soul in a clear and chaste body.

Ralph Waldo Emerson, 'The Poet', from 'Essays and Representative Men', in *The Works of Ralph Waldo Emerson*, George Bell & Sons, 1906, volume I, page 213

I saw also that there was darkness and death, but an infinite ocean of light and love flowed over the ocean of darkness. In that also I saw the infinite Love of God; and I had great openings.

George Fox, *The Journal of George Fox*, J.M. Dent & Sons, 1924, page 11

What is this world? A dream within a dream—as we grow older each step is an awakening. The youth awakes as he thinks from childhood—the full grown man despises the pursuits of youth as a visionary—the old man looks on manhood as a feverish dream—The Grave the last sleep?—no it is the last and final awakening.

Sir Walter Scott, *The Journal of Sir Walter Scott*, Oxford University Press, 1951, page 305

The nature of the mind is such that the sinner who repents and makes an act of faith in a higher power is more likely to have a blissful visionary experience than is the self-satisfied pillar of society with his righteous indignations, his anxiety about possessions and pretensions, his ingrained habits of blaming, despising and condemning.

Aldous Huxley, *Heaven and Hell*, Chatto & Windus, 1956, page 52

So long the city I desired to reach
Lay hid; when suddenly its spires afar
Flashed through the circling clouds; you may conceive
My transport. Soon the vapours closed again,
But I had seen the city, and one such glance
No darkness could obscure; nor shall the present—
A few dull hours, a passing shame or two,
Destroy the vivid memories of the past.
I will fight the battle out; a little spent
Perhaps, but still an able combatant.

Robert Browning, 'Paracelsus', IV, in *The Poetical Works of Robert Browning*, Oxford University Press, 1949, page 47

Prejudice can distort our vision. There is nothing which so destroys a man's judgment as prejudice does. It prevents him from forming the clear, reasonable and logical judgment which it is the duty of any man to form. It blinds him alike to the facts and to the significance of the facts. Almost all new discoveries have had to fight their way against unreasonable prejudice... One of the most necessary things in life is the fearless self-examination which will enable us to see when we are acting on principle and when we are victims of our own unreasonable and unreasoning prejudices. In any man who is swayed by prejudice the eye is darkened and the vision distorted.

William Barclay, *The Gospel of Matthew*, The Saint Andrew Press, 1987, volume I, page 243

Whence, then, comes the stimulation to vision? Two obvious sources readily spring to mind: the Bible and the liturgy. No one surely would be so foolish as to deny the way in which a reading of the Bible can stretch horizons, or the way its self-authenticating passages (e.g. Psalm 23, Isaiah 53, 1 Corinthians 13, Romans 8) have awakened and inspired and sustained many faithful Christians. We depend on the Bible to 'check' our vision of Christ which is such a crucial stimulus to growth...

The other obvious resource of vision is liturgy, since clearly it was originally intended to articulate the vision of God-in-Christ and recreate it week by week for those who participate in it.

Frank Wright, *The Pastoral Nature of the Ministry*, SCM Press, 1980, page 17

The normal limits of the human vision are not the limits of the universe. There are other worlds than that which our senses reveal to us, other senses than those which we share with the lower animals, other forces than those of material nature. If we have faith in the soul, then the supernatural is also a part of the natural. Most of us go through life with eyes half shut and with dull minds and heavy hearts, and even the few who have had those rare moments of vision and awakening fall back quickly into somnolence. It is good to know that the ancient thinkers required us to realise the possibilities of the soul in solitude and silence and transform the flashing and fading moments of vision into a steady light which could illumine the long years of life.

Sir Sarvepalli Radhakrishnan, *Indian Philosophy*, George Allen & Unwin, 1931, volume II, page 373

We all have a consciousness of spiritual beauty. It is part of the experience of prayer to develop this consciousness and to follow the light which it brings. As we follow it, so our capacity for vision increases. Prayer is faith in our own capacity for spiritual vision, and exercise of that capacity. Teaching is faith in the capacity of other people for spiritual vision, and appeal to that capacity.

Our Lord had amazing faith in people's capacity for spiritual vision. When He spoke to that poor, smirched woman of Samaria, He said to her some of the most profound spiritual truths He ever said to any one. It was to her He said, 'God is a Spirit, and they that worship Him must worship Him in spirit and in truth.' He shared with her His own vision of the spiritual kingdom, which was not fettered to Jerusalem or to any place, but into which all spiritual people could enter by the adventure of faith.

In Acts 10 we read of two people who had visions, Cornelius a disciple, and Peter a teacher, and to both these men the vision came when they were at prayer. Cornelius had his vision of the man who was to come to teach him. Peter had his vision of the equality of souls in the sight of God, a vision that broke down his race and class prejudices. The beginning of the... Church was the breaking down of Jewish prejudice, the idea of the God of the nation giving place to belief in the God of the world. It was the appeal of one who had capacity for spiritual vision to another who had that capacity. The vision came to the teacher and to the disciple, and to both the vision came at their prayer.

Father Andrew, SDC., *Meditations for Every Day*, A.R. Mowbray & Co., 1941, page 291

For most of us most of the time, the world of everyday experience seems rather dim and drab. But for a few people often, and for a fair number occasionally, some of the brightness of visionary experience spills over, as it were, into common seeing, and the everyday universe is transfigured. Here is an entirely characteristic description of this transfiguration of the everyday world.

'I was sitting on the seashore, half listening to a friend arguing violently about something which merely bored me. Unconsciously to myself, I looked at a film of sand I had picked up on my hand, when I suddenly saw the exquisite beauty of every little grain of it; instead of being dull, I saw that each particle was made up on a perfect geometrical pattern, with sharp angles, from each of which a brilliant shaft of light was reflected, while each tiny crystal shone like a rainbow... The rays crossed and recrossed, making exquisite patterns of such beauty that they left me breathless... Then, suddenly, my consciousness was lighted up from within and I saw in a vivid way how the whole universe was made up of particles of material which, no matter how dull and lifeless they might seem, were nevertheless filled with this intense and vital beauty. For a second or two the whole world appeared as a blaze of glory. When it died down, it left me with something I have never forgotten and which constantly reminds me of the beauty locked up in every minute speck of material around us.'

Aldous Huxley, *Heaven and Hell*, Chatto & Windus, 1956, page 17

WORD OF GOD

Word of God—Christ as mediator or manifestation of God to men and women

I am very fond of the story of Elijah at Mount Horeb in which the word of the Lord came to him in 'a still small voice'. I believe this is how we should hear the 'word of God' today, though very few of us are quiet enough to hear it.

Our Lord was supremely aware of this 'still small voice'. That is why he spent such a long time in the wilderness and whole nights in prayer, away from everyone so he could listen and hear.

I have been greatly helped by some words of William Dell in which he said that people might feel something *nearer* to them than the Scriptures, which was the *Word in the Heart,* from whence all Holy Scriptures came, which *is Christ within them the Hope of their Glory.* This encourages us to be open to the voice of God who continues to speak to us directly in that 'still small voice.' Michel Quoist also supports this view. He agreed that God speaks to us in his Gospel, but he speaks to us also through life, that new Gospel to which we ourselves add a new page every day.

Someone said it's all very well being open to the word of God in this way, but how does this relate to the Word of God in the Bible, and the overall authority of Scripture? What about those people who claim to hear the voice of God and then commit awful crimes in obedience to the voice of God?

I take as my ultimate authority 'the still small voice', and then use the Bible as a canon or guide to check carefully the authenticity of this *word.* If it is in line with Scripture, OK, if not, then it has to be rejected.

My current practice is to 'reflect' on passages in *Visions of Faith, Hope,* and *Love,* and listen to the word of God which I experience as 'a still small voice.' This is how I hear *that new Gospel.*

But the word is very near you; it is in your mouth and in your heart, so that you can do it.

Deuteronomy 30:14

If I say, 'I will not mention him, or speak any more in his name,' there is in my heart as it were a burning fire shut up in my bones, and I am weary with holding it in, and I cannot.

Jeremiah 20:9

And the Word became flesh and dwelt among us, full of grace and truth.

John 1:14

For the word of God is living and active, sharper than any two-edged sword, piercing to the division of soul and spirit, of joints and marrow, and discerning the thoughts and intentions of the heart. And before him no creature is hidden, but all are open and laid bare to the eyes of him with whom we have to do.

Hebrews 4:12–13

The Word of God tends to make large-minded, noble-minded men.

Henry Ward Beecher, *Proverbs from Plymouth Pulpit*, Charles Burnet & Co., 1887, page 129

The New Testament designs the Christian man to be a child of light and joy.

Henry Ward Beecher, *Proverbs from Plymouth Pulpit*, Charles Burnet & Co., 1887, page 164

The Word of God is a grand encourager of the supreme use of the understanding of men, both in things secular and in things spiritual and divine.

Henry Ward Beecher, *Proverbs from Plymouth Pulpit*, Charles Burnet & Co., 1887, page 134

By dwelling in the one Word dwelt in all, so that the one being constituted the Son of God in power, the same dignity might pass to the whole human race.

St Cyril of Alexandria, in F.C. Happold, *Religious Faith and Twentieth Century Man*, Darton, Longman and Todd, 1980, page 145

The supremest power of divine truth is not when it is uttered forth in idea-form, but when exhibited in heart-form, or as it is evolved in actual life-experience.

Henry Ward Beecher, *Proverbs from Plymouth Pulpit*, Charles Burnet & Co., 1887, page 178

The Word is to be distinguished from any human words, even the words of the Bible. The Word has its centre in Christ, and is attested to by the Bible, but is known only through the grace of God.

John Bowden, in Alan Richardson and John Bowden, editors, *A New Dictionary of Christian Theology*, SCM Press, 1985, page 603

... does not mean telling the old story over and over again, but the offering of channels through which people can discover themselves, clarify their own experiences and find the niches in which the Word of God can take firm hold.

Henri J.M. Nouwen, *The Wounded Healer*, Doubleday, 1979, page 40

Then the word of God shall have come into your souls and clinging to your hearts will form your minds according to the image of the word itself, i.e. that you should desire and do what the word of God wills, and thereby Christ himself will be formed in you.

Origen, 'Homily on Psalm 36', in Mother Mary Clare, SLG, *Encountering the Depths*, edited by Ralph Townsend, Darton, Longman and Todd, 1981, page 15

People are hungry for the word of God that will give peace, that will give unity, that will give joy. But you cannot give what you don't have. That's why it is necessary to deepen your life of prayer. Allow Jesus to take you, pray with you and through you, and then you will be a real, true contemplative in the heart of the world.

Mother Teresa, *Jesus, the Word to be Spoken*, compiled by Brother Angelo Devananda, William Collins Sons & Co., 1990, page 74

The word of God becomes flesh during the day, during meditation, during Holy Communion, during contemplation, during adoration, during silence. That word in you, you give to others. It is necessary that the word live in you, that you understand the word, that you love the word, that you live the word. You will not be able to live that word unless you give it to others.

Mother Teresa, *Jesus, the Word to be Spoken*, compiled by Brother Angelo Devananda, William Collins Sons & Co., 1990, page 27

The word of God is like a seed which enters human hearts with varying results according to the nature of the soil. In some the word is able to take root and to create a response of faith. Although the process is in accordance with divinely pre-ordained laws, no attempt is made to interfere with the soil. Each man is free to respond or not. So it was with all our Lord's teaching.

L.S. Thornton, C.R., *The Common Life of the Body of Christ*, Dacre Press, A. & C. Black, 1950, page 242

... the minister of the Word works to achieve the precision in his utterances which is the poet's power both to be incisive and to extend the range of human consciousness... How men are enlarged and caught continues to be a mystery bound up with the mystery of what is communicated when the Gospel is proclaimed. The words in which it is spoken are the words of life and it is not given to the preacher to manipulate them as he wills.

R.E.C. Browne, *The Ministry of the Word*, SCM Press, 1958, page 73

To achieve the interior act one must assemble all one's powers as it were into one corner of one's soul, where, secreted from images and forms one is able to work. We must sink into oblivion and ignorance. In this silence, this quiet, the Word is heard. There is no better method of approaching this Word than in silence, in quiet: we hear it and know it aright in unknowing. To one who knows naught it is clearly revealed.

Meister Eckhart, in Franz Pfeiffer, *The Works of Meister Eckhart*, translated by C. de B. Evans, John M. Watkins, 1924, volume I, page 13

Within that awful volume lies
The mystery of mysteries!
Happiest they of human race,
To whom God has granted grace
To read, to fear, to hope, to pray,
To lift the latch, and force the way;
And better had they ne'er been born,
Who read to doubt, or read to scorn.

Sir Walter Scott, *The Monastery*, Oxford University Press, 1912, page 118

The Bible is really the guided, inspired word of man about the Word of God, but there is only one real Word of God, and that is our Lord Jesus Christ. The Bible gives us the inspired prophecy that looks forward to His coming, and the inspired memoirs of men who wrote about Him when He came, but the one Word of God that abideth forever is our Lord Jesus Christ. He is the everlasting Word that shall never fail, He is the everlasting Revelation that shall never pass away, the everlasting Life in Whom alone we shall find our perfect peace.

Father Andrew, SDC., *A Gift of Light*, selected and edited by Harry C. Griffith, A.R. Mowbray & Co., 1968, page 76

There is a place where God speaks to you and it's closer than you think—it is in *you*. Stop for a moment, close your eyes and keep quiet. You've arrived. Now listen. Your Lord has just said: 'If anyone loves me he will keep my word, and my father will love him, and we shall come to him *and make our home with him*' (John 14:23).

'But I'm not practising God's Word.'

'You're trying though, aren't you.'

'Yes.'

'Then "they" are there—the Lord said nothing about only loving saints.'

Michel Quoist, *With Open Heart*, translated by Colette Copeland, Gill and Macmillan, 1983, page 181

Robert What did you mean when you said that St. Catherine and St. Margaret talked to you every day?

Joan [of Arc] They do.

Robert What are they like?

Joan (suddenly obstinate) I will tell you nothing about that: they have not given me leave.

Robert But you actually see them; and they talk to you just as I am talking to you?

Joan No: it is quite different. I cannot tell you: you must not talk to me about my voices.

Robert How do you mean? voices?

Joan I hear voices telling me what to do. They come from God.

Robert They come from your imagination.

Joan Of course. That is how the messages of God come to us.

George Bernard Shaw, *Saint Joan*, The Bodley Head, 1924, scene i

Now as the word of God is full of the expression of his love towards man, so all his works do loudly proclaim it: he gave us our being, and by preserving us in it, doth renew the donation every moment. He hath placed us in a rich and well-furnished world, and liberally provided all our necessities; he raineth down blessings from heaven upon us, and causeth the earth to bring forth our provision; he giveth us our food and raiment, and while we are spending the productions of one year, he is preparing for us against another. He sweeteneth our lives with innumerable comforts, and gratifieth every faculty with suitable objects; the eye of his providence is always upon us, and he watcheth for our safety when we are fast asleep, neither minding him nor ourselves.

But lest we should think these testimonies of his kindness less considerable, because they are the easy issues of his omnipotent power, and do not put him to any trouble or pain, he hath taken a more wonderful method to endear himself to us; he hath testified his affection to us, by suffering as well as by doing; and because he could not suffer in his own nature, he assumed ours.

Henry Scougal, *The Life of God in the Soul of Man*, C.J.G. & F. Rivington, 1829, page 62

WORK

Work—expenditure of energy, striving, application of effort to some purpose; task to be undertaken; employment, especially of earning money by labour; laborious occupation

I remember coming across an elderly accountant in Bradford, whom I used to know in Huddersfield. I had recently been ordained and was a Minor Canon on the staff of Bradford Cathedral. He said he wished I was in industry, as he felt I was needed there, and not in the Church.

I thought carefully about his comments, and felt he was making an important point. As an undergraduate in Oxford I tended to move in evangelical circles with an emphasis on Jesus Christ and the Holy Spirit. In that milieu we almost entirely missed out on the Father. Perhaps we did this because God the Father was difficult to understand and we tended to think in black-and-white terms. To be involved in 'grey areas' was considered unsound. So we ignored him—much to our cost.

In theology we think of God the Father as Creator. If we ignore the Creator we become blind to the creation. Thirty years ago in Oxford we were encouraged to be evangelical and convert people to Christ. We missed out on the kingdom of God, with its message of converting not only individual lives, but also the whole of creation. Man and woman, after all, are made in the image and likeness of God with dominion over the earth, with a mandate to run it according to the will of God. I wonder if we need to get back to this fundamental principle.

I think we should work, not just to earn our living, but to transform and redeem the work-a-day world. Vocation should not be limited to a few occupations, but everyone is called to redeem and transform the world we are living in and exercise dominion over the world.

The Lord God took the man and put him in the garden of Eden to till it and keep it.

Genesis 2:15

There is nothing better for a man than that he should eat and drink, and find enjoyment in his toil. This also, I saw, is from the hand of God; for apart from him who can eat or who can have enjoyment?

Ecclesiastes 2:24–25

We must work the works of him who sent me.

John 9:4

But let each one test his own work, and then his reason to boast will be in himself alone and not in his neighbour. For each man will have to bear his own load.

Galatians 6:4–5

Work is not the curse, but drudgery is.

Henry Ward Beecher, *Proverbs from Plymouth Pulpit*, Charles Burnet & Co., 1887, page 37

Joy's soul lies in doing.

William Shakespeare, *Troilus and Cressida*, I. ii. 278

It is a good sign where a man is proud of his work or his calling.

Henry Ward Beecher, *Proverbs from Plymouth Pulpit*, Charles Burnet & Co., 1887, page 36

Men who have been very stingy and very grasping are usually men who have very strong commercial instincts.

Henry Ward Beecher, *Proverbs from Plymouth Pulpit*, Charles Burnet & Co., 1887, page 33

Perpetual devotion to what a man calls his business, is only to be sustained by perpetual neglect of many other things.

Robert Louis Stevenson, *Virginibus Puerisque*, Chatto & Windus, 1906, page 78

Certainly work is not always required of a man. There is such a thing as a sacred idleness, the cultivation of which is now fearfully neglected.

George Macdonald, *Wilfred Cumbermede*, Hurst and Blackett, Publishers, 1872, volume III, page 169

There is no right more universal and more sacred, because lying so near to the root of existence, than the right of men to their own labour.

Henry Ward Beecher, ***Proverbs from Plymouth Pulpit,*** **Charles Burnet & Co., 1887, page 58**

Blessed be the man whose work drives him. Something must drive men; and if it is wholesome industry, they have no time for a thousand torments and temptations.

Henry Ward Beecher, ***Proverbs from Plymouth Pulpit,*** **Charles Burnet & Co., 1887, page 37**

The most important motive for work in the school and in life is the pleasure of work, pleasure in its results and the knowledge of the value of the result to the community.

Albert Einstein, ***Out of my Later Years,*** **Thames and Hudson, 1950, page 35**

The world demands work. Work is needed for the mere maintenance of life; more work is needed for the maintenance of a particular level of civilization; still more work is needed if we look to the future and aim at giving later generations better chances of fuller life.

Sir Julian Huxley, ***Religion without Revelation,*** **C.A. Watts & Co., 1967, page 140**

Love work: for if thou dost not want it for food, thou mayst for physic. It is wholesome for thy body, and good for thy mind. It prevents the fruits of idleness, which many times come of nothing to do, and leads too many to do what is worse than nothing.

William Penn, ***Fruits of Solitude,*** **A.W. Bennett, 1863, page 16**

The story is relevant here of the somewhat pompous parson leaning over the gate with the farmer, viewing a fine crop of barley. 'It is wonderful,' said the parson, 'what can be done when you and God get together.' 'Aye,' said the farmer, 'but you should have seen this field last year when God had it all to Himself.'

George Macleod, ***Only One Way Left,*** **The Iona Community, 1956, page 29**

The great hardship in manual labour is that we are compelled to expend our efforts for such long hours simply in order to exist.

The slave is he to whom no good is proposed as the object of his labour except mere existence.

Accordingly he must either be detached or fall to the vegetative level.

Simone Weil, ***Gravity and Grace,*** **Routledge and Kegan Paul, 1972, page 158**

Some groups of people are being hit particularly hard, especially those who face other difficulties in their lives. Those who suffer ill-health or disability, and younger and older workers, are particularly vulnerable to unemployment. Unemployment rates among people from the minority ethnic communities in the Urban Priority Areas are a particular cause for concern.

Faith in the City, **Church House Publishing, 1985, page 199**

The workman must do everything as if he was doing it for Christ. We do not work for pay; we do not work for ambition; we do not work to satisfy an earthly master. We work so that we can take every task and offer it to Christ. All work is done for God, so that God's world can go on, and so that God's men and women may have the things they need for life and living. All work is work for God.

William Barclay, ***The Letters to the Philippians, Colossians and Thessalonians,*** **The Saint Andrew Press, 1971, page 197**

Most people work so hard developing their power of corresponding with the visible world, that their power of corresponding with the invisible world is left in a rudimentary state. But when, for one reason or another, we begin to wake up a little bit, to lift the nose from the ground and notice that spiritual light and that spiritual atmosphere as real constituents of our human mind; then the whole situation is changed. Our horizon is widened, and at the same time our responsibilities are enlarged.

Evelyn Underhill, in John Stobbart, editor, *The Wisdom of Evelyn Underhill*, A.R. Mowbray & Co., 1951, page 8

Businesses are, in reality, quasi-religious sects. When you go to work in one you embrace a *new faith*. And if they are really big businesses, you progress from faith to a kind of mystique. Belief in the product, preaching the product, in the end the product becomes the focus of a transcendental experience. Through 'the product' one communes with the vast forces of life, nature, and history that are expressed in business. Why not face it? Advertising treats all products with the reverence and the seriousness due to sacraments.

Thomas Merton, *Conjectures of a Guilty Bystander*, Burns & Oates, 1968, page 211

The problem set before us is to bring our daily task into the temple of contemplation and ply it there, to act as in the presence of God, to interfuse one's little part with religion. So only can we inform the detail of life, all that is passing, temporary, and insignificant, with beauty and nobility. So may we dignify and consecrate our meanest of occupations. So may we feel that we are paying our tribute to the universal work and the eternal will. So are we reconciled with life and delivered from the fear of death. So are we in order and at peace.

Henri Frédéric Amiel, *Amiel's Journal*, translated by Mrs Humphry Ward, Macmillan & Co., 1918, page 224

No work done by any man, however great, will really prosper unless it has a distinct religious backing. But what is Religion? I for one would answer: 'Not the Religion you will get after reading all the scriptures of the world. Religion is not really grasped by the brain, but a heart grasp.'

Religion is a thing not alien to us. It has to be evolved out of us. It is always within us: with some, consciously so; with others, quite unconsciously. But it is always there. And whether we wake up this religious instinct in us through outside assistance or by inward growth, no matter how it is done, it has got to be done, if we want to do anything in the right manner, or to achieve anything that is going to persist.

Mohandas K. Gandhi, in C.F. Andrews, *Mahatma Gandhi's Ideas*, George Allen & Unwin, 1929, page 101

Oh, when I think of the industrial millions, when I see some of them,
a weight comes over me heavier than leaden linings of coffins
and I almost cease to exist, weighed down to extinction
and sunk into depression that almost blots me out.
Then I say to myself: Am I also dead? is that the truth?
Then I know
that with so many dead men in mills
I too am almost dead.
I know the unliving factory-hand, living-dead millions
is unliving me, living-dead me,
I, with them, am living dead, mechanical enslaved at the machine.

And enshrouded in the vast corpse of the industrial millions embedded in them, I look out on the sunshine of the South.
And though the pomegranate has red flowers outside the window and oleander is hot with perfume under the afternoon sun
and I am 'il Signore' and they love me here,
yet I am a mill-hand in Leeds
and the death of the Black Country is upon me
and I am wrapped in the lead of a coffin-lining, the living death of my fellow men.

D.H. Lawrence, 'We Die Together', in Vivian de Sola Pinto and Warren Roberts, editors, *The Complete Poems of D.H. Lawrence*, William Heinemann, 1967, volume II, page 629

Work is a central reality of existence; and as soon as there is any division of labour (we cannot imagine any society without it) work is a basic social reality. It can be both a brute necessity and drudgery and also a joy, either because of the creativeness involved in some jobs or because of the social significance work brings, or both. This double aspect of work as toil and a joy is brought out in the biblical 'parables' of Creation and Fall in Genesis. The Bible has a realistic attitude to work and is not at all fastidious, unlike the Greeks. The educated Greek thought ordinary work degrading for a free man, it was for slaves; and a touch of this attitude can be seen in Ecclesiasticus 38, which comes significantly from hellenized Judaism. The Bible may not do enough justice to creative art, but it certainly sees the vast bulk of the world's work positively under God. The New Testament stresses the need to work and not be idle, to work well and cheerfully (cf. 1 and 2 Thessalonians... Colossians 3:23). Work is a vocation...

The Christian doctrine of work sees it as a means of loving God by serving human needs. Needs are interpreted in a broad sense, but not as broad as wants. There are some wants which it is hard to please God by supplying, but in general we should not be too fastidious. If gambling, for instance, is within bounds a legitimate activity, so is the supply of facilities for it. The church has never excommunicated bookmakers. As to choice of jobs, those who have the longest and most specialized training will expect to exercise it, but they usually have a fair choice where to do so, and what life-style they will adopt. Those with the least differentiated skills will find it easiest to change jobs. However, while there may well be a 'right to work' if one lives in a society that evaluates people by their work, there cannot be a right to a particular job if the needs of society change. At the same time the state should so arrange its economic affairs that there is no long-term unemployment. A wise society moves younger rather than older men to new jobs, and provides generous adjustment allowances and retraining facilities when a change of type of job requires this.

Ronald Preston, in James F. Childress and John Macquarrie, editors, *A New Dictionary of Christian Ethics*, SCM Press, 1986, page 666

YOUTH

Youth—being young; adolescence (the vigour or enthusiasm or weakness or inexperience or other characteristic of the period between childhood and full manhood or womanhood)

At the age of eleven I went away to school in ignominy—I had failed to get in at the local grammar school. My parents gave me some valuable advice for the future—'William, remember, you only get out of life what you are prepared to put into it.'

These words guided me throughout youth. I greatly enjoyed my schooldays, and was into everything. This gave me a solid foundation on which to build for the future. I was called up for National Service in the army and put these words into action. They have remained with me ever since and continue to stimulate me on a daily basis.

They proved to be invaluable in the early days of ministry. The then Bishop of Bradford, Michael Parker, took me aside one day and said, 'Come along, lad. I want you to be a chaplain of a boys' club on the outskirts of the city. I'll take you along sometime and introduce you to the warden.' I was apprehensive, having never been into a boys' club before.

We duly went along and met the warden. He asked me to spend an evening a week in the club, and insisted I wore my dog-collar; he wanted the lads to know exactly who I was.

How does one carry out the role of a chaplain of a boys' club in which the Church was anathema? The words of advice above came to my rescue. I used to go into the club in the evening, wearing my dog-collar for ten minutes, making sure everyone saw me briefly. I would then change into sports gear and tracksuit and join in everything—indoor football, table-tennis, trampoline, rugby, and cricket, camping, caving, and potholing in the summer. I even learned to wrestle and nearly lost face in contests. Everyone wanted to wrestle 'wit' vicar'.

So my advice to youth, if asked, would be: 'You only get out of life what you are prepared to put into it.'

The glory of young men is their strength.

Proverbs 20:29

Remember also your Creator in the days of your youth.

Ecclesiastes 12:1

Let no one despise your youth, but set the believers an example in speech and conduct, in love, in faith, in purity.

1 Timothy 4:12

... shun youthful passions.

2 Timothy 2:22

I felt so young, so strong, so sure of God!

Elizabeth Barrett Browning, 'Aurora Leigh', in *The Poetical Works of Elizabeth Barrett Browning*, Henry Froude, 1904, page 391

Youth seldom criticizes the accomplished fact.

E.M. Forster, *A Room with a View*, Penguin Books, 1986, page 113

Excess in youth in regard to animal indulgence is bankruptcy in old age.

Henry Ward Beecher, *Proverbs from Plymouth Pulpit*, Charles Burnet & Co., 1887, page 44

The eye of youth dilates and distorts the images. The focussing process is painful. Youth has no norm.

Norman Douglas, *An Almanac*, Chatto & Windus in association with Martin Secker & Warburg, 1945, page 39

As one who tries to remain youthful in his thinking and feeling, I have struggled against facts and experience on behalf of belief in the good and the true.

Albert Schweitzer, *Memoirs of Childhood and Youth*, translated by C.T. Campion, George Allen & Unwin, 1924, page 102

Youth beholds happiness gleaming in the prospect. Age looks back on the happiness of youth; and instead of hopes, seeks its enjoyment in the recollections of hope.

Samuel Taylor Coleridge, *The Table Talk and Omniana of Samuel Taylor Coleridge*, Oxford University Press, 1917, page 379

Youth is the time to go flashing from one end of the world to the other both in mind and body; to try the manners of different nations; to hear the chimes at midnight.

Robert Louis Stevenson, *Virginibus Puerisque*, Chatto & Windus, 1906, page 62

I remember my youth and the feeling that will never come back any more—the feeling that I could last for ever, outlast the sea, the earth, and all men.

Joseph Conrad, *Youth*, J.M. Dent and Sons, 1946, page 36

But what troubles the sensitive youth most is the inescapable recurrence of his faults. For how late do we learn to realize that in developing our virtues we at the same time cultivate our faults. This is the most difficult aspect of knowledge of one's self, making it well-nigh impossible.

Johann Wolfgang von Goethe, *Wisdom and Experience*, selected by Ludwig Curtius, translated and edited by Hermann J. Weigand, Routledge & Kegan Paul, 1949, page 205

Settle it in your minds, young people, that the first and the last of all virtues and graces which God can give is Self-Control, as necessary for the saint and the sage lest they become fanatics and pedants, as for the young in the hey-day of youth and health.

Charles Kingsley, *Daily Thoughts*, Macmillan & Co., 1884, page 241

... the young men of this land are not, as they are often called, a 'lost' race—they are a race that never yet has been discovered. And the whole secret, power, and knowledge of their own discovery is locked within them—they know it, feel it, have the whole thing in them—and they cannot utter it.

Thomas Wolfe, *The Web and the Rock*, William Heinemann, 1947, page 215

The sum total of man's endeavours is directed upon man as their object through the medium of personality; youth impinges most strongly upon youth, and here we have the purest transmission of human energies. It is this activity of youth which animates the world and preserves it from extinction both morally and physically.

Johann Wolfgang von Goethe, ***Wisdom and Experience,*** **selected by Ludwig Curtius, translated and edited by Hermann J. Weigand, Routledge & Kegan Paul, 1949, page 161**

... People smile at the 'enthusiasm of youth'—that enthusiasm which they themselves secretly look back at with a sigh, perhaps unconscious that it is partly their own fault that they ever lost it... Do not fear being considered an enthusiast. What matter? But pray for tact, the true tact which love alone can give, to prevent scandalising a weak brother.

Charles Kingsley, ***Daily Thoughts,*** **Macmillan & Co., 1884, page 35**

The secret of life... that this fine youthful spirit should never be lost. Out of the turbulence of youth should come this fine precipitate—a sane, strong aggressive spirit of daring and doing. It must be a flexible, growing spirit, with a hospitality to new ideas, and a keen insight into experience. To keep one's reactions warm and true, is to have found the secret of perpetual youth, and perpetual youth is salvation.

Randolph Bourne, ***Youth and Life,*** **Constable & Co., 1913, page 26**

It is a very strange sensation to inexperienced youth to feel itself quite alone in the world: cut adrift from every connection; uncertain whether the port to which it is bound can be reached, and prevented by many impediments from returning to that it has quitted. The charm of adventure sweetens that sensation, the glow of pride warms it: but then the throb of fear disturbs it; and fear with me became predominant, when half an hour elapsed and still I was alone.

Charlotte Brontë, ***Jane Eyre,*** **Oxford at the Clarendon Press, 1969, page 112**

Crabbed age and youth cannot live together:
Youth is full of pleasure, age is full of care;
Youth like summer morn, age like winter weather;
Youth like summer brave, age like winter bare.
Youth is full of sport, age's breath is short.
Youth is nimble, age is lame,
Youth is hot and bold, age is weak and cold.
Youth is wild and age is tame.
Age, I do abhor thee; youth, I do adore thee.
O my love, my love is young.
Age, I do defy thee.

William Shakespeare, ***Poems from The Passionate Pilgrim,*** **xii. 1**

Ah, glorious twenty-one, with your inexhaustible powers of doing and enjoying, eating and hungering, sleeping and sitting up, reading and playing! Happy are those who still possess you, and can take their fill of your golden cup, steadied, but not saddened, by the remembrance that for all things a good and loving God will bring to them to judgement. Happier still those who (like a few) retain in body and soul the health and buoyancy of twenty-one on to the very verge of forty, and, seeming to grow younger-hearted as they grow older-headed, can cast off care and work at a moment's warning, laugh and frolic now as they did twenty years ago, and say with Wordsworth—

'So was it when I was a boy,
So let it be when I am old,
Or let me die.'

Charles Kingsley, *Daily Thoughts*, Macmillan & Co., 1884, page 13

The increase in youth unemployment has disrupted the normal progression of development from home to school to job; and the time during which a young person is dependent on home and family has been extended. The prolonging of financial dependency creates problems both for parents and for their children, who live in a youth culture which relies on an adequate income. But above all it has removed one of the main ways a young person has of valuing himself or herself. Many young people are extremely resilient and seem able to transcend their environment with hope in their hearts. Others have spoken to us of the hurt of watching young people grow through childhood to adolescence and beyond, and as they do so experiencing a transformation from the normal expectancy and hope of the young, through apparent resignation to the inner pain and anger of a life seemingly without hope.

***Faith in the City*, Church House Publishing, 1985, page 316**

How shall I describe Youth, the time of contradictions and anomalies? The fiercest radicalisms, the most dogged conservations, irrepressible gayety, bitter melancholy,—all these moods are equally part of that showery springtime of life. One thing, at least, it clearly is: a great, rich rush and flood of energy. It is as if the store of life had been accumulating through the slow, placid years of childhood, and suddenly the dam had broken and the waters rushed out, furious and uncontrolled, before settling down into the quieter channels of middle life. The youth is suddenly seized with a poignant consciousness of being alive, which is quite wanting to the naïve unquestioning existence of the child. He finds himself overpoweringly urged toward self-expression.

Just as the baby, born into a 'great, blooming, buzzing confusion,' and attracted by every movement, every colour, every sound, kicks madly in response in all directions, and only gradually gets his movements coordinated into the orderly and precise movements of his elders,—as the youth suddenly born into a confusion of ideas and appeals and traditions responds in the most chaotic way to this new spiritual world, and only gradually learns to find his way about in it, and gets his thoughts and feelings into some kind of order.

Randolph Bourne, *Youth and Life*, Constable & Co., 1913, page 3

The time of youth is necessarily a time of danger.

(i) In youth there are temptations which are stronger. The blood runs hotter and the passions speak more commandingly. The tide of life runs strongest in youth and it is a tide which sometimes threatens to sweep a young person away.

(ii) In youth there are more opportunities for going wrong. Young people are thrown into company where temptation can speak with a most compelling voice. Often young people have to study or to work away from home, and away from the influences which would keep them right. The young person is much more of an individual than the older person. The young person has not yet taken upon himself the responsibility of a home and a family; he has not yet given hostages to fortune; and he does not yet possess the anchors which hold an older person in the right way through a sheer sense of obligation. In youth there are far more opportunities to make shipwreck of life.

(iii) In youth there is often that confidence which comes from lack of experience. In almost every sphere of life a young person will approach life more recklessly than an older person, for the simple reason that he has not yet discovered all the things which can go wrong. A young person, to take a simple example, will often drive a motor car much faster than an older person because he has not yet discovered how easily an accident can take place, and on how slender a piece of metal the safety of a car depends. A young man will often shoulder a responsibility in a much more carefree spirit than an older person, because he has not known the difficulties and has not experienced how easily shipwreck may be made. No one can buy that experience; that is something for which only the years can pay. There is a risk, as there is a glory, in being young.

For that very reason, the first thing at which any young person must aim is self-mastery. No one can serve others until he has mastered himself.

William Barclay, *The Letters to Timothy and Titus*, The Saint Andrew Press, 1965, page 287

Index

F

G

H

I

J

K

L

M

U

V

W

Y